# TESOL Teacher Education in a Transnational World

*TESOL Teacher Education in a Transnational World* critically examines theories and practices in contemporary TESOL teacher education to shed new light on the intersection of transnationalism and language teacher education. It emphasizes the scholarship of transnational mobility of language teachers, and showcases critical research from diverse contexts.

The book fills a critical research gap by more fully examining the theory and practice of teacher education in a changing time when national identities and cross-border mobilities continue to figure prominently in scholarly discussions. Through a diverse set of epistemological, historical, and theoretical perspectives along with methodological innovations, contributors of this volume not only index the dynamism of the scholarship of teacher education, but they also offer new forums for lively pedagogical debates. Featuring contributions from diverse educational and geographical contexts, including Europe, Asia, North America, and Latin America, the book moves the existing scholarship forward to more fully examine TESOL teacher education in relation to transnationalism.

This book will be of great interest to academics, scholars, postgraduate students, teacher educators, policymakers, curriculum specialists, administrators, and other stakeholders interested in language teacher education, TESOL, and applied linguistics

**Osman Z. Barnawi** is Associate Professor at the Royal Commission Colleges and Institutes, Yanbu, Saudi Arabia. His research interests include the intersection(s) of language and political economy, social and education policy studies, the cultural politics of education, multilingual and multicultural studies, second language writing, and transnational education.

**Anwar Ahmed** is Assistant Professor in the Department of Languages, Literatures and Linguistics at York University in Canada. His current research interests are language teacher education, second language writing pedagogy, technology, and affect studies.

# Routledge Research in Language Education

The ***Routledge Research in Language Education*** series provides a platform for established and emerging scholars to present their latest research and discuss key issues in Language Education. This series welcomes books on all areas of language teaching and learning, including but not limited to language education policy and politics, multilingualism, literacy, L1, L2 or foreign language acquisition, curriculum, classroom practice, pedagogy, teaching materials, and language teacher education and development. Books in the series are not limited to the discussion of the teaching and learning of English only.

Books in the series include:

**Language Education and Emotions**
Research into Emotions and Language Learners, Language Teachers and Educational Processes
*Edited by Mathea Simons and Tom Smits*

**Attitudes to English Study among Japanese, Chinese and Korean Women**
Motivations, Expectations and Identity
*Edited by Yoko Kobayashi*

**Second Language Pragmatics and English Language Education in East Asia**
*Edited by Cynthia Lee*

**Writing Motivation Research, Measurement and Pedagogy**
*Muhammad M. M. Abdel Latif*

**Pop culture in language education**
Theory, Research, Practice
*Edited by Valentin Werner and Friederike Tegge*

**TESOL Teacher Education in a Transnational World**
Turning Challenges into Innovative Prospects
*Edited by Osman Z. Barnawi and Anwar Ahmed*

For more information about the series, please visit www.routledge.com/Routledge-Research-in-Language-Education/book-series/RRLE

# TESOL Teacher Education in a Transnational World

## Turning Challenges into Innovative Prospects

**Edited by**
**Osman Z. Barnawi and Anwar Ahmed**

Routledge
Taylor & Francis Group
LONDON AND NEW YORK

First published 2021
by Routledge
2 Park Square, Milton Park, Abingdon, Oxon OX14 4RN

and by Routledge
52 Vanderbilt Avenue, New York, NY 10017

*Routledge is an imprint of the Taylor & Francis Group, an informa business*



*British Library Cataloguing in Publication Data*
A catalogue record for this book is available from the British Library

*Library of Congress Cataloging-in-Publication Data*
A catalog record has been requested for this book

ISBN: 978-0-367-44275-0 (hbk)
ISBN: 978-1-003-00866-8 (ebk)

Typeset in Galliard
by Taylor & Francis Books

**We dedicate this volume to English language teachers who are going above and beyond their job requirements to support transnationally mobile students during the global pandemic of COVID-19.**

# Contents

# Illustrations

## Figures



## Tables

# Contributors

**Anwar Ahmed** (PhD, University of Toronto) is an assistant professor in the Department of Languages, Literatures and Linguistics at York University in Canada. He formerly published under the name Sardar Anwaruddin. Anwar's articles have appeared in journals such as *Educational Philosophy and Theory, Professional Development in Education, Discourse, Reflective Practice, Teaching in Higher Education, Educational Studies, Curriculum Inquiry, International Journal of Leadership in Education, International Journal of Research and Method in Education, Oxford Review of Education, CALICO Journal*, and *The Brazilian Journal of Applied Linguistics*. Anwar was an editor of *Curriculum Inquiry* from 2011 to 2016. His recent edited book is *Knowledge Mobilization in TESOL: Connecting Research and Practice* (Brill, 2019).

**Sedat Akayoglu** is currently working as an assistant professor at the Department of Foreign Language Education at Bolu Abant İzzet Baysal University. He is working with pre-service EFL teachers, and his expertise includes computer-assisted language learning, computer-mediated communication, intercultural communication, and teacher education.

**Osman Z. Barnawi** is Associate Professor at the Royal Commission Colleges and Institutes, Yanbu, Saudi Arabia. His research interests include the intersection (s) of language and political economy, social and education policy studies, the cultural politics of education, multilingual and multicultural studies, second language writing, and transnational education. His works have appeared in journals such as *Language and Education, Critical Studies in Education*, and *Language and Literacy*. His recent books are *TESOL and the Cult of Speed in the Age of Neoliberal Mobility* (Routledge, 2020), *Neoliberalism and English Language Education Policies in the Arabian Gulf* (Routledge, 2018), and *Writing Centers in the Higher Education Landscape of the Arabian Gulf* (Palgrave Macmillan, 2017).

**Peter Browning** is a PhD candidate in the Department of Culture, Communication and Media at University College London's Institute of Education. His current ESRC-funded PhD research project explores the ways in which language and language policy play a role in the process of rapid urban change and development in the municipality of Rionegro, Colombia, through a critical sociolinguistic ethnographic lens. Peter's research interests are informed by his first-hand experience as a TESOL teacher and teacher educator in both Colombia and the UK.

**Iara Bruz** (Universidade Federal do Paraná – Brazil) researched the D-TEIL program for her doctoral studies; she took part in the practicum and generated data with the group. Iara is member of the research group New Literacies/Novos Letramentos affiliated with Universidade de São Paulo (USP).

**Yin Ling Cheung** is Associate Professor (English Language and Literature) and Associate Dean (Outreach and Engagement) at National Institute of Education, Nanyang Technological University. She has published in journals such as *System* and *RELC Journal*.

**Xuan Jiang** is an assistant director at the Center for Excellence in Writing at Florida International University. Her research interests include writing tutors' professional development, writing tutors' well-being and morale in the workplace, issues and strategies in academic writing, various instructional scaffoldings, second-generation and 1.5-generation students' academic performance and the factors behind, linguistic and cultural challenges faced by immigrant and international students in K-12 and higher education in the United States, using transnational literature and dialogues to promote culturally responsive teaching and to develop cultural and communicative competence in both English Language Learners (ELLs) and native English speakers.

**Ryuko Kubota** is a professor in the Department of Language and Literacy Education at the University of British Columbia, Canada, where she teaches applied linguistics and teacher education. Her research draws on critical approaches to second language education, focusing on race, culture, and language ideologies. Her publications appear in such journals as *Applied Linguistics, Critical Inquiry in Language Studies, Journal of Multilingual and Multicultural Development, Journal of Second Language Writing, TESOL Quarterly*, and *World Englishes*. She is a co-editor of *Race, Culture, and Identities in Second Language Education: Exploring Critically Engaged Practice* (Routledge, 2009). She has also published actively in Japanese.

**Geoff Lawrence** is an Associate Professor in ESL and Applied Linguistics at York University. Geoff is a teacher educator, researcher, and curriculum designer interested in exploring the potential of online, blended, plurilingual, and intercultural approaches in language teaching and teacher education programs. His research examines online/blended language teaching methodology, teacher beliefs toward educational innovation, and intercultural/plurilingual learning in language and language teacher education.

**Ruberval Maciel** (Universidade Estadual de Mato Grosso do Sul – Brazil).

**Ian Martin** (Glendon College) is member of the research group New Literacies/Novos Letramentos affiliated with Universidade de São Paulo (USP).

**Latisha Mary** is associate professor of language education at the School of Education, University of Strasbourg (France). Her research interests include teacher education for the support of second language acquisition, bi-/plurilingual and intercultural education, teacher language awareness, and language teacher identity. She has been involved in several national and international research and teacher education projects focusing on language awareness, multilingualism, and intercultural education.

**Jim McKinley** is an associate professor at UCL Institute of Education, and director of the MA TESOL Pre-Service program. His research explores implications of globalization for L2 writing, language education, and teaching in higher education. He is an author and editor of several books on research methods in applied linguistics.

**Sarina Chugani Molina** serves as the Associate Dean and Associate Professor in the School of Leadership and Education Sciences at the University of San Diego. She has directed the MEd in TESOL program in the Department of Learning and Teaching for 15 years. She has taught English to students both locally and internationally for over 20 years and trains teacher candidates and teachers both within the United States and abroad. Her research interests include teaching English as an international and transnational language, supporting the needs of marginalized students in academic communities, and TESOL teacher development, particularly as it relates to developing mindful, reflective practitioners from a constructive developmental perspective.

**Benjamin Luke Moorhouse** is an assistant professor in the Department of Education Studies at Hong Kong Baptist University where he teaches on initial English language teacher education programs. His research interests include experiential learning, initial English language teacher education, and primary English language education. His works have appeared in journals such as *Journal of Education for Teaching*, *Asia-Pacific Journal of Education*, *ELT Journal*, *RELC Journal*, and *TESOL Journal*.

**Brian Morgan** (Glendon College) is member of the research group New Literacies/Novos Letramentos affiliated with Universidade de São Paulo (USP).

**Gustavo Moura** (University of Manitoba, doctoral candidate, and MA, Universidade Estadual do Mato Grosso do Sul) participated on two courses and on the practicum for the D-TEIL program in 2016.

**Nashwa Nashaat-Sobhy** is currently an assistant professor of Applied Linguistics at the Polytechnic University of Valencia (UPV). She has a PhD in Philosophy and Linguistics and an MA in Applied Linguistics from La Universidad Autónoma de Madrid (UAM), and an MA in Teaching English as a Foreign Language from the School of Humanities at the American University in Cairo.

She is a member of the UAM-CLIL research group at UAM and the research group GALE at UPV. Her research activities and publications focus on teaching and learning in content and language integrated contexts (CLIL and EMI).

**Kyle Perkins** is a retired professor of TESOL and Foreign Language Education at Florida International University. His research interests include the composing process, reading comprehension, instructional sensitivity, language testing, and Rasch measurement.

**Davinia Sánchez-García** (PhD (Hons.) and MA in Applied Linguistics) is an assistant professor of English Language and Linguistics at Universidad Complutense de Madrid (UCM) and Universidad a Distancia de Madrid (UDIMA). She is actively involved as an educational developer at Universidad Complutense de Madrid (UCM), and member of the EQUiiP project (https://equiip.eu/). Her research interests focus on English-medium education (EME), classroom discourse, and teacher education.

**Cristina Sánchez-Martín** (PhD, Illinois State University) is Assistant Professor in the English Department at Indiana University of Pennsylvania. Her work revolves around investigating how humans are situated in and navigate language and writing practices in transnational spaces. Her research interests also include teacher education, socialization, and identity, mentoring of linguistically diverse students, feminist praxis, and transdisciplinarity. Her work appears in the *Journal of Second Language Writing* and *Poroi*. She is currently serving as an editor for the NNESTs (Non-native English Teachers) TESOL interest section newsletter.

**Xiaoya Sun** is a PhD candidate in the English Language and Literature Academic Group at National Institute of Education, Nanyang Technological University. She has published in *Comunicar* and *System*.

**Babürhan Üzüm** is an associate professor of bilingual education and ESL in the School of Teaching and Learning at Sam Houston State University. His research interests include language teacher education, intercultural communication, computer-mediated communication, telecollaboration, and sheltered instruction of English language learners.

**Li Wei** is a British linguist of Manchu-Chinese parentage. He is a Fellow of the Academy of Social Sciences and a Fellow of the Royal Society of Arts. He is Chair of Applied Linguistics and Director of the UCL Centre for Applied Linguistics at the UCL Institute of Education, University College London.

**Joel Windle** is Assistant Professor of English at the Fluminense Federal University, Brazil, where he coordinates the Centre for Critical Studies in Language, Education, and Society and is a member of the UNESCO Chair on Language Policies for Multilingualism. His current research investigates subaltern transnationalisms in Brazilian urban peripheries. He is the winner of the Raewyn Connell and Stephen Crook prizes for best book in Australian sociology. He is series editor of New Perspectives on Language Education for Multilingual

Matters and associate editor of the Brazilian journal *Papers in Applied Linguistics*.

**Bedrettin Yazan** is an associate professor of TESL teacher education and applied linguistics at the University of Texas, San Antonio educational linguistics in the Department of Curriculum and Instruction at the University of Alabama. His research is focused on language teacher learning and identity, language policy and planning, world Englishes, and collaboration between ESL and content teachers. His recent work has appeared in *World Englishes, International Multilingual Research Journal, TESOL Journal, Teacher Education Quarterly, RECALL*, and *European Journal of Language Policy*.

**Xiaoye You** is Liberal Arts Professor of English and Asian Studies at the Pennsylvania State University, USA, and Yunshan Chair Professor at Guangdong University of Foreign Studies, China. He is the editor of *Transnational Writing Education: Theory, History and Practice* (Routledge, 2018).

**Weiyu Zhang** is a PhD candidate in the English Language and Literature Academic Group at National Institute of Education, Nanyang Technological University. She has published in *International Journal of English Studies* and *The Asian ESP Journal*.

**Dandan Zhu** is a PhD candidate at UCL Institute of Education, University of London, exploring teacher identity of foreign English teachers in China. She is a graduate of the MA TESOL Pre-Service at UCL, and is involved in multiple projects investigating the experiences of Chinese TESOL postgraduate students.

# Acknowledgments

We would like to express our heartfelt gratitude to the authors who have contributed to this volume.

# 1 Introduction

## Preparing language teachers for a transnational world

*Osman Z. Barnawi and Anwar Ahmed*

A rich body of research has emerged in the last three decades under the banner of transnationalism. A growing concern for globalization and its capitalist bent, a right-wing populism and a neo-nationalist protectionist approach to borders have inspired many social scientists to turn to transnationalism as an analytical tool. Today, as we write this introduction, the political borders of most nation-states are closed as an unprecedented measure to curb the spread of the COVID-19 virus. The mobility of people and goods has come to a halt in a way that no one has seen in the recent past. What does transnationalism tell us in this kind of situation? As members of a global TESOL community, what can we learn from transnationalism? Before answering these questions, we should take a look at the meaning and etymology of this important keyword.

### What does transnationalism mean?

The prefix "*trans*" originated from the Old French and Latin. It refers to actions, movements, changes, and shifts as mentioned in the *Etymology Dictionary*:

> "across, beyond, through, on the other side of, to go beyond," from Latin *trans* (prep.) "across, over, beyond," perhaps originally present participle of a verb **trare-*, meaning "to cross," from PIE **tra-*, variant of root *tere- … "cross over, pass through, overcome."
>
> (Online Etymology Dictionary, www.etymonline.com/search?q=trans)

The term "*national*" originates from Middle French *national* and Old French *nacion*. It means:

> "of or pertaining to a nation or a country regarded as a whole; established and maintained by the nation; peculiar to the whole people of a country," 1590s, from Middle French *national* (16c., from Old French *nacion*), and also from nation + -al … Opposed to *local* or *provincial* (or in the U.S., *state*). Meaning "peculiar or common to the whole people of a country" is by 1620s. From 1802 as "established and maintained by the nation or its laws". As a noun, "citizen of a (particular) nation," from 1887.
>
> (Online Etymology Dictionary, www.etymonline.com/search?q=national)

The suffix "ism" implies a doctrine, theory, practice, or system. It originates from:

> French *-isme* or directly from Latin *-isma*, *-ismus* (source also of Italian, Spanish *-ismo*, Dutch, German *-ismus*), from Greek *-ismos*, noun ending signifying the practice or teaching of a thing, from the stem of verbs in *-izein*, a verb-forming element denoting the doing of the noun or adjective to which it is attached.
>
> (Online Etymology Dictionary, www.etymonline.com/search?q=ism)

Taken together, ***trans-national-ism*** refers to multiple ties, interactions, and activities that connect people, institutions, and cultural practices across the borders of nation-states (Vertovec, 1999, 2009). Transnational activities operate in complex and multidirectional ways in today's age of mobility; i.e., mobility of knowledge, ideas, cultural practices, capital, languages, goods, and people. Additionally, recent advancements in information and communication technologies (ICTs) have added a new dimension of "virtual mobility" to an already mobile world. ICTs increase the speed and efficiency of transnational activities in myriad ways. Notably, multiple ties, interactions, and activities in transnational spaces are manifested "in between the life-world of personal interactions, on the one hand, and the functional systems of differentiated spheres or fields, such as the economy, polity, law, science and religion, on the other hand" (Faist & Bilecen, 2017, p. 5). It is for these reasons that transnationalism has been conceptualized and institutionalized differently in different contexts and settings. The primary goal of this volume is to engage with the ways in which transnationalism intersects with the field of Teaching English to Speakers of Other Languages (TESOL). More specifically, the volume examines how transnationalism has been conceptualized, negotiated with, enacted, contested, and justified in different contexts and settings of TESOL teacher education (TE).

## Conceptualizations and institutionalizations of transnationalism

Although scholars have investigated transnational practices since the 1980s (see, for example, Appadurai & Breckenridge, 1988; Kearney, 1995), *transnationalism* as a research paradigm first gained ground and popularity in the field of anthropology back in the early 1990s. Specifically, in their seminal book entitled *Nations unbound: Transnational projects, postcolonial predicaments, and deterritorialized nation-states*, Basch, Schiller, and Szanton (1994), the American anthropologists, used transnationalism as a research paradigm in order to investigate issues surrounding international migrations. Through their work, the concepts of transnationalism and "transnational social field" gained popularity. Basch, Schiller, and Szanton (1994) called for the development of a "transnational analytical framework" by conceptualizing "transnationalism as processes and of the construction of identities that reflect transnational experience, individuals, communities, or states" (p. 9). Since then "transnationalism" has become an important analytical concept and category in various disciplines including history (Iriye, 2004; Saunier,

2013), sociology, language education (Duff, 2015), higher education (Phan, 2017), political sciences (Sikkink, 1998), and curriculum studies, to name a few.

The project of transnationalism, historically speaking, was first developed in the United States. As such, epistemologies, theories, and research practices in the field of transnationalism were predominantly US-oriented during the past decades. Today, however, transnationalism has gained a firm footing in different settings and contexts across Europe, Asia, Africa, the Arabian Gulf, and Latin America with different ontological, epistemological, theoretical, and pedagogical orientations. Scholars in diverse geographical locations have used disciplinary, interdisciplinary, and multidisciplinary approaches to understanding transnational activities—political, economic, social, cultural, and educational—within their respective contexts. Such diversity of scholarly endeavors are evident, for example, in You's (2018) *Transnational writing education: Theory, history, and practice* and Phan's (2017) *Transnational education crossing "Asia" and "the West": Adjusted desire, transformative mediocrity and neo-colonial disguise*. The field of higher education has recently witnessed numerous scholarly endeavors, including projects (e.g., Asia Pacific Economic Cooperation—APEC Transnational Education Data Collection Project—Cross-Border Provider Mobility), special issues (e.g., Mok, Han, & Jiang, 2018; Windle & O'Brien, 2019), edited collections (e.g. Garcés-Mascareñas & Penninx, 2016; You, 2018), articles (e.g., De Fina & Perrino, 2013; Duff, 2015), conferences (e.g., International Conference on Transnational Education), and books (e.g., Phan, 2017) on transnational scholarly activities.

Transnational activities and their durability, in one way or another, have been examined through "their degree of institutionalization" as Mügge (2016, p. 11) and other scholars (e.g., Van Amersfoort, 2001) noted. Transnational activities are institutionalized through "high" versus "low" as well as "below" versus "above" degrees. Other scholars have also "categorized transnational activities by distinguishing between various types of transnationalism" (Mügge, 2016, p. 112; see also Nell, 2007). These categorizations may take five different forms:

> The first is transplanted homeland activities, where habits or conflicts between ethnic groups in the homeland are transplanted to the immigrant community ... The second type is transplanted immigrant activities, which emerge when migrants return to the homeland with skills and ideas acquired in the host country ... The third type is homeland-directed transnational activities. Here, migrants in the country of settlement direct their activities towards their country of origin. The fourth type, diaspora activities, is a subset of homeland-directed transnational activities for groups that do not have a homeland. The fifth category is country of residence-directed transnational activities.
>
> (Mügge, 2016, p. 112)

What is clearly evident in the aforementioned climate is that transnational activities, broadly speaking, are manifestations of globalization and neoliberal free market ideologies. That is,

> globalization has given rise to unprecedented levels of mobility of people and ideas across national borders, [and] it has also drawn attention to the growing levels of cultural diversity in most communities, raising the possibilities of both cultural exchange and conflict.
>
> (Rizvi & Choo, 2020, p. 2)

Social actors in different contexts and settings have their own conceptions of transnationalism guided by commonly held (generalized) beliefs that we all "belong to a single global community" (Rizvi & Choo, 2020, p. 2). These beliefs, within the current turns and debates about Global English (GE), and the use of English in multilingual contexts, are located in a diverse sets of epistemological, theoretical, ideological, linguistic, cultural, ethical, and pedagogical practices (see, for example, Alim, Ibrahim, & Pennycook 2009; Blackledge & Creese, 2010; Blommaert, 2010; Duff, 2015; Li, 2012; Rumbaut, 2002). Collectively, in these scholarly works, the discussions and arguments that English, as a global language, has a potential to bridge boundaries in a transnational world are the key. One recent case in point is Rose and Galloway's (2019) work on *Global Englishes for language teaching*. In it, the authors argue that "[t]he spread of English as a global language has resulted in the emergence of a number of related fields of research within applied linguistics, including English as an International Language, English as a Lingua Franca, and World Englishes" (p. xx). The emergence of these different fields of research also has numerous implications to TESOL policies, curricula, and pedagogical practices. Rose and Galloway's (2019) arguments in many ways support Duff's (2015) position that the field of TESOL/Applied Linguistics is now "increasingly concerned with *identity* construction and expression through particular language and literacy practices across the life span, at home, in diaspora settings, in short-term and long-term sojourns abroad for study or work, and in other contexts and circumstances" (p. 57).

In this volume, we will not only acknowledge the current debates and key theories about Global Englishes, English as a Lingua Franca, language teaching and multilingualism, transnationalism, and identity in relation to mobility, but we will also endeavor to move the existing scholarly debates forward. Specifically, we will take the position that despite the existence of numerous studies on transnationalism in relation to the field of TESOL, the nexus between transnationalism and TESOL teacher education remains relatively silent.

## TESOL teacher education in a transnational world

As a profession and as a multidisciplinary field of scholarly study, TESOL is fundamentally concerned with various aspects of English language education, including pre-service teacher education and in-service teachers' professional learning and development. In 1996, Karen Johnson called on TESOL teacher education programs to "find ways to situate learning about teaching within authentic contexts" so that teachers could make sense of their professional knowledge and act upon it "within the context of real teaching" (p. 770). Since the time of Johnson's writing, the contexts of *real teaching* have changed so much! One of the changes with a significant impact on teaching and learning of the English language is the transnational mobility of people, ideas, pedagogies, and cultural practices. The contexts of teaching are no longer defined and negotiated primarily by nation-states and their priorities. Additionally, recent advancements in ICTs have added a new dimension of "virtual mobility" to an already mobile world. While, as stated earlier, issues of transnational mobility of language, identity, culture, ideology, curriculum, and pedagogy have come to the fore within the contemporary scholarship of TESOL and Applied Linguistics (e.g., De Fina & Perrino, 2013; Duff, 2015; Phan, 2017; Warriner, 2017), the intersection of transnationalism and TESOL teacher education remains under-explored at epistemological, theoretical, historical, and practical levels.

In this edited volume, colleagues frame and examine TESOL teacher education in relation to transnationalism. In the context of TESOL teacher education, transnationalism is understood as "activities in the ground" (You, 2018, p. 2) in which TESOL student-teachers, teacher educators, policy makers, government officials, local communities, curriculum specialists, administrators, and other local stakeholders as well as their social institutions engage in regular and sustained linkages, relationships, and practices across national borders. These activities on the ground are conceptualized and institutionalized differently by different actors in particular social and educational contexts. Our contention is that transnational practices in language teacher education (LTE) may occur in various domains and under various conditions including practicum in multi- and cross-cultural settings, study abroad programs, online teacher education, professional development courses, borrowing and lending of LTE curricula and pedagogies, interactions in virtual communities of teachers, professional learning on social media platforms, and transcultural flow of professional knowledge. In the pages that follow, contributors critically examine transnational practices in contemporary TESOL teacher education. As editors of this volume, we are curious about the explorations of:

1. how transnational practices in TESOL teacher education are institutionalized and conceptualized;
2. how the learning of teaching, the content, and the discourses of language teacher education are taking place in today's linguistically and culturally diverse world;
3. the kinds of curricular and pedagogical innovation and intervention needed for TESOL teacher education in transnational spaces; and
4. the ways in which issues of LTE pedagogies, identities, and different forms of capital (i.e., cultural, linguistic, social, symbolic, or economic) are negotiated in such spaces.

As we engage in these explorations, we are intrigued by contributing authors' works in diverse educational, cultural, political, and geographical contexts. Collectively, the chapters featured in this volume shed light on "the design, enactment, and consequences of language teacher education … in order to meet the needs of current and future English language teachers in an increasingly diverse, mobile, unequal, and globalized world" (Johnson & Golombek, 2018, p. 1). Although most TESOL teacher education programs involve a transnational dimension, there has been an absence of rigorous scholarship that explicitly links TESOL teacher education with transnationalism. A key contribution of this edited volume is, therefore, to fill in this critical research gap and also to move the existing scholarship forward to more fully account for the multifaceted dynamics of TESOL teacher education in a transnational world.

Contributors to this collection provide multiple layers of interventions (including epistemic, economic, ideological, cultural, and material) centred on the mobility of pedagogical knowledge and ideas in relation to TESOL teacher education, with new directions for the growth of our discipline. Specifically, through a diverse set of epistemological, historical, and theoretical perspectives together with methodological orientations, research questions, design, and aims, actors and analytical frameworks crafted in different geographical and political locations, chapter contributors not only index the dynamism of the scholarship of TESOL teacher education in the transnational world, but also offer new spaces for lively pedagogical debates. These debates, which we invite you to engage with, suggest that a wide variety of answers are possible to the key questions we posited earlier.

Taking the diverse group of contributors' interventions together, we propose a *transnational dialogue for TESOL teacher education*. We would like to view this dialogue as an ongoing and dynamic endeavor to (re)think, (re)examine, critique, and (re)present possible knowledge cultures in relation to professional practices so as to keep transnationalism in view in all its complexities. The art of "possible" in transnationalism is aimed at unsettling the monolingual ideologies, displacing nationalist binaries, disrupting knowledge hierarchies, and exploring epistemologically, culturally, linguistically, ideologically, and socio-materially responsive pedagogies in TESOL teacher education. The proposed transnational dialogue also aims to move student-teachers, teacher educators, policy makers, government officials, local communities, and curriculum specialists' minds and bodies into the heart of cultural politics of boundary (re)construction in TESOL teacher education.

## Organization of the book

In terms of organization, the book is divided into four parts. Following the introduction, the volume begins by offering conceptual foundations of transnationalism in relation to education in general and language education in particular. A key intention is to radicalize historical consciousness, and at the same time find new concepts, ideas, questions, and relations between them. It then moves on to deeply engage readers with different cases and examples of on-the-ground realities of transnational practices in TESOL teacher education as experienced by various actors in diverse contexts. Subsequently, the volume immerses readers in cases of professional learning and development at such levels as policy, curricula, and pedagogies. Thus, the volume sets out to bring together a diverse set of explorations of how the learning of teaching, the content, and the discourses of language teacher education are taking place in today's transnational reality. It is our hope that the different cases and examples presented in this book will enrich our transnational perspectives on and engagement in TESOL teacher education at both individual and collective levels. It is also our intention in this collection to present the richness of various conceptualizations and institutionalizations of transnationalism in relation to language teacher education, so as to give readers insights into processes of transnationalism in all its complexities.

All three chapters in Part I render the epistemological, conceptual, ideological, and political battles of transnationalism in relation to TESOL teacher education. Xiaoye You (in Chapter 2) offers epistemological and theoretical exercises to transnationalism and TESOL teacher education. Xiaoya Sun, Weiyu Zhang, and Yin Ling Cheung (in Chapter 3) critically review scholarly works published in English between 1998 and 2018 (a period which witnessed the emergence of transnationalism as a key concept in TESOL). They empirically substantiate the absence of scholarly works that examine the intersection of transnational mobility and TESOL teacher education. Ryuko Kubota (in Chapter 4) makes a convincing case that in order for TESOL teachers "to transform biases, inequities, and marginalities, a critical approach to ELT needs to go beyond challenging ideology and political economy, and exercise *praxis*—critical reflection and action."

The next three chapters in Part II capture spatial grounding of transnational practices in TESOL teacher education. Using a TESOL Initial Teacher Education (ITE) Project in Hong Kong as a qualitative case study, Benjamin Moorhouse (in Chapter 5) examines the experiences of pre-service teachers teaching English in China for two weeks. Peter Browning (in Chapter 6) explores the ways in which transnational dimensions of *Colombia Bilingüe* policy have been rejected and critiqued by local academic and educational practitioners, and how such rejection of transnationalism has led to the emergence of discourses that have an ambivalent relation to transnationalism in the country. Cristina Sánchez-Martín (in Chapter 7) underscores the importance of adopting "critical autoethnography methodology" and "Cultural Historical Activity Theory" in transnational TESOL teacher education programs to make informed pedagogical choices.

Part III comprises four chapters that engage readers with dynamic debates on the ways in which transnationalism is enacted in TESOL teacher education in virtual spaces. Geoff Lawrence (in Chapter 8) acknowledges the "increasingly digital, dynamic and transnational" nature of contemporary TESOL contexts. He then proposes a pedagogical framework that can be utilized in TESOL teacher education programs to support pre-service teachers. Using telecollaboration as a translingual contact zone, Bedrettin Yazan and his colleagues (in Chapter 9) examine how 117 TESOL teacher candidates across three distinct geographical locations (i.e., France, Turkey, and the United States) negotiated and constructed their identities in online contact zones. Through an online language teacher training project, Sarina Chugani Molina (in Chapter 10) explores how to create authentic contexts for Kenyan teacher candidates in order to experience transnational teaching and learning practices. Davinia Sánchez-García and Nashwa Nashaat (in

Chapter 11) investigate how the Two2Tango (T2T) program (a transnational community of practice) supports in-service TESOL teachers across six European countries to construct their professional identities.

Four chapters in Part IV interrogate the ways in which transnational practices are (mis)represented in the policies, curricula, and professional learning trajectories within the broader scholarship of TESOL teacher education. Iara Bruz and her colleagues (in Chapter 12) explore the merit of transnational dialogue in the Certificate Program in the Discipline of Teaching of English as an International Language (D-TEIL). They also show how such a dialogic approach helps them tap their experiential differences in several key themes including "transglocal program design; the ethics of transnational teacher education; dealing with unpredictability" and the like. Kyle Perkins and Xuan Jiang (in Chapter 13) make a case for the incorporation of transnationalism as a curriculum unit or model into a graduate TESOL teacher education programs. They offer four major themes for inclusion, and the "why," "what," "how," and "when" questions for realizing such endeavors. Joel Windle (in Chapter 14) emphasizes human rights as a performative context for transnationalism. He does so by examining how Brazilian student-teachers place "themselves in relation to situations of transnational contact, in an applied linguistics course that drew on concepts of critical intercultural citizenship education." Dandan Zhu and Jim McKinley (in Chapter 15) explore the experiences of 20 transnational students from China pursuing their TESOL degree in the United Kingdom. They offer thought-provoking implications for TESOL program developers and curriculum writers.

By presenting these insightful chapters, we invite you to critically engage with the notion of transnationalism and its potential contributions to TESOL teacher education. While the mobility of people and goods across national borders may be easily tracked, monitored, and controlled, it is difficult to understand how knowledge and ideas move beyond borders and how they are taken up by various stakeholders in diverse contexts. Borders may be shut down, but not ideas. As the chapters in this volume suggest, knowledge and ideas needed to prepare future language teachers follow an unpredictable cartography. They move forward, backward, and sideways, and follow complex trajectories. A matter of great concern is how political borders obstruct and/or facilitate the movement of professional knowledge and ideas. It is also important to examine how borders attach national identity tags to people and their ideas that may have far-reaching consequences for a transformative utilization of transnational knowledge in TESOL teacher education.

## References

Alim, H., Ibrahim, A., & Pennycook, A. (eds.). (2009). *Global linguistic flows: Hip hop cultures, youth identities, and the politics of language*. New York, NY: Routledge.

Appadurai, A., & Breckenridge, C. (1988). Why public culture? *Public Culture*, 1, 5–9.

Basch, L., Schiller, C., & Szanton, C. (1994). *Nations unbound: Transnational projects, postcolonial predicaments, and deterritorialized nation-states*. New York, NY: Routledge.

Blackledge, A., & Creese, A. (2010). *Multilingualism: A Critical Perspective.* London: Continuum.

Blommaert, J. (2010). *The sociolinguistics of globalization.* Cambridge: Cambridge University Press.

De Fina, A., & Perrino, S. (2013). Transnational identities. *Applied Linguistics*, 34(5), 509–515.

Duff, P. A. (2015). Transnationalism, multilingualism, and identity. *Annual Review of Applied Linguistics*, 35, 57–80.

Faist, T., & Bilecen, B. (2017). Transnationalism: Updated. COMCAD Working Papers, 158. Bielefeld: Universität Bielefeld, Fak. für Soziologie, Centre on Migration, Citizenship and Development (COMCAD). https://nbn-resolving.org/urn:nbn:de:0168-ssoar-55393–55395.

Garcés-Mascareñas, P., & Penninx, R. (2016). *Integration processes and policies in Europe: Contexts, levels and actors.* Berlin: Springer.

Iriye, A. (2004). Transnational history. *Contemporary European History*, 13(2), 211–222.

Johnson, K. E. (1996). The role of theory in L2 teacher education. *TESOL Quarterly*, 30(4), 765–771.

Johnson, K. E., & Golombek, P. R. (2018). Informing and transforming language teacher education pedagogy. *Language Teaching Research*, Online First, 1–12. http://doi-org-443.webvpn.fjmu.edu.cn/10.1177/1362168818777539.

Kearney, M. (1995). The local and the global: The anthropology of globalization and transnationalism. *Annual Review of Anthropology*, 24, 547–565.

Li, W. (ed.). (2012). Language policy and practice in transnational, multilingual families and beyond [Special issue]. *Journal of Multilingual and Multicultural Development*, 33(1), 67–83.

Mok, K., Han, X., & Jiang, J. (2018). International and transnational education for whose interests? A study on the career development of Chinese students. *Higher Education Quarterly*, 72(3), 208–223.

Mügge, L. (2016). Transnationalism as a research paradigm and its relevance for integration. In B. Garcés-Mascareñas & R. Penninx (eds.), *Integration processes and policies in Europe* (pp. 109–125). Cham: Springer.

Nell, L. M. (2007). Locally specific transnational political ties: Turkish and Turkish Kurdish immigrants in the Netherlands. In A. Guillou, S. de Tapia, & M. Wadbled (eds.), *Migrations Turques dans un monde globalisé: Le poids du local* (pp. 199–216). Rennes: Rennes University Press.

Phan, L. (2017). *Transnational education crossing "Asia" and "the West": Adjusted desire, transformative mediocrity and neo-colonial disguise.* New York, NY: Routledge.

Rizvi, F., & Choo, S. (2020). Education and cosmopolitanism in Asia: An introduction. *Asia Pacific Journal of Education*, 40(1), 1–9.

Rose, N., & Galloway, N. (2019). *Global Englishes for language teaching.* Cambridge: Cambridge University Press.

Rumbaut, R. (2002). Severed or sustained attachments? Language, identity, and imagined communities in the post-immigrant generation. In P. Levitt & M. Waters (eds.), *The changing face of home: The transnational lives of the second generation* (pp. 43–95). New York, NY: Russell Sage Foundation.

Saunier, P. (2013). Transnational history: Introduction. In *Transnational history.* London: Palgrave Macmillan.

Sikkink, K. (1998). Transnational politics, international relations theory, and human rights. *Political Science and Politics*, 31(3), 516–523.

Van Amersfoort, H. (2001). *Moderne diaspora's, transnationalisme en sociale cohesie.* Amsterdam: Institute for Social Science Research, University of Amsterdam.

Vertovec, S. (1999). Conceiving and researching transnationalism. *Ethnic and Racial Studies*, 22(2), 447–462.

Vertovec, S. (2009). *Transnationalism.* London: Routledge.

Warriner, D. (2017). Theorizing the spatial dimensions and pedagogical implications of transnationalism. *Curriculum Inquiry*, 47(1), 50–61.

Windle, J., & O'Brien, S. (2019). Language, education and transnationalism: An introduction. *Trabalhos em Linguística Aplicada*, 58(1), 1–10.

You, X. (2018). *Transnational writing education: Theory, history, and practice.* New York, NY: Routledge.

# Part I

# Epistemological, theoretical, and historical interventions

# 2 Transnationalism and education

## Epistemological and theoretical exercises

*Xiaoye You*

### The charge

The rise of the nation after the industrial revolution ushered nationalism into the educational domain. Focusing on cultivating national citizens, schools place emphasis on natural and artificial boundaries between peoples, cultures, and languages, differentiating between "us" and "them." In language education, nationalism concretizes in a monolingual ideology and practice: students are taught the national language and literature at the expense of their home language and local literate practice. In TESOL, the monolingual ideology dictates that teachers lead their students toward reified native speaker norms in spelling, pronunciation, vocabulary, and grammar. However, the continuous deepening processes of globalization and the resurgence of nationalism in Asia, Europe and North America urgently requires that TESOL teachers develop a fluid, less-bounded perspective to nation, culture, and language, that is, a transnational orientation to language education.

In this chapter, first, I will suggest that TESOL, despite taking place in multilingual and transnational contexts, has predominantly worked under the monolingual ideology. This ideology has shaped TESOL teachers' identity and epistemology; the latter refers to their beliefs about English and its teaching, and their content knowledge (CK) and pedagogical content knowledge (PCK) required for teaching English as a second or foreign language. Drawing on evidence from Asian countries and focusing on the teaching of writing, an area of my expertise, I demonstrate that teachers there struggled with a monolingual ideology endorsed by the state. Influenced by monolingualism, teachers have often developed a monolingual identity and epistemology, fostering monolithic beliefs about language and culture and losing sight of the multilingual and transnational reality in which they live.

Recent scholarship in applied linguistics and literacy studies (such as Canagarajah, 2013; Cenoz & Gorter, 2011; Fraiberg, Wang, & You, 2017; Pennycook, 2010; You, 2016, 2018) has suggested ways to embrace multilingualism and transnationalism in teaching and research. Next, I propose a transnational approach to TESOL by integrating three theoretical constructs—translingualism, transculturalism, and cosmopolitanism. Taking this transnational approach,

I suggest that as English becomes a Lingua Franca in globalization, it has potential to bridge cultural boundaries if it is conceived and taught in a transnational framework. In this framework, English needs to be understood as practice on the ground, referring to the diverse styles used by people regardless of their birthplace, nation, region, race, and ethnicity. A transnational orientation suggests that English users will interact with diverse dialects and languages in addition to Standard English, a problematic construct with a colonial and nationalist history (Crowley, 1989). Furthermore, they will encounter diverse cultural discourses and, through deep engagement with them, potentially form affinities with the communities and groups behind these discourses. The transnational orientation demands that we seek to cultivate in English users the ability to engage with these cultural discourses through Standard English, other styles of English, other languages, and other semiotic resources.

Coupled with such scholarship, I then propose that knowledge of the multilingual history of TESOL in the local context and the transnational understanding of English and English teaching may encourage TESOL teachers to negotiate with their monolingual ideology and local stakeholders proactively, and to transform their CK. I conclude the chapter by introducing a model of border crossing for TESOL teachers to develop their PCK. When interacting with multilingual students of other nations through information technology, teachers may integrate transnational and historical insights into their PCK and reinvent their teacher identity.

## The monolingual epistemology and teacher identity in TESOL

As part of an "imagined community" (Anderson, 1991), national subjects are engrained by the state with a bounded perspective to language and nation, or monolingualism. Within the monolingual frame, it is assumed that one communicates with other members, sharing a national culture and a national language; other languages are considered ethnic or foreign and best kept at home or in the classroom (Dicker, 2003). An example of monolingual nationalism is still common in the teaching and research of ESL writing these days: whatever languages or dialects have mediated a writing activity, when teachers and researchers focus on a writer's first language, they often assume it is the national code. If someone chose to study me drafting this chapter, for instance, that person would likely focus on the mediation of Putonghua (China's official code) or of the Putonghua-based writing system. However, my first language is not Putonghua but Hakka. I draw on elements of Hakka, Southwest Mandarin, Putonghua, classical Chinese, and English in my composing process. In multilingual societies, students' first languages and dialects do not always coincide with the officially sanctioned codes.

Deeply affected by the monolingual ideology, TESOL teachers often unconsciously come to identify with it, adopting it as part of their professional identity makeup. This identity makeup can be understood in a frames perspective, as suggested by Pennington (2015). She posited that a TESOL teacher identity can be viewed through both practice-based and contextual frames. Some of the practice-based frames are instructional (teaching content, methods, materials, and technologies; teacher roles; and teacher–student relationship), disciplinary (academic affiliation; academic qualifications; areas of teacher knowledge; and research and scholarship), and professional (ethics and standards; teacher education and development; working condition; political influence and power; collegial relations). The contextual frames include global (international orientation; practices related to global flows of people, money, technology, information, ideologies, and language), local (situatedness of practice, institution, community, nation; specific teacher and student groups in a particular locale), and sociocultural (linguistic and ethnic backgrounds of teachers and students; demographics of administrators, teachers, and students) (p. 19). Each of these frames represents different facets of TESOL teacher identity, which together make up a composite identity.

Examined from the frames perspective, TESOL teachers often manifest identification with the monolingual ideology, which in turn shape their knowledge of the discipline, instructional practice (as well as their PCK), and the profession. Let's take English teachers in Asia as an example. In a disciplinary frame, the teachers may view English as foreign because traditionally it is not widely spoken in the local or national context. Take the teaching of English writing as an example. A cursory survey of ESL writing related articles published in academic journals in China, Taiwan, Japan, Korea, Indonesia, and Malaysia shows that a monolingual nationalist ideology is strong in the consciousness of English teachers and researchers there (Chou & Hayes, 2009; You, 2010). In addition to viewing English as the tongue of the other, they uphold the essentialized and idealized "native speaker" norms as the target of teaching and assessing writing. This can be partly attributed to the dominance that second language acquisition (SLA) research holds in the applied linguistics and TESOL programs in the region. For a long time, the cognitive approach to SLA research has viewed students learning a foreign language as moving toward the native speaker norms. English teachers view native speakers as the target audience for their students' speech and writing. English is assumed of pragmatic functions for academic, business, and cultural communication in international contexts rather than for communication within the nation.

The power of monolingualism in shaping identity and epistemology can be similarly observed in an instructional frame. In Lee's (2013) study conducted in Hong Kong, for instance, the in-service teachers came into the MA teacher education course viewing the teaching of writing as primarily teaching grammar and vocabulary and correcting errors. After the course, their perception of teaching writing remarkably expanded. However, their teacher identity and instructional practice continued to be shaped by the monolingual values of their community of practice. Although they had changed their beliefs about the primacy of marking all student errors and developed a preference for focused error feedback, they were mandated by a school policy that required them to mark all student errors. As a result, they followed the policy and marked all student errors. The school policy, as supported by the local community of teachers, administrators, and parents, views correcting all student errors as a must in moving students' written English toward native speaker norms. Despite their active negotiation with the local community values, these teachers ended up submitting to monolingualism in classroom teaching.

In the professional frame, this monolingual ideology has also shaped TESOL teachers in Asia. Implicitly, the profession of English teaching has supported monolingual assumptions and practice (Kam, 2002; Kubota, 1998). For instance, studying the teaching of English writing at a Chinese university, You (2004a) found that in Chinese universities, English writing is taught under the guidance of a nationally unified syllabus and examination system. Influenced by the high stakes of a college English exit exam, teachers are concerned about the teaching of correct form and test-taking skills rather than assisting their students to develop thoughts in writing. Because of their relatively low-income status, teachers have to work extra hours and have little time to spend on individual students or on furthering their professional training. In recent years, as universities compete for prestige, English teachers in Asian nations face mounting pressure to publish in scholarly journals (Liu, 2014; Min, 2014), often without receiving reduced teaching load. With new expectations for research, teachers have less time devoted to teaching, thus often falling back on their old teaching practice that focuses on language correctness and test-taking skills.

From the perspective of a contextual frame, English teacher identity and epistemology has prominently taken a local orientation, which aligns with monolingualism. Entrenched in classroom teaching, for example, writing teachers tend to be interested in practical issues arising from the classroom, such as pedagogy, technology, assessment, feedback to student writing, features of student texts, and writing strategies (Chou & Hayes, 2009; You, 2004b; Zhang, Yan, & Liu, 2015). Attending local academic conferences and reading local journals have reinforced their interest in the practical issues of the local, without encouraging them to understand teaching writing from a transnational perspective.

## Toward a transnational epistemology in TESOL

Recent conversations in applied linguistics, cultural studies, and philosophy have pointed out ways to move beyond nationalism in imagining a more socially just future. Important to TESOL are such constructs as translingualism, transculturalism, and cosmopolitanism. Arising from both historical human experiences and observations on the flows of people, artifacts, products, and literacy practices in globalization, these constructs provide ways for TESOL teachers to understand, cross, and sometimes transcend the boundaries that have circumvented students' reading and writing, and to help forge just social relations.

Translingualism emphasizes the fluid and artificial boundaries among languages and across modes of representation in human communication (Blackledge & Creese, 2010; Canagarajah, 2013; García, 2009; Jordan, 2015). Our sense of language and dialect has been deeply influenced by nationalism, which has taught us rigid rules and forms within lingua-cultural boundaries. In practice, languages are neither discrete nor stable but rather dynamic and negotiated, and writing necessarily involves the negotiation of language difference. Using the term "translingual practice," Canagarajah (2013) intends to break down the boundaries of linguistic codes in a speaker's communicative repertoire. He emphasizes two key points in human communication: first, communication transcends individual languages because languages are always in contact and mutually influencing each other; second, communication transcends words and involves diverse semiotic resources and ecological affordances. Recently, Canagarajah (2018) takes a step further by arguing that translingual practice is deeply connected to a transnational positioning. It is because translingual practice, such as code-meshing, is most commonly found among multilingual speakers who consciously position themselves in a niminal space between nations and between cultures.

Transculturalism is the next critical lens in a transnational approach to ESL education (Guerra, 1997, 2015; Pratt, 1991; Zamel, 1997). First defined by the South American scholar Fernando Ortiz, transculturalism refers to the process of *métissage* (mixing of peoples) as a distinctive character of a culture in the Americas, which developed from both native and immigrant populations. Ortiz views transculturalism in its earliest stage as a synthesis of two phases taking place at the same time: a deculturalization of the past and a *métissage* with the present. As a biological and cultural *métis*, one is always part of the dialectic with the Other. Cuccioletta (2001) suggests that the process of recognizing oneself in the Other will lead to a cosmopolitan citizenship:

> This citizenship, independent of political structures and institutions, develops each individual in the understanding that one's culture is multiple, métis, and that each human experience and existence is due to the contact with *other*, who in reality is like, oneself.
>
> (p. 9, emphasis in the original)

Building on translingualism and transculturalism, I proposed the construct of "transliteracy," emphasizing that in globalization everyone is a cultural and linguistic *métis*, but with salient socio-historical differences. When being respected and taken seriously, one has to, and can, come to recognize oneself in the Other through reading and writing across languages, engaging diverse cultural discourses, and shuttling between communities (You, 2016).

While translingualism and transculturalism describe language and cultural practices people already engage in, *cosmopolitanism* refers to a cross-border disposition to be inculcated in teachers and students. Although the term "cosmopolitanism" has been attributed to Diogenes the Cynic, an ancient Greek, the same ideal can be found in many cultures, such as in the writings of Confucius in China (Chan, 2002), of Immanuel Kant in Germany, and of W. E. B. Dubois, Martin Luther King Jr., and Barack Obama in the United States (Mullen, 2004; Selzer, 2010). Of its various formulations, cosmopolitanism carries a fundamental meaning: though sometimes defined by kindred relations, ethnicity, nation, race, or class, all people are first and foremost members of the human race and as such are morally obligated to those outside their categories; further, they have the agency to develop and sustain new allegiances across cultures, communities, and languages. Taking an antiessentialist stand, the cosmopolitan perspective reminds us of the historicity, artificiality, and rhetoricity of these cultural categories, and more importantly the historical effects of these categories. This perspective enables us to perceive human connectedness as being deeply underpinned in the various accents, styles, and uses of language in everyday life and literary culture. Linguistic, cultural, and ethnic differences are not to be contained but to be respected and appreciated. They need to be explored, in pedagogy and research, to recover and protect the multifaceted, intricate human connections severed by artificial borders.

Together, translingualism, transculturalism, and cosmopolitanism constitute an epistemological framework in English education with a transnational orientation. Translingualism calls our attention to how we use language and other systems of representation in communication, effectively tearing down the linguistic "fences," and by extension that of national, ethnic, and racial boundaries. Transculturalism reminds us that we are always culturally hybrid by nature, however we define "culture." We are always in a state of diaspora if there was ever a "home" in the first place. The way we encounter, blend in, and reconstitute various cultures challenges the idealized original "us." Cosmopolitanism offers an ethical imperative for TESOL. In addition to educating our students as national subjects, we must educate them at the same time as responsible global citizens. Further, as articulated by Surma (2013) and others, cosmopolitanism can serve as a form of resistance to or a critique of the destructive aspects of globalization, particularly of the neoliberal market economy.

To encourage TESOL teachers to embrace a transnational epistemology, historical knowledge on second language (L2) teaching in local contexts becomes critical. It will reveal to the teachers that this history has always been multilingual and thus make them aware of their monolingual orientation. Further, with sociopolitical forces shaping language teaching in the past coming into relief, teachers may be inspired to examine the current sociopolitical situation that has shaped their assumptions about language, culture, and pedagogy. To demonstrate the affordances of historical knowledge in reinventing teacher identity and epistemology, next, I will visit several themes in the historical accounts of teaching L2 writing in Asia. Often focused on instructional issues of the present, TESOL teachers tend to neglect or ignore this history, which, however, bears important implications for their work.

## Retrieving a multilingual history of teaching L2 writing

Asian countries have a long history of teaching L2 writing, a history deeply connected to trade, migration, colonization, and religion. In east and south-east Asia, classical Chinese was widely studied due to the reach of Chinese empire and the circulation of Confucian and Buddhist classics. As early as two millenniums ago, Sanskrit and Persian were taught in Indian temples and academies to speakers of other languages. These classical languages dominated the scene of teaching L2 in Asia until the eighteenth century, when the East India Company entered India and started its colonial rule there. Since then English has become the widely taught additional language in Asia. In various historical accounts of teaching L2 writing in Asia, several themes have emerged. As these themes are connected to broad sociopolitical forces, they tend to evade the attention of local teachers, who are interested in practical issues arising from their immediate context. Those long-standing themes include L2 reading and writing as a local language practice, literary creativity in an L2, the local's ambivalence toward an L2 and its so-called native speakers, and the mediation of L2 literacy in local education and sociopolitical life.

After an L2 is introduced into a local context, it gradually becomes part of the locals' communicative practice. The spread of classical Chinese in Japan, for instance, took place largely through migration and travel. Chinese and Korean immigrants brought classical Chinese into Japan in the fifth century, which became its first major writing system. While for a long time it was only available to the elite class as a foreign language, over time its users transformed it into their own. In the early years, writing in Japan strictly adhered to the syntactic rules of classical Chinese. In the seventh century, Japanese writers started composing kanji (Chinese character) texts using vernacular Japanese syntax and vernacular texts using kanji as phonograms. When the oldest extant chronicle in Japan, Kojiki, was composed in the eighth century, the practice of writing with Japanese syntax while using kanji, partially as phonograms, was firmly established (Seeley, 1991). Once classical Chinese traveled beyond its original cultural bound, its phonological, morphological, syntactic, and pragmatic conventions were reconfigured by its new users to accommodate their meaning making practice.

As part of this local and translocal meaning making practice, writers have used L2 to describe their lives and their imaginations, drawing linguistic and cultural resources from their communities and beyond. Literary works were created using classical Chinese in Korea and Japan, and religious texts using Sanskrit and Persian in India. Examples of using English for literary creativity are abundant in Asia. These creative writers come from, using Braj Kachru's terms, both the Outer Circle and Expanding Circle nations in Asia: Raja Rao from India (Mercanti, 2009); Gregorio Brillantes from the Philippines (Cruz, 2011); Yutang Ling, Ha Jin, and Xiaolu Guo from China (Bolton, Botha, & Zhang, 2015; You, 2016; Zhang, 2002); and Kumut Chandruang and Pongpol Adireksarn from Thailand (Watkhaolarm, 2005). The literary genres are diverse: poem, short story, novel, play, and essay. Using English to capture the lived or imagined experiences of their people, these writers infused unique sensibilities into their creative styles (Kachru, 1990). Their English works have challenged a commonly held assumption in language teaching that there is a fixed, one-to-one relationship between language, culture, and place.

In the context of colonization, learning the colonizer's language tends to create mixed feelings and identities. When comparing English teaching in the Philippines under the American rule and after independence, for instance, Philippine scholars tend to show ambivalence. Alberca (1994) examined the history of English teaching in the Philippines, focusing on the work of American soldier-teachers and

Thomasites, i.e., the American civilian teachers. Drawing on student compositions produced around 1904, he demonstrates that within six years of American colonial rule, local students were able to use English at a high proficiency level. He concludes his study by arguing for the importance of balancing nationalism and internationalism in the teaching of English:

> Put simply, why limit the Filipino child's learning experience to bananas, guavas, and carabaos which he or she already knows? Why not introduce him or her to other worlds which will expand his or her knowledge not only as a nationalist but also as an internationalist?
>
> (p. 71)

Recalling the colonial days certainly does not mean the Philippines have to go back to the colonial rule to produce competent English users. Instead, striking a balance between the nationalist and internationalist orientation, hence in teacher identity and epistemology, is necessary.

In both colonial and postcolonial contexts, the issues of which language should be taught and why, the effects of language on students' identities, and the power and cultural values attached to language education were central concerns to students, teachers, and administrators (Arnold, 2014; Ramanathan, 2003; You, 2010). In Arnold's (2014) study of language attitudes, policies, and pedagogies at the Syrian Protestant College in Beirut in the nineteenth century, for instance, she notes the change of medium of instruction at the college around 1880 from Arabic to English. The faculty initially wrote and translated texts for and taught their courses in Arabic. Then they switched to English because they believed that teaching in Arabic had not proven to be "the best means of Christianizing and civilizing the East" (p. 283, cited in Arnold, 2014). Additionally, as the student population and faculty hires diversified, Arabic was not always a language known to them. It is important to note that before and after the change of medium of instruction, students and faculty were forced to negotiate and switch between English, Arabic, French, and other languages across the college curriculum as writers, readers, and speakers.

When English writing was taught in the colonial period, it was intertwined with the teaching of other subjects in many Asian universities (see Indian universities in Jeyaraj, 2009; and Chinese universities in You, 2010). In universities that were influenced by the American tradition, there were courses called English composition. Universities that were influenced by the British tradition tended to integrate English reading and writing into subject courses. Thus, students' English literacy development was intertwined with and mediated the learning of subject knowledge in a variety of fields. For example, Jeyaraj (2009) examined several dozen student compositions from British parliamentary records, compositions produced between 1817 and 1857 for government scholarship exams or university exit exams. The student essays reveal that by participating in a modernist curriculum, Indian college students internalized modernist values and practices. Some of the values include the belief in an external reality; one making truth claims based on evidence, scientific method, and rationality; the existence of human universals; and language as a transparent tool of representation. English literacy practice actively participated in transmitting and creating knowledge for students and came to shape their worldviews.

Students' English composition not only mediated their learning of subject knowledge but also their sociopolitical life. The Indian students' exam essays were their means to negotiate with the British colonial structure. At St. John's University in Shanghai, Chinese students similarly used English composition to participate in the national struggle against colonial and imperialist forces. During World War II, the war with Japan was a popular topic in the writing class despite the life-threatening risks such a topic could bring to students. Lamberton (1955), an English teacher at St. John's at that time, recalls those dangerous scenarios: Japanese boats continuously passed on the creek flowing around the campus and they were loaded with property taken from the Chinese who lived in Soochow. Unable to bear this sight quietly, often students expressed their hatred of the Japanese in their English compositions. Their teachers often tore up the essays rather than risk them being found on students who might be searched on their way home. Thus, English writing provided the students living in those dreadful circumstances a venue to express their sadness, indignation, and hatred. Their writing subverted the disorder and terror imposed by the Japanese imperialists. Through writing, students and their foreign teachers co-constructed a transnational anti-Fascist discourse. Using this "foreign" language in their fight against imperialist encroachment in Asia, students turned English into their own.

Out of these historical examples emerges a multilingual history of teaching L2 writing in Asia. This history indicates, first, that the teaching and learning of an L2 always takes place in a multilingual context, interacting with the learning and use of other languages. Second, the use of an L2 in the Asian context defies the commonly held view that there is a fixed, one-to-one relationship between language, nation, and place. The use of a second or foreign language has always been part of local people's social practice, mediating their learning of subject knowledge and their sociopolitical and literary actions. By appropriating a second or foreign language for their diverse purposes, the users turned the language into one of their own, thus collapsing the boundaries between "us" (non-native speakers) and "them" (native speakers), our language and their language.

## Integrating transnational and historical insights into TESOL pedagogy

TESOL teachers need to integrate the transnational and historical insights gained from reading professional literature into their pedagogical content knowledge. In the field of education, scholars such as Shulman (1986, 1987) and his colleagues differentiate between content knowledge (CK) and pedagogical content knowledge (PCK). CK is composed of knowledge of the major findings, theories, and investigative procedures of a given field and is shared by both teachers and non-teaching experts in that field. The transnational epistemology in TESOL and the multilingual history of teaching L2 introduced in this chapter fall underneath content knowledge for TESOL teachers. The transnational epistemology requires the teacher (and the researcher) to embrace translingual understanding of English, transcultural understanding of nation, and producing global citizens as the goal for TESOL. Knowledge of the transnational history of TESOL may encourage the teacher to reflect upon and break away from his or her monolingual visions. PCK, in contrast, represents both the process and result of a teacher transforming content knowledge into pedagogically appropriate forms for students. So, for instance, an experienced writing teacher would have a categorically different type of knowledge about writing than a non-teaching professional writer would. In addition to general content knowledge common to both, the teacher would possess knowledge of "the conceptions and preconceptions that students of different ages and backgrounds bring with them to the learning" of writing as well as "the most useful forms of representation, the most powerful analogies, illustrations, examples, explanations, and demonstrations" of writing concepts for learners (Shulman, 1986, p. 9). This knowledge of content for teaching is PCK. Therefore, for teachers interested in taking the transnational approach into their classroom, they need to develop or reformulate their PCK from a transnational perspective. Here, I suggest a border-crossing model for both TESOL teacher development and for writing pedagogy, where TESOL teachers can develop their PCK by drawing on transnational and historical insights.

To develop their PCK from a transnational perspective, it is beneficial that TESOL teachers seek opportunities to engage students and teachers from outside their nations. The model of border crossing I propose here serves as both an institutional program and a pedagogical strategy. In this model, TESOL teachers and multilingual writers are connected through communication technologies, including electronic bulletin boards, blogs, e-mails, instant messaging, teleconferencing, and phones. Student writers share their work and their composing processes with the teachers. Through a dialogical process whereby students and teachers discuss student writings and reflect on their interactions, teachers gain first-hand knowledge of the writers' needs and resources and the features of their writing. In return, writers receive feedback from the teachers. In the interactions the teachers are led to recognize and enlist their own language and cultural experiences to reconceptualize issues of multilingual writing. In this model the teachers cross and re-cross artificial borders: the border between teaching "native" and "non-native" multilingual writers, the border between the teachers' language learning and teaching experiences, and the borders between writing programs, between universities, and even between nations. The model has been employed by You (2016) and Zhang (2018) to transform teachers' conceptions of writer, audience, and language.

In You (2016), American teachers taking a graduate seminar were connected with undergraduate writers from a Chinese university. The teachers read the students' essays and offered their comments. Then they discussed their comments with students online and their interactions with the students in the graduate seminar. In the online and classroom discussions, several key concepts mediated the teachers' development of expertise prominently. These concepts, including "audience," "coherence," "genre," and "language," introduced by the seminar instructor or brought up by the teachers, framed their evaluations of the student essays, their border-crossing correspondence, class discussions, and end-of-semester reflections. While using these concepts to organize and make sense of their experiences working with the Chinese students, the teachers were led to reformulate their understandings of these concepts arriving at the "true concepts" in the Vygotskyan sense.

Tracing the key concepts in the instructors' mental lives shows that they came to understand many of the cultural and rhetorical complexities associated with multilingual writing. Like travelers arriving in a foreign land, they encountered situations that challenged, confused, and even shocked them. For example, they were perplexed by the ambiguity of audiences evoked and positions held in the student essays. Although the Chinese students kept the American teachers in mind, they didn't seem altogether successful in addressing them, as the latter raised a series of questions about audience. The students' "failure" revealed to the teachers the challenges of negotiating double consciousness inherent in multilingual writing. In exploring the pedagogical motivations and sociocultural implications of assigning feature stories in college writing courses, the instructors marveled at the deep cultural meanings associated with teaching English writing in China. Through dialogical engagement with the Chinese students, they experienced first-hand the complex interplay between translocal values and writing in English as an additional language.

The challenging, confusing, and sometimes shocking experiences of the interchange inspired the instructors to confront and to reformulate their conceptions about multilingual writers, audience, and language. In reading the student reports, they learned that these writers juggled several languages and modalities when constructing their feature stories. For example, a group of students interviewed street vendors in Cantonese and Mandarin on how they dealt with urban inspectors, prepared a news report in English, and presented the report as an anchor reporting in a newsroom whiling showing clips of their street interviews. When teacher–student power relations were equalized to some extent in the online space, some Chinese students held fast to their biases about Chinese and American societies, unwavering when confronted with American teachers' suggestions for revision. Assessing writing in a translocal context proved a significant challenge for American teachers, as it forced them to reassess their assumptions about audience. Class discussions on coherence also revealed the opposing values held and contested among the instructors: one teacher connected coherence to the integrity of the writer while a few other instructors preferred to limit the term to the internal consistency of a text. The teachers came to realize that the coherence issue they attributed at first to the Chinese student writers turned out not to be an exclusively multilingual issue. Similarly, some of them didn't find surface-level language challenges a uniquely multilingual issue either. The exchange awakened the teachers to their values and assumptions and challenged them to embrace translingual and transcultural ones.

In Zhang's (2018) study, in addition to transforming teachers' perceptions of multilingual writers, audience, and language, the border-crossing activity reshaped preservice TESOL teachers' identity. In a graduate seminar on TESOL, Zhang connected American teachers with Chinese undergraduates, inviting the former to read and discuss the latter's essays. The activity prompted the teachers to construct new teacher identity with a transnational orientation in discourse, practice, and activity. First, through discourse, i.e., their reflections, teaching philosophy, class discussions, and interactions with Chinese students, the teachers discussed their perceptions of ESL students, ESL writing, and the teacher's role in language education. Second, through practice, i.e., reading and discussing the Chinese student essays, the teachers recognized the strengths of their writing and provided constructive suggestions to address their needs. Their interactions with students enhanced their professional knowledge both theoretically and practically and built up their professional confidence. Third, although most of the teachers did not have much real-life teaching experience, the activity shaped their identity construction from social, cultural, and historical perspectives. Before the activity, the teachers' conceptions of language learners mainly originated from their own foreign language learning experience and their previous monolingual, monocultural learning environment and mindset. Their interaction with Chinese students enhanced their perceptions of themselves, their students, and their future careers. For the few teachers who had taught American students before, this activity made them realize the limitations of their current ESL programs and the necessity of high-quality ESL programs in the American public-school system. The cross-border activity called teachers' attention to sociocultural factors such as their personal experience (foreign language learning experience), educational environment (monolingual student body), educational system (foreign language policies), and work environment, that shaped their teacher identity and epistemology.

The success of our border-crossing activities does not guarantee the model's success in other institutions or in the development of TESOL teachers. To implement this model, a TESOL program needs to embrace transliteracy as its pedagogical goal and to possess the right resources, such as trained or at least interested faculty, technological support, and already well-established connections across borders. The success of our teacher development practices had much to do with the teachers being students at the same time, a group that we could teach and shape. They had the opportunity to take graduate courses and to participate in the exchange. In contrast, most in-service TESOL teachers may not have such opportunities for development. For the fortunate few who are retrained once every few years, a border-crossing activity can be implemented in their training courses. Despite these challenges, hopefully TESOL program administrators and literacy scholars will be inspired by our border-crossing practices and adapt this model in their contexts.

## Conclusion

As the processes of globalization deepen and nationalism simultaneously rises in many parts of the world, TESOL teachers will increasingly feel the push and pull of the transnational and national forces. This chapter argues that they must seriously consider a political and ethical imperative of globalization, i.e., they work to produce not only responsible national but also global citizens. As Alberca (1994) argued, we, English teachers, need to expand our students' knowledge of the worlds "not only as a nationalist but also as an internationalist" (p. 71). In this chapter, I have introduced an epistemological framework for TESOL with a transnational orientation, a framework consisting of three key constructs—translingualism, transculturalism, and cosmopolitanism. To transform teacher identity and epistemology from a national to a transnational framework, first, I suggest that they can be introduced to the history of teaching L2 in the local context, by calling their attention to the multilingual nature of this history. Second, they can then try incorporating the epistemological constructs and historical insights into their instructional practice, ultimately transforming their PCK. I have introduced a border-crossing model for teacher education as an example of pedagogical experimentation. In their own contexts, as also reported by some studies in You (2018), teachers and teacher educators can experiment with ways in which the epistemological framework can come to undergird whatever aspects of English language that they teach. Epistemological and historical exercises that matter to the local context may encourage the teacher to find ways to strike a balance between national and transnational impulses in his or her instructional practice.

## References


Alberca, W. L. (1994). English language teaching in the Philippines during the early American period: Lessons from the Thomasites. *Philippine Journal of Linguistics*, 25(1/2), 53–74.

Anderson, B. (1991). *Imagined communities: Reflections on the origin and spread of nationalism* (revised ed.). New York: Verso.

Arnold, L. R. (2014). "The worst part of the dead past": Language attitudes, policies, and pedagogies at Syrian Protestant College, 1866–1902. *College Composition and Communication*, 66(2), 276–300.

Blackledge, A., & Creese, A. (2010). *Multilingualism: A critical perspective.* New York: Continuum.

Bolton, K., Botha, W., & Zhang, W. (2015). English in China: A contemporary bibliography. *World Englishes*, 34(2), 282–292.

Canagarajah, S. (2013). *Translingual practice: Global Englishes and cosmopolitan relations.* New York: Routledge.

Canagarajah, S. (2018). Transnationalism and translingualism: How they are connected. In X. You (ed.), *Transnational writing education: Theory, history, and practice* (pp. 41–60). New York: Routledge.

Cenoz, J., & Gorter, D. (2011). Focus on multilingualism: A study of trilingual writing. *Modern Language Journal*, 95(3), 356–369.

Chan, K. (2002). Both sides, now: Culture contact, hybridization, and cosmopolitanism. In S. Vertovec & R. Cohen (eds.), *Conceiving cosmopolitanism: Theory, context, and practice* (pp. 191–208). New York: Oxford University Press.

Chou, L., & Hayes, D. M. (2009). An overview of English writing research in Taiwan. *English Language Teaching*, 2(4), 215–222.

Crowley, T. (1989). *Standard English and the politics of language*. New York: Palgrave Macmillan.
Cruz, P. A. T. (2011). Code-switching, resistance, and reflection: Language awareness through Philippine literature in English. *Asian Englishes*, 14(2), 22–39.
Cuccioletta, D. (2001). Multiculturalism or transculturalism: Towards a cosmopolitan citizenship. *London Journal of Canadian Studies*, 17, 1–11.
Dicker, S. J. (2003). *Languages in America: A pluralist view* (2nd ed.). London: Multilingual Matters.
Fraiberg, S., Wang, X., & You, X. (2017). *Inventing the world grant university: Chinese international students' mobilities, literacies, and identities*. Logan, UT: Utah State University Press.
García, O. (2009). *Bilingual education in the 21st century: A global perspective*. Oxford: Wiley-Blackwell.
Guerra, J. C. (1997). The place of intercultural literacy in the writing classroom. In C. Severino, J. C. Guerra, & J. E. Butler (eds.), *Writing in multicultural settings* (pp. 248–260). New York: MLA.
Guerra, J. C. (2015). *Language, culture, identity and citizenship in college classrooms and communities*. New York: Routledge.
Jeyaraj, J. (2009). Modernity and empire: A modest analysis of early colonial writing practices. *College Composition and Communication*, 60(3), 468–492.
Jordan, J. (2015). Material translingual ecologies. *College English*, 77(4), 364–382.
Kachru, B. (1990). *The alchemy of English: The spread, functions, and models of non-native Englishes*. Urbana, IL: University of Illinois Press.
Kam, H. W. (2002). English language teaching in East Asia today: An overview. *Asia Pacific Journal of Education*, 22(2), 1–22.
Kubota, R. (1998). Ideologies of English in Japan. *World Englishes*, 17(3), 295–306.
Lamberton, M. (1955). *St. John's University, Shanghai, 1879–1951*. New York: United Board for Christian Colleges in China.
Lee, I. (2013). Becoming a writing teacher: Using "identity" as an analytic lens to understand EFL writing teachers' development. *Journal of Second Language Writing*, 22(3), 330–345.
Liu, J. Y. (2014). Problems, strategies, and impact of SSCI publication in English: Perceptions and negotiations of Taiwanese researchers. In C. P. Chou (ed.), *The SSCI syndrome in higher education: A local or global phenomenon* (pp. 109–126). Boston: Sense Publisher.
Mercanti, S. (2009). *The rose and the lotus: Partnership studies in the works of Raja Rao*. New York: Rodopi.
Min, H. (2014). Participating in international academic publishing: A Taiwan perspective. *TESOL Quarterly*, 48(1), 188–200.
Mullen, B. V. (2004). *Afro-orientalism*. Minneapolis, MI: University of Minnesota Press.
Pennington, M. C. (2015). Teacher identity in TESOL: A frames perspective. In Y. L. Cheung, S. B. Said, & K. Park (eds.), *Advances and current trends in language teacher identity research* (pp. 16–30). New York: Routledge.
Pennycook, A. (2010). *Language as a local practice*. New York: Routledge.
Pratt, M. L. (1991). Arts of the contact zone. *Profession*, 91, 33–40.
Ramanathan, V. (2003). Written textual production and consumption (WTPC) in vernacular and English-medium settings in Gujarat, India. *Journal of Second Language Writing*, 12(2), 125–150.
Seeley, C. (1991). *A history of writing in Japan*. Leiden, The Netherlands: E. J. Brill.

Selzer, L. (2010). Barack Obama, the 2008 presidential election, and the new cosmopolitanism: Figuring the black body. *MELUS*, 35(4), 15–37.

Shulman, L. S. (1986). Those who understand: Knowledge growth in teaching. *Educational Researcher*, 15(2), 4–14.

Shulman, L. S. (1987). Knowledge and teaching: Foundations of the new reform. *Harvard Educational Review*, 57(1), 1–22.

Surma, A. (2013). *Imagining the cosmopolitan in public and professional writing*. New York: Palgrave Macmillan.

Watkhaolarm, P. (2005). Think in Thai, write in English: Thainess in Thai English literature. *World Englishes*, 24(2), 145–158.

You, X. (2004a). "The choice made from no choice": English writing instruction in a Chinese university. *Journal of Second Language Writing*, 13(2), 97–110.

You, X. (2004b). New directions in EFL writing: A report from China. *Journal of Second Language Writing*, 13(4), 253–256.

You, X. (2010). *Writing in the devil's tongue: A history of English composition in China*. Carbondale, IL: Southern Illinois University Press.

You, X. (2016). *Cosmopolitan English and transliteracy*. Carbondale, IL: Southern Illinois University Press.

You, X. (ed.). (2018). *Transnational writing education: Theory, history, and practice*. New York: Routledge.

Zamel, V. (1997). Toward a model of transculturation. *TESOL Quarterly*, 31, 341–352.

Zhang, C., Yan, X., & Liu, X. (2015). The development of EFL writing instruction and research in China: An update from the International Conference on English Language Teaching. *Journal of Second Language Writing*, 30, 14–18.

Zhang, H. (2002). Bilingual creativity in Chinese English: Ha Jin's *In the Pond*. *World Englishes*, 21(2), 305–315.

Zhang, Y. (2018). English teacher identity development through a cross-border writing activity. In X. You (ed.), *Transnational writing education: Theory, history, and practice* (pp. 197–202). New York: Routledge.

# 3 Researching transnationalism and TESOL teacher education

## Critical review and outlook

*Xiaoya Sun, Weiyu Zhang and Yin Ling Cheung*

## Introduction

### *Transnationalism: a brief overview*

Since the late twentieth century, advances in transportation and communications technologies have fueled the globalization of migration and ever more prevalent intercultural and international encounters (Brittain, 2009). Contemporary globalization, in turn, contributes to the emergence of the phenomenon of transnationalism (de Fina & Perrino, 2013; Warriner, 2017), which has since been subject to empirical and theoretical research attention in the social sciences (Chin & Smith, 2015). The notion of transnationalism has been defined as "sustained cross-border relationships, patterns of exchange, affiliations and social formations spanning nation-states" (Vertovec, 2009, p. 2). One key feature of transnationalism is that movement is no longer unidirectional (Lie, 1995). Instead, people who engage in transnational mobility, aptly termed "transmigrants" or "transnationals," potentially live across geographical and national boundaries, as they integrate into a new community while maintaining economic, social, political, and cultural connections with the old one (Choi, 2017; Guo & Maitra, 2017; Li & Stodolska, 2006; Sánchez & Machado-Casas, 2009). Unlike internationalism, whose entities are often nation-states, transnationalism distinguishes itself by looking at relationships transcending the nation-state (Canagarajah, 2018) and involving mostly non-state actors (Toukan, Gaztambide-Fernandez, & Anwaruddin, 2017).

Casinader (2016, 2017) problematizes Vertovec's interpretation of transnationalism with its emphasis on cross-border population mobility, and calls for an evolved notion that is more reflective of the complex and multifaceted nature of the phenomenon. He maintains that the prefix "trans-" in "transnationalism" should not be perceived in terms of spatial movement, but considered as representing the "changes or shifts in personal and/or cultural identity as a result of global mobility" (Casinader, 2017, p. 12). Transnationalism as such is "far more than a mere geographical transition" (Casinader, 2018, p. 266). Rather, it is fundamentally disassociated from spatial concepts of place, location, and boundaries, with transculturalism as an essential aspect and cultural diversity as an identifier (Casinader, 2016, 2017). This perception, he believes, enhances the value of transnationalism as a powerful tool for making sense of the long-term impacts of the globalization process (Casinader, 2017).

Based on the previous discussion of the concept, transnationalism can be comprehensively conceptualized as the worldwide movements and interchanges of people and ideas and, more importantly, the formation and transformation of transcultural identities and attitudes that they engender.

### *Transnationalism and TESOL teacher education*

In recent years, the notion of transnationalism has evolved as a frame for thinking beyond nation-state borders in education (Donahue, 2018). Educational settings are susceptible to the impact of transnationalism and migration (Rizvi & Beech, 2017). Internationalization of education inevitably involves participation in and creation of space for transnational education (Phan, 2016). The growing phenomenon of transnational educational mobility, a most visible aspect of transnationalism (Baiutti, 2018; Gordon & Liu, 2014; Song, 2011), has brought about more culturally and linguistically heterogeneous classrooms with an ever-diverse student population (Casinader & Clemans, 2018; Phan, 2016). Accordingly, all teachers, even if they are based in one educational context, are potentially teaching cross-culturally with the presence of different ethnic groups and international students in schools and institutions of higher learning around the world (Jurkova & Guo, 2018; Lum, 2018). In the face of this new trend, culturally relevant and responsive educational programs are called for (Burns & Roberts, 2010; Kim & Slapac, 2015) which could cope with the challenges and demands generated by diversity, convert them into pedagogical resources (Jurkova & Guo, 2018), and develop young people's ability to interact with and respond to the multifarious facets of a globally interconnected world (Casinader, 2016).

Transnationalism also gives rise to new challenges to teaching English to speakers of other languages (TESOL) programs. As the accepted language for global exchanges (McKay, 2018), the English language is of crucial importance in constructing and maintaining connections across transnational social fields (Lam & Warriner, 2012). This has resulted in a greater need to master the language and an increased demand for English teaching and teachers of English (McKay, 2018). TESOL programs have been expanding and taking in a growing number of users of English as an additional language, who will graduate to face linguistically and culturally diverse student populations (Kim & Richardson, 2018; Lum, 2018). To adapt to these changes in terms of "who teaches English, who learns English and why, of the sociopolitical and socioeconomic contexts in which English is taught, and of the varieties of English that are being taught and used around the world" (Johnson, 2006, p. 235), TESOL teacher education programs need to "find ways to situate learning about teaching within authentic contexts" (Johnson, 1996, p. 770). In order to account for the transnational experiences of English language teachers from diverse backgrounds, and prepare them to teach English in varying contexts worldwide (Park, 2012), TESOL programs should re-examine English learning and teaching through a transnational lens (Solano-Campos, 2014), and "instil transnational sensibilities and desires together with the languages, cultures and topics being discussed" (Duff, 2015, p. 76).

### *The present review*

Despite how transnationalism has been challenging existing norms and practices of education in general and language teaching in particular, the impact of transnationalism on TESOL teacher education has not been well-represented in existing literature. In view of this gap, the chapter aims to critically review current research of transnationalism and TESOL teacher education to provide an outlook of the field. More specifically, it will:

1 take stock of research output on issues at the intersection of transnationalism and language teacher education;
2 draw implications on how a foundational knowledge of transnationalism can inform the education of future-ready TESOL teachers; and
3 identify gaps in the research base that still need closer scrutiny and further engagement.

This synthesis of literature is organized around three basic questions:

1 What theoretical and conceptual foundations have guided existing research on transnationalism and TESOL teacher education?
2 What methodological approaches have been adopted in empirical research on transnationalism and TESOL teacher education?
3 What implications does transnationalism have for TESOL teacher education?

Through answering questions 1 and 2, we aim to shed light on the potential theoretical, conceptual, and methodological tools that can be adopted in future research of transnationalism and TESOL teacher education. The answer to question 3 will make explicit the emerging trends in TESOL teacher education in the context of transnationalism, which represent the issues to be addressed in future research of the field.

## Search procedure, inclusion criteria, and method of analysis

The review focuses exclusively on research published in English-medium, international refereed journals and books, because they are: (1) widely accessible to the global audience and, (2) have gone through rigorous peer-review processes (Benson, Chik, Gao, Huang, & Wang, 2009). In order to provide a relatively comprehensive description of the current knowledge base, relevant research published during the three decades between 1998 and 2018 was included. The year 1998 was chosen as the starting point because the late twentieth century was when transnationalism emerged as a key concept in the social sciences (Chin & Smith, 2015), and when transnational education started to receive academic attention (Phan, 2016). For the review to be current, the search extended to literature published as recently as the previous year.

The search for relevant research was conducted in three stages. The first stage was a conventional literature search undertaken in Google Scholar, Web of Science, as well as other online databases (e.g., ERIC and Scopus) that were available through the library system in the authors' institution. Key terms, including *transnationalism*, *transnational*, *transnationalization*, *TESOL teacher education*, and *language teacher education*, plus various combinations of these terms, were employed. In stage two, the reference lists of the initially identified articles were trawled through manually, in search of potentially relevant documents whose titles did not include the keywords. Following a closer look at the abstracts of all articles selected in the first two stages, any studies not addressing issues related to transnationalism and/or TESOL teacher education were excluded. Eventually, a total of 26 empirical studies were reviewed to answer the first two research questions, i.e., for a summary of theoretical/conceptual foundations and methodologies, while an additional 59 relevant documents, including journal articles, book chapters, and books, were examined to draw implications for TESOL teacher education and to identify potential directions for future research.

Guided by the three research questions, we first examined the selection of empirical studies for salient themes in the theoretical, conceptual, and methodological tools that have been adopted, then move on to more relevant research to draw implications for TESOL programs in the context of transnationalism, and conclude by proposing the potential issues to be addressed in future research. Correspondingly, the rest of this chapter is presented in four sections, i.e., theoretical and conceptual foundations, a summary of methodologies, implications for TESOL teacher education, and a brief summary and proposal of directions for future research. It is hoped that through offering a critical review of existing literature and an outlook of emerging research trends, this chapter can be of value to future research in the field.

## Theoretical and conceptual foundations

This section summarizes the theoretical and conceptual foundations that have guided existing research on transnationalism and TESOL teacher education. The findings are presented according to the five common themes identified in the research, namely, teacher identity, linguistic imperialism and multilingual practices, language teacher cognition, theory–practice gap in TESOL teacher education, and impacts of transnational experience.

Teacher identity is one of the key concepts in TESOL teacher education literature because it is believed to have important implications for classroom practices. The concept has been investigated from perspectives such as "poststructuralism," which conceptualizes identity as negotiated and constructed in different contexts and thus is dynamic, fluid, and multiple (Barkhuizen, 2016; Duff, 2015). In the context of transnationalism, studies from the poststructuralist perspective problematize the dominant native–non-native dichotomy for examining language teacher identity and advocate for a translingual orientation to legitimize the language proficiency and cultural background of non-native TESOL teachers (Aneja, 2016; Flores & Aneja, 2017). The studies suggest that non-native teachers should be given opportunities to engage in translingual practices to negotiate and construct a multilingual teacher identity and develop pedagogical practices that build on the teachers' shared home language with students.

The research of teacher identity has also been informed by sociocultural learning theories, particularly situated learning (Lave & Wenger, 1991) and communities of practice (Wenger, 1998). The theories hold that learning is a process of "legitimate peripheral participation" in the practices of social communities for newcomers to master the knowledge and skills required for full participation and construct their identities as members in the communities. From this perspective, the study by Kiely and Askham (2012) examines how trainee teachers construct a TESOL teacher identity during their participation in a pre-service training course and how it translates into their abilities for work. The findings were related to the social psychological construct "furnished imagination," which refers to the "combination of knowledge, procedural awareness and skills, dispositions, and identity which the teachers take from the course as the conceptual toolkit for work in TESOL" (Kiely & Askham, 2012, p. 496). The study views identity as future oriented and as a capacity to imagine a transformed and desirable self in the TESOL community, which is furnished through the training course. Shahri (2018) explores the connections between teacher emotion and identity by drawing on the concept of "perezhivanie," which is defined as individuals' "emotional or lived experience" and "subjective sense of their environment and experience" (p. 93). The study shows that teacher identity is rooted in one's emotional experience and manifests in the emotional attachment to a certain self-understanding. In line with the sociocultural theories, the study points out the importance of "mediation" in identity construction, which refers to "the role of cultural tools, signs and concepts in development" (Shahri, 2018, p. 92). As a means of mediation, "biliteracy events" are explored in transnational bilingual teachers' identity construction during their participation in a pre-service training course (Ceballos, 2012). The notion "biliteracy events" is derived from "literacy events," which concerns how literacy is used in everyday lives (Barton, 2007), to emphasize bilingual teachers' use of literacy in two languages. The study suggests that the knowledge of how transnational teachers construct and maintain a biliteracy and bicultural identity can help them better appreciate the multiple literacy practices and identities of their transnational students.

### *Linguistic imperialism and multilingual practices*

The diverse identities and literacy practices of transnational teachers and learners call into question the dominant status of English and the unequal power relations between speakers of native English and the emerging varieties of Englishes (Kachru, 1992). Aligned with the perspectives of linguistic imperialism (Phillipson, 1992) and critical applied linguistics (Pennycook, 2001), Solano-Campos (2014) demonstrates the various linguistic and racial positionings experienced by a non-native TESOL educator working in a transnational context. While critical applied linguistics problematizes social relations and relates language use to cultural and political factors, linguistic imperialism offers a lens to analyze the asymmetrical power relations between native and non-native English speakers. The actions taken by transnational learners to handle unequal power relations are explored through the intersectional approach. The term "intersectionality" refers to oppressions arising from the intersections of race, gender, class, and other social relations of dominance and power (Collins, 2000). Through this approach, Chamakalayil and Riegel (2016) analyzed the experience of a female immigrant dealing with the challenges and discriminations in a transnational education context. The analysis was informed by the concept of "scopes of possibility," which represents "the possibilities and boundaries a person perceives and how these are interpreted with regard to their relevance and potential for realization in their own life" (Chamakalayil & Riegel, 2016, p. 124).

The unequal power relations associated with language and language learning ideology is also investigated in the discourse of "neoliberalism." Neoliberalism proposes that "human well-being can best be advanced by liberating individual entrepreneurial freedom and skills within an institutional framework characterized by strong private property rights, free markets, and free trade" (Harvey, 2005, p. 2). However, Warriner's (2015) study suggests that the neoliberal discourse sustains language ideologies that privilege English and that immigrant learners often cannot survive depending on their skills and competences alone but need to give up their own language and cultures to fully participate in the English-speaking community. In such cases, the immigrants' unique knowledge derived from their transnational living experiences is left unrecognized and undervalued. The unique knowledge of the immigrants is conceptualized as the "transnational funds of knowledge" and the application of such knowledge in education is advocated (Dabach & Fones, 2016).

Some individuals, however, can position themselves flexibly and perform dynamic multilingual practices in a transnational space. The linguistic behaviors of these individuals are investigated under the concept of "translanguaging." The concept is built on the psycholinguist notion of "languaging," which refers to "the process of using language to gain knowledge, to make sense, to articulate one's thought and to communicate about using language" (Li & Zhu, 2013, p. 519). The prefix "trans" highlights the dynamic and flexible linguistic practices by multilingual users that go between different linguistic structures and systems, which provides a window into human cognition, sociality, and social relations (Li, 2011; Li & Zhu, 2013).

### *Language teacher cognition*

Some studies fall within a broader area of "language teacher cognition" research, which addresses research questions concerning teachers' knowledge, beliefs, and perceptions of all aspects of language teaching. This research area has been explored through many theoretical frames including "coherence system," "folk-linguistic theories," and "metaphors." The coherence system is "a system that claims to provide a means for understanding, evaluating, and constructing accounts of experience" (Linde, 1993, p. 164). It represents a system of knowledge that occupies the mid-ground between expert theories and more common-sense beliefs. The common-sense beliefs about language learning are known as folklinguistic theories, which are simplifying paradigms used by learners to interpret their language learning experience (Miller & Ginsberg, 1995). Folklinguistic theories and conceptual metaphors are crucial in the process of teacher development to integrate expertise into individuals' coherence systems (Kinginger, 1997). These theoretical frames are employed to investigate novice TESOL teachers' preconceptions and reveal that the use of metaphors to conceptualize their beliefs of language teaching allows them to structure their experiences into a coherent whole and adapt expert theories into their teaching approaches (Warford & Reeves, 2003).

The knowledge of teachers about the subject matter and the effective ways to make the subject content accessible to learners is conceptualized as "pedagogical content knowledge" (Gleeson & Davison, 2016; LaFond & Dogancay-Aktuna, 2009). This knowledge develops and solidifies through classroom experiences and teachers are unlikely to accept professional education outside their existing epistemology (Gleeson & Davison, 2016). Therefore, for new learning to happen, teachers need to realize the gap between their knowledge, beliefs, and practice.

The perception of student teachers and alumni of TESOL education programs on the importance of linguistic theory in their teaching practices has been examined from the perspective of "language awareness" (LaFond & Dogancay-Aktuna, 2009). Language awareness is people's conscious awareness of and sensitivity to the forms and functions of language and the role it plays in human life (Svalberg, 2007). The results of the study suggest that while most of the student teachers and alumni perceive the knowledge of linguistic theory positively, they also call for more explicit linkages between theory and practice in TESOL education programs.

Underpinned by the theory of "teacher efficacy," which refers to teachers' belief of how well they can affect student learning (Tschannen-Moran, Woolfolk Hoy, & Hoy, 1998), the preparedness and self-efficacy beliefs of novice teachers in a TESOL induction program are explored to find out about what aspects and content of the program these teachers may find useful (Faez & Valeo, 2012). The findings further point to a theory–practice gap between teacher education programs and the realities of language classrooms.

### *Theory–practice gap in TESOL teacher education*

The theory–practice gap is sometimes framed as the disconnect between "grand theory" and "craft theory." Craft theory or "practical knowledge" is constructed by practitioners to inform everyday practices, whereas grand theory or "scholarly knowledge" is constructed by researchers and often "lacks orientation to particular contingencies and tends to pass over important details" (Hennessy & Deaney, 2009, p. 9). Therefore, the grand theory taught in TESOL programs is usually not immediately transformable into teachers' practical knowledge to inform their teaching practices in a particular context (Baecher, 2012a). One effective way to bridge the theory–practice gap is to integrate field experiences in TESOL teacher education programs (Baecher, 2012b). To redesign the programs and improve the field experiences for student teachers, faculty members can follow the procedures of "curriculum mapping," which involve the collection of curriculum-related data and a series of reviews to determine the points for immediate revision or for future research and planning (Jacob, 1997).

### *Impacts of transnational experience*

The increasing globalization has led to more opportunities for individuals to expose to transnational experiences and a few studies we reviewed have examined the impacts of such experiences on both educators and students. For educators, transnational experiences develop their transcultural capacity, which is a necessary skill in classrooms with learners of multicultural backgrounds. One model used to examine educators' development of transcultural capacity is "cultural dispositions of thinking (CDT)," which comprises a spectrum with one end representing individual-focused thinking and the other standing for community-focused thinking (Casinader, 2014). The model posits that individuals' CDT will develop, through transnational experience, toward the center spectrum to a transcultural form. In light of this model, educators' transnational experiences are found to enhance their disposition to effectively communicate within and across social and cultural groups (Casinader, 2018). For some transnational learners, their experience can be explored through the lens of Bourdieu's concept of habitus, which refers to "a set of acquired schemes of dispositions, perceptions, and appreciations, including tastes, which orient our practices and give them meaning" (Thorp, 2010, p. 193). The term "habitus clivé" was used by Bourdieu to depict the consequence of the contradictions he experienced in striving for scholarly distinction with a low social origin (Bennett, 2007). This term is employed to explore the state of unsettling experienced by transnational learners as they enter unfamiliar fields of the host countries, where the capitals they possess in their countries of origin cannot translate into equal value (Soong, Stahl, & Shan, 2018).

## Methodologies of empirical research

In this section, we summarize the methodologies adopted in empirical research on transnationalism and TESOL teacher education. These methodologies are grouped into six categories of different inclusiveness. Some categories represent broader approaches such as "ethnography," whereas others are more specific methods of data collection or analysis, such as "survey study" and "cross-case analysis."

### *Ethnography*

Ethnography is a qualitative research method employed to understand culture and society through the observation of participants. It is one of the most popular methods identified in our review. Data collected for ethnographic studies include observations of activities, recordings, field notes, narratives of participants, retrospective evaluative accounts, literacy artifacts, as well as written documents and talks produced by participants (Gordon & Liu, 2014; Kiely & Askham, 2012; Li & Zhu, 2013; Sánchez, 2007; Warriner, 2015). One of the studies developed a participatory research project where the student participants are invited to become researchers of their own community and authored a meta-narrative of the transnational experience of the larger community (Sánchez, 2007). A useful framework for data analysis is "moment analysis," which seeks to search for linguistic behaviors with immediate and long-term consequences and identify what prompts the behaviors and the consequences, such as other people's reactions (Li & Zhu, 2013).

### *Narrative inquiry*

Narrative inquiry is a way of research based on the stories we tell about our life experiences and the meanings we attach to the experiences (Barkhuizen, 2016). Similar to ethnographic studies, data collected for narrative inquiry include observations of activities, recordings, field notes, semi-structured interviews, photographs, newspaper clippings, journal and blog entries, and academic writing (Aneja, 2016; Solano-Campos, 2014). In the research articles we have reviewed, the method is most often used to understand how TESOL teachers construct their identity. The analysis of data can be done through thematic analysis to identify illuminating themes within or across narratives that contribute to answering the research question. The use of narrative inquiry enables researchers to construct an understanding of the phenomenon under study from the participants' own perspectives.

### *Survey study*

Survey may take many forms, such as electronic or pen-and-pencil questionnaires and interviews, and can be used to collect self-reported data from target individuals. It is often employed in TESOL teacher education research to explore teachers' knowledge and perceptions. Qualitative data collected from surveys, such as answers to open-ended questions and interviews, can be analyzed by identifying and comparing emergent themes (LaFond & Dogancay-Aktuna, 2009); or by connecting the data to emerging theory based on grounded theory (Baecher, 2012a). The quantitative data, such as scores obtained from Likert scales, can be analyzed by running descriptive statistics or statistical tests, like Chi-square, to uncover trends (Faez & Valeo, 2012; Sehlaoui & Shinge, 2013).

### *Classroom discourse analysis*

This method is used to examine disciplinary language use in English-medium instruction (Dafouz, Hüttner, & Smit, 2018). The analysis draws on the perspective of "sociocultural discourse analysis," which focuses on the functions of language in achieving the communicational goals of knowledge construction in the classroom. The analysis focuses on two aspects of oral interactions in classroom discourse: (1) disciplinary-reasoning episodes (DREs), in which knowledge is developed; and (2) language-related episodes (LREs), which clarify terminologies. The results of the analysis provide both a quantitative overview of the frequency distribution of the DREs and LREs across the corpus and a qualitative interpretation of the strategies and tendencies identified in the quantitative data. The analysis of classroom discourse is also employed to explore how transnational curriculum policy is enacted in classrooms (Wahlström, 2018). The study compares the general patterns of discourse in different classrooms and reveals a prevailing pattern of "dialogic recitation," which can be related to the transnational curriculum standards.

### *Cross-case analysis*

Cross-case analysis is a qualitative research method that enables the comparison of research studies in different contexts. This method is applied to investigate teacher involvement in TESOL research (Burton, 1998). An evaluative framework for TESOL teacher research is developed and trialled with six language education projects in five different contexts. The outcomes of the projects are assessed with the evaluative framework and the results are compared to draw links across contexts.

### *Methods for literacy research*

Some research examines the literacy practices of pre-service TESOL teachers. The data collected for this research include official documents such as syllabi and course lectures, written artifacts produced by participants, transcripts of course discussions and interviews, student teacher's drafts and reflections, recordings of meetings, and other course projects (Ceballos, 2012; Flores & Aneja, 2017). The data can be analyzed through textual analysis with an inductive approach (Ceballos, 2012). The analysis is also a reflective process grounded in the data itself and shaped by the researcher's own experience. The data can also be analyzed by a hybrid inductive and deductive approach to identify emergent themes (Flores & Aneja, 2017).

## TESOL teacher education in the transnational world: some implications

In today's interconnected world, where language education occurs "in multiple contexts with diverse populations" (Dogancay-Aktuna, 2006, p. 281), TESOL teacher educators and curriculum developers should aim to nurture teachers' capacity for analysing the demands of new contexts of teaching with transnational students, and making more socioculturally informed pedagogical decisions (Kim & Richardson, 2018). On the basis of the empirical studies reviewed above, and an examination of other related research, three major implications can be drawn on how TESOL teacher education can rise up to the challenge of transnationalism, through embracing diversity, cultivating intercultural competence, and reconceptualizing English language teaching.

### *Embracing diversity*

To prepare current and future English language teachers for the multifaceted and demanding instructional contexts, teacher education programs should take into account the emerging population of transnational learners and the ensuing diversity, and help language teachers develop teaching practices that are responsive to the impact of cross-national mobility of students (Song, 2011).

One manifestation of the diversity is the increasing number of international student teachers enrolled in TESOL programs worldwide, who are poised to be a large and important future force in the profession (Flores & Aneja, 2017; Liu, 1998). Instead of viewing the considerable linguistic and cultural diversity that these transnational student teachers represent as a problem or a hindrance, TESOL educators should capitalize on such diversity as a rich repertoire of pedagogical resources (Kumaravadivelu, 2007; Menard-Warwick, 2008). To this end, future language teachers' cultural backgrounds and language varieties should be incorporated as part of teaching practice (Li, 2017), with spaces created in the classroom for them to draw on their transnational funds of knowledge (Dabach & Fones, 2016; Kim & Richardson, 2018; Kim & Slapac, 2015) and engage in reflection on and discussions of transnationalization as a concept and lived experiences (Menard-Warwick, 2008; Schneider, 2017). In addition, TESOL educators should work closely with international students to identify elements in the programs that may not be relevant to their local contexts (Liu, 1999), and tailor the curricula to meet their academic and professional needs (Park, 2012).

Besides acknowledging and tapping into future English language teachers' own diversity, TESOL programs are also tasked to adequately prepare these teachers for the diverse contexts they will encounter in their teaching careers. Instead of sticking to a one-size-fits-all curriculum, which might "discriminate against students' linguistic, racial, ethnic, and class backgrounds" (Loh & Liew, 2016, p. 275), there is a need for more culturally responsive pedagogies. The arrival of increasing immigrant and refugee students in traditionally largely monolingual classrooms warrants attention and action on the part of teacher education programs. Teachers' understandings of these immigrant/refugee students' unique situations must be enhanced, and their awareness raised of how they can differentiate support for such students, who may vary in terms of their educational backgrounds and literacy experiences at home (Carhill-Poza, 2018).

In contexts where English is taught and learned as a foreign language, on the other hand, an emerging challenge related to transnational educational migration is that brought by students who have engaged in overseas studies and then returned to their home educational contexts (Song, 2011). Teacher education programs should prepare future teachers for leveraging these students' strengths, i.e., the advanced English skills and intercultural competence that they have acquired through their transnational experiences, to enrich their teaching practices, rather than experiencing these advantages as a threat to their authority. Integrating and carefully executing the practicum component in TESOL programs has been proposed as an effective measure for boosting teacher readiness for the variety of contexts they are about to face and aligning their expectations with the realities (Faez & Valeo, 2012). Including more context-specific electives is also believed to benefit students who plan to teach in different contexts (Stapleton & Shao, 2018).

### *Cultivating intercultural competence*

In the era of transnationalism, intercultural competence, or the ability to relate to and work with others in a culturally heterogeneous setting, is a crucial skill (Trede, Bowles, & Bridges, 2013; Wang, 2011). For TESOL teachers, intercultural competence can build up their capacity for and confidence in working in multicultural education settings (McCalman, 2014). Teacher preparation programs should therefore integrate systematic intercultural training (Senyshyn, 2018; Yang, 2018) to enable teachers to develop both linguistic and intercultural competence necessary for the enriching experience of interacting with people of other cultures (Trede et al., 2013), and guide them to adopt the same approach with their future students (Li & Huh, 2018).

Various means have been proposed for engineering the learning experience to foster learners' intercultural competence. Teacher education programs that include a transnational element, where students study in a different country for part of their education, are considered more effective than those conducted entirely in the home environment (Macalister, 2016). There is some merit to this belief, as international mobility experiences expose student teachers to the new and different in diverse environments, thereby facilitating the development of transcultural and professional readiness and the ability to handle cultural complexity (Casinader & Clemans, 2018). However, it must be noted that immersion in culture alone does not necessarily translate into intercultural learning. To maximize the potential of international experiences in preparing students for an intercultural globalized world, a purposeful pedagogy must be in place, with opportunities for students to critically reflect on and systematically explore what they have experienced and learned from their intercultural experiences (Senyshyn, 2018).

In cases where such transnational mobility is unrealistic, a particular form of transnationalism where no physical cross-border movement is necessary provides an alternative. Instructional materials, even imperfect ones with overly simplistic representations of culture and cultural differences, are potential facilitators of intercultural competencies (McConachy, 2018). This can be achieved through the classroom activity of helping learners engage in a critical scrutinization of cultural representations in instructional materials "against the backdrop of globalization and the transnational flow of information, goods and people" (Curdt-Christiansen & Weninger, 2015, p. 5). Another possibility is to translate local access to linguistically and culturally diverse students into learning opportunities. Engaging in direct interaction and meaningful experiences with these students can enhance pre-service teachers' readiness to work with them (Senyshyn, 2018). Encouraging online communication with people in other parts of the world is yet another time-saving and cost-effective option for sparking learners' interest in different cultures (Schwieter, Ferreira & Miller, 2018).

### *Reconceptualizing English language teaching*

With the growing trend of transnationalism and its impact on language use, traditional approaches to English language teaching, which have placed native English norms at the center of classroom practices (Rose, 2017), have been challenged. The fundamental principles of English learning and teaching, as well as where, why, how, and to what end English language teachers are being prepared (Johnson, 2006; Johnson & Golombek, 2018), are undergoing massive changes. A global community of English speakers, including the native-speaking populations and learners of English as an additional language, are likely to use different varieties of the language in various contact situations with a diverse range of interlocutors (Donahue, 2018; Rose, 2017). Language teacher education must keep in step with these changes in the specific contexts where teachers learn and teach (Johnson, 2006).

To reflect the globalized contexts in which a diverse set of Englishes are used, TESOL teacher education programs need to reconsider their purposes, that is, whether they are preparing teachers to teach an idealized "standard English," or to teach English as a pluricentric, global language to diverse groups of learners (Marlina, 2017). In the latter case, language teachers should be professionally guided to shift away from the dichotomous native–non-native perspective (Song, 2011), move beyond the assumption of a homogeneous, monolingual classroom (Schreiber, 2018), and develop an openness toward different varieties of English and norms in which the learners have gained competence through their transnational experience (Shin & Kubota, 2008). TESOL teacher training programs should reconceptualize, re-evaluate, and modify the type of knowledge and skills that they reinforce (Li, 2017), and communicate to the future generation of teachers an informed understanding of today's English, including its global forms, functions, and users (Dogancay-Aktuna & Hardman, 2017; Matsuda, 2017). Teachers should be helped to adapt their teaching according to the particular demands of specific learning contexts (Dogancay-Aktuna & Hardman, 2017), and develop a context-sensitive language pedagogy that places emphasis on students' ability to use English effectively with speakers of the language from various backgrounds (McKay, 2018).

## Conclusion and directions for future research

This chapter offers a comprehensive and up-to-date synthesis of the current evidence base on transnationalism and its implications for TESOL teacher education. More specifically, the review sheds light on the theoretical, conceptual, and methodological tools adopted in previous research and offers our thoughts on how TESOL programs can thrive in today's deeply transnational world. Our examination of existing literature has also identified several emerging trends that merit more scholarly attention.

Research on transnationals' learning should re-direct some of its focus on immigrants to an elite group of transnationals which is growing in number and likely to be in possession of considerable future influence in the world (Choi, 2017). One such group is consisted of students from Outer Circle countries studying in Inner Circle or Expanding Circle (Kachru, 1992) countries. More research should be carried out on the impact that this student population have on the educational and linguistic landscape in their source and host countries, and what implications they have for language teacher education (Song, 2011). Particularly, more scholarship is called for regarding topics on the educational reintegration of these students when they return to their home countries, such as returnee students' struggles to adjust to the educational context at home, and how the linguistic capital and new practices and perspectives they bring in might influence the domestic context of language learning and teaching. With an increasing number of higher education institutions setting up branch campuses and offering degrees in locales outside their (often Anglophone) bases, another much neglected group is students worldwide who study for "international" degrees and academic qualifications in their home educational contexts. Although the degrees these students obtain are labeled as "transnational education," they involve no or very limited transnational mobility on the part of the students. The kind of student experience acquired through such transnational education, and the intersections between transnational (im)mobility and access to international/transnational education or educational opportunities are in need of further research (Waters & Leung, 2013).

The study of the emotional dynamics of transnationalism and migration, and their impact on education, is another worthwhile direction for future research. Transnational circumstances exert considerable influence on people's emotional well-being (Li & Stodolska, 2006). For academic staff, transnational teaching experience may challenge their long-held perceptions of teaching and learning (Bovill, Jordan, & Watters, 2015), and induce changes in the development of their classroom practice (Shahri, 2018). The emotional dimension of teaching has received less research attention than the intellectual demands of the profession (Loh & Liew, 2016). Especially, there is a dearth of studies on how transnationalism complicates the emotional investments of English teaching in different sociocultural contexts. In the case of transnational students, emotional problems may arise due to their exposure to an alien environment (Li & Stodolska, 2006).

Immigrants and refugees, in particular, have experienced complex and ambivalent emotions (Anwaruddin, 2017). All these emotions may have consequences in educational settings. More explicit attention is needed for an examination of "what the entanglement of transnationalism, migration and emotions implies for educators, students, parents and their communities" (Zembylas, 2012, p. 163). Such an investigation will inform policy-makers, educators and researchers in weighing the pedagogic significance of these emotional dynamics (Zembylas, 2012).

Initially emphasizing the movement of people, transnational education now also features the movement of programs (Phan, 2016). This leads to the promising research field of how the establishment of English-medium-instruction programs in institutions of higher education where English is not the native language can be construed as a form of transnational education. With the English language and English-medium education increasingly endorsed worldwide (Phan, 2016), the internationalization of curricula, an essential goal of education in the age of globalization (Wu, 2018), becomes intertwined with the Englishization thereof (Rose, 2019). As a result, many local universities in Outer or Expanding Circle countries, such as those in Japan, Singapore, Malaysia, Thailand, and Vietnam, seek to follow the "internationalization at home" trend (Rose, 2019) and offer English-medium programs which are inherently mobile and transnational in not just medium of instruction, but also ideas, structures, and contents (Phan, 2016). TESOL teacher educators also need to create their own English-medium programs, courses or workshops. As they do so, "existing programs, materials, course syllabi, and lectures from other English-medium programs developed elsewhere" (Phan, 2016, p. 7) constitute a frequently visited source of ideas and inspirations. The ways in which these programs are developed transnationally, whether they are compatible with the local educational context and the learning styles of local students, the extent to which they are pedagogically effective, and how students and faculty experience and perceive of them, are all topics that can be meaningfully investigated for a critical understanding of these programs and their future improvement.

Finally, research into how the new dimension of "virtual mobility" can be useful for language teacher education will be relevant. Advancements in information and communication technologies have helped forge an already mobile world, where contact and exchanges between languages and their speakers may take place either face to face or in increasingly diverse virtual or digital environments (Prior, 2018). With the assistance of technology, transnational instructional spaces can be reconstructed or created (Lam & Smirnov, 2017), where geographically distributed learners are allowed the opportunity to experience intercultural encounters, engage in collaborative learning, develop global mindedness, and build transnational identities (Liu, 2018; Wu, 2018). Exploring the affordances of this virtual mobility in facilitating the cultivation of teaching capacity and intercultural competence, especially when opportunities are scarce for transnational movement in the physical sense, will open up new options for language teacher education and language teaching alike.

## References


Aneja, G. A. (2016). (Non) native speakered: Rethinking (non) nativeness and teacher identity in TESOL teacher education. *TESOL Quarterly*, 50, 572–596.

Anwaruddin, S. M. (2017). Emotions in the curriculum of migrant and refugee students. *Curriculum Inquiry*, 47, 112–124.

Baecher, L. (2012a). Feedback from the field: What novice PreK–12 ESL teachers want to tell TESOL teacher educators. *TESOL Quarterly*, 46, 578–588.

Baecher, L. (2012b). Integrating clinical experiences in a TESOL teacher education program: Curriculum mapping as process. *TESOL Journal*, 3, 537–551.

Baiutti, M. (2018). Fostering assessment of student mobility in secondary schools: Indicators of intercultural competence. *Intercultural Education*, 29, 549–570.

Barkhuizen, G. (2016). Narrative approaches to exploring language, identity and power in language teacher education. *RELC Journal*, 47, 25–42.

Barton, D. (2007). *Literacy: An introduction to the ecology of written language*. Oxford: Blackwell.

Bennett, T. (2007). Habitus Clivé: Aesthetics and politics in the work of Pierre Bourdieu. *New Literacy History*, 38(1), 201–228.

Benson, P., Chik, A., Gao, X., Huang, J., & Wang, W. (2009). Qualitative research in language teaching and learning journals, 1997–2006. *The Modern Language Journal*, 93, 79–90.

Bovill, C., Jordan, L., & Watters, N. (2015). Transnational approaches to teaching and learning in higher education: Challenges and possible guiding principles. *Teaching in Higher Education*, 20, 12–23.

Brittain, C. (2009). Transnational messages: What teachers can learn from understanding students' lives in transnational social spaces. *The High School Journal*, 92, 100–113.

Burns, A., & Roberts, C. (2010). Migration and adult language learning: Global flows and local transpositions. *TESOL Quarterly*, 44, 409–419.

Burton, J. (1998). A cross-case analysis of teacher involvement in TESOL research. *TESOL Quarterly*, 32, 419–446.

Canagarajah, S. (2018). Transnationalism and translingualism: How they are connected. In X. You (ed.), *Transnational writing education: Theory, history and practice* (pp. 41–60). New York, NY: Routledge.

Carhill-Poza, A. (2018). Bilingual and multilingual immigrant youth and language learning and use. In J. I. Liontas (ed.), *The TESOL encyclopedia of English language teaching*. London: Wiley-Blackwell.

Casinader, N. (2014). *Culture, transnational education and thinking: Case studies in global schooling*. Abingdon, UK: Routledge.

Casinader, N. (2016). Transnationalism in the Australian curriculum: New horizons or destinations of the past? *Discourse: Studies in the Cultural Politics of Education*, 37, 327–340.

Casinader, N. (2017). *Transnationalism, education and empowerment: The latent legacies of empire*. Abingdon, UK: Routledge.

Casinader, N. (2018). Transnational learning experiences and teacher transcultural capacity: The impact on professional practice – a comparative study of three Australian schools. *Intercultural Education*, 29, 258–280.

Casinader, N., & Clemans, A. (2018). The building of the transcultural capacities of preservice teachers to support their employability in a globalised world: A pilot study. *Intercultural Education*, 29, 589–608.

Ceballos, C. B. (2012). Literacies at the border: Transnationalism and the biliteracy practices of teachers across the US–Mexico border. *International Journal of Bilingual Education and Bilingualism*, 15, 687–703.

Chamakalayil, L., & Riegel, C. (2016). Negotiating potentials and limitations in education in transnational migration contexts: A case study. *European Education*, 48, 120–136.

Chin, K.-S., & Smith, D. (2015). A reconceptualization of state transnationalism: South Korea as an illustrative case. *Global Networks*, 15, 78–98.

Choi, T.-H. (2017). Identity, transnationalism, and bilingual education. In O. García, A. M. Y. Lin, & S. May (eds.), *Bilingual and multilingual education* (pp. 175–189). Dordrecht: Springer International.

Collins, P. H. (2000). *Black feminist thought: Knowledge, consciousness, and the politics of empowerment*. New York, NY: Routledge.

Curdt-Christiansen, X. L., & Weninger, C. (2015). Introduction: Ideology and the politics of language textbooks. In X. L. Curdt-Christiansen & C. Weninger (eds.), *Language, ideologies and education: The politics of textbooks in language education* (pp. 1–8). New York, NY: Routledge.

Dabach, D. B., & Fones, A. (2016). Beyond the "English learner" frame: Transnational funds of knowledge in social studies. *International Journal of Multicultural Education*, 18(1), 7–27.

Dafouz, E., Hüttner, J., & Smit, U. (2018). New contexts, new challenges for TESOL: Understanding disciplinary reasoning in oral interactions in English-medium instruction. *TESOL Quarterly*, 52, 540–563.

de Fina, A., & Perrino, S. (2013). Transnational identities. *Applied Linguistics*, 34, 509–515.

Dogancay-Aktuna, S. (2006). Expanding the socio-cultural knowledge base of TESOL teacher education. *Language, Culture and Curriculum*, 19, 278–295.

Dogancay-Aktuna, S., & Hardman, J. (2017). A framework for incorporating an English as an International Language perspective into TESOL teacher education. In A. Matsuda (ed.), *Preparing teachers to teach English as an international language* (pp. 19–31). Bristol, UK: Multilingual Matters.

Donahue, C. (2018). Rhetorical and linguistic flexibility: Valuing heterogeneity in academic writing education. In X. You (ed.), *Transnational writing education: Theory, history and practice* (pp. 21–40). New York, NY: Routledge.

Duff, P. A. (2015). Transnationalism, multilingualism, and identity. *Annual Review of Applied Linguistics*, 35, 57–80.

Faez, F., & Valeo, A. (2012). TESOL teacher education: Novice teachers' perceptions of their preparedness and efficacy in the classroom. *TESOL Quarterly*, 46, 450–471.

Flores, N., & Aneja, G. (2017). "Why needs hiding?" Translingual (re)orientations in TESOL teacher education. *Research in the Teaching of English*, 51, 441–463.

Gleeson, M., & Davison, C. (2016). A conflict between experience and professional learning: Subject teachers' beliefs about teaching English language learners. *RELC Journal*, 47, 43–57.

Gordon, J. A., & Liu, X. (2014). Preparation for transnationalism: Changes in China's top secondary schools. *Journal of International Education and Leadership*, 4, 1–14.

Guo, S., & Maitra, S. (2017). Revisioning curriculum in the age of transnational mobility: Towards a transnational and transcultural framework. *Curriculum Inquiry*, 47, 80–91.

Harvey, D. (2005). *A brief history of neoliberalism*. Oxford: Oxford University Press.

Hennessy, S., & Deaney, R. (2009). "Intermediate theory" building: Integrating multiple teacher and researcher perspectives through in-depth video analysis of pedagogic strategies. *Teachers College Record*, 111, 1753–1795.

Jacob, H. H. (1997). *Mapping the big picture: Integrating curriculum and assessment K-12*. Alexandria, VA: Association for Supervision and Curriculum Development.

Johnson, K. E. (1996). The role of theory in L2 teacher education. *TESOL Quarterly*, 30, 765–771.

Johnson, K. E. (2006). The sociocultural turn and its challenges for second language teacher education. *TESOL Quarterly*, 40, 235–257.

Johnson, K. E., & Golombek, P. R. (2018). Informing and transforming language teacher education pedagogy. *Language Teaching Research*, 1–12.

Jurkova, S., & Guo, S. (2018). Connecting transculturalism with transformative learning: Toward a new horizon of adult education. *Alberta Journal of Educational Research*, 64, 173–187.

Kachru, B. B. (1992). World Englishes: Approaches, issues and resources. *Language Teaching*, 25, 1–14.

Kiely, R., & Askham, J. (2012). Furnished imagination: The impact of preservice teacher training on early career work in TESOL. *TESOL Quarterly*, 46, 496–518.

Kim, J., & Richardson, E. (2018). Transnational students and language use. In J. I. Liontas (ed.), *The TESOL encyclopedia of English language teaching*. London: Wiley-Blackwell.

Kim, S., & Slapac, A. (2015). Culturally responsive, transformative pedagogy in the transnational era: Critical perspectives. *Educational Studies*, 51, 17–27.

Kinginger, C. (1997). A discourse approach to the study of language educators' coherence systems. *The Modern Language Journal*, 81(1), 6–14.

Kumaravadivelu, B. (2007). *Cultural globalization and language education*. New Haven, CT: Yale University Press.

LaFond, L., & Dogancay-Aktuna, S. (2009). Teacher perspectives on linguistics in TESOL teacher education. *Language Awareness*, 18, 345–365.

Lam, W. S. E., & Smirnov, N. (2017). Identity in mediated contexts of transnationalism and mobility. In S. L. Thorne & S. May (eds.), *Language, education and technology*. Dordrecht: Springer International.

Lam, W. S. E., & Warriner, D. S. (2012). Transnationalism and literacy: Investigating the mobility of people, languages, texts, and practices in contexts of migration. *Reading Research Quarterly*, 47, 191–215.

Lave, J., & Wenger, E. (1991). *Situated learning: Legitimate peripheral participation*. Cambridge: Cambridge University Press.

Li, G. (2017). Preparing culturally and linguistically competent teachers for English as an International Language education. *TESOL Journal*, 8, 250–276.

Li, G., & Huh, S. (2018). Implicit curriculum. In J. I. Liontas (ed.), *The TESOL encyclopedia of English language teaching*. London: Wiley-Blackwell.

Li, M. Z., & Stodolska, M. (2006). Transnationalism, leisure, and Chinese graduate students in the United States. *Leisure Sciences*, 28, 39–55.

Li, W. (2011). Moment analysis and translanguaging space: Discursive construction of identities by multilingual Chinese youth in Britain. *Journal of Pragmatics*, 43(5), 1222–1235.

Li, W., & Zhu, H. (2013). Translanguaging identities and ideologies: Creating transnational space through flexible multilingual practices amongst Chinese university students in the UK. *Applied Linguistics*, 34, 516–535.

Lie, J. (1995). From international migration to transnational diaspora. *Contemporary Sociology*, 24, 303–306.

Linde, C. (1993). *Life stories: The creation of coherence*. New York, NY: Oxford University Press.

Liu, D. (1998). Ethnocentrism in TESOL: Teacher education and the neglected needs of international TESOL students. *ELT Journal*, 52, 3–10.

Liu, D. (1999). Training non-native TESOL students: Challenges for TESOL teacher education in the West. In G. Braine (ed.), *Non-native educators in English language teaching* (pp. 197–210). New York, NY: Routledge.

Liu, J. Y. (2018). The affordances of Facebook for teaching ESL writing. In X. You (ed.), *Transnational writing education: Theory, history, and practice* (pp. 203–221). New York, NY: Routledge.

Loh, C. E., & Liew, W. M. (2016). Voices from the ground: The emotional labour of English teachers' work. *Teaching and Teacher Education*, 55, 267–278.

Lum, C. M. K. (2018). Developing intercultural competence in the language classroom. In J. I. Liontas (ed.), *The TESOL encyclopedia of English language teaching*. London: Wiley-Blackwell.

Macalister, J. (2016). Tracing it back: Identifying the impact of a trans-national language teacher education programme on classroom practice. *RELC Journal*, 47, 59–70.

Marlina, R. (2017). Practices of teaching Englishes for international communication. In A. Matsuda (ed.), *Preparing teachers to teach English as an international language* (pp. 100–113). Bristol, UK: Multilingual Matters.

Matsuda, A. (2017). Introduction. In A. Matsuda (ed.), *Preparing teachers to teach English as an international language* (pp. xiii–xxi). Bristol, UK: Multilingual Matters.

McCalman, C. L. (2014). International instructor preparing teachers for multicultural classrooms in the United States: Teaching intercultural communication competence online. *New Directions for Teaching and Learning*, 138, 73–81.

McConachy, T. (2018). Critically engaging with cultural representations in foreign language textbooks. *Intercultural Education*, 29, 77–88.

McKay, S. L. (2018). Globalization, English language teaching, and teachers. In J. I. Liontas (ed.), *The TESOL encyclopedia of English language teaching*. London: Wiley-Blackwell.

Menard-Warwick, J. (2008). The cultural and intercultural identities of transnational English teachers: Two case studies from the Americas. *TESOL Quarterly*, 42, 617–640.

Miller, L., & Ginsberg, R. B. (1995). Folklinguistic theories of language learning. In B. Freed (ed.), *Second language acquisition during study abroad* (pp. 293–315). Amsterdam: John Benjamin.

Park, G. (2012). "I am never afraid of being recognized as an NNES": One teacher's journey in claiming and embracing her nonnative-speaker identity. *TESOL Quarterly*, 46, 127–151.

Pennycook, A. (2001). *Critical applied linguistics: A critical introduction*. Mahwah, NJ: Lawrence Erlbaum.

Phan, L. H. (2016). *Transnational education crossing "Asia" and "the West": Adjusted desire, transformative mediocrity and neo-colonial disguise*. New York, NY: Routledge.

Phillipson, R. (1992). *Linguistic imperialism*. Oxford: Oxford University Press.

Prior, M. T. (2018). Globalization and the dilemmas of linguistic identity. In J. I. Liontas (ed.), *The TESOL encyclopedia of English language teaching*. London: Wiley-Blackwell.

Rizvi, F., & Beech, J. (2017). Global mobilities and the possibilities of a cosmopolitan curriculum. *Curriculum Inquiry*, 47, 125–134.

Rose, H. (2017). A global approach to English language teaching: Integrating an international perspective into a teaching methods course. In A. Matsuda (ed.), *Preparing teachers to teach English as an international language* (pp. 169–180). Bristol, UK: Multilingual Matters.

Rose, H. (2019). The future of English in global higher education: Shifting trends from teaching English to teaching through English. *CALR Journal*, 9. Retrieved from http://web.aou.edu.lb/online-journals/calr-issue9.

Sánchez, P. (2007). Cultural authenticity and transnational Latina youth: Constructing a meta-narrative across borders. *Linguistics and Education*, 18, 258–282.

Sánchez, P., & Machado-Casas, M. (2009). At the intersection of transnationalism, Latina/o immigrants, and education. *The High School Journal*, 92, 3–15.

Schneider, C. (2017). Transnationalisation within school education: The interconnection between actors, structures and mechanisms. *Globalisation, Societies and Education*, 15, 607–620.

Schreiber, B. R. (2018). Epilogue: A perspective on transnational writing education from a New York City subway train. In X. You (ed.), *Transnational writing education: Theory, history, and practice* (pp. 244–252). New York, NY: Routledge.

Schwieter, J. W., Ferreira, A., & Miller, P. C. (2018). Study abroad learners' metalinguistic and sociocultural reflections on short- and long-term international experiences. *Intercultural Education*, 29, 236–257.

Sehlaoui, A. S., & Shinge, M. (2013). The pursuit of quality over quantity in TESOL teacher education: Coursework versus test only. *TESOL Journal*, 4, 106–128.

Senyshyn, R. M. (2018). Teaching for transformation: Converting the intercultural experience of preservice teachers into intercultural learning. *Intercultural Education*, 29, 163–184.

Shahri, M. N. N. (2018). The development of teacher identity, emotions and practice: Before and after graduation from an MA TESOL program. *System*, 78, 91–103.

Shin, H., & Kubota, R. (2008). Postcolonialism and globalization in language education. In B. Spolsky & F. M. Hult (eds.), *The handbook of educational linguistics* (pp. 206–219). Malden, MA: Blackwell.

Solano-Campos, A. (2014). The making of an international educator: Transnationalism and nonnativeness in English teaching and learning. *TESOL Journal*, 4, 412–443.

Song, J. (2011). Children's study abroad, and transnationalism as an emerging context for language learning: A new task for language teacher education. *TESOL Quarterly*, 45, 749–758.

Soong, H., Stahl, G., & Shan, H. (2018). Transnational mobility through education: A Bourdieusian insight on life as middle transnationals in Australia and Canada. *Globalisation, Societies and Education*, 16, 241–253.

Stapleton, P., & Shao, Q. (2018). A worldwide survey of MATESOL programs in 2014: Patterns and perspectives. *Language Teaching Research*, 22, 10–28.

Svalberg, A. M. L. (2007). Language awareness and language teaching. *Language Teaching*, 40, 287–308.

Thorp, H. (2010). Bourdieu, gender reflexivity, and physical culture: A case of masculinities in the snowboarding field. *Journal of Sport and Social Issues*, 34(2), 176–214.

Toukan, E. V., Gaztambide-Fernández, R., & Anwaruddin, S. M. (2017). Shifting borders and sinking ships: What (and who) is transnationalism "good" for? *Curriculum Inquiry*, 47, 1–13.

Trede, F., Bowles, W., & Bridges, D. (2013). Developing intercultural competence and global citizenship through international experiences: Academics' perceptions. *Intercultural Education*, 24, 442–455.

Tschannen-Moran, M., Woolfolk Hoy, A., & Hoy, W. K. (1998). Teacher efficacy: Its meaning and measure. *Review of Educational Research*, 68, 202–248.

Vertovec, S. (2009). *Transnationalism*. Abingdon, UK: Routledge.

Wahlström, N. (2018). When transnational curriculum policy reaches classrooms: Teaching as directed exploration. *Journal of Curriculum Studies*, 50, 654–666.

Wang, P. (2011). The effects of cross-cultural competence on my teaching and studying in the UK context. *Intercultural Education*, 22, 513–519.

Warford, M. K., & Reeves, J. (2003). Falling into it: Novice TESOL teacher thinking. *Teachers and Teaching*, 9, 47–65.

Warriner, D. S. (2015). "Here, without English, you are dead": Ideologies of language and discourses of neoliberalism in adult English language learning. *Journal of Multilingual and Multicultural Development*, 37, 495–508.

Warriner, D. S. (2017). Theorizing the spatial dimensions and pedagogical implications of transnationalism. *Curriculum Inquiry*, 47, 50–61.

Waters, J., & Leung, M. (2013). Immobile transnationalisms? Young people and their *in situ* experiences of "international" education in Hong Kong. *Urban Studies*, 50, 606–620.

Wenger. E. (1998). *Communities of practice: Learning, meaning and identity.* Cambridge: Cambridge University Press.

Wu, Z. (2018). Technology-mediated transnational writing education: An overview of research and practice. In X. You (ed.), *Transnational writing education: Theory, history and practice* (pp. 170–186). New York, NY: Routledge.

Yang, P. (2018). Developing TESOL teacher intercultural identity: An intercultural communication competence approach. *TESOL Journal*, 9, 525–541.

Zembylas, M. (2012). Transnationalism, migration and emotions: Implications for education. *Globalisation, Societies and Education*, 10, 163–179.

# 4 Critical engagement with teaching EFL

## Toward a trivalent focus on ideology, political economy, and praxis

*Ryuko Kubota*

### Introduction

Transnationality, as observed in the global flow of people, goods, and information, is not a new phenomenon. However, the current amount and speed of the transnational flow appears unprecedented, compelling educators and policymakers to respond to the demands arising from this flow. Under these circumstances, the concept of English as a global language has been highlighted, promoting English language teaching (ELT) in many parts of the world. Although the global presence of English includes a vast diversity in terms of the form, practice, and user of English, enduring ideologies afford a legitimate status to only some variants, while marginalizing others. Furthermore, not only ideologies but also material conditions and economic interests shape language education practices and policies. It is thus important to critically examine how inequities and biases in language education policies and practices are shaped ideologically and sustained in the political economy, rather than simply taking the increased emphasis on ELT and related practices at face value. Moreover, in order to transform biases, inequities, and marginalities, a critical approach to ELT needs to go beyond challenging ideology and political economy, and exercise *praxis*—critical reflection and action.

In this chapter, I will focus on teaching English as a foreign language (EFL) specifically in the context of Japan and critically examine the following four topics in relation to ideology and political economy: English, English users, culture, and language-in-education policies. The discussion will be contextualized by five concrete anecdotes that I have recently encountered. I will begin my discussion by briefly examining the trend of critical perspectives in language studies to lay out a conceptual orientation.

### Synergy between ideology and materiality in critical inquiry

In pursuing critical approaches to language studies since the 1990s, scholars have mainly critiqued dominant ideologies and discourses regarding language, educational practices, teacher or learner identities, and policies (see Kubota & Miller, 2017). Earlier, Freirean critical pedagogy was introduced (Auerbach, 1992; Auerbach & Burgess, 1985) and ideological critiques and debates on the linguistic imperialism of English attracted critical scholars' attention (Brutt-Griffner, 2002; Phillipson, 1992). Subsequently, Foucauldian poststructuralism viewed Marxist-informed concepts of ideology and hegemony as too rigid and deterministic, suggesting concepts such as discourse, subjectivity, and governmentality for analysis (Miller, 2012; Pennycook, 2001). Furthermore, postcolonial orientations have influenced other critical work and problematized colonial relations of power operating historically and symbolically in postcolonial and settler colonial societies (e.g., Canagarajah, 1999; Mazrui, 2002; Ramanathan, 2005, 2013; Shin, 2006). Through these critical perspectives, taken-for-granted assumptions related to ELT have been questioned. As I examine in more detail in the following sections, critical approaches have scrutinized inequalities and marginalization related to English, attributes of English users (e.g., race, ethnicity, gender, sexual identity), and culture, exploring fluid, hybrid, and complex understanding of learners, teachers, and educational practices.

Overall, much of the critical scholarship has tended to advocate broadening the understanding of what is deemed legitimate in language education in order to overcome the problems of marginalization, oppression, and inequity embedded in teaching, learning, teachers, learners, and educational environments. Citing Nancy Fraser (2015), Block (2018) characterizes this orientation, mainly grounded in poststructuralist thought, as *recognition politics* in the sense that it promotes the importance of recognizing and affirming difference in seeking criticality. However, recognizing and affirming difference alone cannot transform societal inequality and injustice, since these problems are not merely conceptual or cultural but also material. Block (2018) thus proposes to direct our attention more toward *redistribution politics* to scrutinize the socioeconomic injustices of economic exploitation, marginalization, and deprivation that divide and hierarchize groups of people. Pointing out the omission of material conditions from understanding, for example, the significance of translanguaging for different groups, he proposes "a bivalent (or even multivalent) approach to inequity, one that would examine the intersection of what, in effect, is ethnolinguistic racism, with a particular class position in society" (Block, 2018, p. 252). Following this perspective, I will illuminate both the ideological and socioeconomic facets of each of the four ELT topics. Also, I will further suggest that we add *praxis* for our critical engagement in ELT to pursue actual transformation.

## Episodes

As a critical scholar and teacher educator working in North American higher education, I have been making efforts to promote linguistic, cultural, and human diversity and equity through scholarly activities, mostly publishing. Although academic publications in English have enabled me to share critical perspectives with other scholars and teacher educators, they are typically accessed only by professionals who are users of English usually working in Anglophone countries. Thus, the conventional method of scholarly publishing and presenting in academic venues tends to result in merely preaching to the choir, so to speak. As I began to provide more professional development for EFL teachers and observe how normative ideologies persisted, my feelings of frustration became greater. This partly led me to publish a paperback in Japanese targeting the general audience in Japan in order to introduce scholarly knowledge that demystifies common beliefs about English language teaching and learning (Kubota, 2018). Through these experiences, I have had pedagogical and non-pedagogical encounters that demonstrate narrow, normative, or prescriptive understandings of language, culture, and language users. Below, I will present these instances in order to contextualize my discussion. All five episodes describe what I have encountered in Japan in recent years. To protect the privacy of some of the individuals mentioned in the episodes, some details are slightly altered.

### *Episode 1*

Mr. A, a Japanese high school teacher of English, conducted a study lesson in his school.[1] He delivered classroom instruction, which was observed by 15 other teachers visiting from the same school district. The lesson was almost entirely conducted in English and the level of students' engagement was quite high. The lesson was followed by a reflective discussion in English between Mr. A and the observers, including me. During the discussion, the following interaction took place:

> Observer: You should have corrected the pronunciation error of a student. It should be "catalog" [pronouncing in a "nonstandard" accent]
> Mr. A: Sorry? [not recognizing what was said]
> Observer: Catalog [repeating]
> Mr. A: Sorry? I don't understand.
> Kubota: Catalog.
> Mr. A: Oh, I see.

The observer attempted to point out the student's pronunciation error, but the observer himself could not pronounce the word intelligibly.

### *Episode 2*

I gave a presentation to a small group of people in Japan who were interested in issues of ELT and educational issues of Canada, where I work. After the presentation, the audience and I engaged in informal discussion in Japanese. One participant, a retired high school teacher of mathematics, hesitantly revealed that he had never traveled abroad. To my question "Why?", he responded "I don't speak English well, and I am afraid of being laughed at" (original in Japanese).

### *Episode 3*

Since 2007, the Japanese government has administered national achievement tests every year in mathematics and Japanese for students in Grades 6 and 9.[2] In 2019, an English subtest was added for the first time in Grade 9. In an item that combines listening and writing, students heard the following recording and were prompted to write advice in English:

> Hello. I'm Nick. I'm looking forward to meeting you. I'm going to stay in your country for two weeks. I hear that there are a lot of club activities in Japanese schools. I want to try some! Which club activities can I try? Can you give me some advice? I'm waiting for your answer. Thank you.

Later, scoring criteria and item response analysis were released. It was explained that the correct answers should include concrete club name(s) or activities conducted in a club in order to respond to Nick's question. Thus, answers such as "You can decide after you arrive in Japan" or "You can ask your teacher" were marked incorrect.

### *Episode 4*

An experienced Japanese high school teacher of English was quite confident and creative. During the class I observed, she used authentic audiovisual materials, which seemed motivating for the students. I was intrigued by the teacher's repeated mention of the word "foreigner" to describe the white people in the video and other materials used in the lesson. During the debriefing session after class, I asked, "To you, who is a 'foreigner'?" After a few seconds of contemplation, she replied, "People who don't look Asian."

### *Episode 5*

Professor Emeritus Youn-ok Song (real name), a Japanese-Korean feminist scholar, gave a public talk in Japanese in Tokyo on Korean women who resisted Japanese colonialism in the first half of the twentieth century. In her talk, she touched upon Umeko Tsuda, a well-known Japanese pioneering woman who promoted women's education around that time. Professor Song pointed out the fact that Tsuda was enraged by Western missionaries' belittlement of the Japanese, while at the same time she looked down upon Koreans. In critiquing her hypocritical attitude, Professor Song shared her own experience of learning English in high school in Japan. In teaching the word "wasteland," the Japanese teacher associated the word with the scenery of colonized Korea he saw from Manchurian border during his travels. Professor Song was deeply hurt by the offensive description of her homeland. Even after 50 years, the pain is still ingrained in her memory.

## Ideologies and political economy regarding English

Despite scholarly criticisms, normative beliefs about language, including the superiority of the so-called standard or mainstream linguistic forms, persists. In ELT, it is believed that the legitimate English is standard inner-circle varieties of

English (i.e., those used in the United States, Canada, England, Australia, and New Zealand). Accordingly, the instructional model or *correct* English is believed to be one of such varieties, especially American and British English. This belief is reflected in Episodes 1 and 2. In Episode 1, the teacher who observed Mr. A's class pointed out a student's non-standard pronunciation, which, in my observation, did not seem to have negatively affected communication in the classroom. Ironically, the teacher was unable to pronounce the word in a standard accent or in an intelligible way. This case exemplifies the teacher's desire for prescribed correctness even though the quest is out of reach. In Episode 2, a fear of making errors in English had kept the man from traveling outside of Japan for so many years. In everyday contexts where communication is the primary concern, we rarely ridicule linguistic deviations; rather, we typically collaborate to understand one another. The fear was perhaps developed by the correctness-driven method of teaching, learning, and assessing English.

The power of standard English, observed in these episodes, has been destabilized in academic discussions. Valorizing diverse linguistic forms of English, scholars have proposed alternative perspectives, such as world Englishes, English as a lingua franca, and English as an international language, which can be consolidated and called *global Englishes* (Rose & Galloway, 2019). Overall, the scholarly knowledge rejects the idea that American or British mainstream English should be the desired model for ELT, since English is a language used globally by diverse people for various purposes, and thus EFL learners are no longer expected to use English only with mainstream English speakers. Although the use of mainstream English is expected for high-stakes writing for academic theses, publications, grant proposals, and so on, not all EFL learners will be obtaining higher degrees in English dominant institutions, nor will they uniformly obtain employment that requires proficiency in standard English. What is necessary for many of these learners is to develop proficiency to understand diverse forms of English and to make themselves intelligible. It is also important to note that intelligibility is established not only by the information sender's communicative ability but also the receiver's willingness to understand (Rajagopalan, 2010). This implies the limitation of focusing only on the development of linguistic skills in English, including the ability to use mainstream English, for language education that fosters competence for global communication.

In ELT, efforts have been made to integrate the diverse nature of English by introducing concepts such as world Englishes (Rose & Galloway, 2019). Although some positive learning outcomes are reported, they tend to be restricted to the learners' superficial recognition of diversity without fundamental changes in their attitudes (e.g., Sung, 2015; Suzuki, 2011). This challenge indicates the pervasiveness of the normative ideologies.

More recently, the concept of translanguaging has attracted scholarly attention in sociolinguistics and language education (e.g., Blackledge & Creese, 2017; García & Li, 2014). Translanguaging in language education challenges the monolingual normative expectations imposed on plurilingual students by reconceptualizing their linguistic competence as an individually unique repertoire drawn from their available linguistic resources, rather than a sum of abilities of languages separated in a compartmentalized manner. Thus, the perspective of translanguaging encourages students to deploy their individually unique linguistic repertoires instead of acquiring a complete set of linguistic ability analogous to that of the imagined native speaker. However, pedagogical practice of translanguaging alone would not transform the hegemony of standard language ideology or marginalization of minoritized learners, since issues in broader society, such as racism, sexism, economic inequality, and other injustices, continue to privilege dominant groups that benefit from the normative ideology, while marginalizing others.

The persistence of normative beliefs about language is especially reinforced by language tests that are calibrated to the prescriptive forms of mainstream language. Furthermore, as Episode 3 demonstrates, scoring criteria can be overly regimented to the extent that a correct answer excludes what is possible in authentic communication.

As discussed later, the neoliberal emphasis on accountability has increased the use of tests in order for learners to prove their ability. Similarly, programs and institutions are held accountable for yielding positive outcomes of the educational services that they provide. The national achievement test shown in Episode 3 is a prime example. Although the test item itself seems appropriate as it elicits open-ended responses for meaningful communication, the scoring criteria undermine communicative authenticity. The problem of compromising authenticity may be inevitable given the fact that nearly one million students' responses need to be scored consistently (National Institute for Educational Policy Research, n.d.). A negative washback effect is obvious—it is likely that test takers are compelled to obtain higher scores by adhering to the prescribed answers that may not reflect authentic communication. Such preoccupation with correctness may also cause a fear of making errors, as seen in Episode 2.

The test-oriented culture also generates huge economic benefits for the testing and related industries. The global teaching of EFL creates a huge market for large enterprises and organizations, such as major publishers and the British Council. Phillipson (2017) argues that the notion of English as a lingua franca or global English appears to be divorced from the colonial power of the past, but it is indeed "a project to establish English as the language of neoliberal empire serviced by global finance whatever the consequences for other cultures" (p. 317). This indicates that the seemingly progressive ideas of English as a lingua franca or world Englishes can be co-opted by the hegemonic forces of the political economy. I will discuss this problem in more detail later in relation to language-in-education policies.

## Ideologies and political economy regarding English users

Linguistic normativity is closely linked to the prevalent belief about who legitimate language users are. The obvious category is the native speaker. The idea that the native speaker is the ideal model for ELT has been problematized by critiques of linguistic imperialism of English (Phillipson, 1992) as well as the advocacy movement for nonnative English-speaking teachers (NNESTs) (e.g., Braine, 1999; Kamhi-Stein, 2004; Park, 2012; Selvi, 2014). Research on NNESTs has illuminated their professional strengths and resilient identities. Research has also revealed the co-constructed and fluid nature of native or nonnative speaker identities (Faez, 2011). Indeed, native or nonnative speakerness is a matter of identity and social positioning. Moreover, the linguistic features that native speakers use are multiple, reflecting global Englishes. However, the native speaker of English in everyday discourses in schools, universities, the media, and education policies often indexes speakers of mainstream Englishes in inner-circle countries.

Furthermore, in these discourses, the native speaker typically indexes whiteness, as Episode 4 implies. Episode 4 contains two fallacies: first, the concept of "foreigners" in Japan is falsely associated only with English speakers, an assumption that does not reflect the reality. In fact, the 2018 statistics show that, of the visitors from overseas arriving in Japan, 73.4% were from East Asian countries (i.e., South Korea, China, Taiwan, and Hong Kong) and 11.2% from South and Southeast Asia, whereas only 11.6% were from Europe, the Americas, and Australia. Of course, such statistics do not perfectly overlap with the racial backgrounds of the visitors. Nonetheless, this fallacy is widespread in teaching English. Second, non-Japanese Asian people are excluded from the teacher's definition of "foreigner," and by extension, Asian people are not regarded as native or nonnative English speakers. This is consistent with the marginality and discrimination experienced by Asian native speakers of English in teaching English, mirroring students' expectations that English teachers are white (Kubota & Fujimoto, 2013; Jenks, 2019; Lee, 2011; Rivers & Ross, 2013). The indexical meaning of "foreigner" in Episode 4 overlaps with the general public's discourse in Taiwan, as exemplified by online reactions to an incident captured in a video, in which an "American-born Chinese" man aggressively confronted a bus driver in English. In subsequent online postings, he was indexically positioned as neither a "foreigner" nor a legitimate speaker of English (Lee & Su, 2019). All in all, the concept of the native speaker in popular discourses typically indexes a white native speaker of inner-circle mainstream English.

The ideologically constructed superiority of the white native speaker of mainstream English is exploited by the ELT industry. Businesses that recruit and hire English language teachers typically prefer white mainstream English speakers, packaging their services and products to boost their market appeal for the customers (Ruecker & Ives, 2015). In referring to the situation in South Korea, Jenks (2019) argues, "the branding of ELT instruction as a racialized commodity recalibrates supply and demand (cf. Lury, 2004) in the market by drawing attention to the (perceived) importance of Whiteness in language teaching" (p. 529). Other scholars have also pointed out the common practice of using the indexical image of whiteness attached to native speakers of English in promotional materials for selling English language programs and hiring English language teachers in Japan (Bailey, 2006; Takahashi, 2013). Especially in business-run ELT settings in Japan, the image of white English speakers is gendered and exploited to evoke or respond to female English learners' romantic desire (Bailey, 2006; Kubota, 2011a;

Takahashi, 2013). The notion of the native speaker, together with its double indexical meanings (i.e., whiteness and mainstream inner-circle English speakerness), normalizes who the legitimate English users are in the ELT market in many parts of the world.

More recently, a new ELT marketing trend has emerged. It capitalizes on the neoliberal ideology of human capital, promoting the idea that proficiency in English would boost one's entrepreneurial worth in the global labor marketplace. For example, in Japan and South Korea, analyses of recent advertisements for ELT businesses uncovered their tendency to emphasize success in the global marketplace as a major benefit of learning English (Jenks, 2019; Nuzke, 2019; Simpson, 2018). In these advertisements, the previous marketing strategy shifts from using images of learning English from white teachers to using images that evoke economic success or supplements them with the symbolism of entrepreneurial accomplishment.

The marketing shift toward entrepreneurship seems to be taking place in parallel with the global expansion of the ELT supply market. Being justified by the concept of global Englishes, this expansion capitalizes on the instrumental purpose of learning English for transnational communication. The ELT supply market has indeed spread outside of traditional inner-circle countries, reflecting the economic interest coming from both supply and demand.

For instance, the Philippines has become a popular destination for study abroad or online tutorials for students in South Korea (Choe, 2018; Jang, 2018) and Japan (Tajima, 2018). It has indeed become a niche market for ELT, providing customers with more affordable options for learning English compared to studying in inner-circle countries from native English-speaking teachers. Teaching English in the Philippines also offers employment opportunities to educated Filipinos who were previously excluded from the traditional ELT supply market dominated by white native speakers of mainstream English. This new niche market is promoted and rationalized by the seemingly progressive postcolonial orientation of global Englishes and the professional legitimacy of NNESTs. However, as Lorente and Tupas (2013) point out, this market still exists in the racially, linguistically, and culturally hierarchized ELT world and, as it is entrenched in the capitalist pursuit of profit, it does not fundamentally change the ideologies behind the existing norms. Furthermore, even though the Philippine English used by these teachers is marketed as *neutral* in terms of accent (Choe, 2018), it represents a variety of educated Philippine English spoken by middle-class and upper-middle-class Filipinos, which is positioned higher in the hierarchy of Philippine English*es* (Tupas, 2019).

Here, the Philippines and (privileged) Philippine English are co-opted by capitalist tactics—they are integrated into the global ELT market with a new reformist image. This is illustrated by promotional online information for study abroad programs targeting Japanese students. This Japan-based business supports study abroad in the Philippines along with Australia, New Zealand, Canada, and the United States. Of many pieces of promotional information in Japanese, one webpage poses the question, "Is a native speaker the best teacher?" and cites my aforementioned book in Japanese (Kubota, 2018), in which I critiqued the conflation of native speakers of English with white people and described NNESTs' professional strengths as identified by scholarly discussions.[3] On a separate webpage, providing a list of general advantages of learning English in the Philippines, the instructional strengths of NNESTs are also listed along with affordability of one-on-one instruction. However, the list also includes instructors speaking in a clear *American accent*, which, according to the website, is also used by Filipino operators in call centers for US-based companies.[4]

This illustrates the challenge of promoting critical perspectives on linguistic norms only through the *recognition politics* (Block, 2018). That is, merely advocating the diversification of English speaker norms can easily be co-opted by a capitalist pursuit of profit making, while the international and intranational linguistic hierarchies of power, which socioeconomically affect English speakers and non-English speakers, are kept intact.

## Ideologies and political economy regarding culture

The discussions thus far demonstrate how diverse Englishes and English users are ideologically stratified along the lines of what is deemed legitimate or not. Also, such ideological stratifications are exploited by capitalist interests, further solidifying the ideologies and socioeconomic inequalities. Ideologies of Englishes and English users are also related to the ideas of cultural legitimacy.

The global spread of English implies the fallacy of the one-nation-one-language assumption, questioning the traditional approach to teaching about culture in ELT, which typically associates English only with inner-circle countries and especially white middle-class mainstream people. However, the persistent focus on the traditional view of culture associated with English (e.g., Yamada, 2015) continues to ignore and marginalize other(ed) cultures and the perspectives of diverse English-speaking populations. Continuing to privilege white middle-class mainstream cultures in ELT would not lead to the fostering of respect, understanding, and affirmation of cultural and human diversity in the world.

Episodes 4 and 5 illustrate this problem. In Episode 5, the English teacher's insensitive and derogatory reference to Professor Song's homeland perhaps coexisted with his positive attitudes toward American and British cultures, which were probably more prominent at that time. This ambivalence also seems to underlie the teacher's exclusion of Asian Others from the "foreigner" in Episode 4. Professor Song's parents belong to an ethnically minoritized transnational group created by Japanese colonialism. While *zainichi* Koreans still constitute a large ethnically minoritized group in Japan, the number of newcomers with other types of transnational background has greatly increased in recent years. Teachers, especially English language professionals, who are tasked to foster students' understanding of cultural, linguistic, and human difference, must affirm minoritized learners' culture and heritage.

While this vision should be a central goal of education, the global expansion of businesses also necessitates sensitivities for various kinds of difference. Although this rationalization of diversity and inclusion constitutes neoliberal multiculturalism—a form of multiculturalism for the sake of capitalist expansion—it can be appropriated and integrated into education for critical purposes (Kubota, 2016).

However, such critical vision does not seem to influence the ELT industry. For instance, under the increased emphasis on teaching English to younger learners, the ELT businesses take advantage of cultural elements to allure young learners. Mainstream holidays and festivals celebrated in inner-circle countries, such as Halloween, Christmas, and Easter, are employed to offer superficial enjoyment to children, further reinforcing cultural biases attached to English.

## Ideologies and political economy in language-in-education policies

As discussed, neoliberal capitalist ideologies have galvanized English language education in various parts of the world. The basic premise of neoliberal capitalism as applied to ELT is that the ability to use English as an international language will ensure the economic success of individuals and nation states and that the success is achieved through competitions, implying that individuals and institutions are held accountable for staying competitive and expected to prove their competitiveness in an objective way (Bernstein et al., 2015; Kubota, 2015).

Such neoliberal capitalist ideologies have compelled many expanding circle countries to design and implement policies to promote ELT, such as teaching English to young children, English medium (i.e., monolingual) instruction, hiring native English-speaking teachers, and using standardized tests. Without exception, these language-in-education policies have been implemented in Japan (Bradford & Brown, 2018; Hashimoto, 2011; Kubota, 2018; Toh, 2014). Of these policies, language assessment, an instrument to measure accountability, displays a contradiction of neoliberalism; that is, assessing English language skills through large-scale tests goes against the educational aim to foster communication skills in global Englishes.

The aforementioned Episode 3, describing a test item that appeared in the national achievement test, illustrates this problem. To give a brief background, the national achievement test in Japan was reinstated in 2007, after its failed implementation in the 1960s. It now assesses all Grade 6 and Grade 9 students' academic achievement of *kokugo* (language arts) and mathematics every year and science every three years. The reinstatement was intended to increase the academic competitiveness of the students as well as schools and school districts (see Kubota, 2011b). As mentioned earlier, an English subtest for Grade 9 was added in 2019. Although the English test administered in 2019 was designed to measure all four skills (i.e., listening, speaking, reading, and writing), the computer-based speaking test items were given only in selected schools equipped with technology. Assessing the four skills is part of the government initiative for developing communication ability (*komyunikēshon nōryoku*) in English language education (MEXT, 2015). The emphasis on communication ability emerged in the national curriculum in the 1990s, consistent with the prominence of the discourse of internationalization and globalization.

Nonetheless, in Episode 3, the narrow scoring criteria reject multiple possible answers, failing to assess genuine ability to communicate, which is characterized by malleable, open-ended, and co-constructed interactions, rather than a static, prescriptive, and compartmentalized linguistic performance. In fact, research on language education has illuminated the co-constructed nature of communication. This is represented by the concept of *interactional competence* (Kramsch, 1986; Young, 2011), which highlights communication achieved by negotiated interaction between speaker/writer and listener/reader, rather than the isolated linguistic knowledge of individuals as conceptualized in the previous concept of *communicative competence* (Canale & Swain, 1980). While the Japanese government has been keenly advocating the development of communication ability, what is actually promoted is the acquisition of the four linguistic skills measurable by widescale tests under the neoliberal accountability scheme. This practice is likely to discourage students from using English for fear of making mistakes, as seen in Episode 2.

The contradiction between the preoccupation with developing communication ability and the reliance on tests is also observed in a government document assessing the achievement of goals delineated in a five-year education plan set by MEXT (MIC, 2017). A core objective in the education plan is fostering global *jinzai* (human resources), a concept including attributes such as language ability and communication competence. However, the document (MIC, 2017) mainly reports quantitative data, such as students' and teachers' scores on standardized English tests, and the final recommendations merely mention the need to improve students' and teachers' English ability without mentioning communication competence. In other words, communication in English is conflated with the four skills measurable by tests. The same document presents results from a corporate survey on companies' views on the effectiveness of the policy for fostering global *jinazai*, but interestingly, this conflated understanding was not entirely shared by representatives of Japanese corporations with overseas operations. Some open-ended corporate comments indicate broader understandings of communication competence beyond the four skills in English, resonating with *interactional competence* and the results of a study on Japanese transnational workers' communicative experiences in Asia (Kubota, 2013; Kubota & Takeda, 2019).

While the inconsistency between the government's emphasis on the development of isolated four skills and the corporate needs for global *jinzai* with wider-ranging communication competence is quite peculiar, what is clear is the fact that the emphasis on developing the four measurable skills certainly benefits the ELT industry, including testing companies. For instance, the aforementioned achievement tests for Grades 6 and 9 are outsourced to private corporations selected through a bidding process (Kubota, 2011b).

An even more apparent link between the promotion of the four skills and tests is observed in the recent controversy surrounding a proposed new policy for university admissions, which would replace the existing common national test with commercially available wide-scale tests of English.[5] Applicants would be encouraged to take one of the designated tests up to twice and submit the higher score.

This privatization of the examination system would bring huge profit margins to the testing industry, as each of approximately 500,000 test takers has to pay for a test up to twice. It has been pointed out that the committee set up by MEXT to discuss this new scheme was partly constituted by representatives from testing companies (Abe, 2017). Moreover, many of these test developers sell materials and services for test preparation, generating additional profits. Similar cases of a conflict of interest involving non-profit testing organizations—a US-based test developer and a Japan-based test distributor—have been reported by the media (see Kubota, 2011c).

Business interests are associated with not only testing but also the entire activity of ELT. The neoliberal ideologies surrounding English, globalization, competition, and accountability are exploited by the synergetic interest between private businesses and neoliberal governments.

## Seeking praxis in ELT

I have examined how ideologies and political economy are intertwined in shaping educational practices in ELT. While the bivalent approach to *recognition politics* and *redistribution politics* (Block, 2018) is essential for developing a deeper understanding of the existing problems in language education, pursuing these two orientations still seems to end in intellectual exercise only. In order to achieve actual transformation, it is necessary to proactively engage in *praxis* or "reflection and action upon the world to transform it" (Freire, 1998, p. 33). In other words, transformation requires a trivalent approach to critically engaging in ELT that embraces *recognition* and *redistribution politics* as well as *praxis*.

One strategy for enactment is public scholarship—writing and speaking to a broader audience, including teachers, parents, and ordinary people—to share and suggest scholarly and professional ideas. This includes writing to the media and producing affordable and accessible publications. Also, plurilingual ELT professionals can make intranational and transnational efforts multilingually to share knowledge with not only scholars but also non-academic audiences. Another strategy would be to engage in scholarly activism collaboratively with others. Activities may include generating or signing petitions, sending feedback to the government or other organizations, writing to the lawmakers, and attending and speaking out in public meetings. Although these activities are likely to take place locally, developing online professional networks can be done transnationally. Sharing advocacy strategies and supporting each other on the transnational platform would facilitate local praxis. It is certainly not easy to achieve actual change in policies, practices, and beliefs. However, these efforts, made collectively, would be indispensable for actual transformation.

## Conclusion

The promotion of ELT in globalized societies is closely tied to the neoliberal capitalist interest in making greater profit, further perpetuating the common beliefs about the legitimacy of particular forms of language, cultures, and language users in teaching and learning English. It is necessary for English language teachers, teacher educators, and scholars to recognize how taken-for-granted beliefs, policies, and systems reproduce unequal linguistic, cultural, racial, and economic relations of power as well as the regimented understanding of communication, which would fail to fix such inequalities. Critical inquiry in ELT has tended to problematize ideologies and discourses that reproduce inequity and injustice, but this approach is likely to only result in the circulation of critical discourse among those who are already committed or interested. Critical approaches for actual change must break this impasse. The global spread of English and associated ideologies and material conditions can be challenged by creating transnational coalitions of scholars and practitioners for sharing information, strategies for advocacy, and reflections of actions for further transformative engagement. A trivalent critical engagement that combines *recognition politics*, *redistribution politics*, and *praxis* would provide an alternative strategy for achieving actual change.

## Notes

1 For study lesson, see Fernandez and Yoshida (2004).
2 Compulsory education in Japan is from Grade 1 to Grade 9.
3 www.over-seas.jp/news/1974.html (accessed December 4, 2019).
4 www.over-seas.jp/philippines.html (accessed December 4, 2019).
5 The implementation of the new policy has recently been postponed due to a public outcry against geographical and economic inequities among applicants.

## References


Abe, M. (2017). *Shijō saiaku no eigo seisaku: Uso darake no "4 ginō kanban"* [*English education in chaos: Confusion and dishonesty in Japanese government policy*]. Tokyo: Hitsuji shobō.

Auerbach, E. R. (1992). *Making meaning, making change: Participatory curriculum development for adult ESL literacy*. Washington, DC: Center for Applied Linguistics.

Auerbach, E. R., & Burgess, D. (1985). The hidden curriculum of survival ESL. *TESOL Quarterly*, 19, 475–495.

Bailey, K. (2006). Marketing the eikaiwa wonderland: Ideology, akogare, and gender alterity in English conversation school advertising in Japan. *Environment and Planning D: Society and Space*, 24, 105–130.

Bernstein, K. A., Hellmich, E. Y. A., Katznelson, N., Shin, J., & Vinall, K. (2015). Critical perspectives on neoliberalism in second/foreign language education. *L2 Journal*, 7, 3–14.

Blackledge, A., & Creese, A. (2017). Translanguaging and the body. *International Journal of Multilingualism*, 14, 250–268.

Block, D. (2018). The political economy of language education research (or the lack thereof): Nancy Fraser and the case of translanguaging. *Critical Inquiry in Language Studies*, 15, 237–257.

Bradford, A., & Brown, H. (Eds.) (2018). *English-medium instruction in Japanese higher education: Policy, challenges and outcomes*. Bristol: Multilingual Matters.

Braine, G. (1999). *Nonnative educators in English language teaching*. Mahwah, NJ: Lawrence Erlbaum Associates.

Brutt-Griffler, J. (2002). *World English: A study of its development*. Clevedon: Multilingual Matters.

Canagarajah, S. A. (1999). *Resisting linguistic imperialism in English teaching*. Oxford: Oxford University Press.

Canale, M., & Swain, M. (1980). Theoretical bases of communicative approaches to second language teaching and testing. *Applied Linguistics*, 1, 1–47.

Choe, H. (2018). Identity formation of Filipino ESL teachers teaching Korean students in the Philippines. *English Today*, 32(1), 5–11.

Faez, F. (2011). Are you a native speaker of English? Moving beyond a simplistic dichotomy. *Critical Inquiry in Language Studies*, 8, 378–399.

Fernandez, C., & Yoshida, M. (2004). *Lesson study: A Japanese approach to improving mathematics teaching and learning*. Mahwah, NJ: Lawrence Erlbaum Associates.

Fraser, N. (2015). The fortunes of socialist feminism: Jo Littler interviews Nancy Fraser. *Soundings*, 58, 21–33. doi:10.3898/136266215814379664.

Freire, P. (1998). *Pedagogy of the oppressed*. New York, NY: Continuum.

García, O., & Li, W. (2014). *Translanguaging: Language, bilingualism and education*. Basingstoke: Palgrave Macmillan.

Hashimoto, K. (2011). Compulsory "foreign language activities" in Japanese primary schools. *Current Issues in Language Planning*, 12, 167–184.

Jang, I. C. (2018). Legitimating the Philippines as a language learning space: Transnational Korean youth's experiences and evaluations. *Journal of Sociolinguistics*, 22, 216–232.

Jenks, C. (2019). English for sale: Using race to create value in the Korean ELT market. *Applied Linguistics Review*, 10, 517–538.

Kamhi-Stein, L. (2004). *Learning and teaching from experience: Perspectives on nonnative English-speaking professionals*. Ann Arbor, MI: University of Michigan Press.

Kramsch, C. (1986). From language proficiency to interactional competence. *Modern Language Journal*, 70, 366–372.

Kubota, R. (2011a). Learning a foreign language as leisure and consumption: Enjoyment, desire, and the business of eikaiwa. *International Journal of Bilingual Education and Bilingualism*, 14, 473–488.

Kubota, R. (2011b). The politics of school curriculum and assessment in Japan. In Y. Zhao et al. (Eds.), *Handbook of Asian education: A cultural perspective* (pp. 214–230). New York, NY: Routledge.

Kubota, R. (2011c). Questioning linguistic instrumentalism: English, neoliberalism, and language tests in Japan. *Linguistics and Education*, 22, 248–260.

Kubota, R. (2013). "Language is only a tool": Japanese expatriates working in China and implications for language teaching. *Multilingual Education*, 3(4). doi:10.1186/2191-5059-3-4.

Kubota, R. (2015). Inequalities of Englishes, English speakers, and languages: A critical perspective of pluralist approaches to English. In R. Tupas (Ed.), *Unequal Englishes: The politics of Englishes today* (pp. 21–41). Basingstoke: Palgrave.

Kubota, R. (2016). The multi/plural turn, postcolonial theory, and neoliberal multiculturalism: Complicities and implications for applied linguistics. *Applied Linguistics*, 37, 474–494.

Kubota, R. (2018). *Eigo kyōiku gensō* [*Misconceptions of English language teaching and learning*]. Tokyo: Chikuma shobō.

Kubota, R., & Fujimoto, D. (2013). Racialized native-speakers: Voices of Japanese American English language professionals. In S. A. Houghton & D. J. Rivers (Eds.), *Native-*

*speakerism in Japan: Intergroup dynamics in foreign language education* (pp. 196–206). Bristol: Multilingual Matters.

Kubota, R., & Miller, E. R. (2017). Re-examining and re-envisioning criticality in language studies: Theories and praxis. *Critical Inquiry in Language Studies*, 14, 129–157.

Kubota, R., & Takeda, Y. (2019, March). *The monolingual approach to global language education in the multilingual world*. Paper presented at the American Association for Applied Linguistics Conference, Atlanta, GA.

Lee, E. (2011). Ethical issues in addressing inequity in/through ESL research. *TESL Canada Journal*, 5, 31–52.

Lee, W.-H., & Su, H.-Y. (2019). "You are in Taiwan, speak Chinese": Identity, language ideology, and sociolinguistic scales in online interaction. *Discourse, Context & Media*, 32, https://doi.org/10.1016/j.dcm.2019.100339.

Lorente, B. P., & Tupas, T. R. F. (2013). (Un)emancipatory hybridity: Selling English in an unequal world. In R. Rubdy & L. Alsagoff (Eds.), *The global-local interface and hybridity: Exploring language and identity* (pp. 66–82). Bristol: Multilingual Matters.

Lury, C. (2004). *Brands: The logos of the global economy*. London: Routledge.

Mazrui, A. A. (2002). The English language in African education: Dependency and decolonization. In J. W. Tollefson (Ed.), *Language policies in education: Critical issues* (pp. 267–281). Mahwah, NJ: Lawrence Erlbaum Associates.

MEXT (Ministry of Education, Culture, Sports, Science and Technology) (2015). *Seito no eigoryoku kōjō suishin puran* [*Plans for improving and advancing students' English ability*]. Retrieved from www.mext.go.jp/a_menu/kokusai/gaikokugo/__icsFiles/afieldfile/2015/07/21/1358906_01_1.pdf.

MIC (Ministry of Internal Affairs and Communication) (2017). *Gurōbaru jinzai no ikusei suishin ni kansuru seisaku hyōka hyō* [*Evaluation of the policies promoting global human resources*]. Retrieved from www.soumu.go.jp/menu_news/s-news/107317_00009.html.

Miller, E. R. (2012). Performativity theory and language learning: Sedimentating appropriating, and constituting language and subjectivity. *Linguistics and Education*, 23, 88–99.

Motha, S. (2014). *Race, empire, and English language teaching*. New York, NY: Teachers College Press.

National Institute for Educational Policy Research (n.d.). Heisei 31 nendo zenkoku gakuryoku/gakushū chōsa, hōkokusho, chūgakkō eigo [2019 national survey on achievement and learning status: Report on junior high school English]. Retrieved from www.nier.go.jp/19chousakekkahoukoku/report/data/19meng.pdf.

Nuzke, K. (2019). Vehicle of erotic liberation or instrument of career survival? Japan's ideologies of English as reflected in conversation school advertisements. *Discourse, Context & Media*, 31, https://doi.org/10.1016/j.dcm.2019.100319.

Park, G. (2012). "I am never afraid of being recognized as an NNES": One teacher's journey in claiming and embracing her nonnative-speaker identity. *TESOL Quarterly*, 46, 127–151.

Pennycook, A. (2001). *Critical applied linguistics: A critical introduction*. Mahwah, NJ: Lawrence Erlbaum Associates.

Phillipson, R. (1992). *Linguistic imperialism*. Oxford: Oxford University Press.

Phillipson, R. (2017). Myths and realities of "global" English. *Language Policy*, 16, 313–331.

Rajagopalan, K. (2010). The soft ideological underbelly of the notion of intelligibility in discussions about "world Englishes." *Applied Linguistics*, 31, 465–470.

Ramanathan, V. (2005). *The English-vernacular divide: Postcolonial language politics and practice*. Clevedon: Multilingual Matters.

Ramanathan, V. (2013). A postcolonial perspective in applied linguistics. In M. R. Hawkins (Ed.), *Framing languages and literacies: Socially situated views and perspectives* (pp. 83–104). New York, NY: Routledge.
Rivers, D. J., & Ross, A. S. (2013). Idealized English teachers: The implicit influence of race in Japan. *Journal of Language, Identity & Education*, 12, 321–339.
Rose, H., & Galloway, N. (2019). *Global Englishes for language teaching*. Cambridge: Cambridge University Press.
Ruecker, T., & Ives, L. (2015). White native English speakers needed: The rhetorical construction of privilege in online teacher recruitment spaces. *TESOL Quarterly*, 49, 733–756.
Selvi, A. F. (2014). Myths and misconceptions about nonnative English speakers in the TESOL (NNEST) movement. *TESOL Journal*, 5, 573–611.
Shin, H. (2006). Rethinking TESOL from a Sol's perspective: Indigenous epistemology and decolonizing praxis in TESOL. *Critical Inquiry in Language Studies*, 3, 147–167.
Simpson, W. (2018). Neoliberal fetishism: The language learner as homo œconomicus. *Language and Intercultural Communication*, 18, 507–519.
Sung, C. C. M. (2015). Implementing a global Englishes component in a university English course in Hong Kong. *English Today*, 31(4), 42–49.
Suzuki, A. (2011). Introducing diversity of English into ELT: Student teachers' responses. *ELT Journal*, 65, 145–153.
Tajima, M. (2018). Gendered constructions of Filipina teachers in Japan's Skype English conversation industry. *Journal of Sociolinguistics*, 22, 100–117.
Takahashi, K. (2013). *Language learning, gender and desire: Japanese women on the move*. Bristol: Multilingual Matters.
Toh, G. (2014). English for content instruction in a Japanese higher education setting: Examining challenges, contradictions, and anomalies. *Language and Education*, 28, 299–318.
Tupas, R. (2019). Entanglements of colonialism, social class, and unequal Englishes. *Journal of Sociolinguistics*, 23, 529–542.
Yamada, M. (2015). *The role of English teaching in modern Japan: Diversity and multiculturalism through English language education in globalized era*. New York, NY and London: Routledge.
Young, R. (2011). Interactional competence in language learning, teaching, and testing. In E. Hinkle (Ed.), *Handbook of research in language learning and teaching* (pp. 426–443). New York, NY: Routledge.

# Part II

# Spatial interventions

# 5 Teaching abroad during TESOL initial teacher education

## The case of a project in China

*Benjamin Luke Moorhouse*

## Introduction

As our world becomes increasingly globalized, we see unprecedented growth in human mobility and an insatiable desire to learn the English language. English has become "the unrivalled and perhaps unassailable global lingua franca" (Evans, 2016, p. 2). There are an estimated 1.5 billion users of English in the world (Myers, 2015), with the majority no longer residing in countries where English is the first language (Crystal, 2012). This has inevitably affected the Teaching English to Speakers of Other Languages (TESOL) profession, with classrooms becoming more diverse and teaching teams becoming more internationalized. In addition, there is an extraordinary global demand for TESOL professionals (Crystal, 2012). These TESOL professionals find themselves teaching in diverse and complex contexts, very different from the context in which they received their initial teacher education (ITE), in roles for which they may not feel adequately prepared (Johnson & Golombek, 2018; Castro, 2010; Amero-Jiménez, 2012). The understanding is growing that a strong command of English and pedagogical knowledge is not enough. TESOL professionals must also be culturally responsive (Gay, 2010) and able to adapt to changing contextual conditions (Gao, 2015). In addition, globalization and human mobility have led to an increase in the diversity of learners from different contexts and cultures in domestic English-language classrooms (Santoro, 2014).

In recent years, graduates from the TESOL ITE program at the author's university in Hong Kong have gone on to teach English in countries in Asia, Europe, and North America. There has been a steadily increasing number of immigrants to Hong Kong from Mainland China and South East Asia who share languages, histories, and cultures different from those of the local population (Chan & Gao, 2014; Shen, 2016). Therefore, graduates need the "ability to communicate and collaborate effectively with people whose attitudes, values, knowledge and skills may be significantly different from their own" (Cushner, 2007, p. 27), while being personally reflective, understanding that their lived experiences and identities (e.g., race, religion, class) influence their decisions and actions as a teacher (Goodwin, 2010). These understandings have led to calls for TESOL ITE providers to re-examine their practices (Johnson & Golombek, 2018, p. 2).

Historically, TESOL ITE has involved students attending universities or higher-education institutions where they receive taught courses and participate in domestic teaching practicums. The combined experience of the taught courses and practicum aims to prepare students for their future careers, with the practicum as an integral part (Farrell, 2008). Richards and Crookes (1988) write that the practicum in initial TESOL education serves to provide preservice teachers with "the practical skills and knowledge needed to function as effective language teacher[s]" (p. 9).

Many scholars in TESOL and the wider field of teacher education find the traditional structure of programs that rely solely on taught courses and domestic practicums to prepare preservice teachers to be problematic (Farrell, 2008; Darling-Hammond, 2006; Zeichner, 2010; Tomaš, Farrelly, & Haslam, 2008). Challenges can lie in the limited experiences that the domestic practicum offers. First, during the practicum, preservice teachers may work with a group of learners with whom they share a first language and culture. This linguistic and cultural homogeneity may not prepare them for working in other countries or with learners from different cultures. Furthermore, preservice teachers may interact with students or teachers with different cultural backgrounds without having an immersion experience in those cultures. They may hold stereotypes of certain learners from different cultural backgrounds (Sleeter, 2008) or fail to notice "cultural, ethnic, or racial differences between themselves and their students" (Pilonieta, Medina, & Hathaway, 2017, p. 22). In Hong Kong, preservice English-language teachers have been found to perceive new immigrants from Mainland China negatively and see them as deficient when compared to "local" students (Chan & Gao, 2014). Second, conducting the practicum in the educational context in which they received their education may lead them to take its practices as common sense and limit their critical evaluation of the methods that the teachers adopt. They can become "socialized" into the teaching profession by following the practices of the teaching practicum school and mentor, rather than the skills and knowledge they are learning in their university-based courses (Farrell, 2008; Cahn, 2014). In Hong Kong, preservice English teachers often feel pressured to adapt to school practices and norms by having to implement rigid and standardized curriculums and teaching approaches (Trent, 2018). Finally, student-teachers can lack interaction and the opportunity to learn collaboratively with their peers (Cho & Peter, 2017), often because of placements in different schools (Tomaš et al., 2008). Tomaš et al. (2008) state that "although some practicum programs encourage preservice teachers to give each other feedback through peer response, preservice teachers are not generally able to engage in intensive observations of each other's work in the cooperative classroom or to collaborate on lesson planning" (p. 660).

Despite these potential limitations, domestic practicums remain an important part of professional TESOL ITE programs (Funk & Hoffman, 1982; Farrell, 2008; Trent, 2018). However, ITE providers are exploring ways to address some of these limitations by offering additional and diverse supplemental experiences. These include service learning, community-based projects (e.g., Amero-Jiménez, 2012; Harfitt & Chow, 2018), cultural-immersion experiences (see Smolcic & Katunich, 2017), and study-abroad programs (e.g. Lee, 2009; An, 2016). One such experience that is becoming increasingly common in TESOL ITE, due to its perceived benefits for students combined with the obvious desire around the world to learn English, is "teaching abroad" (Barkhuizen & Feryok, 2006; Kabilan, 2013; Trent, 2011).

This chapter presents a general overview of teaching-abroad experience from the relevant literature. It then explores one such experience, now in its third year, offered by an ITE institution in Hong Kong that involves preservice TESOL teachers teaching English in a primary school in China for two weeks. Drawing on the reflections of the preservice TESOL teacher-participants and the author's observations as the project leader, this chapter reports on the project's development and implementation. A critical reflection follows on the effectiveness of the experiences in preparing the preservice TESOL teachers for their future roles in a transnational world. The chapter concludes with suggestions for the future development of such experiences in TESOL ITE.

## Teaching-abroad experiences during TESOL ITE

The literature has referred to teaching abroad as "international field experiences" (Pence & Macgillivray, 2008), "overseas student teaching" (Cushner & Mahon, 2002), and "teaching practicum abroad" (Tomaš et al., 2008). While various scholars have referred to such experiences by different names, they essentially mean projects involving preservice teachers teaching in different countries from the one in which they pursue their ITE (Cushner, 2007).

Along with its different names, teaching-abroad experiences reported in the literature are tremendously diverse. They vary in length from two or three weeks (Trent, 2011; Willard-Holt, 2001; Tomaš, et al., 2008) to six weeks (Ateşkan, 2016; Kabilan, 2013; Cho & Peter, 2017). Some involve preservice teachers teaching alone (Santoro, 2014), while others involve teaching in pairs or teams (Trent, 2011; Ateşkan, 2016). Some report on native-English speaking preservice teachers going to EFL contexts (Cho & Peter, 2017; Santoro, 2014); others involve non-native English speakers going to contexts in which English is the first language (Ateşkan, 2016; Trent, 2011); and still others see non-native English speakers going to other EFL contexts (Kabilan, 2013). The kind of supervision and support they receive also differs. Host schools can provide primary support (Santoro, 2014), as can partner ITE institutions in the host countries (Trent, 2011; Ateşkan, 2016) or tutors from their own ITE institutions (Cho & Peter, 2017). The host schools can be primary schools, secondary schools, tertiary institutions, special schools, and either government schools or international schools.

While there is a diversity of experiences, most studies report benefits of these experiences for the participants (Kabilan, 2013). A study by Willard-Holt (2001) involving North American preservice teachers teaching in Mexico found that participants developed greater global awareness, flexibility, and reflectivity in teaching, along with a heightened sense of professionalism in collaborating with colleagues and teaching students in other countries. Kabilan (2013) made similar observations of six preservice Malaysian English-language teachers who taught English for six weeks in the Maldives. The literature shows other benefits, including an increase in participants' confidence in their ability to teach, enhanced interpersonal skills, greater empathy, and an increase in intercultural competencies (Ateşkan, 2016; Hepple et al., 2017). Studies of non-native English-speaking preservice teachers find an increase in their confidence in speaking and using English to teach (Ateşkan, 2016; Kabilan, 2013). The overwhelming benefits found in most studies have led to calls for more students to receive such experiences to supplement the domestic teaching practicums. Cushner (2007) states:

> More than ever, there is the need for preservice teachers to have significant cross-cultural experiences that enable them to teach with, work with, and continue to learn from people different from themselves. Overseas student teaching can be the catalyst that starts teachers on a path of learning from others; their students, their colleagues, their community, and their world.
> (p. 37)

Santoro (2014) reminds us that any benefits of teaching-abroad experiences depend upon the development and implementation of such experiences. She reports on a study in which Australian preservice teachers went to India to teach English in orphanages and schools for the disabled. She found that the experience reinforced cultural stereotypes and biases around race, ethnicity, and poverty (Santoro, 2014). She attributed this to limited opportunities for students to critically reflect on the experiences, a lack of space to mediate what they were experiencing with their development as a teacher, and the reliance on a third party without expertise in teacher education to organize the experience. In addition, Santoro (2014) argues that the host schools could have been too different from participants' previous experiences for them to make adequate connections. Similar experiences have been criticized for their costs, creating ethical issues because only some students can afford them, and they provide little benefit to the host communities (Palacios, 2010) and are seen as an exotic vacation in a foreign country rather than an educationally rigorous project (Gray & Campell, 2007). Some experiences involve non-education majors or students from different subject disciplines usually going abroad to teach English as a foreign language (Smolcic & Katunich, 2017). This may reinforce the myth that "anyone who can speak English can teach English" or place students in situations for which they feel ill-prepared.

Therefore, it is important when developing and implementing such experiences to acknowledge the possibilities of negative consequences or hidden curriculum, to learn from previous cases and to develop teaching-abroad projects in a principled way. That was the goal of this project.

## The project: a teaching-abroad experience in China

In 2015/2016, the Faculty of Education at the University of Hong Kong began to reform its ITE programs to ensure they would better prepare students for their future role in both local and international contexts. These reforms involved several new faculty initiatives, including service-learning opportunities, experiential-learning projects, and teaching-abroad experiences (see Harfitt & Chow, 2018). Credit-bearing and non-credit-bearing projects and courses have been initiated in partnerships with community partners, such as Oxfam and Hong Kong Ocean Park; and schools and other organizations in both Hong Kong and other international contexts, including Vietnam, Cambodia, and Mainland China. Students from all subject disciplines can join a suite of different projects, in the hope that these experiences can help develop skills transferrable to their teaching (Harfitt & Chow, 2018).

The teaching-abroad project reported here began in the 2016/2017 academic year, in response to reforms, with the author as the project leader, and it ran again in 2017/2018 and 2018/2019. A credit-bearing program, it was offered to students studying for the five-year undergraduate double degree, namely a Bachelor of Arts and Bachelor of Education (Lang-Ed) English program. The program qualifies graduates to teach English as a second/foreign language in both primary and secondary schools. During the program, the students have four domestic teaching practicums, two in Year Three, one in Year Four, and one in Year Five.

### *Project development*

As stated in the literature review, it is important to develop and implement teaching-abroad projects in a principled way. Accordingly, this project team established some key principles to guide the development of this teaching-abroad experience:

1 all eligible students regardless of their financial situation should be able to join the project;
2 only English-language majors with relevant teaching-practicum experiences in Hong Kong should be recruited;
3 care should be taken to ensure the project maintains academic rigor and provides participants with professional learning that supplements their domestic course and practicums;
4 the host school should benefit from the project and these benefits should be sustainable;
5 students should feel fully prepared and supported during the project; and
6 opportunities for ongoing guided reflection should be provided throughout the project.

Fortunately, an external donor (The Trust) approached the project team and showed an interest in collaborating, agreeing to pay for the flights and accommodations of all participants. This meant students could join regardless of their financial situation. The project was made available to senior-year English-language students who had already taken part in a domestic practicum. It was felt these students would have greater experiences on which to draw and more knowledge and skills to share with the teachers in the host school. It was important that the students had relevant pedagogical and subject knowledge in teaching English as a foreign language. In this way, the project would supplement their university-based learning. The students could sign up freely on a first-come-first-served basis when selecting courses, with a course cap of ten students. The practicum counted as one of their free electives. The project was promoted to the targeted student population through email and orientation sessions each summer during course registration. This promotion focused on the project's objectives to ensure that students would see it as a part of their teaching development and not as a vacation (Santoro, 2014).

The Trust had been working with a school in Ningbo and was looking for partners to help them develop the English-language teaching in the school. The Ningbo school (host school) is a government through-train school (primary, middle, and high school) of approximately 2,200 students, with class sizes of 45–50 students. Due to the size of the school and limited resources, the project team decided to conduct the project in the primary section. The school has five grades, with students entering the school at six or seven years old and moving to the middle school at 11 years old. The primary section has 30 classes and 11 English teachers. The students receive five 40-minute periods a week of English lessons, and they start learning English in primary one. Due to restrictions in China, the teachers must use a specific government-approved English-language textbook.

To ensure the project would benefit the school, a pre-project trip was arranged. During the trip, the author and a colleague went to Ningbo for three days. They observed lessons, held meetings with the school management and English-language teachers, and reviewed teaching materials and assessment tasks. They noted that the textbook and lessons tended to be too easy for the students. Teachers informed us of their frustration with the materials and felt they lacked subject-specific teaching knowledge. The trip proved invaluable for providing students with greater contextual information and artifacts (e.g., teaching materials and lesson recordings) that could help them prepare for the experience. It also allowed development of complementary academic-focused objectives for both the faculty and the school (see Table 5.1). The project team strongly believed that the project should be a collaboration and not going to China to "improve" the English-language teaching.

During the pre-visit trip, it was agreed that the teach-abroad experience would take place in January and last for two weeks. The time chosen was a university holiday, during which the Ningbo school still had classes. The lessons would be developed and taught by two preservice teachers and one host teacher, creating a teaching team. These teams would teach one grade. The team would teach two or three classes in each level, adopting the lesson-study approach (Fernandez, 2002), where the team would develop a lesson, teach the lesson, receive feedback from the project leader or peers, and reteach the lesson to another class. In this way, teams would feel supported and encouraged to try new teaching methods. As the project team and the teachers felt the textbook was too restrictive, it was agreed that the teams would have autonomy to develop their own teaching units and materials.

*Table 5.1* Objectives of the project

| *Faculty objectives* | *Host school objectives* |
|---|---|
| 1. Preservice teachers develop skills and knowledge of curriculum and professional development including needs analysis, collaborative planning and teaching, objective-setting, and lesson reflection and evaluation. | 1. Host-school English teachers develop knowledge and skills in key areas such as curriculum and materials design, task-based learning and teaching, teaching input on reading skills, and using authentic texts in English lessons through collaborative planning and teaching. |
| 2. Preservice teachers develop a greater understanding of their roles as education professionals and the need as professionals to share their knowledge and skills in the wider educational community. | 2. Host-school English teachers gain exposure to activities that motivate the school students' interest in learning English. |
| 3. Preservice teachers gain a better understanding of English teaching in China and the needs of the students in different contexts. | 3. Host-school English teachers learn ways to create a more holistic and engaging school-wide English environment. |

The project team felt it was important to involve the author as project leader in all aspects of the project's development and implementation. To ensure academic rigor and maximize learning (Pilonieta et al., 2017; Santoro, 2014), the author developed the taught sessions and attended the two-week placement in Ningbo. This enabled support for the participants at every stage: reading and commenting on lesson plans and materials, observing lessons, attending co-planning meetings, and guiding students to reflect on their experiences. In addition, he agreed to teach a demonstration lesson during the placement. The focus was selected by the school teachers. Having taught in primary school in Hong Kong for several years, and having had previous opportunities to visit schools and observe lessons in China, the author was familiar with the teaching contexts in Hong Kong and China.

To prepare students for the experience, five taught sessions were developed and held biweekly in the semester leading up to the experience. In these sessions, students become aware of the project objectives, view a video on the current teaching practices in the school and identify areas of support. They make initial plans for the English activities and create materials for use in the English lessons. They are put in teaching teams for the English lessons. Each student creates a short bio to share with teaching partners in the schools, to whom the bios are sent prior to the project members' arrival.

One challenge of credit-bearing projects is assessing them. Accurately considering what aspects must or should be assessed can be difficult. As a result, the university approved the project as a pass/fail course. Students must attend the full two weeks and complete two key assessment tasks:

1 An individual portfolio: the individual learner's ongoing reflections on learning (four entries minimum, each entry 100–200 words, including those on understandings of target communities/social groups, learning/teaching,

personal development, ethical issues, intercultural communication, or project impact) and materials and/or artifacts prepared for the project (e.g., lesson plans, curriculum documents, task sheets) and related project documentation (e.g., video recordings, pictures).

2 A multimedia presentation: students prepare and present their projects and project experiences through a multimedia presentation (in groups) after the completion of the project.

These tasks are designed to help the students reflect on the experiences, allow for self-inquiry, make connections to their university learning and "reconstruct" and "reinterpret their experiences as learners of teaching" (Johnson & Golombek, 2018, pp. 9–10). Prompts were developed to help guide the reflections (see Table 5.2). The presentation provides them with a way to disseminate their learning to a wider audience, including students interested in joining the project.

### *Project implementation*

Every year, students show great interest in the project and all student places have been filled. According to students' pre-project reflections, they primarily enrol to gain a better understanding of the education system in China and to gain more experience teaching primary-school English-language learners. This shows the academic nature of the project and that students' expectations match the project objectives.

During the taught sessions, students were keen to learn about the current practices of the school and try out new approaches and methods in the unfamiliar context. Students have stated that in their domestic teaching practicum, they often

*Table 5.2* Prompts provided to preservice teachers for their reflections

| |
|---|
| *Pre-project (at least one reflective writing)* |
| • Your motivation for joining the course and project, your hopes and aspirations for learning, your challenges and concerns. |
| • Your beliefs about learning of English language at the primary school and creating an effective learning environment in relation to the teaching of English in China. |
| • Your growing understanding of the needs of the school learners and teachers. |
| *During project (at least two reflective writings)* |
| • Your reflections on your experience at the school, including planning, implementing, refining, and reflecting on the lessons you teach. |
| • One or more critical incidents reflecting ethical issues or communication issues you encountered and what you learned about yourself, the school, the project, and, more widely, education in a globalized society. |
| *Post-project (at least one reflective writing)* |
| • Your most significant learning. |
| • How you have changed as a person, as a prospective education professional. |
| • How your experience with the school has influenced your understanding of teaching and learning. |

felt restricted by prescribed curricula, teaching plans, and textbooks (Trent, 2018). The opportunity to develop materials and lessons without these constraints was appealing. They see the chance to connect with the teachers in the school as valuable—they can get feedback on their developing ideas and gain more awareness of the context. In the second and third year, previous project members were invited to share their experiences and give feedback on the students' ideas.

During the two-week placement in Ningbo, the students teach about eight lessons to three different classes of the same grade. This is considerably less than they teach during a domestic practicum, but it gives them time to co-plan and observe their peers. The participants particularly value the opportunity to teach multiple classes of the same grade. As they had limited knowledge of the context and had often taught prescribed curricula during the domestic teaching practicum, few of them had experience in designing and teaching a lesson from scratch. This meant the first lesson often had room for improvement. However, after each lesson, a discussion of the lesson's strengths and weaknesses followed, with suggestions for improvement is carried out. The author was able to observe most lessons and engage students in reflecting on the lesson taught. This involvement was important, as the student-teachers often struggled to identify areas for improvement and synthesize the feedback they received from their teaching team and peers. Through detailed mediated reflective meetings, participants were able to talk through the lessons and agree concrete actions to be taken. Then, the teams would work on modifying plans and materials before teaching the lesson to another class. This provided them with space to take risks that they may not have otherwise. The extract below from one student's reflections shows his satisfaction in being able to teach the same lesson more than once:

> Through this process of "re-teaching" the same lesson to a different class, I have made stark changes to different stages of the lessons. While in Hong Kong, it is rare that a teacher can teach 2 English classes of the same grade, let alone 3 classes of the same grade. It is truly beneficial to "re-teach" the same lesson … It is really rewarding and satisfying to see the changes in the same lesson leading to better response and participation on students' part.

They also value the opportunity to observe each other, as this student reflected:

> We can now observe our classmates' lesson; we have learnt much from them as we can have discussion and feedback session after each teaching. Moreover, some of our classmates had conducted a really good lesson that we can learn their teaching strategies and classroom management as well.

Throughout the project, the participants needed to work closely with the host teachers as they planned and observed lessons together. There were some clear differences of opinion between the preservice teachers and host teachers, with regard to what they considered effective English-language teaching and different expectations of the learners' abilities. An example of this came in the first year.

One team wanted to create English "Fai Chuns" with their grade-two class, as Chinese New Year was a few weeks away. The host teachers felt this would be too challenging. However, once they tried the activity, the opinion changed. One preservice teacher reflected on this and the importance of providing students with more challenging activities:

> At first, we were told that the Grade 2 students were not able to write a whole word as they were still learning the alphabet. However, sometimes, students needed to be pushed out of their comfort zone so that they could go beyond themselves with the help of teachers. And in fact, the students could actually write words to express their own meaning on the "Fai Chun" which was quite fascinating to teachers.

While the student-teachers have faced similar differences in their domestic teaching practicum, the team-teaching approach means they must spend more time discussing their rationale and reasons for their approaches. As this student's reflection shows:

> I think this project helped me to disagree respectfully and to compromise and come to an agreement eventually in a better way. Since the lessons are co-planned and co-taught, the lessons will require a consensus and collaboration with my teaching partners. We may not agree with each other all the time and sometimes there will be heated debate over certain issues. But I reminded myself that we all have the good will to make our lesson better.

Through these discussions, the participants start to understand each other's perspectives and ideas, leading to mutual learning through the "pedagogical exchange" of ideas (Goodwin, 2010). This reflection shows the mutual learning the project provided:

> This trip has taught me that teaching should be collaborative. Teachers should work together to learn from each other and to gain new ideas. I learned from teachers in [the host school] and they also learned from [project leader], my classmates and I.

Throughout the project, the written reflections provided an avenue for the student-teachers to reflect on their experiences. They were observed making connections between their experiences teaching in Hong Kong, discussing cultural differences between themselves and the teachers in the school, and contemplating their future roles. The reflection below shows how one student-teacher reflects on the difference between Ningbo and Hong Kong experiences and the impact this has on her future plans:

> The project was a chance for me to reflect on what kind of teacher I want to be and what impact I want to make on students. I feel that I could offer more

> to the students in Ningbo than what I could offer to the students in Hong Kong. Teachers in Hong Kong often struggle with restrictions from the curriculum, the parents and also the assessments ... I commit myself to be a change maker in terms of content and pedagogies to teach English language.

Overall, students have left Ningbo each year with a positive view of the experience and feel they have developed, both personally and professionally (Moorhouse, 2018a). The following extract from one student's reflection encapsulates the feeling of several participants:

> I will definitely say that I developed most as a teacher during the trip to Ningbo. Being able to teach in an unfamiliar environment and given the opportunity to try out different styles of teaching, I was able to recognize my strengths and weaknesses as a teacher.

### *Personal insights*

While the project showed positive benefits to the participants, it is important to acknowledge the challenges the author faced as the project leader and how these challenges were overcome. Developing and implementing a project which crosses geographical and cultural boundaries inevitably leads to miscommunications, misunderstandings, and different expectations of a "good" English lesson. This was particularly true in the first year of the project. Although the pre-visit had helped develop the author's contextual knowledge and clarify expectations, he still had limited knowledge of TESOL teacher education in China and sociocultural factors that impacted on the teaching of English. It was important to set up a dialogue with the teachers in the school and understand their beliefs, ideas, and real and perceived contextual constraints before making judgments or offering suggestions. Sometimes suggestions, which seemed like common sense to the author and his students, were challenged by the host teachers who were used to teaching in different ways or felt bound by established practices. They had to find ways to justify ideas, acknowledging their concerns as legitimate and find approaches that would work and made the teachers and students feel comfortable within the context. The author felt the demonstration lesson he taught went a long way to model his beliefs in practice and clarify his ideas of teaching. The host teachers could see in action the practices he was proposing and how the school students responded to his approaches. This, coupled with the regular co-planning meetings, has led to greater mutual understanding and the sustainability of the project over three years.

## Critical reflection

The following section critiques the effectiveness of the teaching-abroad experience in preparing the preservice TESOL teachers for their future roles in a transnational world. It explores the effectiveness in three areas: personal reflectivity, increased adaptability and enhanced communication and collaborative abilities, and important attributes of teaching in a transnational world (Johnson & Golombek, 2018).

### *Personal reflectivity*

Students come to TESOL ITE with beliefs about teaching and learning from their experience as a student and a language learner. In their home context, they will often observe practices that seem familiar to their own learning experience (Johnson & Golombek, 2018). This project revealed that by taking students from their home context and into a new space, where practises seem different and people hold different beliefs, they become more aware of themselves and their own beliefs. Therefore, they can reflect on these experiences and explore if or how they might be relevant or appropriate for different contexts or learners. This may mean challenging misconceptions or contradictions in their beliefs about teaching, learners, or themselves. However, they need guidance. After lessons, they struggle to identify areas for improvement; after co-planning meetings with a host teacher, they struggle to understand their perspectives. On the ground and able to observe these difficulties, the author could ask questions and help guide them to explore their own practices and different beliefs of the host teachers. This led in turn to deeper reflections and a greater understanding of themselves and others. Going abroad is not enough to develop personal reflectivity (Santoro, 2014). Creating opportunities for students to reflect on their own conceptions is essential in TESOL ITE for students to become more open-minded about differences and the constantly adapting and changing field. However, these opportunities must be pursued in a safe and guided way. Developing projects that are explicitly designed to benefit the host communities can help students reflect on their contribution to education globally and their place within the world.

### *Increased adaptability*

As Goodwin (2010) mentions, preparing preservice teachers for every possible situation is impossible. Instead, we can "provide ways of thinking about teaching and children, with problem-solving, problem-posing, and information gathering skills" (p. 24). During a domestic teaching practicum, preservice teachers report few opportunities to go beyond the prescribed curriculum or standardized school practices (Trent, 2018). This limits their opportunities to address learners' needs and can lead to frustration in both preservice (Trent, 2018) and in-service teachers (Moorhouse, 2018b).

Experiences such as teaching abroad, which provide participants with the chance to adapt lessons to meet learners' needs and different expectations, while being able to teach lessons again with input from peers or tutors, allows them to consider problems and implement solutions. This freedom gives students the chance to engage with essential skills necessary for curriculum development, including critically assessing and adapting materials and creating new materials to meet the pedagogical needs of learners. As classrooms become more diverse, it is important for TESOL professionals to feel capable and confident in their ability to adapt their teaching to meet the needs of their learners or their context.

### *Enhanced communication and collaborative skills*

As people move around the world, they bring with them different ideas, cultures, and beliefs. Teachers must respect these differences (Goodwin, 2010) while working collaboratively with diverse groups of people (Cushner, 2007) from different cultures (Gay, 2010). China and Hong Kong have a complex relationship for historical and political reasons—a tense relationship at times. Hong Kong preservice English-language teachers have viewed students from Mainland China in their practicum classrooms negatively (Chan & Gao, 2014). But projects such as this give them the chance to work and learn together. They can learn more about each other and develop mutual respect (Cushner, 2007; Goodwin, 2010). The preservice teachers were able to work closely with the host teachers to the benefit of their students, even though they had different views and opinions regarding students' capabilities and effective teaching practices. Opportunities to work with others who hold different views, opinions, and ideas can strengthen preservice TESOL teachers' collaboration skills, and at the same time help them to question the rationale for their practises as they communicate that rationale to others.

## Conclusion

This chapter describes teaching-abroad experiences and their development in response to the changing roles, needs, and expectations of TESOL ITE. Such experiences can benefit the preservice TESOL teachers, as a supplement to their domestic teaching practicum, providing a mediated space for students to become more personally reflective and adaptable while developing their ability to communicate with diverse groups of people. These are required qualities for TESOL professionals to function effectively in an increasingly complex transnational world (Johnson & Golombek, 2018). However, to achieve these benefits, the projects must be developed in a principled way with specific academic-focused objectives. Following are suggestions for developing TESOL ITE accordingly.

"Realistically … not all preservice teachers can benefit from the international teaching practicum and experience due to constraints and limitations such as capability, time and demanding course requirements" (Kabilan, 2013, p. 200). Nonetheless, finding ways to reduce barriers where possible, particularly financial barriers (such as collaborating with a sponsor) must be a project goal. At the same time, thought must go into the eligibility requirements of such projects, to ensure that participants and hosts can gain maximum benefit from such experiences. Ideally, only students studying to be TESOL professionals, who have experienced teaching in their home countries, should be recruited for such projects.

Teacher educators from the preservice teachers' ITE must be involved in the development and implementation of such experiences. This allows them to make connections between the participants' experiences in their courses and domestic practicum and the project (Moorhouse, 2018a). It helps to ensure the project is primarily educational and academically rigorous (Santoro, 2014). Participants can get expert feedback on their teaching in the new context, which, in turn, provides them with opportunities to try new approaches and ideas that they may be unable or reluctant to try during a domestic teaching practicum. These teacher educators should be familiar with teaching English in the host country.

Host schools and partner organizations must be chosen carefully, and effort spent to ensure the project benefits them. Through our pre-visit, we got a much better understanding of the school's needs and provided important contextual information to the project participants. The long-term partnership with the school has meant these benefits can be sustained (Harfitt & Chow, 2018).

Students must be adequately prepared for the experience and supported throughout. Pre-project sessions can be organized which focus on raising students' cultural and contextual awareness and give them time to develop lesson plans and materials. During the experience, we must guide them to revise and improve their lessons to meet the needs of the learners. Teaching in teams was beneficial in this project.

Finally, students must engage in ongoing reflections throughout the experience. Prompts, such as those in Table 5.2, can help them focus on specific events or areas on which to reflect. Regular reflective meetings can be arranged where students can be invited to speak freely about their observations, thoughts, and ideas.

Due to globalization and the increase in human mobility, it seems almost inevitable that TESOL professionals will be working with learners with links across national and territorial borders or in contexts different from the ones they were educated in. Therefore, preparing preservice TESOL teachers for such inevitabilities in our transnational world is paramount. To do this, it is important to provide experiences in diverse classrooms and contexts, where they can meet, work, and collaborate with people who share lived experiences, values, attitudes, and skills different from their own (Cushner, 2007).

This chapter suggests that including teaching-abroad experiences, as a form of transnational practice, in curricula is one way ITE providers can better prepare students for their future classrooms. However, while providing positive benefits to students, these experiences must be developed with specific academic-focused objectives and in a principled way. Students will always be attracted to the opportunity to go abroad to teach, and universities are under pressure to internationalize their curriculums (Santoro, 2014). Often, these projects will involve English-language teaching, due to the world's demand for more English and language barriers that come with teaching other subjects. We must ensure that we do not reinforce the myth that "anyone who can speak English can teach English," and that such experiences maintain academic rigor.

## References

An, H. (Ed.). (2016). *Handbook of research on efficacy and implementation of study abroad programs for P-12 teachers*. Hershey, PA: IGI Global.

Amero-Jiménez, C. (2012). Service learning: Preparing teachers to understand better culturally and linguistically diverse learners. *Journal of Education for Teaching*, 38(2), 211–213.

Ateşkan, A. (2016). Pre-service teachers' cultural and teaching experiences abroad. *Journal of Education for Teaching*, 42(2), 135–148. doi:10.1080/02607476.2016.1144634.

Barkhuizen, G., & Feryok, A. (2006). Pre-service teachers' perceptions of a short-term international experience programme. *Asia-Pacific Journal of Teacher Education*, 34(1), 115–134.

Cahn, L. V. (2014). Great expectations: The TESOL practicum as a professional learning experience. *TESOL Journal*, 5(2), 199–224.

Castro, A. J. (2010). Themes in research on preservice teachers' views of cultural diversity implications for researching millennial preservice teachers. *Educational Researcher*, 39(3), 198–210.

Chan, W. (Brad) Y., & Gao, X. (2014). Pre-service English teachers' perceptions of newly arrived children from mainland China. *Journal of Education for Teaching*, 40(2), 140–154.

Cho, H., & Peter, L. (2017). Taking the TESOL practicum abroad: Opportunities for critical awareness and community-building among preservice teachers. In W. Paterson (Ed.), *Handbook of research on efficacy and implementation of study abroad programs for P-12 teachers* (pp. 149–171). Hershey, PA: IGI Global.

Crystal, D. (2012). *English as a global language*. Cambridge: Cambridge University Press.

Cushner, K. (2007). The role of experience in the making of internationally minded teachers. *Teacher Education Quarterly*, 34(1), 27–39.

Cushner, K., & Mahon, J. (2002). Overseas student teaching: Affecting personal, professional, and global competencies in an age of globalization. *Journal of Studies in International Education*, 6(1), 44–58.

Darling-Hammond, L. (2006). *Powerful teacher education: Lessons from exemplary programs*. San Francisco, CA: Jossey-Bass.

Evans, S. (2016). *The English language in Hong Kong*. London: Palgrave Macmillan.

Farrell, T. S. (2008). "Here's the book, go teach the class": ELT practicum support. *RELC Journal*, 39(2), 226–241.

Fernandez, C. (2002). Learning from Japanese approaches to professional development: The case of lesson study. *Journal of Teacher Education*, 53(5), 393–405.

Funk, F., & Hoffman, J. (1982). The cooperating teacher as most significant other: A competent humanist. *Action in Teacher Education*, 4(2), 31–38.

Gao, A. (2015). Promoting experiential learning in pre-service teacher education. *Journal of Education for Teaching*, 41(4), 435–438. doi:10.1080/02607476.2015.1080424.

Gay, G. (2010). *Culturally responsive teaching* (2nd ed.). New York, NY: Teachers College Press.

Goodwin, A. L. (2010). Globalization and the preparation of quality teachers: Rethinking knowledge domains for teaching. *Teaching Education*, 21(1), 19–32.

Gray, N. J., & Campell, L. M. (2007). A decommodified experience? Exploring aesthetic, economic and technical values for volunteer ecotourism in Costa Rica. *Journal of Sustainable Tourism*, 15(5), 463–482.

Harfitt, G. J., & Chow, J. M. L. (2018). Transforming traditional models of initial teacher education through a mandatory experiential learning programme. *Teaching and Teacher Education*, 73, 120–129.

Hepple, E., Alford, J., Henderson, D., Tangen, D., Hurwood, M., Alwi, A., … & Alwi, A. (2017). Developing intercultural learning in Australian pre-service teachers through participating in a short term mobility program in Malaysia. *Teaching and Teacher Education*, 66, 273–281.

Johnson, K. E., & Golombek, P. R. (2018). Informing and transforming language teacher education pedagogy. *Language Teaching Research*. Advance online publication. https://doi.org/10.1177/1362168818777539.
Kabilan, M. K. (2013). A phenomenological study of an international teaching practicum: Pre-service teachers' experiences of professional development. *Teaching and Teacher Education*, 36, 198–209.
Lee, J. (2009). ESL student teachers' perceptions of a short-term overseas immersion programme. *Teaching and Teacher Education*, 25, 1095–1104.
Moorhouse, B. L. (2018a). Taking an active role in our pre-service teachers' overseas teaching experiences: A report on an experiential learning project in China. *Journal of Education for Teaching*, 44(2), 241–242.
Moorhouse, B. L. (2018b). Standardized homework practices and teacher autonomy: Experiences of primary English language teachers in Hong Kong. *The Asia-Pacific Education Researcher*, 25(5), 345–354.
Myers, J. (2015, October 13). Which languages are most widely spoken? Retrieved from weforum.org/agenda/2015/10/which-languages-are-most-widely-spoken/ (retrieved August 7, 2019).
Palacios, C. (2010). Volunteer tourism, development and education in a postcolonial world: Conceiving global connections beyond aid. *Journal of Sustainable Tourism*, 18(7), 861–878. doi:10.1080/09669581003782739.
Pence, H. M., & Macgillivray, I. K. (2008). The impact of an international field experience on preservice teachers. *Teaching and Teacher Education*, 24(1), 14–25.
Pilonieta, P., Medina, A. L., & Hathaway, J. I. (2017). The impact of a study abroad experience on preservice teachers' dispositions and plans for teaching English language learners. *The Teacher Educator*, 52(1), 22–38.
Richards, J. C., & Crookes, G. (1988). The practicum in TESOL. *TESOL Quarterly*, 21(1), 9–27.
Santoro, N. (2014) "If I'm going to teach about the world, I need to know the world": Developing Australian pre-service teachers' intercultural competence through international trips. *Race Ethnicity and Education*, 17(3), 429–444. doi:10.1080/13613324.2013.832938.
Shen, S. (2016). *Hong Kong in the world*. London: Imperial College Publishing.
Sleeter, C. (2008). An invitation to support diverse students through teacher education. *Journal of Teacher Education, 59(3)*, 212–219.
Smolcic, E., & Katunich, J. (2017). Teachers crossing borders: A review of the research into cultural immersion field experiences for teachers. *Teaching and Teacher Education*, 62, 47–59.
Tomaš, Z., Farrelly, R., & Haslam, M. (2008). Designing and implementing the TESOL teaching practicum abroad: Focus on interaction. *TESOL Quarterly*, 42(4), 660–664.
Trent, J. (2011). Learning, teaching, and constructing identities: ESL pre-service teacher experiences during a short-term international experience programme. *Asia Pacific Journal of Education*, 31(2), 177–194.
Trent, J. (2018). "Fitting in" or "being different"? Integration, separation, and identity construction during a teaching practicum in Hong Kong. *Teacher Development*, 22(4), 571–586.
Willard-Holt, C. (2001). The impact of a short-term international experience for preservice teachers. *Teaching and Teacher Education*, 17, 505–517.
Zeichner, K. (2010). Rethinking the connections between campus courses and field experiences in college and university-based teacher education. *Journal of Teacher Education*, 61(1–2), 89–99. doi:10.1177/0022487109347671.

# 6 Rejecting the transnational in TESOL teacher training

## The propagation, spread, and hybridization of a critical pedagogic register of TESOL teacher training in the *Oriente Antioqueño*, Colombia

*Peter Browning*

### Introduction

As the current iteration of Colombia's national English language in education policy *Colombia Bilingüe* (2004–19) comes to an end, it seems appropriate to explore some of the debates the policy implementation has opened up regarding TESOL teaching and teacher training in the country. In this chapter, I will pay attention to the ways in which academics critical of the *Colombia Bilingüe* policy have framed their critique around a rejection of the transnational dimensions of the policy.

In a recent special edition of the thought-provoking journal *Trabalhos em Linguística Aplicada*, dedicated to "Language, Education and Transnationalism," Joel Windle and Sarah O'Brien define the scope of scholarly work at the confluence of these areas as considering "the ways in which transnational movements of populations, linguistic practices, ideology, knowledge and capital shape educational policies and practices related to language. It is concerned with migration, internationalisation of educational provision, student mobility, and global communications" (2019, p. 1).

In this chapter, I pay particular attention to the transnational mobility of knowledge, specifically expertise related to English language teaching and learning, and explore its impact on TESOL policy and teacher training practice. As will become clear in the course of the chapter, the "movement of knowledge" and expertise in the context of TESOL in Colombia is often understood as a being one-way, thus transnationalism can be understood in the context of the present discussion as the involvement of non-Colombian organizations and their associated expertise in TESOL policy and practice. I explore how this transnational involvement, emblematic here is the British Council, is rejected by local academics and educational practitioners and describe how the production and circulation of such critique means that an oppositional stance to transnationalism in TESOL has become a key element of a critical pedagogic register, now an established register in TESOL teaching and teacher education in the country. I will then turn my attention to how this register travels, and consider my own attempts to introduce this critical pedagogic register to an institution in which an outright rejection of transnationalism would have been counter to the institutional orientations, and consider then how this led to the emergence of an alternative, hybridized, critical pedagogic register which has an ambivalent relation to the transnational, rather than an outright rejection of it. I offer some final thoughts reflecting on the fact that this "hybridized" register ultimately leads to the acceptance of the knowledge mobilized by transnational organizations and considering how this register may provide privileged access to the labor market.

In turning my attention to my own role in propagating a hybridized, critical pedagogic register, I hope to do so in the spirit of "uncomfortable reflexivity" (Pillow, 2003), that is to say I reflexively engage with my being as a white, European, British, English "native-speaker" in order to give account for my role; to give account in both the sense of "telling the story," "documenting the process" and in the sense of "being accountable." This imperative is given extra weight in light of the colonial framing of the local critiques of transnationalism; my role in voicing these local critiques and ultimately contributing to their hybridization – a process that relies on essentialist discourses and thus reproduces colonial structures (Cusicanqui, 2019) – indeed leads me to a place of uncomfortable reflexivity, and needs me to give account.

A quick, but important, note on terminology. The experiences recounted in the remainder of this chapter have all taken place within *licenciatura* programs, specifically *licenciaturas en lenguas extranjeras (inglés, francés)*. This is an official denomination authorized by the Colombian Ministry of Education, *licenciatura* meaning that on completion of the eight-semester-long degree program, students will be licensed teachers; in this case teachers of *lenguas extranjeras (inglés, francés)* foreign languages (English, French). Given the focus of this discussion, I will use the term TESOL (although this term has little currency outside of the "TESOL International Association" in the Colombian context, practitioners more likely to conceive of what they do under the concept of ELT) to refer to the English element of these *licenciatura* programs, without wanting to ignore or invisibilize the French element, but to give direction to the discussion in line with the book's focus. Finally, I have chosen to follow the title of the book and talk about teacher "training," though I acknowledge that this, in and of itself, may be interpreted as an orientation to a transnational norm in TESOL. As I myself align (although now more reflexively and tentatively) with a critical pedagogic register, I, and many of my Colombian colleagues of the same orientation, would prefer the term teacher "formation" (a calque of the Spanish *formación*), or at best teacher "education" to talk about a more holistic, humanistic process, which we would see as being in opposition to a more instrumentalist, technical approach to teacher education as encapsulated in the concept of "training," this conceptual and terminological rift will be echoed in much of the forthcoming discussion.

## TESOL teacher training at the *Universidad de Antioquia*: the regional campus and Medellín

It seems fitting that the first time I went to the *Universidad de Antioquia* (*UdeA*) regional campus was to a yoga class. The campus is small and very green, if you sit on the grass, the *manga* to drink a coffee or have an improvised picnic (as is obligatory if you go with an alumni student as they will tell you that this is one of their favorite memories of their time there), before too long you can forget that you are at a university at all; you can see exotic birds, you can hear the sound of water splashing into the lake from a water fountain, and you can start to feel what Colombians will tell you: that the *manga* will take away any bad energies you have and allow you to relax. The *UdeA* regional campus was originally housed in a *finca* (farmhouse) but over the years new offices and blocks have been built to cater for a growing student population, however the natural feel of the place remains intact. Indeed, even the most modern building which houses new "smart classrooms" and the state-of-the-art library is built with large internal courtyards filled with plants, blurring the lines between the in- and outdoors.

The *UdeA* regional campus was the first place in the *Oriente Antioqueño* region of Colombia to offer TESOL training and continues to be an important center of TESOL training and of higher education and professionalization in general. The *Oriente Antioqueño* is a sub-region of the department of Antioquia. It is known for being an area rich in agriculture and floriculture and home to Colombia's second international airport. The *Oriente Antioqueño* region is made up of 23 municipalities, the largest and most important being Rionegro, the *de facto* capital of the sub-region. The *UdeA* regional campus is about 20 minutes outside of Rionegro by bus on the road to La Ceja, although administratively it belongs to El Carmen de Viboral. The *UdeA* is often the number one choice of university for students in the *Oriente Antioqueño*, it not being common to move away to study, most students commute from all over the sub-region for up to two hours each day to study in order to become "professionals." As a public university, the *UdeA* is open to all students provided they pass an admissions exam, this exam is defined by program, but all are notoriously difficult. If accepted, students pay fees depending on their socio-economic strata.

In the Colombian context, university degrees are conceptualized as "professionalization courses," this is against a backdrop in which your *títulos*, your level and certificates of education, are linked very strictly to the kind of employment you can seek (OECD, 2016). Without any *títulos*, most people either cannot work, or work as day laborers, farmhands, often in the unregulated economy. On graduating high school, you gain the title of *bachiller* which gives you access to so-called "unskilled jobs"; so-called "semi-skilled" jobs require you to have a *técnica* and so-called "skilled" jobs or "professions" require a university degree in the specific area: to work in accountancy you must have studied to become an accountant; to work in communications you must have studied to become a communicator; to work in business administration you must have studied to be a business administrator; and so on. You will not be asked by Colombians "what did you study at university?", rather "what is your profession?". The rigidity of the system seems odd to somebody brought up in the British education system in which many people end up working in areas only loosely connected to their studies, especially in the arts and humanities (areas which are drastically under-represented in Colombian higher education), and where your experience can still outweigh your *títulos*, this is, however, certainly not the case in Colombia. In this context, then,

TESOL teacher training can be understood as a necessary rite of passage for all English teachers, the training processes explicitly conceptualized as a process of "making English teachers." The contents of such programs, the knowledge and expertise drawn on, play an important role in defining what is understood by "English language teaching." Every TESOL teacher training program is designed around a *perfil del egresado* (alumnus profile) which outlines the "type" of professional the process is designed to "make," in the case of the *UdeA* this is "teachers who promote respect for different cultures and social and ethnic diversity and who identify problems in their surroundings and take critical and transformational positions towards them"[1] (UdeA, 2018), what would locally be understood as a critical pedagogic conception of a TESOL practitioner. The TESOL training program offered at the *UdeA* regional campus is aligned to the program approved by the *UdeA*'s central body but offered at the regional campus on a cohort basis in order to respond to the economic demands of the *Oriente Antioqueño*. In order to trace the origins of the alumnus profile and to better understand the TESOL training program at the *UdeA* regional campus, it is illuminating to briefly turn our attention to the main university *sede* as it is the epicenter of the knowledge that informs the alumnus profile and its critical pedagogic orientation.

The main campus of the *UdeA* is in the north of the city of Medellín, emblematic of the university is a fountain crafted by the Antioqiuian sculptor Rodrigo Arias Betancourt that sits at the center of a concrete plaza around which the numerous blocks of offices, classrooms, laboratories, the theater, sports center, swimming pool, banks, and restaurants sprawl. Here too there is a *manga*, affectionately referred to as "*el aeropuerto*," the "airport," because it is here that students go to smoke marijuana and "fly high," although in recent years this space has taken on darker connotations; with the arrival of "peace" and the fracturing of the traditional centers of the narco industry, it is said that the *aeropuerto* has become one of the centers of micro-trafficking in the city of Medellín. In many respects, the *UdeA* regional and main campuses are worlds apart. It is, however, important to remember that it is within the *UdeA* main campus that the critical pedagogic register of TESOL education is forged, the politicized nature of this register becoming apparent taking this context into account.

For me, used to the *campestre*, Arcadian *UdeA* regional campus, what is most striking about the buildings of the *UdeA* is not only their number, but that seemingly each and every wall is covered by political murals, graffiti, or posters. Murals are not uncommon in public universities in Colombia, a recent study in the *UdeA* documented 110 murals and categorized them as depicting: social struggles, political struggles, memory, history, identity, revindication of women, and revindication of nature (Hecemos Memoria, 2018). What these murals point to is what everyone here knows about the *UdeA*: it is a very politicized place. There is tight security on entering the university campus, I have been refused admittance on various occasions, this is typical during *asambleas* (student assemblies), elections, or any other time when political tensions are heightened and anti-imperialist feeling can build up, my being "visibly foreign" (read: white, European, though often taken as US American) being enough to preclude being allowed in.

The *UdeA* is known for having been the site of violent clashes during the 1980s and 1990s, with university students and teachers falling victim to violence at the hands of armed groups, often right-wing civil defense and paramilitary groups, this because of the reputation of the *UdeA* for being sympathetic to leftist politics, it is even said that some university teachers would use their classes as platforms to recruit students to the FARC guerrilla group. It is also said that the government planted agents from the DAS (Department of Homeland Security) in the university to keep tabs on the left-wing activity. This is a lot of hearsay, but this is because ultimately there is a lot that is unknown, untold, or indeed untellable about this period in Colombia's history (Hacemos Memoria, 2017), but the circulating stories about the *UdeA* at this time serve to illustrate the politicized environment that still exists at the university to this day and informs the critical orientations to transnationalism in TESOL training.

Although the political fervor of the *UdeA* does sometimes still spill over into violence (it is not uncommon to hear of *encapuchados* appearing at events), the university's left-leaning agenda is packaged in its commitment to social engagement (and transformation) and critical thought, clearly evidenced in the TESOL teacher alumnus profile. It should be understood that in the Colombian context, it is still hard for left-of-center opinions, politics, and theories to be read outside of the context of insurgent guerilla forces. Expressing any sort of left-wing opinion then can be read as tantamount to expressing support for these groups and make one a target of civilian defense/paramilitary violence. According to a recent report from the Political-Electoral Democracy Observatory (Observatorio Político-Electoral de la Democracia) between October 2018 and June 2019, 265 political, social, and community leaders (environmental activists, LGBTI activists, women's rights campaigners, amongst others) have been the victims of violence, 75 being assassinated; that is an average of one leader assassinated every three days (Observatorio Político-Electoral de la Democracia, 2019). This trend is worryingly on the increase, 37 *líderes sociales* reported to have been assassinated in the first six months of 2020 (El Tiempo, 2020). Being an alumnus of the *UdeA*, especially from socially engaged programs (education, social work) then comes with specific expectations, although in discussions with colleagues who studied at the regional campus they are keen to tell me that they do not fully identify with the *UdeA* of the main campus, they do recognize the political weight of their *títiulo*. This difference is also evidenced when they meet other English teachers and their response to the standard "where did you graduate from?" question, "Universidad de Antioquia," instigates the follow-up question, "in Medellín, or in the regional campus?".

It is perhaps unsurprising that the regional campus of the *UdeA* is less overtly political than the Medellín campus given its location. If Antioquia is known as being a conservative, religious, and federalist region, the *Oriente Antioqueño* subregion crystalizes these characteristics. To people in Medellín the *Oriente Antioqueño* is quaint, rural, and *montañero* – lacking finesse and a hangover from a past time. Of course, this image is contested by people living in the *Oriente Antioqueño*, but people tend to be more socially conservative and the Catholic church still holds a great sway over the population. The *Oriente Antioqueño* can also be seen as the heartland of *Uribismo* – a political-ideological cult centered around ex-president Álvaro Uribe Vélez who lives in, and has close family ties in, the sub-region.

Álvaro Uribe came to prominence as the mayor of Medellín before becoming the governor of Antioquia and finally taking the office of president in 2002. Originally a member of the Colombian Liberal Party, Uribe broke away from the liberal party and won his presidential campaign as an independent candidate backed by private funders under the populist banner of *Primero Colombia* – Colombia First, and the campaign slogan: *mano firme, corazón grande* – firm hand, big heart. The first president to break with Colombia's Conservative/Liberal political hegemony, Uribe served two terms in office (having changed the Constitution in order to do so) before aligning himself to the *Partido de la U* – the Social Party of National Unity, and founding the currently governing *Céntro Democrático* party which holds the same *mano duro, corazón grande* motto. Uribe is a decisive figure (to put it lightly!), his presidency marred by controversies and his links to paramilitary and civil defense groups are still under investigation. Characteristic of Uribe's presidency was a rapprochement between Colombia and the United States under George W. Bush, in whom he found a political ally. This lead to the intensification of the "Plan Colombia" strategy, a far-reaching US aid, diplomacy, and military package designed to weaken the hold of the FARC and to secure the viability of the Colombian state via US expertise-backed bombing raids, military training, weaponry, and crop eradication program. It is also within the framework of this "special relationship" that the wheels were set in motion for the signing of a Free Trade Agreement (FTA) between the United States and Colombia.

The signing of this FTA heralded a new insistence on the need for Colombians to speak English and a boom in TESOL. If the country is to be doing business with the United States, Colombians need to interact in English (Valencia, 2013). Up until this point both French and English had a role within the Colombian education system, understood as being important European languages for forming citizens in culture and literature, however the FTA set in motion a shift in language education to focus solely on English and away from "cultural" perspectives toward more "instrumentalist" notions of language teaching and learning (Usma Wilches, 2009). The FTA also set in motion a series of policy and legislation moves toward the institutionalization of the teaching of English in schools (for a comprehensive overview of the intricacies of these policy moves, see Bonilla Carvajal & Tejada-Sánchez, 2016). Foundational in this respect is the *Plan Nacional de Bilingüismo* (PNB), its introduction of the Common European Framework of Reference (CEFR) and the publishing of the "*Guía 22*" guide that establishes a competence-based framework for the teaching of English in Colombia. The legislative moves associated with the national English language in education policy have been criticized by Colombian scholars working in TESOL teacher training at the *UdeA* who have critiqued the transnational dimension (importing of non-Colombian knowledge and expertise) of the policy, a critique that must be understood within the context of the emergence of the PNB as part, and product, of the US–Colombia rapprochement. In the following section, I will explore this critique and how it contributes to the critical pedagogic register of TESOL teaching and training.

## Public policy, not epistemology: transnationalism and the critical pedagogic register

I have come to understand that central to the critical pedagogic register of the *UdeA* is opposition to the transnational dimension of the national English language in education policy, centering on the role of the British Council, an organization that has played a part in TESOL in Colombia for a number of years. The British Council published a damming report in 1989 about the situation of English language teaching and learning in Colombia in which they "conjured the crisis" of the state of English language proficiency and teaching in the country; in many ways creating the "problem of English" they would later be invited to "solve." The British Council were involved in the design and implementation of the PNB, their involvement seen as a betrayal of Colombian academics and previous efforts made to improve standards of TESOL teaching and learning, namely the Colombia Framework for English (COFE) project.

The COFE project carried out between 1991 and 1997 was "the result of a complementary arrangement between the government of the United Kingdom of Great Britain and Northern Ireland and the Republic of Colombia concerning technical cooperation for the improvement in the teaching of English" (Rubiano et al., 2000, p. 38). This project is generally positively valued in the literature, and understood as a "collaborative approach" (González, 2010, p. 340) between a transnational entity, Thames Valley University (now the University of West London), brokered by the British Council, and major Colombian universities. This collaborative project sees the lines between Colombian and UK knowledge and expertise blurred, conceived of as a bi-directional transnationalism, and sits in stark contrast to the reaction to the PNB and the role of the British Council in English language in education policy in Colombia. In elaborating the PNB, the National Ministry of Education (MEN) adopted a program developed and implemented by the British Council, rather than Colombian universities based on the COFE experience. This has contributed to a deep and ongoing rift between the language school of the *UdeA* and the MEN. This tension is ongoing, one of the senior members of the language school recently joking at a public event that there is probably a dartboard with their picture on it in the offices of the MEN and a senior civil servant in the MEN confiding in me words to the effect of "these academics are over-the-top and don't realize that these programs are about public policy, not epistemology."

In a highly influential 2007 paper, "Professional development of EFL teachers in Colombia: Between colonial and local practices," Adriana González Moncada, the then Director of the School of Languages at the *UdeA*, articulated this critique of the MEN and in turn set in motion the rejection of transnationalism in Colombian TESOL training. In the paper, she draws heavily on critical applied linguistics and postcolonial studies to justify the rejection of the role of the British

Council and the importation of the TKT,[2] the CEFR, and the technification of teaching, leading her to conclude that, "[t]he current teacher development model is a representation of colonial, traditional, and central discourses in ELT that must be reshaped by the new, local, and peripheral knowledge constructed by Colombian ELT scholars and teachers" (2007, p. 326). This paper sets the distinction between the "us" of local Colombian scholars and the "them" of transnational actors and points to mobility of knowledge and expertise about TESOL as being one-way, a movement conceived of in terms of the "centre" and "periphery."

This paper, and the concepts it crystalizes, has had a big impact on the research into TESOL teaching and education coming from the *UdeA* and represents what I call an "oppositional stance" to transnationalism in TESOL teacher education. This oppositional stance gives emphasis to, justifies, and is itself justified by, the critical pedagogic orientation of the *UdeA* and currently forms a central part of a discourse register allowing for the bringing together of concepts such as Linguistic Imperialism (Phillipson, 1992), Circles of English (Kachru, 1982), Pedagogy of the Oppressed (Freire, 2007), Post-method teaching (Kumaravadivelu, 1994, 2003), symbolic violence and language testing (Shohamy, 1998, 2017), and critiques of native speakerism (Graddol, 1999). These concepts have been given authority though the presence of some of these key scholars (including Kumaravadivelu and Shohamy) at workshops and research events organized by one of the Language School's research groups and find their coherence through the rejection of knowledge produced in the "inner circle" (Kachru, 1982) and understanding its imposition as a violent practice imbued by colonial logics.

In line with this rejection of the transnational, "inner circle" knowledge and expertise about TESOL teacher training, the *UdeA* Language School ascribes a principle of radical "situated knowledge." All the research produced by the undergraduate students, a core component of their training courses, fits within an Action Research paradigm, and the university runs a successful continual professional development program for teachers whose name, *in situ*, speaks to the preference for praxeological, local (read: not transnational) epistemology. It is worth pointing out that the preference for Action Research within TESOL teacher training courses can be traced back to the aforementioned COFE project (Gónzalez Moncada, 2007). What is interesting in the present discussion is how this transnational link is erased in favor of an understanding of Action Research articulated in terms of Kumaravadivelu's rejection of the "teacher–researcher" dichotomy, in which "outer-circle" teachers are understood to be dependent on "inner-circle" knowledge producers, researchers. A turn to Action Research then is seen as a way of overcoming this dichotomy, a way of rejecting the authority of "inner circle," "transnational" theory and "reclaiming" "local(ized)" practice (Kumaravadivelu, 1994, 2003).

Recent research from the *UdeA* Language School still has this "critical" and praxeological current but has reoriented slightly, drawing on critical language policy studies, critical media literacy, critical interculturality, and the coloniality of knowledge, all of which can be characterized as following Gónzalez Moncada's 2007 invitation to resist the "transnational" in favor of the "local." In July 2019, the *UdeA*'s biannual conference on Foreign Language Teacher Education and Development was, in part, merged with the International ELF conference, the first time that the latter has been held outside of Europe. I understand this embracing of the "ELF paradigm" within the logics that English in Colombia needs to be about recognizing "Colombian English" as a legitimate variety and rejecting native speaker ideologies – in short, using an ELF paradigm once again to favor the local over the transnational. This logic became clear in the opening address by Adriana, whereby she took the opportunity to highlight the importance of "locally produced knowledge" and, with reference to the controversial Netflix series *Narcos*, reject imperialist ideas and discourses about what Colombia is like – the conclusion being that only those *in situ* can understand the reality and respond to it, just as with TESOL teacher education, transnational "expertise" is therefore devalued, questioned, and outright rejected.

Having briefly characterized the critical pedagogic register in TESOL training as it is produced by scholars working at the *UdeA* and seen how it coalesces around a rejection of transnational knowledge and expertise, I will now turn my attention to the way this register travels and becomes embedded, and hybridized, in another context, the *Universidad Católica de Oriente*, the other center of TESOL teacher training in the *Oriente Antioqueño* where I was working as a TESOL teacher educator. I will first set the scene of the university in the hope of illuminating some of the similarities and differences to the *UdeA* (Medellin and regional campuses) before exploring the institutional orientation to transnational knowledge and expertise with respect to TESOL teacher training.

## TESOL teacher training at the *Universidad Católica de Oriente*: traveling registers

Walking around the *Universidad Católica de Oriente* (*UCO*) you can't help but be struck, first and foremost, by the incline of the campus, the academic buildings built up a steep hill, but also the greenery, as you walk from one part of campus to the next through trees, seeing squirrels running around, feral cats and adopted dogs. Built on the site of an old country farmhouse, over the past couple of years the university has grown considerably and has recently been accredited by the national government (September 2019), firmly establishing it as a center of professionalization in the *Oriente Antioqueño* region. The *UCO* is a private, fee-paying university which, as its name suggests, has a Catholic foundation (the dean, or rector, is a ecclesiastical appointment, the university, its own parish, belonging to the Diocese of Sonson-Rionegro); if you fail to pass the admissions exam to study at the *UdeA* and you live in the *Oriente Antioqueño*, there is a high probability that you will decide to study at the *UCO*. Given its Catholic foundations, the *UCO* has a Catholic-humanist philosophy, meaning that alongside professional skilling, the institution pays close attention to the development of the *ser*, the "being," and has a stated vocation for the region.

The *UCO* has a good reputation in the region for language teaching. The Language Center, recently rebranded *Idiomas UCO*, has been running for over

25 years and offers generalist classes in English, Portuguese, French, Italian, German, and Spanish for foreigners (they have on occasion also offered courses in Colombian Sign Language, Japanese, Chinese-Mandarin, and Estonian Culture). The Language Centre as an academic and administrative unit was born out of the Faculty of Economic Sciences and the *Comercio Exterior*, International Business program. In 2011, the Language Centre, with input from the Faculty of Education Sciences, created a *licenciatura*, Initial Teacher Training program in foreign languages: English and French. This program was accepted by the Ministry of Education and over the past eight years has built up a reputation as being an important site of TESOL training in light of the ever-increasing demand for highly-trained English language teachers thanks to the ongoing impact of the national English language in education policies outlined above.

The establishment of the *licenciatura* program meant the expansion of the Language Centre, and it increased from having two full-time members of staff and one coordinator to having seven full-time members of teaching-research staff in addition to the coordinator, the rest of the teaching on the program covered either by staff from the Faculty of Education Sciences or adjunct professors. With a couple of exceptions all of the full-time positions and the vast majority of the adjunct positions on the *UCO* TESOL training program, have been filled by professionals who studied at the *UdeA*, the majority of those at the regional campus. There is a tangible link between the *UCO* and the *UdeA* not only in terms of teaching and research staff, but thanks to ongoing collaboration in terms of research, conferences, the ubiquity of adjunct (and even full-time) professors who have contracts to teach at both institutions, and both adjunct and full-time professors taking Master's degrees at the *UdeA* (the *UCO* not yet having any postgraduate programs in TESOL).

The alumnus profile for the TESOL training course at the *UCO* is, however, noticeably different from that of the *UdeA*. The idea of social engagement is still present (though here couched in terms of "development" as opposed to "transformation"), but what is clear is the explicit alignment to the National Ministry of Education guidelines and the reference beyond the local context.

> An alumnus of the *Universidad Católica de Oriente* with the *licenciatura en lenguas extranjeras* with emphasis in English *título* will have a solid humanist formation which reflects the social and ethical reality of the region, the country and the globalized world. An alumnus will have the level of English as a foreign language in line with the current Colombian context and the National Ministry of Education guidelines for alumni of foreign language programs. They will be trained to work as teachers in formal education both *básica* (1st–9th grade) and *média* (10th and 11th grade) in both public and private institutions; they will be a promotor and agent of social development in their surroundings.
>
> In addition, this professional will be able to work as a bilingual teacher, within the parameters outlined in law, for work-related training and will be competent in designing and delivering such programs and projects in public and private institutions.

> An alumnus of the *licenciatura en lenguas extanjeras* with emphasis in English will have the theoretical, conceptual, research and practical formation to allow them to study postgraduate programs, both nationally and internationally, related to the teaching-learning of foreign languages and education sciences, or related areas. In other words, they will be able to develop professionally in the country, or abroad.
>
> (PEP, 2019)

Within the TESOL teacher training program at the *UCO*, and what is clear from the alumnus profile, there is an ambivalent relationship to "critical" approaches to teaching English and especially to the relationship between the "local" and 'transnational' tendencies in TESOL teacher training. The *licenciatura* sits within the Faculty of Education Sciences, students therefore receive pedagogical theory taught in Spanish, directly from the Faculty. The Faculty of Education Sciences, in keeping with the *UCO*'s Catholic-humanist vision, promotes *pedagogía social* and *pedagogía del texto*, both of which can be understood as falling under a broad "critical pedagogy" umbrella. This pedagogical orientation sits well within the broader program of TESOL teacher training at the *UCO* and serves to ratify some of the "locally-oriented" praxeological discourse present in the *UdeA* script of resistance to transnational norms that becomes enacted at the *UCO* by professionals, alumni of the *UdeA*, working on the training course.

This is perhaps most evident in the *UCO*'s *semillero* (research incubator) *Semillero de Educación Rural* (*SER*). The work done in this incubator in relation to TESOL teaching and training is led by the co-director of research, Jacqueline Marín Gómez, whose collaborative Master's thesis, completed at the *UdeA*, looked at rural-Colombian ELT teachers and concluded that not only are rural teachers often unaware of the training that is offered by the State for the implementation of "bilingualism," but also that this training does little to reflect the realities of teachers "on the ground" (García Pérez & Marín Gómez, 2015) – a clear articulation of the critical pedagogic register relying on the vindication of the "local." In many ways, *SER* takes these findings as its starting point and works on the basis that transnational models of TESOL cannot be implemented in a rural Colombian (read: local) context, and thus students and professors attached to this research incubator take for granted the critical, oppositional stance previously outlined.

On the other hand, the history of the Language Center, its having been born out of the International Business program, has been very present with the TESOL teacher training program. The Language Center and the *licenciatura* program have been enmeshed not only with each other, but also with the Office for International Relations,[3] this, in part, has led to a clear influence of transnational TESOL practices, including the adopting of "inner circle" textbooks, training sessions offered by "inner circle" publishing houses, and the direct involvement of both Fulbright and British Council through the presence of English Language assistants.

I myself arrived to the *UCO* in 2010 as a British Council English Language Assistant, the second that the university had had, and since that time the TESOL teacher training program has continued to be part of the British Council English language assistant program, organized through the Colombian academic mobility agency ICETEX. Additionally, they have been accepted as part of the Fulbright English Language Assistant program, administered directly by the Ministry of Education, as well as having an English language assistant through the AISEC program, Chinese-Mandarin assistants, and French assistants. The practice of bringing English language assistants to the TESOL training program not only speaks to the symbolic acceptance of the "inner circle" transnationalism – language assistants symbolically embodying the native speakerism much criticized in critical spheres – but also a material acquiescence to UK and USA subordination, the language assistant being a conduit of state soft power (Codó & McDaid, 2019). Interestingly, the TESOL program offered at the *UdeA*, to the best of my knowledge, has never participated in English language assistantship programs.

Another clear example of where the *licenciatura* embraces transnational TESOL teacher training practices is in its use of international exams, indeed *Idiomas UCO* is an official British Council testing center and a Cambridge certification center. Students studying initial TESOL teacher training must sit the British Council proficiency Aptis test halfway through their studies to ensure their English level is sufficient (CEFR B2) for them to continue to study content-based classes in English and begin their teaching practice. Furthermore, in order to graduate, to ensure compliance with *decreto 1075* of 2015, which states that graduates from TESOL teacher training programs must achieve a CEFR C1 level, students must take the IELTS, managed by the British Council, IDP Education, and University of Cambridge English Language Assessment. All teachers employed at the *UCO* in either full-time or adjunct positions must also take the IELTS every two years. Again, these practices are much more in keeping with a transnational than a local orientation to TESOL teacher training and therefore can be understood as reflecting a departure from the oppositional stance of the *UdeA* and a seeming alignment with and embracing of a competency and standards based model of TESOL.

What should be clear from the above account is that TESOL training at the *UCO* can be characterized by its ambivalent relation to transnationalism, that is to say inner circle knowledge and expertise. Although space is made for a rejection of transnational discourse and the voicing of a kind of critical, pedagogic register in the research incubator, this sits alongside the main program of study and is an optional space in which students can partake if they desire. Within the TESOL training program itself, with the inclusion of language assistants and obligatory language tests being emblematic, there seems to be an orientation *toward* transnational practices and an embracing of the British Council and associated "inner circle" agencies. In what follows, I document my own attempt to bring a critical, pedagogic register into the main program and describe some of the struggles and contradictions this posed, reflecting especially on orientations to the transnational dimensions of TESOL training, and present some of the hybridized registers that emerged from negotiating "local" and "transnational" knowledge and expertise.

## Navigating the transnational and the local: a hybridized register?

Although I was not trained at the *UdeA*, having been active in academic/research circles at the university and having been professionally socialized with colleagues who *did* study at the *UdeA*, I learnt to identify with the critical pedagogic register in part, I think, as an attempt to justify my position and gain professional ratification in striving to manage my categorization as what Usma Wilches, expanding Popkewitz's original concept (2000), has labeled

> indigenous foreigners … [i]n the case of applied linguistics in Colombia, members of this group tend to speak English as their mother tongue, which makes them more attractive to local communities in search for interaction with "native" speakers of this dominant international language. This critique does not mean that members of this club may not serve important educational and social causes, or illuminate studies and investigations like this one, but implies that in the context of cultural globalization the knowledge and experience of some northern elites are privileged over local practitioners.
>
> (2015, pp. 49–50)

My adopting the critical pedagogic register meant that at a research event, an influential teacher at the *UdeA*, after an eloquent dismantling of native speaker ideology and a strident critique of native speaker teachers in Colombia, within the logics of them not having any pedagogical skills, publicly announced words to the effect of: "not you Peter, you're a different – you're a native speaker, but you're on our side." Embodying the critical pedagogic register then, at least on this occasion, allowed me to perform a certain kind of locally ratified, professional-academic identity. As Soto and Pérez-Milans (2018) show, being able to enact specific pedagogic registers affords specific benefits, in this case the benefit to me was being read as a serious, academically informed TESOL practitioner, which, in turn I am sure, also contributed to my being given considerable responsibility within the TESOL training program at the *UCO*.

In 2015, I was given the responsibility of redesigning the curriculum for the English Language component of the TESOL teacher training program, aligning the contents over five modules with the CEFR so as to prepare students to take the Aptis exam at the end of their English language courses, a requirement for students to demonstrate that they were ready to continue to the content-based subjects on the degree program. Given the need to incorporate the CEFR and the Aptis exam, both transnational, "inner circle" elements, into the modules, I could not fully inhabit the critical pedagogic register because, as I have outlined, this register requires a rejection of the transnational, this led me to lean into a kind of "pragmatism" in relation to the transnational and thus led to the emergence of what I understand as a "hybridized register."

The initial tension I faced was born out of the Communicative Language Teaching framework that had been in place at the *UCO*. It could be argued that in Colombia, Communicative Language Teaching (CLT) is one of the most pervasive features of a "technified transnational TESOL"; ubiquitous in Colombia, CLT is often taken as tantamount to what "good," "up-to-date" English language teaching looks like. On the other hand, in "critical" circles CTL is considered an anaphora for "inner circle" and "colonial" teaching. CLT is understood to inflate the value of the "linguistic model" over the value of pedagogical knowledge, thus sustaining native speaker ideologies. The value traditionally assigned to English teachers' explicit metalinguistic knowledge is minimized, what is valuable under a CLT model is rather having a "feel" of the language and its use. This is seen as accompanying a devaluing of "local" TESOL practices, the *in situ* pedagogical knowledge of teachers becoming replaced with non-context-specific, didactic techniques. Personally identifying with a critical pedagogic orientation, I was attuned to these critiques and reticent to espouse CLT, and yet had to align the modules to the CEFR and the Aptis, both of which have a "communicative focus."

I set about researching alternatives to CLT looking for different "localized" ways of conceptualizing communication in other "expanding circle" countries. Due in large part to the unequal distribution of access to academic literature, the *UCO*, as many other universities, is precluded from purchasing licenses to prestigious, "top-ranking" journals by the high fees put in place by the publishing companies, and as such I was restricted to searching for Open Access material. Whilst searching on Google Scholar, I stumbled across the notion of Communication Oriented Language Teaching (COLT)[4] first proposed by William Littlewood in 2004 and revisited by the same author in 2013. I had not come across COLT, and to the best of my knowledge its impact in TESOL has been limited. COLT is essentially a hybrid approach to language (English) teaching which is clear about the central goal of teaching as achieving "communicative competence," but is pragmatic about the process by which this is achieved, "allowing" for non-communicative activities during the process. This idea is summed up in Littlewood's "Communicative Continuum" (see Table 6.1).

I saw this continuum as an important heuristic in allowing for a recognition of "local expertise," whilst buying into the central logics of communication-as-goal. Having elaborated this approach and how it could be implemented at the *UCO*, I was in charge of running Continual Professional Development sessions for the other teacher educators to ensure we had a coherent basis for our English training program. Looking back on the materials (PowerPoints and worksheets) I produced for this course of training sessions, I can clearly see that I set out to distance the program from CLT. On a slide titled "Why *not* Communicative Language Teaching?" (emphasis in original) I presented the idea that CLT is "too general, means everything and yet, nothing – vague strategies" (PPT) and that in Colombia "'authentic communication' [is] all but impossible in the EFL classroom" (PPT). Both of these statements voice a skepticism of the "inner circle" CLT norm and implicitly question the authority of the transnational knowledge and expertise in TESOL, both moves coherent with a critical pedagogic register. On the next slide, "Why COLT?", I key the pragmatism of the hybrid script stating COLT is "explicit about the communicative goal of ELT, but space made

*Table 6.1* Reproduced from Littlewood (2013)

| Analytic Strategies | | ← → | Experiential Strategies | |
|---|---|---|---|---|
| Non-Communicative Learning | Pre-Communicative Language Practice | Communicative Language Practice | Structured Communication | Authentic Communication |
| Focusing on the structures of language, how they are formed and what they mean | Practising language with some attention to meaning but not communicating new messages to others | Practicing pre-taught language but in a context where it communicates new information | Using language to communicate in situations which elicit pre-learnt language but with some degree of unpredictability | Using language to communicate in situations where the meanings are unpredictable |
| Example: Substitution exercises, inductive 'discovery' and awareness-raising activities | Example: Describing visuals or situational language practice – 'questions and answers' | Example: Information gap activities or 'personalized questions' | Example: Structures role-play and simple problem-solving | Example: Creative role-pay, more complex problem-solving and discussion |
| Focus on form and meanings | | ← → | Focus on meanings and messages | |

for pre-communicative tasks" and that "space [is] made for focus on form (how this is done based not reliant on the approach but based on our principles)" (PPT). In this model then, as I presented it, there is an explicit foregrounding of the "local" knowledge and expertise over the transnational "inner circle" expertise. A move to reclaim the importance of teachers' metalinguistic knowledge, by emphasizing the need to "focus on form," and yet the overall aim of the COLT approach is coherent with the communicative imperative as conditioned by the CEFR and the Aptis, there is therefore not an outright "rejection" of the transnationally informed parameters of action, but rather a negotiation of the critical, pedagogic register *within* these parameters; although on a surface level the adopting of COLT *seems* to be a critical pedagogic move, and to some extent it could be argued that it *is*, it ultimately relies on a tacit acceptance of the transnational. This tacit acceptance, and thus perpetuation, of the transnational is recurrent within the "hybridized" register I championed at the *UCO*. I will now turn my attention to the aforementioned concept of "pedagogical principles" to further explore this tension.

The concept of pedagogical principles, akin to principled-based language teaching, draw on a post-method orientation to English language teaching (Kumaravadivelu, 1994, 2003) which rejects the very concept of having a "method" for teaching as a colonial construct propagated by the "center" in order to exert domination over the "periphery." Kumaravadivelu's "post-method condition" calls for teachers to become reflexive, research-oriented practitioners who are able to reflect and develop their own "methods" *in situ*. It is also Kumaravadivelu's "post-method condition" that informed González Moncada's (2007) original proposal to reimagine TESOL training in Colombia and Kumaravadivelu who left the attendees in no doubt after a workshop I attended with him at the *UdeA* in which he presented his paper "The decolonial option in English teaching: Can the subaltern act?", that "indigenous foreigners" could not "manage" their roles, and that the decolonial, critical pedagogic register could not be inhabited by somebody from the "global north" – I was the only "global northerner" in attendance – a rejection of "inner circle" knowledge and expertise is at the very core of the post-method project.

Kumaravadivelu's rejection of "method" as an organizing principle in the TESOL classroom gives support to widespread critiques within TESOL in Colombia that TESOL has become technicized, the "art" or "craft" of teaching having been lost and replaced by the "how to" of method-oriented, technicized approaches. At the *UCO* this is often expressed through the idea that TESOL in Colombia has "lost" its pedagogical dimension and is rendered didactic (this distinction relies on the calquing of the Spanish and other Romance language cognates *pedagogía* and *didáctica* respectively. Seen as two halves of the whole of teaching, we can simplify, for illustration, by saying that *pedagogía* focuses on the reflective, existential *why* we teach *what* to *whom*, whereas *didáctica* focuses on the *how* we teach).

I also contributed to naturalizing the idea that TESOL in Colombia had "lost" its pedagogic component, elaborating a proposal for "reclaiming" "Pedagogy in the times of didactics" (Browning, 2017) and socializing this widely at research events both at the *UCO* and in other TESOL teacher training centers (including the *UdeA*). In this proposal, I mobilized a critical pedagogic register and promoted various strategies to encourage students' "critical awakening" (Freire, 2007) about the *pedagogic* dimensions of TESOL. It is this discussion that makes it slightly uncomfortable to talk of TESOL "training" as this is clearly aligned to a "didactic," "how to" notion of teaching as opposed to TESOL "formation" which would emphasize a more "pedagogic" dimension. It is within this background that the concept of "pedagogical principles" gains value. To talk about "pedagogical principles" is to invoke the didactics/pedagogy discussion and to take a "critical," pedagogically aligned stance. However, within the COLT model proposed, these pedagogical principles are used as a starting-point and are articulated with traditional, inner-circle transnational TESOL teaching methods; therefore, rather than showing an outright rejection of the "didactics" of TESOL they betray an ambivalent relationship, and really only seek to "rebalance the scales" rather than representing an outright rejection of "method" and the "technicization" of TESOL. I will explain briefly an example to show how this logic works in practice.

The propagator where I sowed the seeds of the "pedagogical principles" logics at the *UCO* can be seen in the core module of "General Didactics" on the TESOL training course which I taught and developed over three years. The module was explicitly designed to give students an overview of the key trends and developments in TESOL, a kind of "potted history" of TESOL methods over the past century (Grammar Translation, The Natural Approach, The Silent Way, Suggestopedia, Communicative Language Learning, Task-Based Teaching, CLT, etc.). The ongoing coursework assessment for this module was the completion of a portfolio in which students had to reflect on each of the methods and approaches studied and consider its applicability to their teaching realities – drawing on the critical pedagogic register, students were encouraged to see these methods and approaches as products of specific "inner circle" transnational academic traditions and were invited to be skeptical of their applicability in Colombia, an invitation not extended to "local" TESOL knowledge which was assumed to be readily applicable. The ambivalence toward this transnationalism, however, comes with the introduction of the pedagogical principles. Once again drawing on Littlewood's work on COLT and "Developing a context-sensitive pedagogy for Communication-Oriented Language Teaching" (2013), the use of pedagogical principles here formed the basis of students' final assessment for the module.

Students were encouraged to reflect on their own pedagogical principles, what they believed to be key ontological features of TESOL. Having settled upon their own principles (of course inspired by authors such as Kumaravadivelu, Brown, Littlewood, etc.), students then had to think about how they could materialize these principles, how they could bring them into being in the classroom (see Table 6.2). In order to do this, and to demonstrate an appropriate command of the TESOL didactics module contents, students were asked to associate each of their principles with techniques and strategies from the methods and approaches seen during the module. The result was the production of what I have been calling a hybridized register: although starting from a "critical" premise, questioning the validity of transnational expertise in TESOL in Colombia, it ultimately, albeit on localized terms, relies on the acceptance of transnational knowledge and expertise to become "materialized". This "hybridization" then, although able to provide an aesthetics of criticality, does very little to address the underlying transnational logics. This kind of hybridized register is not only present in the TESOL teaching and learning at the *UCO*, but also in the knowledge produced within the program, in the TESOL research component.

Research training is seen as an important part of all undergraduate professionalization in Colombia, particularly within teacher training programs. Research is given equal importance alongside teaching and outreach as one of the "substantive

*Table 6.2* An example of pedagogical principles and articulation from *Idiomas UCO* (where the concept was also implemented)

| *Principle* | *Converses with* | *Specific strategies* |
|---|---|---|
| 1. Language learning is an emotional, socio-affective experience | Community Language Learning<br>(De) Suggestopedia | • Weekly check-in and teacher-led diary<br>• Traffic lights (for understanding and feelings)<br>• Spanish OK for discussion about feelings/emotions<br>• Use of appropriate music in class to help students relax<br>• Seating (horseshoe with teacher also seated – get the desk out of the way)<br>• Non-threatening environment: back monitoring/crouching |

functions" of training programs in order for them to be accredited by the National Ministry of Education, within TESOL training at the *UCO* this takes the shape of four modules in research methods as well as the successful submission of an original research paper. By the end of the program, students are expected to have acquired "*el espíritu investigativo*" – the research spirit (Decreto 1075, 2015, 3.4).

The research component of the TESOL teacher training program at the *UCO* is influenced by the research training received by the core members of staff, mainly from the *UdeA*; they have acquired a research spirit which is praxeological and action-oriented. When it comes to students carrying out their own research, this spirit comes into contact with transnational concerns and research agendas, the tension seeming to arise along the *didáctica-pedagogía* fault line. The vast majority of students want to carry out methodological research, perhaps because they have been socialized to be skeptical of the application of "inner circle" transnational expertise and methods in their contexts, perhaps because the research component sits alongside the practicum component of the TESOL training program, or perhaps because it is in keeping with more general trends in TESOL research, students tend to carry out research into the implementation of a methodological strategy in their local context. A typical research project could be paradigmatically rendered: *Using [transnational TESOL strategy] to foster [skill] in [local context]: a case study*. The didactic bent of these studies is "softened" by the invocation of the specificity of the contexts in which they are being implemented, here we *do* see resonances of the skepticism of the appropriacy of transnational TESOL methods in specific contexts that is central to a critical register. What is taken for granted, however, is the basic tenet of teaching skills, be they: communication, speaking, listening, reading, writing, or increasingly (in line with transnational trends) metacognitive strategies and intercultural awareness, once again there is a tacit acceptance of the basic, transnational, rules of the game.

In the last three or four semesters, since I left my position as a full-time teacher at the *UCO*, I have noticed a gradual shift away from the *Using [transnational TESOL strategy] to foster [skill] in [local context]: a case study* paradigm toward a *Using [transnational TESOL strategy] to foster [skill] in [local context]: a systematization of experience* framework. The "systematization of experiences" approach to research has a strong grounding in Latin American critical social sciences (see for example Jara Holliday, 2013) and has gained a lot of acceptance amongst critical scholars in a number of disciplines. The systematization of experiences is an approach to education research that is praxeological and rooted in the production of knowledge from lived experiences *after* the event with an attention paid to enabling future action and to promoting social justice (see a special issue of *Decisio* edited by Ghiso, 2011 for an insightful overview of systematization). This sort of approach to research, given that it requires the object of research to be a lived experience that was not initially conceived of as a "research" experience, the very point to systematize the traces of knowledge(s) produced during a given experience, is perhaps not fully coherent with the kind of intervention/implementation carried out by many students at the *UCO*, "systematization" in this context, rather, seems to take on a methodological weight that could be recast as "thick description." As was the case with "pedagogical principles," I would argue that in this context, the "systematization of experiences" label serves less as a statement of ontology, but rather as a way of evoking a critical pedagogic register with its shades of local expertise, praxis, social justice, and politics. However, although this register is evoked, ultimately transnational TESOL strategies are still being implemented and indeed their implementation somehow considered acceptable when seen within the critical pedagogic framing.

## Final thoughts

In this chapter, I set out to show how rejection of the transnational dimension of TESOL training, understood locally as the one-sided involvement of non-Colombian organizations, their knowledge and expertise, forms the basis of a critical pedagogic register of TESOL training in the *Oriente Antioqueño*, Colombia. I have explored how this register was forged at the *UdeA* in Medellín and propagated via the regional campus to the *Oriente Antioqueño* region before traveling to the *UCO*. I have outlined three instances in which this outright rejection of the transnational in TESOL training is not possible at the *UCO* due to institutional limitations and in which a "pragmatic," "hybrid" register is forged. What I hope has become clear is that given the decolonial, anti-imperial genesis of the critical pedagogic register and its associated rejection of transnational influence in TESOL training, the fact that the "hybrid" register falls short of rejecting the transnational means that the "hybrid" register can only provide a kind of aesthetics of criticality which ultimately is used as a justification to embrace transnational organizations and expertise, albeit "on local terms."

In closing this chapter it is worth briefly returning to the question of the commodification of pedagogical registers (Soto & Pérez-Milans, 2018) and noting that just as inhabiting the critical pedagogic register was beneficial for me to access the academic labor market, inhabiting the "hybrid" register seems to bring benefits for accessing the local English teaching labor market. Monica, who neither studied at the *UdeA* nor the *UCO*, a friend and experienced English teacher at a public school, recently told me words to the effect of:

> Alumni from the *UdeA* are theoretically very strong, they're very critical, but put them in front of a class and they struggle at first ... an alumnus from the *UCO*, however, is great in the classroom, they're very didactic ... they may not be as theoretically strong, but they're still critical enough.

What Monica's words point to is that whilst being "critical" is valued (Monica is representative of teachers especially in the public sector who see their work as socially engaged, political actors, akin to social workers) the labor market ultimately seems to value those who can deploy just "enough" criticality, but who are also able to bring a didactic approach to TESOL, i.e., those who can navigate a hybridized register may have a better chance at accessing the local labor market than those who fully inhabit a critical pedagogic register. This difference is perhaps unsurprising given the political-ideological orientations of the two institutions in which these registers are forged and, indeed not being "valued" by market logics (especially under current conditions in which demand for TESOL teachers far outweighs the supply, and so material implications of not meeting market logics are hypothetical – i.e., you will still get a job may well be the best endorsement of the critical pedagogic register by its own standards. As the national English language in education policy *Colombia Bilingüe* (2004–19) comes to an end, and market demand for English language teachers fluctuates, it remains to be seen what the future influence of transnational organizations, their knowledge and expertise will be in TESOL training in Colombia and how the key institutions for TESOL training in the *Oriente Antioqueño* will align to them.

## Acknowledgments

The thoughts in this chapter are a snapshot of ongoing discussions with colleagues both in Colombia and the UK whose input has been invaluable over a number of years. In particular, I'd like to thank Carlos Andrés García Builes and Carlos Mario Gómez Benavides, both of whom were key in igniting for me the initial sparks of the present discussion as well as the numerous colleagues at UCO, UdeA, and UCL who have kindled the ideas presented here. Additionally, I would like to thank Alfonso del Percio for his insightful comments and guidance. Some of the data presented in the chapter come from fieldwork carried out during an ESRC Studentship. Any shortcomings are, of course, my own.

## Notes

1 Translation my own.
2 The TKT (Teaching Knowledge Test) is a modular, basic-teaching qualification offered by Cambridge English and promoted by the British Council.
3 At the time of writing this chapter, this situation is changing, with the arrival of a new rector, the *licenciatura* has had a change of coordination, and office space, symbolically marking that it now *only* depends on the Faculty of Education Sciences. The Language Centre and Office for International Relations have stayed interconnected but completely independent from the TESOL teacher training program. The impact this will have on the orientation to local and international knowledge and its circulation is, of course, yet to be seen.
4 This is not to be confused with the Communicative Orientation of Language Teaching (COLT) – an approach to classroom observation coined by Fröhlich, Spada, and Allen (1985), Communication Oriented Language Teaching refers to a methodological approach to language teaching-learning.

## References

Bonilla Carvajal, C. A., & Tejada-Sánchez, I. (2016). Unanswered questions in Colombia's foreign language education policy. *Profile: Issues in Teachers' Professional Development*, 18, 185–201.

Browning, P. C. (2017). Pedagogy in the time of didactics: An experience of teaching sociolinguistics on a *licenciatura en lenguas extranjeras* programme. In Universidad de la Amazonia (Ed.), *English in a globalized world*. Florencia: Universidad de la Amazonia.

Codó, E., & McDaid, J. (2019). English language assistants in the 21st century. *Language, Culture and Society*, 1(2), 219–243.

Cusicanqui, S. R. (2019). Ch'ixinakax utxiwa. *Language, Culture and Society*, 1(1), 106–119.

Decreto 1075 (2015). *Por medio del cual se expide el Decreto Único Reglamentario del Sector Educación*. 26 May. Ministerio de Educación Nacional.

El Tiempo (2020, July 9). En 2020 han sido asesinados 37 líderes sociales: Gobierno. Retrieved from https://www.eltiempo.com/politica/gobierno/cuantos-lideres-sociales-han-sido-asesinados-en-colombia-516050 (accessed 15 Sept 2020).

Freire, P. (2007). *Pedagogy of the oppressed*. New York: Continuum.

Fröhlich, M., Spada, N., & Allen, P. (1985). Differences in the communicative orientation of L2 classrooms. *TESOL Quarterly*, 19(1), 27–57.

García Pérez, X., & Marín Gómez, J. (2015). Política Lingüística en Contextos Rurales: Vivencias de Maestros de Inglés. Unpublished MA thesis, Universidad de Antioquia.

Ghiso, A. M. (Ed.). (2011). *Sistematización [Special Issue] Decisio: Saberes para la acción en educacción de adultos*, 28.

González, A. (2010). English and English teaching in Colombia: Tensions and possibilities in the expanding circle. In A. Kirkpatrick (Ed.), *The Routledge handbook of world Englishes* (pp. 332–351). London: Routledge.

González Moncada, A. (2007). Professional development of EFL teachers in Colombia: Between colonial and local practices. *Íkala, revista de lenguaje y cultura*, 12(1), 309–332.

Graddol, D. (1999). The decline of the native speaker. *AILA Review*, 13, 57–68.

Hacemos Memoria. (2017, August 23). Las violencias de la Universidad de Antioquia [video file]. Retrieved from: www.youtube.com/watch?v=aHHj5dDcEzw.

Hacemos Memoria. (2018, September 4). Murales y grafitisL testigos de memoria en la Universidad de Antioquia [video file]. Retrieved from: www.youtube.com/watch?time_continue=14&v=ENv2n8lAi6M.

Jara Holliday, Oscar (2013). *La Sistematización de Experiencias, Práctica y Teoría para otros mundos posibles*. EPPAL, Biblioteca de Educación Popular: Montevideo.

Kachru, B. B. (Ed.). (1982). *The other tongue: English across cultures*. Urbana: University of Illinois Press.

Kumaravadivelu, B. (1994). The postmethod condition: (E)merging strategies for second/foreign language teaching. *TESOL Quarterly*, 28, 27–48.

Kumaravadivelu, B. (2003). *Beyond methods: Macrostrategies for language teaching*. New Haven, CT: Yale University Press.

Littlewood, W. T. (2004). The task-based approach: Some questions and suggestions. *ELT Journal*, 58(4), 319–326.

Littlewood, W. (2013). Developing a context-sensitive pedagogy for communication-oriented language teaching. *English Language Teaching*, 68(3), 3–25.

Observatorio Político-Electoral de la Democracia. (2019). Informe sobre violencia poliítica desde el inicio del calendario electoral (27 de octubre de 2018 a 27 de junio de 2019). Retrieved from Misión de Observación Electoral: https://moe.org.co/wp-content/uploads/2019/07/20190627_Informe_ViolPol.pdf.

OECD. (2016). *Education in Colombia: Reviews of national policies for education*. Paris: OECD Publishing.

Phillipson, R. (1992). *Linguistic imperialism*. Oxford: Oxford University Press.

Pillow, W. S. (2003). Confession, catharsis, or cure? Rethinking the uses of reflexivity as methodological power in qualitative research. *International Journal of Qualitative Studies in Education*, 16(2), 175–196.

Plan Educativo Programa (PEP). (2019). *Licenciatura en Lenguas Extranjeras con énfasis en inglés.*

Popkewitz, T. (2000). Globalization/regionalization, knowledge, and the educational practices: Some notes on comparative strategies for educational research. In T. Popkewitz (Ed.), *Educational knowledge: Changing relationships between the state, civil society and the educational community* (pp. 3–27). Albany, NY: State University of New York Press.

Rubiano, C. I., Frodden, C., & Cardona, G. (2000). The impact of the Colombian Framework for English (COFE) project: An insiders' perspective. *Íkala, Revista De Lenguaje Y Cultura*, 5, 37–56.

Shohamy, E. (1998). Critical language testing and beyond. *Studies in Educational Evaluation*, 24, 331–345.

Shohamy, E. (2017). Critical language testing. In E. Shohamy, I. Or, & S. May (Eds.), *Language testing and assessment: Encyclopedia of language and education* (3rd ed.).

Soto, C., & Pérez-Milans, M. (2018). Language, neoliberalism, and the commodification of pedagogy. *Language and Intercultural Communication*, 18(5), 490–506.

*Universidad de Antioquia* (*UdeA*). (2018). *Licenciatura en Lenguas Extranjeras.* Retrieved from: www.udea.edu.co/wps/portal/udea/web/inicio/institucional/unidades-academicas/escuelas/idiomas/programas-academicos/programas-pregrado/!ut/p/z1/ldJBb4IwFAfwz-KBK30ohbJbg2WT4VBRZL0suLDKgtQgk6-_Jp6crMq7tfn9–5L3ijjKEK_zcynytpR1XqnzO3c-iOePLWpD9LwKfaCOT5mbpDh1MdpqgJUuHcQH5eOXgChgU2_ixVbCrIF5eLUw0CVbvK1jfzENx4_l4Z-iMLD_LeD657eI61qEiasHUwZacNmBDgTzG9CzhWtAgARqzOuI2Zs5QIz_gp493JtEiLio5O7y6Wi9mxCBeFN8FU3RmD-Nut637fH0ZIABXdeZQkpRFeanPBjQF9nLU4uya4mOh42qDMpZOfvG1Tmio9EvAxyLJA!/?1dmy&urile=wcm%3apath%3a%2FPortalUdeA%2FasPortalUdeA%2FasHomeUdeA%2FasInstitucional%2Funidades-academicas%2FasEscuelas%2FIdiomas%2FProgramas%2Bacad%2521c3%2521a9micos%2FProgramas%2Bde%2Bpregado.

Usma Wilches, J. A. (2009). Education and language policy in Colombia: Exploring processes of inclusion, exclusion and stratification in times of global reform. *Profile: Issues in Teachers' Professional Development*, 123–141.

Usma Wilches, J. (2015). *From transnational language policy transfer to local appropriation.* Blue Mounds, WI: Deep University Press.

Valencia, M. (2013). Language policy and the manufacturing of consent for foreign intervention in Colombia. *Profile: Issues in Teachers' Professional Development*, 1–17.

Windle, J., & O'Brien, S. (2019). Language, education and transnationalism: An introduction. *Trabalhos em Linguística Aplicada*, 58(1), 1–9.

# 7 Critical autoethnography in TESOL teacher education

## A translingual and Cultural Historical Activity Theory perspective for transnational spaces

*Cristina Sánchez-Martín*

### Introduction: a transnational journey of identity reconstruction and agency

In the narrative for the first-semester evaluation report for my department's tenure committee, I wrote the following introduction:

> As a new tenure-track faculty member, I began my first semester in the English Department with a robust research agenda. Before coming to IUP, I conducted a research study about how linguistically and culturally diverse teachers navigate spaces deemed "monolingual" and the sorts of situations that emerge as they find avenues to perform their dynamic identities to promote critical pedagogies. As a newcomer at IUP during an extremely polarized political climate, I found myself reflecting on the spaces I was entering and how a symbiotic relationship between my identities and the spatio-temporal elements I was located in could function best to enable my students' learning and the enhancement of diversity as a moral imperative for social justice.

It had just been one semester since I had graduated and defended my dissertation. During my first six months, I had been learning to understand and navigate a new context to which I was bringing antecedent knowledge, including embodied experiences and affective responses as well as theoretical, methodological, and pedagogical notions learned throughout my education working across geographies (Spain, UK, US), disciplines (applied linguistics, TESOL, rhetorics and composition, translation), and named-languages (mostly Spanishes and Englishes, but considering linguistic knowledge of Italian, German, French, and Catalan). During the first few weeks at my institution, I found myself reflecting on how I had dealt with new environments in the past and imagining what the future would bring as I would have to teach a number of new courses during my first couple of years. How had I successfully managed to respond to new situations previously? What types of learning and unlearning did I go through? How much emotional labor did I put forth as I was wrestling to understand my own positionalities and identities in relation to new environments? What transformations did I go through? And, most importantly, how can those experiences inform my pedagogies and mentoring at my new institution?

The introduction in the "Narrative of Teaching/Professional Responsibilities, Scholarly Growth, & Service" points at some of the analytical concepts I was paying attention to as I learned to think how my body and identities were responding to and constructing the practices I was part of the "Composition and Applied Linguistics" (CAL) graduate program. These included TESOL and applied linguistics courses, participating in faculty meetings, assessment practices, and so on and the writing courses I had been assigned to teach during my first semester: two sections of first-year composition for so-called "monolingual" students and one section of multilingual writing.

This study provides an account of how I developed my teacher identity dynamically, across time-space, and by increasingly recognizing my agency as a linguistically diverse teacher of writing in order to enact pedagogies for social justice. Ultimately, the purpose of this study is to offer detailed insights into critical autoethnography for teacher education programs by considering epistemological congruity amongst theories of learning, writing, language, and identity for transnational spaces. This study demonstrates how critical autoethnography from a CHAT (Cultural Historical Activity Theory) and translingual perspective can be systematically utilized to identity salient tools and concepts that impact teachers' transnational pedagogical and identity journeys.

## An autoethnography methodology for teacher-identity

Autoethnography functions as a research and teaching tool that helps individuals trace their identities and their trajectories across communities and spaces and to bring back to life experiences, impressions, and embodied knowledge that might have gone unnoticed but tacitly shaped situations. The methodological principles of autoethnography revolve around the point of view of the "self" as opposed to positivist approaches to knowledge-making based on the premise of detachment of the self from the study (Canagarajah, 2012).

As demonstrated by Canagarajah (2012) and Yazan (2019), autoethnographic writing has the potential to strongly assist novice teachers in developing their identities as they enter and inhabit different institutional and educational contexts with varying student demographics. This approach aligns with the view of teaching as identity work in line with Motha, Jain, and Tecle (2012), Alvarez et al. (2017), and Zhang (2018).

In this sense, autoethnographic approaches involve the use of narratives as data and reporting mechanisms as claimed by Park (2017) and Pavlenko (2007), a somewhat unorthodox practice in applied linguistics, that nonetheless renders researcher reflexivity (Starfield, 2013). Autoethnographic work also brings attention to the lived experiences of individuals as they enter and participate in teaching-learning environments (Sánchez-Martín & Seloni, 2019). In other words, autoethnography contributes to making visible the types of sociocultural and ecological factors that shape and co-construct language, writing, and teaching-learning practices as perceived and sensed by the subject herself. In this sense, autoethnography allows the teacher-researcher to make sense of embodied, affective, and cognitive knowledge. As Canagarajah points out, "autoethnography is a valuable form of knowledge construction in our field, as TESOL professionals in diverse communities can use this genre to represent their professional experiences and knowledge in a relatively less threatening academic manner" (2012, p. 262). Therefore, novice teacher-scholars can take advantage of autoethnographic tools to become more cognizant of how they transition into new academic and pedagogical spaces that in an era of transnationalism are constantly being redefined by those who inhabit them and their complex intersectional identities (Sánchez-Martín & Seloni, 2019).

In addition, autoethnography paired with Cultural Historical Activity Theory (CHAT) and translingualism functions as an analytical framework to identify and map put the sociocultural and ecological factors influencing and being constructed by teaching, writing, and languaging in a multilayered and symbiotic relationship. CHAT postulates that composing, and any other human endeavor, is a human activity historically constructed and mediated by other humans through division of labor, other agents such as institutions, tools, technologies, objects, semiotic resources (including named-languages), and rules among which the subject finds herself situated and working to accomplish a specific goal (Engeström, 2001) in relation to sociocultural and ecological environments (Prior et al., 2007). Attention to these aspects has also been called for through a translingual lens in order to understand language (Canagarajah, 2012; Min-Zhan & Horner, 2016). In addition, I draw on Busch's definition of linguistic repertoires as comprising the following dimensions: observable linguistic repertoires; linguistic ideologies; and Spracherleben (the lived experiences of affective and embodied language practices) (2015). Therefore, to look at the intersections between writing and language, I combine these theoretical frameworks in order to maintain epistemological consistency.

This autoethnographic analysis investigates how I transitioned and constructed my identity as a linguistically diverse teacher of writing for a majority of students who identified as white and monolingual. In particular, I will refer to two articles that I wrote around issues of language for the undergraduate journal used as a textbook in the writing program where I taught. Before proceeding into the analysis, the following section presents an unconventional literature review of the theories that inform my understanding of the concepts mentioned above. In this review of the literature, I provide a dialogic and personal account of my own interactions with these concepts throughout my transnational trajectory as a teacher-scholar.

## Review of literature

### *Dynamic identities*

Investigating my own teacher identity became a self-empowering practice as I continued to engage and interact with different student demographics, my peer writing instructors, and the different academic spaces I participated in. However, at the very beginning of my journey as a graduate teacher of writing, I wasn't fully aware of how specific theoretical approaches to identity in the fields of applied linguistics and TESOL didn't allow me to complicate my own identity. Like many other accounts of professionals demonstrate (Kamhi-Stein & Vandrick, 2013) I was tacitly assigned a "non-native" English teacher identity, especially in an English-studies program and writing classes where the majority of the students were white and monolingual. I had a sense that my identities weren't perceived in the same way depending on whether I was in the language department or in the English department, but could not explicitly address that fact. Once I read literature around the false binary between native and non-native speakers (Brutt-Griffler & Samimy, 2001) in a course on writing pedagogies, I started to reflect on my identity and the "master narratives" (Park, 2017) that had shaped my own self-perceptions. In the reading response for that course on the week of September 20, 2013, I wrote the following:

> One of the conclusions we have reached out after discussing this week readings is that the dichotomy between native and non-native is very blurry and a social construct ... I have to be critical of myself, too. I often have the excuse of not being confident because I am not a native speaker. Therefore, I feel under pressure and thus, my level of confidence decreases in particular environments. I think people have higher expectations about my linguistic performances than they actually do. So I, myself, also set the barrier of being a non-native speaker of English and thus, being somehow inferior to native speakers because *I have been exposed to the native and non-native dichotomy as the only way of conceptualizing writers/speakers until now.*

I became "critical" in my own words in part because I was encouraged to engage with the Brutt-Griffler and Samimy piece "Transcending the nativeness paradigm" (2001) at that moment. Later on, my program continued to expose me and encourage conversations around the intersections between writing and language in global-local contexts and to engage with pieces like "The myth of linguistic homogeneity" by Paul K. Matsuda (2006), which continued to provide avenues to complicate static and categorical notions of identity. Other moments of realization took place as I took up and responded to poststructuralist scholarship in applied linguistics that postulates that language identities are fluid, socially constructed, and contextual in line with the work of Rudolph et al. (2015) and Aneja (2016). Finally, feminist approaches to identity proved to be insightful in guiding me to understand the intersectional nature of my identities across geographical and sociocultural contexts in a circular continuum of privilege and marginalization (Park, 2017) as well as the gendered expectations of my work as a teacher-scholar (Sánchez-Martín & Seloni, 2019).

Five years after my first encounter with the false binary between native and non-native speakers and throughout conscious, systematic, and emotional work around my teacher-scholar identity, I am better equipped to respond to situations that continue to inadvertently but damagingly reinforce simplistic, categorical, and uncritical identity perceptions. For example, over six months ago, at the first meetings with faculty in the humanities in my new institution I was introduced as a new tenure-track professor whose work simply investigated "non-native" issues. Therefore, I was strategically ascribed the role of working with and mentoring "non-native" graduate students, or that was my impression after numerous interactions with other faculty. My goal in pointing this out is not to shame anyone or to complain about the nature of my work, which in fact I am honored to do, but to raise the question of how dichotomies permeate and define the division of labor (Matsuda, 1999) of faculty in specific disciplines, professional identities that at the same time are assigned based on simplistic linguistic and racial traits. However, as previously mentioned, this time I saw myself as much more prepared to identify the problems regarding those statements and how institutional dynamics are going to influence the types of work that I do in a specific environment. Most importantly, an understanding of how others perceive my identities gives me agency in determining my future trajectory as a teacher-scholar.

### *Linguistic diversity in transnational spaces*

As Canagarajah (2013a) and Donahue (2018) remind us, a number of concepts and frameworks have emerged in the past two decades to investigate the meaning of language and what language looks like in and through different geographical areas. Among these concepts we find "translanguaging," "code-meshing" (Canagarajah, 2013a), or more overarching frameworks such as "translingualism," "plurilinguisme," "metrolingualism," "cosmopolitanism," and "heteroglossia" (Donahue, 2018). What these analytical and theoretical tools indicate is a move toward understanding the complexities involved in language practice in transnational spaces (Donahue, 2018, pp. 25–31) and, therefore, a move against structuralist and territorialized conceptualization of language and speakers' labels.

While all these labels offered specific nuances to how we theorize language, a translingual orientation has been the most useful approach to investigate the intersections between language, writing, and identity in transnational spaces. Originally, the term "translingual" was employed by Liu in 1995 to investigate the practice emerging in a Chinese context in relation to Japanese and European language and cultural practices (You, 2018, p. 5). Applied linguist Pennycook referred to the idea of language as local practice (2010), a notion taken up by other applied linguistics scholars in the United States like Canagarajah (2012, 2013) and, later, composition scholars Min-Zhan and Horner, who describe a translingual orientation to language as performative, "not something we have but something we do" (2016, p. 208). Aside from an emphasis on the performative nature of language, the most salient aspects that constitute a translingual orientation have to do with the relevance of the ecology and sociocultural contexts in meaning-making language and writing practices. Moreover, a significant component of a translingual approach to language has to do with efforts of decolonization. Considering that translingualism is a recently developed theoretical framework (although as practice it has always existed) (Canagarajah, 2013a), it has been criticized for not having fully addressed the potential flattening effects of seeing all language as emergent practice without accounting for minority languages that have been delegitimized in the past (Guerra, 2016). However, as a decolonizing theoretical framework, translingualism aims to recognize the space for "endangered" or "threatened" languages not just as linguistic codes that have to be recovered or sustained, but also as an approach that can guide us in "leveling the social, epistemic, semiotic, and linguistic hierarchies that (de)humanize us all" (Cushman, 2016, p. 236).

Perhaps most importantly in relation to the purpose of this chapter is the notion of how translingualism proves itself to help writers locate themselves in a different space for "identity construction, ideological reflection, and communicate practice" (Canagarajah, 2018, p. 41), a liminal transnational spaces that enables detachment from monolingual and territorialized language ideologies. For teachers interested in investigating and reflecting the realities of English language practices across the world in uneven social contexts, doing critical autoethnographic work by engaging in these liminal spaces affords them the deconstruction of master narratives and discourses (Yazan, 2019) around language myths. In fact, working from a translingual and transnational epistemological stance means, in Canagarajah's words, "deconstructing the limiting language ideologies, being reminded of 'horizons larger than oneself', and becoming comfortable with constructing identities and repertoires that are more creative and critical" (2018, p. 58).

## Mapping the trajectory of teacher identity through translingualism and CHAT

This analysis draws on Lee's understanding of identity as "activity" (2013), and thus, on activity theory as a framework to "understand the factors that influence the negotiation of teachers' identities in the writing" (2013, p. 332). Activity theory understand human activity as historically and socially mediated and shaped by tools (including semiotic means), other agents, technologies, norms, and division of labor in specific ecologies. In applied linguistics, Lantlof and Thorne have used activity theory to conceptualize language as "communicative activity." In writing, Prior et al. (2007) proposed a remapping of classical rhetorical analysis grounded in Cultural Historical Activity Theory (CHAT). In their perspective, classical rhetoric and its emphasis on delivery "does not focus attention on the possible rhetorical configurations of distribution, mode, and other mediations" (p. 8). For Prior et al. (2007), rhetorical activity could be re-situated and broken down into seven components for analysis, namely, production, reception, representation, distribution, socialization, activity, and ecology.

Additionally, a translingual orientation to language informs the analysis, since it emphasizes and prioritizes the performative nature of language as something "we do, not as something we have" (Min-Zhan & Horner, 2016). Translingual language practice also involves all semiotic tools available in the environment, including modalities (textual, aural, gestural, spatial, visual) and emergent linguistic repertoires (Busch, 2015). Both theoretical approaches, CHAT and translingualism, also involve attention to the ecology where practice takes place, meaning the environment with physical and biological forces that impact and are constitutive of human activity, as well as the sociocultural factors that also mediate it.

Finally, navigating teaching as language and identity activity systems allows me to account for the ten principles of transdisciplinary language teaching reported by De Costa and Norton (2017) and grounded in the "10 fundamental themes related to learning" by the Douglas Fir Group. De Costa and Norton's principles describe language teaching as: semiotic, "situated and attentionally and socially gated," "multimodal, embodied, and mediated," involving "variability and change," as "identity work," and mediated by literacy and language, as well as language ideologies and emotion and affect (2018, p. 8).

With these principles in mind, the following autoethnographic analysis of two articles informed by activity theory and Prior et al.'s remapping of rhetorical activity (2007) reflects teaching as identity and language activity systems in and through transnational spaces and provides a framework for emergent teacher-scholars to investigate the intersections of language and identity work and pedagogical activity as multidimensional and embodied (more or less consciously) in time-space networks. It is important to mention that Prior's model was originally conceptualized to analyze the literate activity around texts rather than pedagogies; however, my understanding of teaching as rhetorical allows for the repurposing and adaptation of such model.

The two articles I will refer to in my analysis are "Word choice: Global challenges in academic writing" (2015), written during my first year as a composition instructor and Ph.D. student, and "Language variation across genres: Translingualism here and there" (2016), written a year later in a journal published by the writing program. Both articles emerged and functioned as resources for professional development of other teachers as well as to help students in the writing courses to become familiar with issues of language in global-local contexts. At the same time, writing these two articles created a sense of belonging that, as a linguistically diverse teacher in a context of homogenizing English language practices, was much needed. Not only was I contributing to integrating conversations about language in the writing classroom, my teaching identity was developing as "more legitimate" in my own eyes in a reciprocal relationship with the environment of the writing program.

Teaching as identity and language activity systems enables me to think about the tools, technologies, and forms of knowledge that I employ when I am teaching in specific contexts. Production, according to Prior et al., "merges individual and collective invention with the mediated force of technologies, genres, discourses, and practices" (2007, p. 21). In this sense, as I teach, questions related to the production of my identity as a teaching activity emerge, for example: what tools exist and are accessible to me as a teacher? What are those tools like? Which ones do I use and how? As a linguistically diverse teacher of writing, I transitioned from seeing my linguistic background as an obstacle in the context of the writing program due to my previous exposure to language myths like monolingualism (Matsuda, 2006) to thinking about my linguistic metacognitive knowledge as a place for learning as the first article, "Word choice," demonstrates. For instance, it is particularly relevant that the word "challenge" appears in the title of the article and frames the majority of the article portraying a deficit view of the language knowledge of instructors like myself (who I refer to as second or third language writers following an additive view of language). Other instances where I convey a view of language as limiting include saying on the first page "I know I will be stuck on sentences for several reasons and that I will never be satisfied with all the decisions I make throughout all the writing process" (p. 41), a statement that reflects wanting to achieve ideal language standards; on another occasion, I use the self-deprecating expression "I feel so dumb ... for not having spelled the word right" (p. 45), once again measuring my language abilities not on the basis of meaning-making but on the formal features of a view of language as textual codes. Therefore, the main discourses that were mediating the production of my teaching identity were informed by deficit views and language as cognitive processes and formal features. At the same time, other knowledges, like conversations around the native versus non-native binary (Brutt-Griffler & Samimy, 2001) in the graduate program I was participating in started to became tools for the production of my teacher identity. The environment of the graduate and writing programs where other instructors and faculty members worked, as well as the material conditions in it, played a role in the construction of my teaching activities as well. Prior et al. refer to this notion as ecology and define it as the "biotic and natural world, which enables and constrains all the previous functions and which may also be a domain of rhetorical action." The significant impact of the environment and the types of socialization (interactions that contributed to the development of my teaching identity) is clear when we analyze the trajectory of the discourses and knowledges that mediated the construction of my identity. For example, while my article "Word choice" was framed from a structuralist view of language as codes consisting of a binary of signifier and signified, the conclusion hints at how I was processing more complex understandings of language as always hybrid no matter who the speaker is. In fact, the following statement extracted from the concluding paragraph illustrates a transition in my understanding of language, and thus my teacher identity:

> I do so much research to fulfill the readers' expectations, to the point that the boundaries between grammatical correctness and real language use are so fuzzy they do not seem to exist, sometimes it is up to you, reader, to be more or less tolerant towards writers and to invest more or less energy in approaching intelligibility from a more inclusive or narrower perspective.
>
> (p. 51)

When this article was produced and distributed (disseminated) in different classes I realized that its reception had not been exactly what I intended it to be. Prior et al.

define reception as the "actual reading/viewing/hearing and response, how meaning is made under what conditions and for what ends. It is a mental and social activity. Reception can be, and often is, actively shaped by writers or distributors" (2007, p. 21). The emphasis on the deficit view of linguistic diversity was the most widespread uptake among other instructors and students. In my conversations in and outside the classroom, I noticed that the concluding statements about the shared efforts for intelligibility, or as Lippi-Green calls it, the "communicative burden" (2012) between readers and writers, had not clicked with many of my students and even peer-instructors, so I continued to ponder over the questions "What knowledge-making and language practices am I bringing in with me from other contexts? In what ways can they be used to enhance students' learning?" The notion of representation became essential in thinking about how to design, reorient, and enact my identity and pedagogical practices in specific classroom spaces. I necessarily had to think about the fact that the way I was conceptualizing my teaching was "entextualized in talk, text, and mind" (Prior et al., 2007, p. 21), in other words, discourses about the meaning of teaching and learning become visible in my choices as a teacher, consciously or unconsciously made. In fact, my dissatisfaction with the reception of "Word choice" as well as new knowledges about language (specifically my new process of socialization into translingualism) developed throughout my graduate education that year prompted a desire to address the issue by writing another piece for the same journal. This time, to better exercise my agency in the representation I considered questions like: "Who are my students? What about my peer instructors? What do they know about language? What don't they know? What are they expecting to learn? What do they need to learn? What are their intersectional identities based on lived experiences, gender identification, sexuality, abilities, race, ethnicity, nationality, language, economic, sociocultural, religious backgrounds, etc.? In what ways do their identities function in the specific classroom context? How are they visible in the classroom space, course materials, and class interactions?" These questions were important in the conceptualization of my article "Language variation across genres: Translingualism here and there" (2016). For example, I kept in mind that language as emergent practice always involves a combination of modalities (or semiotic means) including textual, visual, aural, spatial, and gestural components and that, to successfully communicate my ideas, I had to point at and discuss the lived experiences and interests of the demographics I was surrounded by in that specific environment in the US Midwest (what I have earlier referred to as ecology). For example, the article includes multiple references to language practices in the United States such as dialectal traits, language emerging from hip-hop genres, and linguistic practices of social media and popular culture. These examples were discuss in conjunction with other ones more relevant to global-local interactions like the emergence of so-called "Chinglish" or British English practices. By attempting to paint a wider picture of language issues across the world and most importantly pertinent to students' lives, I considered making my argument more accessible and robust, while creating a more positive teaching identity. Instead of measuring my linguistic identity against

American Standard English and grammatical accuracy from a structuralist point of view, I was portraying it as part of a wide array of creative possibilities in a complex, diverse, and interconnected world.

The construction of my teaching identity as contextual and co-constructed in an activity system (Lee, 2013) became more evident as more nuanced conversations around language issues in global contexts became more relevant to the sociocultural and ecological context which I was progressively becoming more vocal in. My identity was enhanced by the space made in the program for linguistic diversity and vice versa, the space became more explicitly open to these conversations because of the presence of linguistically diverse instructors like myself and other colleagues.

Growing interdisciplinary and bidirectional conversations between applied linguistics and composition studies (Horner et al., 2011; Tardy, 2017) also mediated the construction of my teaching identity as a legitimate and successful linguistically diverse teacher of writing in predominantly white and monolingual classrooms. Socialization into these types of discourses was therefore essential. Prior et al. define socialization as:

> the making of people and the making of society in concrete history. As individuals engage in cultural practices, they are involved in apprenticeship, learning, and development. As situated engagement in cultural practices unfolds, society is (re)produced, that is, transmitted and transformed in activity.
>
> (2007, p. 21)

In other words, my teaching identity was shaped by interactions between my work and the existing institutional structures and other agents. Questions such as the following ones prove to be useful in order to understand how socialization impacts teacher identity construction: "What institutional practices interact with my teaching? To what administrative unit does my course respond to? How do I negotiate and practice rule-following as well as my own personal teaching style, approach, and philosophies?" The fact that I was encouraged to write and teach writing by drawing on applied linguistics was facilitated as mentioned earlier by the philosophies of the writing program and also by the specific requirements of the graduate degree I was pursuing. For example, one of the exams that all Ph.D. students take prior to becoming Ph.D. candidates involves putting two disciplinary traditions into conversation to answer a research question. Interdisciplinarity was not just promoted, but also required. Therefore, bringing in notions from applied linguistics into the writing classroom and creating a transdisciplinary identity (Sánchez-Martín & Seloni, 2019) was in part enabled by these rules and expectations within the system of activities. In this regard, it is worth noting that experiencing "contradictions" in systems of activity as noted by Russell (1995) and Fraiberg (2018) helps to uncover routines about the ways we think about our activities (in this case, teacher identity) and identify the mediating agents that make both positive and negative impacts on them. For example, as another requirement in the program I was pursuing, I taught a course entitled "Integrated reading and writing" in the English Language Institute at the same university. While at that time I was constructing my translinguistic identity (Motha, Jain, & Tecle 2012) and moving beyond using the native/non-native dichotomy to conceptualize my identity, the institutional environment where I was then teaching became more restrictive in facilitating the types of teaching identity I had been progressively developing based on a translingual orientation to language and writing. While no specific language policies were in place, the English Language Institute had been part of a long history of tacit English-only ideologies as well as approaches to learning based on ideal native speakerism. Alvarez et al. (2017) give an account of how teachers' ethnic and linguistic identities are constructed in relation to specific school-based discourses and practices by both teachers and students who, through a translingual framework, find avenues for complicating assigned simplistic labels. Similarly, Sánchez-Martín, Hirsu, Gonzales, and Alvarez (2019) give an account of how teachers negotiate institutional expectations and discourses to embrace pedagogies of digital composing that honor students' linguistic practices. In this case, how I negotiated my emerging teaching identity was determined by the types of interactions I had with peers and students from various places in the world whose socialization into English writing had been filtered through standard language ideologies and monolingualism.

## Discussion and final thoughts

The multidirectional and unequal journey of my teaching identity as activity continues as I move back and forth between student demographics, geographic and symbolic transnational social spaces, discourse and disciplinary communities, and language practices. Identity as activity is an ongoing quest and a balancing act between adjusting to the rules and expectations existing in certain sociocultural and ecological contexts and, at the same time, pushing against the constraints created and reinforced by language myths and made visible through language policies that have material effects on human beings.

The linkages among identities, language, writing, and teaching is "an ideological project" that involves, as Canagarajah has mentioned, "deconstructing the limiting language ideologies, being reminded of 'horizons larger than oneself', and becoming comfortable with constructing identities and repertoires that are more creative and critical" (Canagarajah, 2018, p. 58). To engage in this process of deconstructing limiting language ideologies and constructing one's translinguistic and transnational identities as teachers, this study demonstrates that using a framework consisting of CHAT and translingualism directs our attention to the myriad of factors that mediate our activity as humans, including our identity in and across classroom spaces.

In practical terms, this approach could be used in teacher education courses or workshops in which teachers learn about other practitioners' use of "identity as pedagogy" (Motha, Jain, & Tecle, 2012). Besides reading these personal accounts, incoming teachers can be asked to analyze, from a CHAT approach, how the writers' uses of "identity-as- pedagogy" are enacted in specific environments and sociocultural contexts by responding to questions such as:

- What concepts and discourses do they use to construct their identities?
- What are the historical trajectories of such concepts and discourses?
- How are those concepts and discourses used by specific sociocultural groups?
- In what ways does the environment determine or influence identity construction? Which identity traits are prioritized in which environments?
- What agents, tools, technologies, and semiotic means (languages) influence identity construction?

In other words, they can analyze identity as activity (Lee, 2013) historically constructed, mediated by knowledges, discourses about language and other traits, and shaped by specific ecologies and communities with certain shared values. Once incoming teachers have analyzed others' identities, the same framework can be utilized to investigate specific critical moments pertaining to their identities. To be introspective of their identities, a transnational feminist perspective brings value to the embodied knowledge of their lived experiences. The following questions can help teachers to detect critical moments for identity construction: "What does it mean to experience anxiety, comfort, or other sensations in specific spaces? What identities and intersectional traits are being represented as mainstream and which ones are marginal across contexts? What discourses influence notions of privilege and marginalization in relation to identity? How does language intersect with other identity traits and in what ways do linguistic identity perceptions change across environments?" Finally, once teachers are cognizant of their identities as well as the factors that impact them, they can better respond to language-related myths in the classroom space by bringing criticality to language learning through their own experiences.

With these recommendations in mind, I acknowledge that future research should pay more attention, in line with De Fina and Perrino's claims, to describing the "finer scalar distinctions and dynamics" of transnational teacher identity (2013) as well as the intersections of identity in different scales to continue complicating and defining the networks by which identity as activity is constructed by and constitutive of. A potential avenue for addressing this gap might lie in analyzing teachers' literacy autoethnographic work or literacy autobiographies.

## References

Alvarez, S. P., Canagarajah, S., Lee, E., Lee, J. W., & Rabbi, S. (2017). Translingual practice, ethnic identities, and voice in writing. In B. Horner & L. Tetreault (Eds.), *Crossing divides: Exploring translingual writing pedagogies and programs* (pp. 31–47). Logan: Utah State University Press.

Aneja, G. A. (2016). Rethinking nativeness: Toward a dynamic paradigm of (non) native speakering. *Critical Inquiry in Language Studies*, 13(4), 351–379.

Beach, K. (2003). Consequential transitions: A developmental view of knowledge propagation through social organizations. In T. Tuomi-Gröhn & Y. Engeström (Eds.),

*Between school and work: New perspectives on transfer and boundary-crossing* (pp. 39–62). Amsterdam: Pergamon Press.

Brutt-Griffler, J., & Samimy, K. K. (2001). Transcending the nativeness paradigm. *World Englishes*, 20(1), 99–106.

Busch, B. (2015). Expanding the notion of the linguistic repertoire: On the concept of Spracherleben—The lived experience of language. *Applied Linguistics*, 38(3), 340–358.

Canagarajah, A. S. (2012). Teacher development in a global profession: An autoethnography. *Tesol Quarterly*, 46(2), 258–279.

Canagarajah, A. S. (2013a). *Translingual practice: Global Englishes and cosmopolitan relations.* New York: Routledge.

Canagarajah, A. S. (2013b). Negotiating translingual literacy: An enactment. *Research in the Teaching of English*, 40–67.

Canagarajah, S. (2018). Transnationalism and translingualism: How they are connected. In X. You (Ed.), *Transnational writing education: Theory, history, and practice* (pp. 57–76). New York: Routledge.

Cushman, E. (2016). Translingual and decolonial approaches to meaning making. *College English*, 78(3), 234–242.

Engeström, Y. (2001). Expansive learning at work: Toward an activity theoretical reconceptualization. *Journal of Education and Work*, 14(1), 133–156.

De Costa, P. I., & Norton, B. (2017). Introduction: Identity, transdisciplinarity, and the good language teacher. *The Modern Language Journal*, 101(S1), 3–14.

De Fina, A., & Perrino, S. (2013). Transnational identities. *Applied Linguistics*, 34(5), 509–515.

Donahue, C. (2018). Rhetorical and linguistic flexibility: Valuing heterogeneity in academic writing education. In X. You (Ed.), *Transnational writing education: Theory, history, and practice* (pp. 37–56). New York: Routledge.

Fraiberg, S. (2018). From activity to mobility systems: Tracing multilingual literacies on the move. In X. You (Ed.), *Transnational writing education: Theory, history, and practice* (pp. 156–169). New York: Routledge.

Guerra, J. C. (2016). Cultivating a rhetorical sensibility in the translingual writing classroom. *College English*, 78(3), 228–233.

Horner, B., Lu, M. Z., Royster, J. J., & Trimbur, J. (2011). Language difference in writing: Toward a translingual approach. *College English*, 73(3), 303–321.

Johnson, K. E. (2006). The sociocultural turn and its challenges for second language teacher education. *Tesol Quarterly*, 40(1), 235–257.

Kamhi-Stein, L., & Vandrick, S. (2013). *Narrating their lives: Examining English language teachers' professional identities within the classroom.* Ann Arbor, MI: University of Michigan Press.

Lee, I. (2013). Becoming a writing teacher: Using "identity" as an analytic lens to understand EFL writing teachers' development. *Journal of Second Language Writing*, 22(3), 330–345.

Lippi-Green, R. (2012). *English with an accent: Language, ideology and discrimination in the United States.* London: Routledge.

Matsuda, P. K. (1999). Composition studies and ESL writing: A disciplinary division of labor. *College Composition and Communication*, 50(4), 699–721.

Matsuda, P. K. (2006). The myth of linguistic homogeneity in US college composition. *College English*, 68(6), 637–651.

Min-Zhan, L., & Horner, B. (2016). Introduction: Translingual work. *College English*, 78(3), 207–218.

Motha, S., Jain, R., & Tecle, T. (2012). Translinguistic identity-as-pedagogy: Implications for language teacher education. *International Journal of Innovation in English Language Teaching and Research*, 1(1), 13–28.

Park, G. (2017). *Narratives of East Asian women teachers of English: Where privilege meets marginalization*. Bristol: Multilingual Matters.

Pavlenko, A. (2007). Autobiographic narratives as data in applied linguistics. *Applied Linguistics*, 28(2), 163–188.

Pennycook, A. (2010). *Language as a local practice*. Bristol: Routledge.

Prior, P., Solberg, J., Berry, P., Bellwoar, H., Chewning, B., Lunsford, K. J., Rohan, L., Roonzen, K., Sheridan-Rabideau, M. P., Shipka, J., Van ittersum, D., & Walker, J. (2007). Re-situating and re-mediating the canons: A cultural-historical remapping of rhetorical activity. *Kairos*, 11(3), 1–29.

Roth, W. M. (2007). Emotion at work: A contribution to third-generation cultural-historical activity theory. *Mind, Culture, and Activity*, 14(1–2), 40–63.

Roth, W. M., & Lee, Y. J. (2007). "Vygotsky's neglected legacy": Cultural-historical activity theory. *Review of Educational Research*, 77(2), 186–232.

Rudolph, N., Selvi, A. F., & Yazan, B. (2015). Conceptualizing and confronting inequity: Approaches within and new directions for the "NNEST movement." *Critical Inquiry in Language Studies*, 12(1), 27–50.

Russell, D. R. (1995). Activity theory and its implications for writing instruction. In J. Petraglia (Ed.), *Reconceiving writing, rethinking writing instruction* (pp. 51–77). Mahwah, NJ: Erlbaum.

Sánchez-Martín, C. (2015). Word choice: Global challenges in academic writing. *Grassroots Writing Research Journal*, 41–52.

Sánchez-Martín, C. (2016). Language variation across genres: Translingualism here and there. *Grassroots Writing Research Journal*, 33–43.

Sánchez-Martín, C., & Seloni, L. (2019). Transdisciplinary becoming as a gendered activity: A reflexive study of dissertation mentoring. *Journal of Second Language Writing*, 43, 24–35.

Sánchez-Martín, C., Hirsu, L., Gonzales, L., & Alvarez, S. P. (2019). Pedagogies of digital composing through a translingual approach. *Computers and Composition*, 52, 142–157.

Starfield, S. (2013). Researcher reflexivity. In C. A. Chapelle (Ed.), *The encyclopedia of applied linguistics* (pp. 1–7). Malden, MA: Wiley-Blackwell.

Tardy, C. M. (2017). Crossing, or creating, divides? A plea for transdisciplinary scholarship. In B. Horner & L. Tetrault (Eds), *Crossing divides: Exploring translingual writing pedagogies and programs*. Logan: Utah State University Press. [Kindle Version].

Thorne, S. L., & Lantolf, J. P. (2007). A linguistics of communicative activity. *Disinventing and Reconstituting Languages*, 62, 170–195.

Vertovec, S. (2009). *Transnationalism*. New York: Routledge.

Yazan, B. (2019). Toward identity-oriented teacher education: Critical autoethnographic narrative. *TESOL Journal*, 10(1), 1–15.

Yazan, B., & Rudolph, N. (2018). Introduction: Apprehending identity, experience, and (in) equity through and beyond binaries. In *Criticality, teacher identity, and (in) equity in English language teaching* (pp. 1–19). Cham: Springer.

You, X. (Ed.). (2018). *Transnational writing education: Theory, history, and practice*. New York: Routledge.

Zhang, Y. (2018). English teacher identity development through a cross-border writing activity. In X. You (Ed.), *Transnational writing education: Theory, history, and practice* (pp. 187–202). New York: Routledge.

# Part III

# Technological and virtual interventions

# 8 A pedagogical framework to support teachers in today's dynamic, digital, intercultural, and transnational learning environments

*Geoff Lawrence*

## Introduction

The use of English, like other languages, has been dramatically changing in recent decades. Today's English 'language' teaching (ELT) contexts are increasingly digital, intercultural, transnational, and dynamic. Rapidly evolving information and communication technologies (ICTs) continue to complexify and "transnationalize" ELT practices and the inherent nature of communication itself (Kessler, 2018; Van Camp, 2016). English is increasingly used through technology-mediated media like SMS, Twitter, email, Google Docs, where the medium is transforming not just the message but the nature and use of the language.

Learners of English today bring into classes a range of digital media literacies and familiarity with participatory online cultures along with an "expectation that teachers will use social technologies in ways that align with students' social practices" (Kessler, 2018, p. 201). The rapidly evolving communicative demands in today's digitally dependent societies have intensified the mobility and hybridity of "language" learning landscapes, redefining the needs of TESOL education. Language learners, like many of us, are increasingly socialized into transnational communities both materially and virtually with a diversity of linguistic, cultural, and imagined experiences that are increasingly technology-mediated and often dynamic and emergent. Such transnational lived experience is increasingly the norm, particularly in the language "classroom" (Lin, 2013; Warriner, 2017). Teaching communication skills nowadays requires much more than just a linguistics focus. To effectively function and contribute in today's inherently plurilingual, pluricultural, and transnational communities, students need a range of communication-related competencies, well beyond those defined by notions of communicative competence (Lin, 2013; Piccardo, 2013, 2019a). Language learners communicate in a range of digital discourse spaces (Sykes, 2017, p. 128) using Facebook, YouTube, Twitter, and fanfiction sites, among others. Such communication is bound within a culturally and contextually framed communicative purpose where social relations and individual identities are negotiated within certain expectations and norms (Kramsch & Thorne, 2002). This requires multimodal literacy, pragmatic and strategic competence to navigate these emerging communicative landscapes. Skills like global citizenship, information literacy, intercultural and cosmopolitan communicative competence, collaboration, and critical thinking are increasingly seen as relevant, transferable, and needed skills (Dede, 2010, p. 5) that synergistically complement language teaching outcomes. Problem-solving skills and genre awareness are also needed to navigate these highly diverse and dynamic linguistic, cultural, and transnational environments.

Today's digital landscapes are inherently intercultural and transnational in nature. The contemporary scholarship of TESOL and Applied Linguistics has reinforced the value and relevance of working with the intercultural dimension in language teaching and learning for several decades. There are a number of theoretical frameworks that have been proposed to clarify notions of intercultural learning and development that can be applied to language learning and ELT. For example, Byram (1997) defined the model of Intercultural Communicative Competence (ICC) by framing it around three dimensions, attitudes, knowledge, and critical discovery/interpretation and reflection skills. Milton Bennett's Developmental Model of Intercultural Sensitivity (1986) defines intercultural learning as a developmental process moving from ethnocentric to ethnorelative orientations to cultural difference, facilitated by critical reflection and empathic strategies. Recognizing the hyper-diverse, fluid interactions in digital communicative contexts and the need to move beyond static, monolithic views of nation-based culture, some have turned to notions of cosmopolitan communicative competence (CCC) (Beck, 2006) as a more nuanced framework for online language teaching/learning (Risager, 2007). CCC seeks an understanding of universalism through engagement with the particular, recognizing and negotiating the fluidity of cultural associations through a range of meaning-making resources.

Some ELT programs have integrated aspects of intercultural language learning. Yet the challenge remains on how to work with the intercultural dimension and notions around transnationalism in dynamic digital communicative environments, and how to make this relevant for learners, an area that's often left for individual teachers to navigate. Chapelle and Sauro (2017) and fellow contributors in their edited volume have redefined the need to focus on "langua-technoculture" (p. 461) in today's language learning landscapes as this characterizes the current intersection of technology, culture, and language, more aptly qualifying the inherently intercultural, technology-mediated discourse spaces that language learners need to consistently navigate.

Research into language teaching has also highlighted the need to more fully leverage learners and teachers' linguistic and cultural resources in the language learning classroom and to build awareness of plurilingual, pluricultural competence that can synergistically facilitate the development of a target language and intercultural competence. Studies examining language learning and teaching have highlighted the relevance of a plurilingual approach in ELT (Lin, 2013; Piccardo, 2013), the need to move away from a monolingual focus on language pedagogy to a more humanistic, situated approach where learners can use/develop their full range of communicative resources in the learning of a "target" language, simultaneously valuing the social, historical, and cultural importance of languages and their plurilingual selves (Cho, Piccardo, Lawrence, & Germain-Rutherford, 2018).

## The call for an innovative, beliefs-centred approach to TESOL

This emerging understanding of "language" teaching has highlighted the need to situate TESOL education in the beliefs of teacher-learners toward effective technology use, perceptions around intercultural learning in ELT, the use of learners' first languages/cultural resources in practice, and to actively work with teacher-learners' idealized views of language teaching and learning (Borg, 2006; Hubbard & Kessler, 2017; Johnson, 2006; Richards, 2015). Such belief-focused teacher education practices can contribute to the development of critical, reflective teaching practices that can sustain and innovate over time. This has fueled the call for a critical, reflective, intercultural, and technology-mediated approach to TESOL education to prepare English language teachers to meet the needs of today's often digitally and transnationally aligned learners.

However such pedagogical and curricular innovation in TESOL education is challenging. The integration of technology is often an afterthought, a supplementary workshop or series of seminars on the "how to" of technology that often neglects a focus on tech-mediated pedagogy, enabling educators to leverage the affordances of specific technologies/modalities to effectively meet the communicative needs of today's learners. The goals of many ELT programs are often acculturation into English-speaking communicative contexts rather than an interculturally negotiated approach where learners build on their cultural and linguistic resources to negotiate nuanced, broadened identities and to help facilitate transnational understandings of their cultural selves, of others, and of communication processes. Many TESOL programs still frame English language learning through a monolingual lens, neglecting or overtly dismissing the rich linguistic and cultural repertoire learners bring into a language learning program. Methodology is still often framed with a progression toward an idealized, linguistically focused, native speaker model, a goal that frustrates learning and seems increasingly irrelevant in today's inherently plurilingual and intercultural societies.

This chapter will examine the demands and challenges faced by English language teachers given today's complex technology-mediated, mobile, and inherently intercultural communicative landscapes and will outline the needs of TESOL education programs. It will discuss current thinking in teacher education research that advocates for a critically reflective and situated approach to language teacher education, actively working with teacher beliefs and realities in teacher education (Borg, 2006; Johnson, 2006; Lawrence, 2018). The chapter will then outline and discuss a pedagogical framework to help support a critical, technology-mediated, intercultural, and plurilingual approach to TESOL education and ELT. The chapter will conclude with a summary of resources to support the integration of this framework into TESOL teacher education programs.

## A transformative turning point in TESOL

In their state-of-the-art handbook on technology and second/additional language (L2) education, Chapelle and Sauro (2017) emphasize that we're at a transformative turning point in L2 teaching and learning. They identify three themes shaping the future of language teaching in today's contexts: the multimodal and technocultural nature of language use that needs to be taught to meet students' digital communicative practices; the need for teachers to reconceptualize themselves as innovative practitioners that reflect today's dynamic language teaching and learning landscapes; and, finally, the integral role of research in designing and evaluating learning activities to inform effective teaching practices (p. 459).

Fully online, blended, flipped, technology-enhanced, and mobile-assisted ELT programs are offering a range of unique pathways to English language learning. Intensely interactive Web2.0 technologies are spawning emergent literacy practices involving new approaches to English language use, interaction, and new ways of seeing learner autonomy and notions of community (Gee & Hayes, 2011; Hockly & Dudeney, 2018; White, 2016). Web2.0 technologies offer transformative approaches to student interaction, multimodal linguistic production, and opportunities for nuanced feedback and participatory collaboration. Tools like wikis, online presentation applications (e.g., Prezi, Google slides) can engage learners in intensely collaborative writing and planning where language production is mediated by peer feedback, interaction, combined with task design, teacher facilitation, and enacted learner autonomy. Mobile devices with video, close captions, translation tools, and grammar checkers can potentially enhance language acquisition and language awareness for a range of learning styles; interactive social media platforms like blogs, Twitter, and Google Docs provide a heightened sense of audience and can encourage collaborative writing, peer feedback, and attention to grammatical accuracy (Kessler, 2009). Tasks designed with such technology-mediated tools can result in enhanced time spent with language input, with output, planning, revisions, with a focus on linguistic form, error, and editing awareness. Such tasks can also offer individualized pathways to participation, reducing anxiety and enhancing a sense of peer connection and community.

Approaches like telecollaboration, virtual exchanges can involve learners – and teachers – in mobile transnational virtual communities of learning where learners and teachers engage in online intercultural interaction and collaboration projects that can promote intercultural awareness and cosmopolitan communicative competence (O'Dowd, Sauro, & Spector-Cohen, 2019; You, 2016). Such projects have the potential of building online learning environments that can facilitate student-centered communicative, plurilingual, and intercultural competencies along with identity investment, transferable digital literacies, learning strategies, and 21st century skills (Lawrence, 2013; Stockwell, 2012) to establish learning communities beyond the classroom. Such virtual exchanges can allow teachers to work in transnational communities of practice, leveraging experiences and knowledge from teachers working in a range of contexts, countries, with diverse curricular and educational systems. Such learning can facilitate a co-constructed transnational understanding of English language use, teaching practices, of technology integration, and an experiential understanding of intercultural teaching and learning (Koehler & Mishra, 2009; Lawrence & Spector-Cohen, 2018).

## The challenges

To leverage these transformative opportunities, however, teachers face considerable challenges. Teaching practices embedding intercultural teaching and learning are often unclear and hard to conceptualize, particularly when integrated with technology. Working with an intercultural dimension can prompt fears around perpetuating stereotypes, perceived lack of "cultural" knowledge/strategies, concerns around keeping the focus on "language" learning, and issues around cultural appropriation. Actively working with learners' first languages in the learning of English needs buy-in from institutions, learners, communities, and teachers who may be used to working in English-only contexts.

In terms of technology use, English language educators often face increasing pressures from schools, institutions, and administrators to implement technology-enhanced pathways/approaches. At the same time, teachers are often responsible for doing this with very little training or support (Hubbard, 2008; Hubbard & Kessler, 2017; Richards, 2015). Teaching English online requires a range of unique skills that often are not taught in TESOL programs. As scholars have warned we cannot simply computerize traditional classroom practices; we must think of new ways of doing new things with new tools (Garrett, 2009; Kessler, 2018). New approaches to pedagogy must be developed that leverage the affordances of various tools/media and curricular innovation with updated teaching practices. Teachers must be skilled at critically assessing the affordances of new technologies and strategically assessing how they can best be integrated into context-relevant teaching practices to target specific learning outcomes.

Teaching with technologies often requires substantial time, ongoing peer mentoring, resources, access, an adaptive curriculum, tech support, and a knowledge of techno-pedagogical competence (Guichon & Hauck, 2011). Research examining technology use in English for academic purposes (EAP) programs across North America found that the majority of EAP teachers used classroom available technologies that included learning management systems, classroom projectors, desktop computers, and facilitated programs in a traditional, more teacher-centred manner (Lawrence, Ahmed, Cole & Johnston, 2020). In this study, teachers complained about a lack of techno-pedagogical training, citing the limitations of one-shot technology-focused workshops that prioritized the "how to" of technology not the "why" of technology use in EAP teaching/learning contexts. Teachers complained about the lack of time to integrate technological tools that included the need to orient students and build learner autonomy to work effectively in tech-based approaches. In related research, both language learners and teachers have been found to compartmentalize the use of technology in their personal lives, viewing the personal and professional uses of technology as separate (Cementina, 2016). In an examination of technology views toward technology use in language teaching, Cementina (2016) found that while teachers recognized and valued the benefits of digital tools in their own lives, they failed to see the transferability of these tools in language teaching practices. These teachers viewed the personal and professional uses of technology as distinct and thus framed language teaching practices around low technology use with more traditional approaches to pedagogy even though their everyday uses of technology were socially mediated and more fully integrated into their lives.

Digitally mediated learning pathways are blurring traditional notions of time, space, teacher vs. learner roles, complexifying teaching. For example, there is an increasing lack of clarity between "face-to-face" classroom learning and "face-to-face" online learning when teachers use a videoconference and communicate with students in real-time in both contexts. A similar lack of clarity exists between online teaching modalities like blended vs. hybrid vs. technology-enhanced and flipped learning that can use technologies in similar ways (Lawrence, Valeo, & Irwin, 2018; Lawrence, Ahmed, Cole, & Johnston, 2020). When using such modalities, teacher and learner roles often change dramatically, requiring completely new approaches to pedagogy, notions of "presence," learner autonomy, interaction, and engagement.

Teaching online requires the need to build and sustain teaching, social, and cognitive presence in an online learning environment (Garrison, Anderson, & Archer, 2000). This is very different than in traditional classroom settings where notions of presence are often not explicitly attended to. However in online learning environments, community formation that results from social, teaching, and cognitive presence must be actively facilitated and sustained. Online presence must explicitly be scaffolded and supported through a critical appreciation of technology's affordances, through curriculum design and innovative teaching practices that support collaborative inquiry and learner success. In spite of the omnipresent nature of technology in today's societies, we (still) can't assume learners have egalitarian digital access and appropriate digital literacies. Although learners may be digitally literate in many aspects of their everyday lives, they may have little experience with language learning online, with online collaboration, and with highly autonomous learning, time management, and other skills needed in these self-paced online learning environments.

## The call for a critical, reflective, developmental approach to TESOL education

As Chapelle and Sauro (2017) stress, due to these rapidly changing contexts in which languages are taught, "the practice of seeking out, creating, and trying innovative approaches to teaching needs to become normal" (p. 461). Pedagogical practices that leverage the affordances of specific technological tools and that integrate learner-centred intercultural, transnational, plurilingual ELT approaches targeting the needs of today's learners must be encouraged. However this is not an easy task. Teacher education practices must help orient new teachers to the complexities of ELT in today's technology-mediated communicative landscape while grounding them in learner-centred language teaching practices and encouraging them to research and innovate in practice.

This task is challenging as while initial teacher education offers promise, there has been criticism that teacher education programs have little impact on how teachers actually teach (Borg, 2006, 2011; Freeman & Johnson, 1998; Johnson,

2009; Richards, 2015). Except for the student teaching component, preservice teacher education has been critiqued as a relatively weak intervention in innovating teaching practices (Johnson, 2009; Richards, 1996). The rigidity of teacher beliefs and the nature of teaching where teacher-learners have been conditioned in years of schooling into a set culture and vision of teaching and learning (Borg, 2004) creates resistance to educational innovation in teacher education, unless there is active work with teacher beliefs, teacher experience, and ongoing reflection (Johnson, 2006; Johnson & Golombek, 2016). In spite of the increasing digitization of language use, research has found that language education continues to resist new ways of thinking about teaching/learning when using technology (Cementina, 2016; Cuban, 1990; Habbu, 2017; Lawrence, Haque, & King, 2013). School structures have continued in many ways to resist technological change over the past century (Cuban, 1986, 1990; Lawrence, 2018).

Borg (2004, 2011) affirms that teacher beliefs and orientations to practice are strongly influenced by teachers' experiences as learners that act as filters that interpret and/or reject new approaches to teaching practice. Research has confirmed that teacher beliefs play a major role influencing efforts to integrate technology and innovative approaches into teaching practices (Albright, Clement, & Holmes, 2012; Borg, 2006; Burton, 2009). As a result, Johnson (2006) argues for an ongoing, in-depth, and reflective approach to language teacher education practice that actively works with teacher participation, experience, and practitioner knowledge as essential mechanisms for change in classroom practice. Teacher education that engages active reflection on beliefs and conceptualizations of teaching is reported to have the most potential to refine beliefs and teaching practices (Borg, 2006; Johnson & Golombek, 2016).

## Pedagogical framework

Recognizing the transformative potential of today's ELT practices and the challenges inherent in TESOL education, there is a need for TESOL programs to work with a critically reflective model examining the use of technology and intercultural dimensions in language teaching practices. The pedagogical framework outlined in Figure 8.1 examines three approaches that can be integrated into TESOL programs to more effectively prepare new teachers to meet the emerging needs of today's increasingly transnational English language learners.

As noted in Figure 8.1, programs can benefit by embedding, layering, and integrating these three approaches to learning throughout their core curricula. These areas are proposed as approaches to scaffold a critical, reflective practice, to actively work with teacher beliefs and understandings around ELT practices, and to foster openness and innovation. This framework is cyclical and open-ended on purpose to reflect the flow that influences teacher learning, that can be influenced by these *and* other dynamic forces that can emerge from context, community, actions, and from within the individual.

First, core learning in TESOL programs needs to be proactively mediated through a critically reflective approach that actively examines teachers' situated

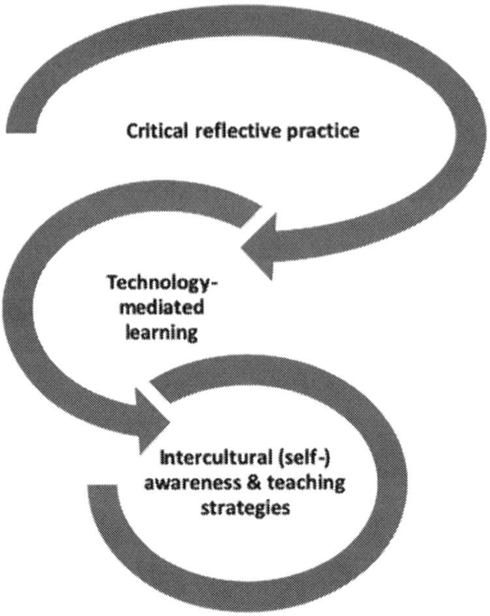


*Figure 8.1* A critically reflective, cyclical TESOL education pedagogical framework

beliefs around all aspects of TESOL content, technology use, teaching practices, notions of culture, transnationalism and intercultural learning, the value of first and other languages/language learning experiences to refine understandings of what it means to be an English "language" educator in the 21st century. TESOL education needs to be facilitated through a range of technology-mediated modalities so teacher-learners experience online learning first-hand, working in these digital learning environments as learners. This can encourage teachers to critically reflect on and assess the affordances of these technological tools, modalities, and pedagogical approaches used with them, helping them to envision the use of digital approaches in their future teaching. Finally, given the inherent intercultural nature of ELT, TESOL curricula also needs to proactively integrate an explicit, intercultural dimension into language teaching and teacher education. This can help develop critical intercultural (self-)awareness which is crucial for teachers as cultural mediators, facilitating discovery and interpretive strategies needed in today's diverse intercultural, communicative contexts. These areas are discussed in detail below.

## A critical reflective practice

TESOL education programs have often approached teacher education through a cognitive lens, defining what teachers need to know from an applied science model, presuming that knowledge from core theoretical areas like linguistics and second language acquisition can be shared with teachers who then will use this to inform and define practices (Johnson, 2009). Less attention has been paid to the perceptions teachers have of this knowledge, their experience as learners, their transnational experiences and identities, their envisioned and context-specific teaching priorities, and how they situate practices in practitioner knowledge (Borg, 2011; Johnson, 2009; Johnson & Golombek, 2016; Richards, 2015). The sociocultural turn in language teacher education and the reflective teaching movement recognizes the need for critical reflective work with teacher beliefs, previous learning experiences along with teacher-learners' evolving understanding of the disciplinary knowledge that has been the dominant focus in TESOL education programs (Borg, 2011; Freeman & Johnson, 1998; Johnson, 2006).

Such reflective, teacher-centred work can legitimize practitioner knowledge and can become a foundational approach in TESOL education programs. Active reflective work can help teachers navigate, internalize, and mediate areas of curricular innovation like technology use and intercultural approaches in envisioned teaching practices. As outlined below, if teachers are learning about ELT through technology-mediated environments where specific pedagogies, teacher/learner roles are being used, there is a need for teacher-learners to temporarily and regularly "step out" of these environments, reflect on assumptions, anticipations, revisit tensions in beliefs to make this part of the legitimate content in their teacher development. The same should be done for intercultural learning where teachers can actively reflect on assumptions about culture, bias, cultural identities, stereotypes, and approaches to work with these tensions in their practice. Teacher journals, private blogs, or audio/video postings that the teacher educator and teacher-learner have access to can fuel such reflection. With these resources the teacher educator can then identify common themes in class reflections to highlight/discuss with the class cohort to fuel further reflection and understanding. Such a critical reflective practice can be juxtaposed with the value of action research so teacher-learners recognize the value of introspection and ongoing research and innovation within their own practices.

## Technology-mediated experiential learning

Technology-mediated language teaching represents "a dynamic complex in which technology, theory and pedagogy are inseparably interwoven" (Garrett, 2009, p. 720). Digital environments afford learners and teachers distinctly unique ways of interacting, dynamic roles and notions of time, space, and of learning environments. The time-space compression that digital technologies offer transforms teacher and learner roles, enhances learner autonomy, and can potentially transform approaches to language activity that engage creativity and imagination where learners are social agents needing to leverage critical, reflective learning strategies (Kessler, 2018). The most effective manner to familiarize teachers with the affordances and limitations of such emerging learning environments is through experiential learning within these contexts.

Given the demands on English language teachers to integrate technology into their programs, technology-mediated teaching and learning needs to be integrated as a consistent, normalized modality of learning within TESOL programs. Such modalities and tools can be used to create learning environments where a range of TESOL topics are discussed and examined through various technology-mediated approaches. In this way teacher-learners can then become students in digitalized approaches, experiencing the impact of techno-pedagogical competence from the teacher educator that can, in turn, help develop these teacher-learners' sense of techno-pedagogical competence.

Such situated, experiential learning can help make technology-mediated practices more concrete. A range of tools, modalities, and teaching approaches should be used so teachers can experience and "feel" the impact of varied tools/approaches on their individual learning. This should be supported by a discussion of the notion of "affordances" so teachers appreciate that these perceived benefits of a tool change with use, context, and approach (Stockwell, 2012). Examining the evolving affordances of a historical range of educational technologies can be useful at this stage to build schema around types of affordances like connectedness, multimodality, experimentation, support, organizational abilities, and collective intelligence (Tour, 2015). Discussions of the Community of Inquiry framework (Garrison, Anderson, & Archer, 2000) examining notions of social, teaching, and cognitive presence are useful to tune educators into the fact that in some technology-mediated modalities, it is the teacher's role to facilitate and help learners sustain these notions of presence (Johnston & Lawrence, 2018). The use of various tools/modalities should be sequenced and scaffolded using a critically reflective approach where teachers reflect on their experiences as learners within these environments and share these reflections to see how colleagues experience similar environments. Such collective critical reflection on tech-mediated learning can help teachers develop the ability to critically assess the affordances of new tools for current and future ELT practices, a skill that is crucial to navigate the overwhelming range of educational technologies available (Haines, 2015; Kessler, 2018). Working with other educators in an online environment using a personal, critical, experiential approach can also help forge a professional community of practice that can extend beyond the TESOL program, providing a community of mentor-teachers to support each other with questions/concerns around ELT technology use in future practices (del Rosal, Ware, & Montgomery, 2016).

Adopting a critical inquiry-based approach to technology use can help teachers appreciate the crucial role of a techno-pedagogical competent teacher to shape technology-mediated ELT practices. This can help build an understanding of the need to adapt pedagogical practices with varied tools/modalities and enable teachers with strategies to innovate their practices (Baran, Correia, & Thompson, 2011). Such TESOL education practices can also help demystify the "wow" factor with technology that continues to fuel the ill-informed use of educational technology.

Ensuring that teachers use a range of technologies and critically reflect on their collective perceived affordances and limitations can also help teachers overcome *the visioning dilemma* (Lawrence, 2014) where teachers are unable to visualize how emerging technologies can potentially be used in an ELT practice without having seen them in practice. For example, a teacher never having seen or experienced interactions within a 3D virtual environment will be limited in what she/he can understand about the potential affordances of these environments for language learning without having experienced, or at least seen, interactions in these environments.

## Building critical intercultural (self-)awareness

As noted above, English language learning programs are increasingly recognized as fertile ground for the promotion of not just English communication skills but intercultural communicative competence: the ability to see oneself operating within a cultural context, to develop interpretation, discovery, and relating skills and adapt communication to specific audiences (Alptekin, 2002; Byram, 1997). The ELT classroom can be a place of cultural intersection, a safe "third space" (Kramsch, 1993) where learners and educators can use their cultural/linguistic resources to explore plurilingual, pluricultural, and transnational perspectives (Piccardo, 2013) to gain critical insight into their multilayered identities while learning about otherness. This is where teachers can explore the normality of transnational experience and identity that leverage plurilingual and pluricultural competence. Explicitly integrating this transnational, intercultural dimension into ELT practices adds a humanistic, reflective focus that can build relevant communication skills, identity investment, and intercultural agency for today's often highly hybridized, transnational language learners (Moeller & Nugent, 2014). Such a focus is crucial in TESOL education programs as teachers become intercultural mediators in the classes they teach.

To work effectively with the intercultural dimension in ELT, TESOL programs need to introduce, develop, and embed intercultural learning through a critically reflective practice throughout their programs. This should include an overview of theories examining intercultural communication in language teaching that include: Byram's framework of intercultural communicative competence (1997); the concept of cosmopolitan communicative competence that examines notions of global citizenship and the dialectic of universalism – particularly in today's hyper-connected world (Beck, 2006), and Bennett's Developmental Model of Intercultural Sensitivity (1986) examining culture general principles,[1] critical self-reflection, and a developmental pathway to ethnorelative orientations to difference.

The treatment of intercultural learning should be approached through critical reflection and a dialogic discussion of principles and strategies in the class. Teachers should start with the "me" in activities where they discuss conceptualizations of culture, the role of culture in language learning, and where they become aware of their cultural selves, their assumptions, biases, and discomforts. Focusing on the "complexity of me" can provide a framework to help teacher-learners see the complexity in others and more effectively interpret cultural behavior (Lawrence, 2013). Michael Agar (2006) argues that culture often only becomes visible when it is being construed from an outsider's perspective. Culture is somewhat of an artificial construction built to enable translation of perceived areas of difference between the source and target cultures. "There is no culture of X, only a culture of X for Y" (Agar, 2006, p. 6). This relational nature of culture can fuel a valuable and essential critically reflective approach to intercultural learning where learning about the "other" can enhance a critical understanding about "me," both as complex cultural beings (Byram, 1997; Kramsch, 1993). Such an approach to culture learning is "decentring" and thereby has the potential to build critical self-awareness, humility, and an ethnorelative perspective to cultural learning and communication, crucial to the development of ELT educators. Canagarajah (1999, p. 186) notes that "learners must be encouraged to become reflexive about themselves, i.e., how their values, community membership, historical background, and subject-positions motivate them to negotiate language and knowledge in particular ways."

Building comfort, or at least familiarity with *dis*comfort is key in developing an intercultural, transnational ELT practice. ELT educators should be encouraged to think outside the frames of nation-based culture, to deterritorialize language, ethnicity, identity, and norms (Lin, 2013; Piccardo, 2019b; Warriner, 2017). Asking teachers to problematize notions of culture, of power, and to critically reflect on their individual dynamic and potentially transnational identities is key, and examining the role of local and global factors, language use and experience in negotiating identities. Teachers should critically reflect on the dynamic nature of language and identity, examining instances where identities may not be tied to territory or place but are instead influenced by flows that transcend culture, linguistic, or national boundaries (Duff, 2015; Warriner, 2017, p. 52). This is where experiential learning can be useful. Activities like critical incident analyses and the *Describe, Interpret, Evaluate Intercultural Activity*[2] can help build critical awareness and curiosity by enabling cognitive flexibility and frame of reference shifting. Such reflective work can build awareness about hidden assumptions, strategies to suspend judgment, and can help teachers critically question their own perspectives while welcoming alternative interpretations and leveraging a range of cultural/linguistic experiences (Ogilvie, 2013), crucial skills for English language teachers. Through such critical self-awareness and an exploration of professional and personal identities, teachers can begin to recognize the socially and situated nature of their beliefs, values, knowledge, and their language use, and can then more effectively facilitate this learning among their students (Canagarajah, 1999; Johnson, 2006).

Discussions should examine around how to negotiate a safe classroom space where different views can be shared, tensions can sit, be reflected on and used as rich points (Agar, 2006) for learning and further examination. This is where working in a "third" space (Kramsch, 1993) is crucial where neither teachers nor learners may have the answers but where principles and strategies should guide discussions and learning. Any challenges that arise through these discussions should be actively used for further critical reflection, where teacher-learners actively apply and work with the *Describe, Interpret, Evaluate Intercultural Framework* noted above. Teacher-learners should be encouraged to suspend judgment, negotiate a common description of the challenge, seek alternative interpretations and possible evaluations before suggesting potential resolution strategies. This is where tolerance of ambiguity should be encouraged, not as a barrier but as an opportunity for growth, reinforcing that teachers do not always have the answers and can offer critical, analytical strategies but sometimes nothing more. In these cases, time can play an important role where any problematic, unresolved challenge can be assigned for longer-term critical reflection and revisited after a period of time has passed, again applying these critical, intercultural reflective strategies to potentially gain enhanced perspectives on a specific challenge. Again, the key to this process is negotiating a safe learning environment along with strategies to critically analyze, reflect on, and learn from challenges.

Deardorff (2011) identifies a list of key skills and strategies needed to attain intercultural competence (as cited in Leeds-Hurwitz, 2013, p. 24).

- Respect ("valuing of others");
- Self-awareness/identity ("understanding the lens through which we each view the world");
- Seeing from other perspectives/worldviews ("both how these perspectives are similar and different");
- Listening ("engaging in authentic intercultural dialogue");
- Adaptation ("being able to shift temporarily into another perspective");
- Relationship building (forging lasting cross-cultural personal bonds);
- Cultural humility ("combines respect with self-awareness").

These can be additional strategies to discuss with teachers and have teacher-learners examine how these strategies can be actualized in classroom and technology-mediated practices through lesson planning and practicum teaching. Teacher-learners can examine how these strategies can be embedded in discussions of ELT methodology to explore language development, genre awareness, sociolinguistic competence, and the impact of this approach on learner identities, strategic competence, and the affective dimension of learning.

## Conclusion

Teachers of English today face considerable challenges in navigating practice. Teachers need to prepare for an inherently technology-mediated, transnational, and plurilingual ELT practice and playing a crucial role as mediators of intercultural relationships, facilitating digital literacies and strategies for life-long learning. This proposed framework is a starting point for TESOL programs to help teachers proactively confront these challenges, turning them into opportunities and innovative approaches to practice.

Learning through a dialogic, critical reflective lens can help teachers develop an innovative, learner-centred practice, critically assessing technologies and appropriate pedagogies to facilitate relevant learning within community. In today's age of increasingly polarized, nativist discussions around migration, identity politics, and language use, adopting an intercultural and transnationally oriented ELT approach can be a validating and transferable tool for learners and teachers, helping reinforce learner and teacher transnational identity and agency. This can help both teachers and learners value their cultural and linguistic resources, learning how to deconstruct stereotypes and recognize relationships between power, language use, and identity. Adopting a critical, affordance-focused approach to technology-mediated learning can help engage technology when it adds substantial, unique benefits, building community and facilitating language acquisition, moving well beyond the "wow" factor. Integrating interactive, intercultural approaches informed by techno-pedagogical competence can help teachers meet the needs of English language learners in an increasingly diverse, mobile, and transnational world.

## Selected additional resources

Chapelle, C. A., & Sauro, S. (Eds.) (2017). *The handbook of technology and second language teaching and learning*. Wiley-Blackwell. www.wiley.com/en-ca/The+Handbook+of+Technology+and+Second+Language+Teaching+and+Learning-p-9781118914038.

- A comprehensive state-of-the-art overview examining the transformative potential of technology-mediated language teaching and learning to facilitate language acquisition, 21st century skills and intercultural communicative competence.

Farrell, T. (2017). *Research in reflective practice in TESOL*. Routledge. www.routledge.com/Research-on-Reflective-Practice-in-TESOL-1st-Edition/Farrell/p/book/9781138635906.

- An examination of research in reflective practice in TESOL practices, focusing on the spiritual, emotional and moral dimensions of reflection and highlighting the relevance of dialogic, critical, reflective practices in the ongoing development of English language educators.

Hastings, C. & Jacob, L. (Eds.) (2016). *Social justice in English language teaching*. TESOL International Press. https://sites.tesol.org/ItemDetail?iProductCode=14027&Category=TEACHED&WebsiteKey=62ea1393-07ea-402b-b723-0e66240ee86b.

- A presentation of various voices discussing a range of topics related to social justice in ELT and TESOL education, related to power, inequities, intercultural learning, discussions of race, gender, identity, and peace-building.

Johnson, K. E., & Golombek, P. R. (2018). Informing and transforming language teacher education pedagogy. *Language Teaching Research*. https://doi.org/10.1177/1362168818777539.

- A sociocultural examination of approaches to language teacher education and practice, arguing for greater attention to the design, enactment, and consequences of language teacher education pedagogy to meet the needs of English language teachers in today's programs.

Leeds-Hurwitz, W. (2013). *Intercultural competences: Conceptual and operational framework*. UNESCO. https://unesdoc.unesco.org/ark:/48223/pf0000219768.

- An overview of intercultural competence and strategies to conceptualize and operationalize intercultural teaching and learning.

## Notes

1 Culture general learning involves the examination of culturally learned behavior that is sometimes embedded in language use like rituals (greetings, leave-taking, complimenting), communication styles (high vs. low context) and value orientations (attitudes to time, hierarchy, age, family, relationship building).

2 The Describe, Interpret, Evaluate Framework Intercultural Activity was developed by Janet and Milton Bennett at the Intercultural Communication Institute (www.intercultural.org) to use ambiguous objects, pictures, and this framework to understand bias and develop strategies to suspend judgment. See: http://files7.webydo.com/91/9185608/UploadedFiles/8D7E526D-3840-1204-F84E-A15FD8EB832D.pdf.

## References


Agar, M. (2006). Culture: Can you take it anywhere? *International Journal of Qualitative Methods*, 5(2). Retrieved from www.ualberta.ca/~iiqm/backissues/5_2/pdf/agar.pdf.

Albright, J., Clement, J., & Holmes, K. (2012). School change and the challenge of presentism. *Leading and Managing*, 18(1), 78–90.

Alptekin, C. (2002). Towards intercultural communicative competence in ELT. *ELT Journal*, 56(1), 57–64.

Baran, E., Correia, A., & Thompson, A. (2011). Transforming online teaching practice: Critical analysis of the literature on the roles and competencies of online teachers. *Distance Education, 32*(3), 421–439. https://doi:10.1080/01587919.2011.610293.

Beck, U. (2006). *Cosmopolitan vision*. Cambridge: Polity.

Bennett, M. J. (1986). A development approach to training for intercultural sensitivity. *International Journal of Intercultural Relations*, 10(2), 179–196.

Borg, M. (2004). The apprenticeship of observation. *ELT Journal*, 58(3), 274–276. doi:10.1093/elt/58.3.274.

Borg, S. (2006). *Teacher cognition and language education: Research and practice*. London: Continuum.

Borg, S. (2011). The impact of in-service teacher education on language teachers' beliefs. *System*, 39(3), 370–380. https://doi.org/10.1016/j.system.2011.07.009.

Burton, J. (2009). Reflective practice. In A. Burns & J. C. Richards (Eds.), *The Cambridge guide to second language teacher education* (pp. 298–307). New York, NY: Cambridge University Press.

Byram, M. (1997). *Teaching and assessing intercultural communicative competence*. Clevedon: Multilingual Matters.

Canagarajah, A. S. (1999). *Resisting linguistic imperialism in English teaching*. Oxford: Oxford University Press.

Cementina, S. (2016). Language teachers' digital mindsets: Links between everyday use and professional use of technology (Unpublished Major Research Paper). York University, Toronto, Canada.

Chapelle, C. A., & Sauro, S. (Eds.) (2017). *The handbook of technology and second language teaching and learning*. Hoboken, NJ: Wiley-Blackwell.

Cho, K., Piccardo, E., Lawrence, G., & Germain-Rutherford, A. (2018). LINCDIRE (Linguistic and Cultural Diversity Reinvented): Integrating western & indigenous perspectives to redefine language education practices. *The Language Educator*, May/June 2018, 44–48.

Cuban, L. (1986). *Teachers and machines: The classroom use of technology since 1920*. New York, NY: Teachers College Press.

Cuban, L. (1990). Reforming again, again, and again. *Educational Researcher*, 19(1), 3–13. doi:10.3102/0013189X019001003.
Dede, C. (2010). Comparing frameworks for 21st century skills. In J. A. Bellanca (Ed.), *21st century skills: Rethinking how students learn* (pp. 51–76). Bloomington, IN: Solution Tree Press.
del Rosal, K., Ware, P., & Montgomery, N. (2016). Mentoring teachers of English learners in an online community of practice. *International Journal of Computer-Assisted Language Learning and Teaching*, 6(3), 1–17. doi:10.4018/IJCALLT.2016070101.
Duff, P. A. (2015). Transnationalism, multilingualism, and identity. *Annual Review of Applied Linguistics*, 35, 57–80.
Freeman, D., & Johnson, K. E. (1998). Reconceptualizing the knowledge-base of language teacher education. *TESOL Quarterly*, 32(8), 397–417.
Garrett, N. (2009). Computer-assisted language learning trends and issues revisited: Integrating innovation. *The Modern Language Journal*, 93, 719–740.
Garrison, D. R., Anderson, T., & Archer, W. (2000). Critical inquiry in a text-based environment: Computer conferencing in higher education. *The Internet and Higher Education*, 2(2–3), 1–19.
Gee, J. P. & Hayes, E. R. (2011). *Language and learning in the digital age*. New York, NY: Routledge.
Guichon, N. & Hauck, M. (2011). Teacher education research in CALL and CMC: More in demand than ever. *ReCALL*, 23, 187–199.
Habbu, S. (2017). Why ESL teachers do or do not use technology in their classrooms: A replication study (Unpublished Major Research Paper). York University, Toronto, Canada.
Haines, K. J. (2015). Learning to identify and actualize affordances in a new tool. *Language Learning & Technology*, 19(1), 165–180.
Hockly, N., and Dudeney, G. (2018). Current and future digital trends in ELT. *RELC Journal*, 49(2), 164–178.
Hubbard, P. (2008). CALL and the future of language teacher education. *CALICO Journal*, 25(2), 175–188.
Hubbard, P., & Kessler, G. (2017). Language teacher education and technology. In C. Chapelle & S. Sauro (Eds.), *The handbook of technology and second language teaching and learning* (pp. 278–292). Hoboken, NJ: Wiley-Blackwell.
Johnson, K. E. (2006). The sociocultural turn and its challenges for second language teacher education. *TESOL Quarterly*, 40(1), 235–257.
Johnson, K. (2009). *Second language teacher education: A sociocultural perspective*. New York, NY: Routledge.
Johnson, K. E., & Golombek, P. R. (2016). *Mindful L2 teacher education: A sociocultural perspective on cultivating teachers' professional development*. New York, NY: Routledge.
Johnston, K., & Lawrence, G. (2018). A theoretically-informed approach to collaborative EAP learning communities using intensely collaborative technologies. In J. Perren, K. Kelch, J. Byun, S. Cervantes, & S. Safavi (Eds.), *Applications of CALL theory in ESL and EFL environments* (pp. 1–21). Hershey, PA: IGI Global Publishing.
Kessler, G. (2009). Student-initiated attention to form in wiki-based collaborative writing. *Language Learning & Technology*, 13(1), 79–95.
Kessler, G. (2018). Technology and the future of language teaching. *The Foreign Language Annals*, 51, 205–218.
Koehler, M. J., & Mishra, P. (2009). What is technological pedagogical content knowledge? *Contemporary Issues in Technology and Teacher Education*, 9(1), 60–70.

Kramsch, C. (1993). *Context and culture in language teaching*. New York, NY: Oxford University Press.

Kramsch, C., & Thorne, S. (2002). Foreign language learning as global communicative practice. In D. Block & D. Cameron (Eds.), *Language learning and teaching in the age of globalization* (pp. 83–100). London: Routledge.

Lawrence, G. (2013). A working model for intercultural learning and engagement in collaborative online language learning environments. *Intercultural Education*, 24(4), 303–314. doi:10.1080/14675986.2013.809247.

Lawrence, G. (2014, July). The "visioning" dilemma in exploratory CALL research. Selected plenary presented at the International CALL Conference, Antwerp, Belgium.

Lawrence, G. (2018). The role of language teacher beliefs in an increasingly digitalized world. In B. Zou & M. Thomas (Eds.), *Integrating technology into contemporary language learning and teaching* (pp. 140–160). Hershey, PA: IGI Global.

Lawrence, G., Ahmed, F., Cole, C., & Johnston, K. (2020). Not more technology, but more effective technology: Examining the state of technology integration in EAP programs. *RELC Journal*, 51(1), 101–116.

Lawrence, G., Haque, E., & King, J. (2013). *Rationale and recommendations for implementing e-learning in Ontario non-credit adult ESL programs: A feasibility report*. Toronto: The Toronto Catholic District School Board.

Lawrence, G., & Spector-Cohen, E. (2018). Examining international telecollaboration in language teacher education. In D. Tafazoli, E. Gomez Parra, & C. A. Huertas Abril (Eds.), *Cross-cultural perspectives on technology-enhanced language learning* (pp. 322–345). Hershey, PA: IGI Global.

Lawrence, G., Valeo, A., & Irwin, P. (2018). *Review and evaluation of TCDSB e-learning pilots: Online citizenship, flipped French language learning, flipped ESL learning*. Toronto: The Toronto Catholic District School Board.

Leeds-Hurwitz, W. (2013). *Intercultural competences: Conceptual and operational framework*. UNESCO. Retrieved from https://unesdoc.unesco.org/ark:/48223/pf0000219768.

Lin, A. (2013). Toward paradigmatic change in TESOL methodologies: Building plurilingual pedagogies from the ground up. *TESOL Quarterly*, 47(3), 521–545.

Moeller, A. J., & Nugent, K. (2014). Building intercultural competence in the language classroom. In S. Dhonau (Ed.), *Unlock the gateway to communication* (pp. 1–18). Eau Claire, WI: Crown Prints. Retrieved from http://digitalcommons.unl.edu/teachlearnfacpub/161.

O'Dowd, R., Sauro, S., & Spector-Cohen, E. (2019). The role of pedagogical mentoring in virtual exchange. *TESOL Journal*. https://onlinelibrary.wiley.com/doi/epdf/10.1002/tesq.543.

Ogilvie, G. (2013). Promoting principled intercultural education in second language pedagogy: An analysis of various conceptualizations of intercultural. In S. May (Ed.), *LED 2011: Refereed conference proceedings of the 3rd international conference on language, education and diversity* (pp. 1–30). Auckland: University of Auckland.

Piccardo, E. (2013). Plurilingualism and curriculum design: Toward a synergic vision. *TESOL Quarterly*, 47(3), 600–614.

Piccardo, E. (2019a). "We are all (potential) plurilinguals": Plurilingualism as an overarching, holistic concept. *OLBI Working Papers*, 10, 1001–1021. doi:10.18192/olbiwp.v10i0.3825.

Piccardo, E. (2019b). Rethinking plurality in our liquid societies. In F. Bangou, D. Fleming, & M. Waterhouse (Eds.), *Deterritorializing language, teaching, and learning:*

*Deleuzo-Guattarian perspectives on second language education* (pp. 58–86). Ottawa: University of Ottawa Press.

Richards, J. C. (1996). Teachers' maxims in language teaching. *TESOL Quarterly*, 30(2), 281–296.

Richards, J. C. (2015). The changing face of language learning: Learning beyond the classroom. *RELC Journal*, 46(1), 5–22.

Risager, K. (2007). *Language and culture pedagogy: From a national to a transnational paradigm*. Clevedon: Multilingual Matters.

Stockwell, G. (2012). *Computer-assisted language learning: Diversity in research and practice*. Cambridge: Cambridge University Press.

Sykes, J. (2017). Technologies for teaching and learning intercultural competence and interlanguage pragmatics. In C. Chapelle & S. Sauro (Eds.), *The handbook of technology and second language teaching and learning* (pp. 118–133). Hoboken, NJ: Wiley. https://doi.org/10.1002/9781118914069.ch9.

Tour, E. (2015). Digital mindsets: Teachers' technology use in personal life and teaching. *Language Learning & Technology*, 19(3), 124–139.

Van Camp, J. (2016). Tech is upending the ways we write, speak and even think. *Digital Trends*. Retrieved www.digitaltrends.com/features/dt10-language-and-tech/.

Warriner, D. (2017). Theorizing the spatial dimensions and pedagogical implications of transnationalism. *Curriculum Inquiry*, 47(1), 50–61.

White, J. (2016). Local norms in CALL language practice. *International Journal of Computer-Assisted Language Learning and Teaching*, 6(1), 40–54. doi:10.4018/IJCALLT.2016010103.

You, X. (2016). *Cosmopolitan English and transliteracy*. Carbondale, IL: Southern Illinois University Press.

# 9 Telecollaboration as translingual contact zone

## Teacher candidates' translingual negotiation strategies

*Bedrettin Yazan, Babürhan Üzüm, Sedat Akayoglu and Latisha Mary*

### Introduction

Telecollaboration (also known as virtual intercultural exchange) has emerged as a learning activity in language teaching and teacher education as a novel example of transnational educational practices. Telecollaboration is part of the innovative pedagogies introduced by computer-mediated communication technologies in education and mainly involves creating transnational virtual communities to foster intercultural learning (O'Dowd, 2007, 2016). It is defined as an Internet-based collaborative practice in which teachers or teacher educators gather students or teacher candidates from varying ethnolinguistic/national backgrounds and geographically remote places in order to discuss intercultural issues and learn (Guth & Helm, 2010). Initially telecollaboration was used in language teaching settings to support language learners' linguistic and cultural developments (Chun, 2011), but recently teacher educators from different educational contexts adopted this virtual tool to construct transnational communities to enhance teacher candidates' learning (Dooly, 2009). Earlier research on telecollaboration in language teacher education explores teacher candidates' intercultural learning through virtual exchanges (e.g., Çiftçi & Savaş, 2018; Uzum, Akayoglu, & Yazan, 2020), creating online professional communities and collaborative learning of teaching methods (e.g., Dooly, 2011; Dooly & Sadler, 2013, 2020; O'Dowd, Sauro, & Spector-Cohen, 2020), teachers' cultural identities (Menard-Warwick, 2008; Menard-Warwick, Heredia-Herrera, & Palmer, 2013; Tanghe & Park, 2016), and the ways in which teacher candidates discuss critical issues of social justice in relation to language education (Schreiber, 2019; Uzum, Yazan, Avineri, & Akayoglu, 2019). O'Dowd (2016) identified this last strand as one of the areas which needed more attention from teacher educators and researchers in order to return to telecollaboration's original transformative learning goal to foster critical intercultural conversations that attend to social inequities and injustices in participants' contexts with particular emphasis on sociocultural, political, economic, and historical issues. Therefore, we designed the current telecollaborative project as a response to O'Dowd's call. Additionally, we endeavored to move culture teaching from national to transnational orientation as proposed by Kumaravadivelu (2008) and Risager (2007) and explored by Menard-Warwick (2008) and Menard-Warwick et al. (2013).

We conceptualize the virtual spaces in which telecollaboration participants, teacher candidates in this case, communicate as "translingual contact zones" (Canagarajah, 2013). Our project emerged from the transnational professional relationships amongst four TESOL teacher educators (who are the authors of this chapter) and intended to construct similar relationships for their teacher candidates. In that sense, the telecollaborative project is situated at the nexus of translingual and transnational relationships because "language contact, code meshing, and shuttling between repertoires are not an option, but a necessity, for voice and identity for everyone in the context of transnational relations" (Canagarajah, 2018, p. 41). Within their groups of six, the participants in this study, 112 teacher candidates from three different educational contexts (France, Turkey, United States), engaged in conversations on social justice topics revolving around immigration, (language) education, gender, sexual orientation, and ethnicity. Their conversations included translingual negotiation strategies, namely, envoicing, recontextualization, interactional, and entextualization (Canagarajah, 2013). Reporting on the data from three groups, this chapter addresses the following research questions: How do teacher candidates negotiate and construct cultural identities in online translingual contact zones? How do they use translingual negotiation strategies as they negotiate and construct these identities?

Before moving forward, we want to underscore the fact that we situate this project at the intersection of our practices as teacher educators who are committed to educating teachers with social justice orientations and our research endeavors as researchers of transnational TESOL teacher education. We believe that the dual role of this project makes it even more meaningful and is also framed within the self-study research (Sharkey & Peercy, 2018) since we view our involvement in this project as a significant part of our growth as transnational teacher educators.

## Methods

This qualitative study draws upon a more extensive study that included two-semester-long telecollaboration projects amongst three teacher education programs located in France, Turkey, and the United States. The researchers adopted a qualitative inquiry approach with a naturalistic interpretive paradigm (Lincoln & Guba, 1985). Based on this approach, the study focused on understanding the translingual negotiation strategies utilized by teacher candidates in the virtual translingual contact zones.

### *Context and participants*

The 112 teacher candidates from three teacher education programs in three different countries, namely France, Turkey, and the United States, participated in this project in the fall semester of the 2017–18 academic year. The participants were teacher candidates preparing to work with English language learners in their respective university-based teacher education programs. Of these teacher candidates, 43 were from France, 34 were from Turkey, and 35 were from the United States. The ones in the US university were in their third year in the program in which they were trained to teach content area courses, such as Language Arts, Social Studies, Math, and Science in sheltered instruction classrooms for English language learners. The teacher candidates in Turkey were in their third and fourth years to be teachers of English as a foreign language in K-12 public schools in Turkey. After they graduate, they take an exam to be assigned to public schools by the Ministry of Education, and most newly graduated start working in rural areas. As for the teacher candidates in France, they were in their first year of a Master's in Education preparing for the national competitive teaching exam which takes place at the end of the first year of the Master's program. Although they were trained in all subject areas they were expected to teach English as a foreign language in public primary schools in France. At the time of the study, all teacher candidates were enrolled in teacher education courses offered by their programs. Table 9.1 presents a list of participants whose data were included in the current chapter.

*Table 9.1* Participants from three university-based teacher education programs

| *Group* | *Participant pseudonyms* | *Institution pseudonyms* |
|---|---|---|
| Group 1 | Aysegul | Northern Anatolian University |
| | Baize | University of Northeastern France |
| | Denise | City State University |
| | Bastina | University of Northeastern France |
| | Aslihan | Northern Anatolian University |
| | Becky (Rebecca) | City State University |
| | Gisele | University of Northeastern France |
| Group 2 | Ajda | Northern Anatolian University |
| | Camille | University of Northeastern France |
| | Clemence | University of Northeastern France |
| | Lily | City State University |
| | Beyza | Northern Anatolian University |
| | Molly | City State University |
| | Seraphine | University of Northeastern France |
| Group 3 | Banu | Northern Anatolian University |
| | Clément | University of Northeastern France |
| | Colette | University of Northeastern France |
| | Mary | City State University |
| | Bahar | Northern Anatolian University |
| | Marta | City State University |
| | Clairette | University of Northeastern France |

### *Data collection procedure*

In the larger study, we used different types of student work produced in this project as data sources in order to maintain the data triangulation and consistency across three contexts. That is, we had students (a) write pre-project expectations and post-project reflections essays; (b) asynchronously discuss the topics of culture in the global context, immigration, gender, religion, ethnicity, and education; and (c) conduct two video-conference interviews with their peers in their groups of six. For the purposes of this study investigating asynchronous virtual translingual discussions, we used online discussions from 18 participants in three groups as the main data sources. However, to contextualize the project for the reader who might be interested in implementing a telecollaboration, the details of the pre-project expectations and post-essays are provided in Table 9.2.

The online discussions lasted for six weeks, and the teacher candidates were asked to discuss six critical topics, namely, culture in the global context, immigration, gender, religion, ethnicity, and education. We grouped teacher candidates in groups of six or seven on a learning management system, Edmodo (www.edmodo.com), and posted the initiating questions to all groups. One teacher educator was assigned to each group as a facilitator (Muller-Hartmann & Kurek, 2016; O'Dowd et al., 2020). Table 9.3 shows the prompts.

The participants also interviewed their peers in small groups using a synchronous video conferencing tool, Zoom (https://zoom.us). They prepared interview questions before meeting online and these questions were mostly geared toward gathering more detailed information about their peers' cultures. These sessions were recorded and uploaded to YouTube by the participants and shared as unlisted so that researchers could watch these sessions.

Apart from its benefits for teacher education, the implementation of this transnational teacher education project included challenges for us as teacher educators and facilitators and our teacher candidates as participants. These challenges were pertinent to the individuals, project design, socio-institutional context, and intercultural interactions (Hauck, 2007; Helm, 2015; O'Dowd & Eberbach, 2004; O'Dowd & Ritter, 2006).

### *Data analysis*

Analyzing the data, we considered the virtual spaces in telecollaboration as translingual contact zones. We focused on the teacher candidates' uses of translingual negotiation strategies, namely, "envoicing, recontextualization, interactional, and entextualization" (Canagarajah, 2013, p. 79). *Envoicing* is a set of strategies that speakers employ to "accentuate their differences from others by moving away from uniform uses and shared norms" (p. 89). In other words, speakers perform unique identities and make strategic linguistic choices to achieve persuasive advantage in a given interaction. Envoicing might include using L1 while communicating in L2, or coining a non-existing L2 word drawing from their L1. Speakers might perform gendered identities and use unique persuasive strategies for effective communication. In *recontextualization*, speakers contextualize their talk and create frames to

*Table 9.2* Prompts for pre-project expectations and post-project essays

| | | | |
|---|---|---|---|
| Pre-project expectations | October 9–15, 2017 | Pre-essay: initial expectations and language learning history (and how they see culture impacting their lives). Students briefly respond to following questions. | 1. Do you speak an additional language(s)? If so, how did you learn it? What were your school and/or learning experience like? In what situations do you use this language? Please describe briefly.<br>2. What do you think about the role of culture in learning an additional language and/or learning in the classroom in general? How did you learn about the culture for your additional language? What do you think are some good practices to teach culture? Are you planning to integrate culture in your classes? If yes, how? How do you plan to teach it in the future?<br>3. What do you think about the role of culture in learning and teaching? How do your culture and your students' culture impact learning and teaching in the schools?<br>4. What do you expect to learn in this telecollaboration experience about the United States, Turkey, and France? What do you already know about these places? What do you think a teacher's life is like in these places?<br>5. What kind of language teacher do you expect to be? What qualities best describe your identity as a teacher of English language learners/teacher in general? |
| Post-essay | November 27–December 3, 2017 | Post-essay: final reflections (revisiting the initial expectations) and evaluating their cultural learning throughout the project. | 1. Please briefly describe what you learned about the United States, Turkey, and France throughout the telecollaboration activity. You can focus on parts that affirmed your current beliefs, stood out to you in some way, surprised you, or challenged your understanding.<br>2. How do you think the life of a teacher in the United States, France, and Turkey compares to yours? What similarities or differences did you observe, concerning the life of a teacher and their expectations of what it is going to be like to be a teacher in their respective contexts?<br>3. How do you think this telecollaborative experience can contribute to your becoming a teacher? Please briefly describe what knowledge, skills, and dispositions (values) the experience might have helped you develop. What else could have been done to better improve your competences as an emerging teacher? |

*Table 9.3* Prompts for weekly asynchronous group discussions

| | | | |
|---|---|---|---|
| Week 1 | October 16–23, 2017 | Introductions<br>Culture in a global context | • Please introduce yourself briefly to the other group members. You can write about your name, city, hobbies/interests, and future aspirations as a teacher.<br>• Culture in a global context: How do you define the role of culture in the globalizing world? What is the role of culture in schools? Is it possible to teach culture in schools? If so, what are the best practices to learn and teach culture addressing the needs of such global environments? |
| Week 2 | October 23–29, 2017 | English language learners/ foreign language learners<br>Refugees and immigration | • How would you describe English language learners/foreign language learners in general in your future classrooms? What is their background, and what are their experiences like? How is linguistic and cultural diversity taken into account at the schools in your context?<br>• How is your country managing the process of refugees and immigration? What are some public and administrative attitudes about this? How would you best describe your own position in this topic? Please watch Melissa Flemming's interview with TED radio on refugees and displaced identities and briefly describe your understanding here along with its implications in your own context. |
| Week 3 | October 30–November 5, 2017 | Culture/ethnicity/ nationality/religion | • What factors or elements do you think makes up culture? What is the role of language in culture and identity? What role does ethnicity, nationality, and religion play in people's creating an identity? How would you best describe your cultural identity? |
| Week 4 | November 6–12, 2017 | Gender in culture | • What do you think about the role of gender in culture? Were your experiences as a teacher candidate affected by your gender? What do you think about the status of gender equality in your environment? What do you think can be done for better gender equality in general? |

| | | | |
|---|---|---|---|
| Week 5 | November 13–19, 2017 | Education system | • What do you think about the education system in your environment? What are some strengths, weaknesses, opportunities, and threats in your education system (SWOT analysis)? How do you think the current education system has served you and is serving current students? What do you intend to do to improve the learning experiences of your future students? |
| Week 6 | November 20–26, 2017 | Critical topics in education | • There are a variety of topics in education that can be addressed critically. Please choose one of these topics and reflect on its impact in your immediate environment and how they can be addressed, including what you can personally do as a teacher. The topics include: ableism (the education system suitable for the needs who are able-bodied, but are not suitable for those with disabilities); the role of social media on teaching and learning; culture of protest and demonstration; inequities in education and the need for social justice (locational inequities, gender inequities, social class) |

achieve appropriate footing. This strategy draws from two major constructs: framing and footing. Originally developed by Goffman (1981), framing establishes the discourse context of a text or talk while footing can be defined as the (dis) agreement and (mis)alignment of speakers in the interaction. Speakers may communicate from different cultural norms and expectations and may need to adjust their strategies in order to achieve intelligibility.

*Interactional* strategies include collaborative (e.g., agreement, harmony) and reciprocal (e.g., disagreement) strategies. Speakers may not always be interested in establishing harmony, but may also deploy reciprocal strategies to show their disalignment. In order to express themselves or to understand their interlocutors better, speakers use negotiation strategies, such as clarification requests, comprehension checks, and follow-up questions. The communication objective is not necessarily agreement, but intelligibility. Therefore, some mistakes may be ignored with a "let-it-pass" principle, and clarification questions would be reserved for fragile moments in which an accurate understanding of the topic would be critical (Pitzl, 2010). A fragile moment is associated with delicate subjects in which different interpretations may drastically change the communicative outcome. The final category proposed by Canagarajah is *entextualization*. This strategy is commonly used when speakers or writers edit, omit, or revise their grammatical and rhetorical choices. Speakers may carefully monitor their speech and choose their words effectively, showing awareness of the different competencies of their interlocutors. Speakers show sensitivity to the norms and framing of the translingual contact zone and preemptively differentiate their language to achieve intelligibility.

We adopted this taxonomy while coding the data in order to understand the negotiation strategies teacher candidates adopted during their conversations. In the first stage, the researchers assigned open codes to the interaction data. They provided their code suggestions while explaining the translingual negotiation of meaning strategies used by the participants. In the second stage, these open codes were examined; some codes were merged, and some codes were renamed so that the number of codes decreased. Finally, these codes were compared with the codes in the literature, with the taxonomy created by Canagarajah (2013) in this case.

## Findings

The findings suggest that the telecollaborative space provided to the teacher candidates in France, Turkey, and the United States served as a translingual contact zone and opened up discursive spaces for teacher candidates to engage on translingual negotiation strategies as they discussed matters of social justice. The teacher candidates employed: (a) envoicing strategies as they narrated their cultural identities; (b) recontextualization strategies in an effort to create multicultural framing and create a collaborative environment; (c) interactional strategies through clarification requests when communication broke down; and (d) entextualization strategies in which they anticipated gaps and preemptively explained cultural and procedural differences across their respective contexts.

### *Envoicing: narrating self through hierarchies, time, and place*

In their telecollaborative conversations, teacher candidates deployed envoicing strategies and projected their identities and personal histories in their narratives by creating hierarchical orders and situating themselves in time and place. Teacher candidates envoiced a variety of identities (e.g., teacher candidate, female, sister, daughter, religious, artist, activist, etc.) and these identities were often negotiated in a seemingly hierarchical order of importance. Sometimes, they self-corrected (e.g., interactional strategy) and edited the order of importance by situating the said elements close to or further from themselves. For example, in excerpt 1[1] below, Aslihan leads with "religion" as the first important factor shaping one's (or her) cultural identity and gives examples illustrating its importance, but later introduces family as the most important factor, marked with the discourse marker "actually" in line 13: "maybe family is the one which matters most."

*Excerpt 1: envoicing hierarchies and place in narratives*

| *Line* | *Transcript* |
|---|---|
| 1 | Aslihan: Actually, there are countless elements of culture but I think the most important |
| 2 | ones are religion, hometown or the place that you grow up, family, language |
| 3 | and your educational level. By saying educational level I don't mean your |
| 4 | school, it is not about that. It is about what you read, what you see. First of all |
| 5 | religion, mostly it determines what is wrong, what is sin and what is good. For |
| 6 | example in Turkey drinking is bad as it is a sin. In our country you cannot buy |
| 7 | a drink after 10pm, it is forbidden. If our religion hadn't forbidden it, you might |
| 8 | have drunk it with relief. Secondly, your hometown or the place you grown up |
| 9 | determines your identity also. Even it determines how you dress. As for my |
| 10 | part I grew up in Karabuk, a small city. In there if you wear mini skirt, people |
| 11 | may judge you due to your clothe but if you wear the same in İzmir, seaside |
| 12 | city, it is quite normal. I mean even cities have their own values and perspectives. |
| 13 | Another important element is family. Actually, maybe family is the one which |
| 14 | matters most. It decide how behave how you react the things happen arounds you, |
| 15 | how you see the outer world and so on. Even it determines which team you |
| 16 | support. I have only few friends who support different team from their families. To |
| 17 | talk more general your family gives you an identity outline to you and it is up to |
| 18 | you how you fill in the blanks. You fill these blanks according to things you read, |
| 19 | you saw, you heard, the people that you know. So I'm trying to say it is not up to |
| 20 | choose where we born but it |
| 21 | is up to us to improve ourselves, to fill in our blanks |

In this example, Aslihan explains her cultural identity outlining the elements that helped shape her identity. The order these elements that emerged is not haphazard, but represents the hierarchies of importance in how much of Aslihan's identity relies on these factors. This hierarchy becomes more explicit when she employs an interactional strategy and edits this order in line 13 and 14 by bringing family before religion. Religion can still be a second most important factor for her since she gives detailed examples on it. A third factor that comes up is place and she presents herself as someone from a small city which observes religious norms more closely than a larger coastal city in lines 9–12. Aslihan's hometown is Karabuk, but she studies in Bolu where her university is located. Her hometown and the associated values still seem to be with her in her new context and becomes part of her identity as she envoices these places as critical aspects of her cultural narrative.

In a similar example, Camille, a teacher candidate from France, employs envoicing strategies by placing herself and her family in time, and narrates different time periods of France throughout her history. These periods become landmarks or critical reference points in her narrative as she compares France when she was a child, a teenager, a college student, and as an adult now.

*Excerpt 2: envoicing time in narratives*

*Line* *Transcript*

Camille: Hi everybody! My name's Camille and I come from France. I live in a little village in the North East of the country. I'm 44 years old, so, as you can see, I'm not a young student. I have 2 daughters: Fabienne, who is 17 and Francine, who is 12. I decided to go back to school to become a teacher for young children (before middle school). I am a nurse since 2010 (at that time, when I was 34, I also decided to go back to school to become a nurse). The job is too hard and in hospitals we have a lot of strains that made me become almost sick. So I decided to change once again. I have always hesitated between a job in Health care and Education. When I was a young student in the 90's I studied English and American literature and civilization. I tried not to forget all the things I studied but it's very difficult because I haven't practiced English for a lot of years. Today, I hope I will get my exam. I would like to be a teacher who will be able to find the right balance between sense of humor and firmness. I will try to be tolerant, caring and approachable for the pupils to help them becoming confident. Concerning the culture, I think today it's more accessible, especially, thanks to the social networks. We can meet people from all over the world. I like learning about foreign civilizations and other cultures and traditions.

...

Camille: The mixture of cultures is the best way to live in peace. I love learning about other traditions and meeting people from different culture. My father is Italian and he came to France with his parents when he was 7. Unfortunately, I don't speak Italian but Italian culture is a part of me! A part of my Italian grand father went to New-York in the 50s, but I have no contact with them. So I can say that the story of my family is part of American story!;-)

*a part of my Italian grand father's family

....

Camille: My daughters are kind teenagers now and are quite autonomous. So it's easier than when I studied in order to become a nurse (10 years ago)! And my "husband" is very nice too! Concerning my painting and sculpting, I began these activities for only 4 or 5 years but it's difficult to find time.

In lines 1–6, Camille envoices her identity through place and time by stating that she lives in a little village in the North East of France, is 44 years old, a mother of two, and a nurse since 2010. In her narrative, the time periods when certain events took place in her life are important and are marked with reference points. In lines 14–16, Camille appreciates the social networking opportunities that are more readily available today, implicitly compared to what she had experienced when she was a college student for the first time in the 1990s. In response to a telecollaborative partner, Camille brings up her grandparents, envoicing an identity of immigrant background and creating historicity to her cultural identity in lines 19–23. In another response to a different peer who commented that it must be difficult raising two daughters, Camille responds with a comparison between having two daughters now and 10 years ago when she was a nursing student. In a different exchange, Lily responds to Camille with the words: "It is amazing that you have personal firsthand knowledge of the ways that France was in the past and have something to compare it to." While many teacher candidates integrated time and place in their envoicing strategies to various degrees, Camille's envoicing is remarkably different since she frequently makes references to time and place together, which points to the spatio-temporality of cultural identity negotiation. Other teacher candidates use time references for their childhoods and space references to outline the different places they have lived in, but Camille makes time references for France in general, reflecting on its evolution throughout time as she has witnessed it.

### *Recontextualization: multicultural framing, communication, and collaboration*

In their telecollaborative conversations, teacher candidates also engaged in recontextualization strategies, by creating multicultural framing, aligning with their interlocutors, establishing rapport, and by preparing their interlocutors for the possible cultural differences and norms. The most common strategy is managing topics. Teacher candidates usually wanted to express their agreement with their interlocutors. They did so by explicitly agreeing with them, bringing up similar experiences or opinions from their context, and asking follow-up questions to learn more about their experience. Sometimes, they did not write additional comments or raise follow-up questions, but usually wrote that they agreed, probably in order to indicate they have read the posts and are engaged in the group conversation.

In their early posts, teacher candidates created multicultural framing and set the stage for a harmonious exchange. They did so by stating their commitment to multicultural education and openness to learn about other cultures. These values became the parameters of the exchanges and created a framing of intercultural communication, as the remaining topics were discussed from this perspective and positionality. While their openness to cultural differences and commitment to multicultural education were critical in establishing footing, they also used other strategies such as small talk and interactional strategies to maintain this footing. In the example below, Denise opens with such commitment and openness.

*Excerpt 3: creating multicultural framing*

| Transcript |
|---|
| Denise:...When multiple cultures come together, I feel like it is eye opening experience! We can all learn from different peoples perspectives, experiences, and view points! Everyone is unique and brings different strengths to the table and in different ways, so by coming together we can strengthen and broaden our own knowledge and schema. I have personally already been impacted by this, simply from being in class with students from different cultural backgrounds. I love learning from others, seeing the different ways that they may learn, hearing about the daily experiences that they have, and overall hearing things from other peoples perspectives! |

A second strategy was to use safe-talk or small-talk which help the interlocutors have productive conversations without offending anyone. While the prompts were often meant to challenge teacher candidates to grapple with difficult topics, they were able to still discuss these topics after establishing the multicultural framing and building on common grounds that they identified in their early conversations. Teacher candidates did so by praising each other, supporting their comments, and creating a third space in which the most important goal for interlocutors becomes intelligibility and therefore they can transform a conflict into one of collaboration and learning (Gutierrez, 2008). This underlying theme of "intelligibility" and "communication" was maintained throughout their collaboration. In the conversation below, Bastina's peers support her and do not mind her mistakes.

*Excerpt 4: recontextualizing through alignment and collaboration*

| Transcript |
|---|
| Bastina: Being French I can talk about my own experience about English language Learning. Learning English has never been traumatic for me but it was never easy and again now. Besides, I apologize for my mistakes. I think that the hardest when we learn a foreign language is to speak in front of the class. Indeed, we are scared that others make fun of our accent. For my part, I have chance because I haven't problems concerning my pronunciation. In France there isn't problem with immigration and refugees. I think it's normal because everyone can move in the country that he wants. |
| Aysegul: Hi, be cool about your pronounce and grammar. Because, English is a lingua-franca and the most important thing is communication |
| Aslihan: Don't worry about your mistakes and don't forget that mistakes are signs of learning! We all can make mistakes |
| Becky: You are doing a great job |
| Bastina: Thanks for your understanding ώ |

In this example, when Bastina apologizes for her "mistakes," her peers renegotiate and adjust the norms and values in the conversation by refocusing Bastina's goal of grammatical correctness to the intelligibility and providing encouragement. Such alignment as a footing helps the translingual participants understand each other and maintain rapport here through collaboration and safe-talk (i.e., conversations that are not part of the main objective of the interaction).

### *Interactional strategies: clarification requests and elaborations*

After establishing rapport in the early interactions and maintaining the established parameters of multicultural framing, teacher candidates employed interactional strategies when communication broke down and especially at fragile moments in which a "let-it-pass" principle was not appropriate, and the uptake hinged on a few possible interpretations. In those moments, teacher candidates asked clarification questions, and their interlocutors elaborated on these points using entextualization strategies. In the example below, teacher candidates address a tense topic and exchange their ideas around immigration and the refugee crisis in their respective contexts.

*Excerpt 5: clarification requests on language differences*

| *Transcript* |
|---|
| Becky: ...There is a lot of fear regarding refugees and immigration in America. Due to attacks, regardless of it is related or not, has caused hesitation within public officials. In recent news, President Trump was in great criticism about the Muslim Ban. This is a great example about the fear I speak of. This was a ban on visas to the US to nationals from seven countries: Iraq, Iran, Libya, Somalia, Sudan, Syria and Yemen, which are all Muslim-majority nations. In recent news as well, the Trump administration has also decided to end the program DACA, Deferred Action for Childhood Arrivals. DACA was a program that allowed for undocumented children and young adults to have a work permit and social security that was established by the Obama Administration. These things would allow children of immigrants that were brought to the United States undocumented to have a possibility of life. These are children that grew up as Americans and are American in every single aspect except on paper. My position is that regardless of what the American government says, I fully support refugees and immigrants. There are qualities that they possess that need to be harnessed and celebrated. There is resiliency and bravery in them. They are humans and our duty as humans is to help one another. As a future educator, I want to accept and do everything in my power to help refugee and immigrant children to help them develop as students and people. There is benefit of having more than one culture, language, backgrounds in a classroom. This helps everyone grow beyond biased views and be more aware and appreciate differences. |
| Aysegul: What do you think about the attitude of your country? In terms of the ABD nation. Are they like-minded with Trump? |

(*continued*)

| *Line* | *Transcript* |
|---|---|
| 25 | Becky: What is an ABD nation? As for the country I think there is a huge split in |
| 26 | the middle. Trump has created such separation through his policies, tweets, actions, |
| 27 | and |
| 28 | attitude. There are supporters and non-supporters. As of now both sides are |
| 29 | represented in the country. |
| 30 | Aslihan: What do you mean by saying 'celebrate it'? I didn't get it. Could you |
| 31 | please explain? |
| 32 | Becky: By informing students, parents, and faculty you are creating awareness of |
| 33 | other cultures where they can be respected and understood and therefore creating |
| 34 | an environment where there is tolerance for differences. |

In this example, Becky envoices the identity of a caring teacher and supports her position with a well-researched narrative. As an entextualization strategy which indicates her critical cultural awareness, she explains the DACA program to an unfamiliar audience along with its abbreviation, definition, history, and implications in lines 6–12. In response, Aysegul wants clarification on whether people in the United States are in agreement with the president in lines 23–24. To Becky, this is a critical and fragile question. The part in the question "are they like-minded with Trump?" is not grammatically "correct," but it is understandable. However, there is still one unknown element in the question "ABD nation" (i.e., ABD is the United States in Turkish). She first seeks clarification on what ABD nation meant in line 24 and continues to address the question as much as she understood. Becky first rejects the generalization in the question "the attitude of your country," employing a reciprocal strategy and explains that there are mixed opinions, supporters, and nonsupporters. She presents a balanced view, capturing the complexity of the problem and acknowledging the heterogeneity of the population while still operating within the principles of multicultural education. Aslihan joins in the conversation in line 30 and seeks clarification on the word "celebrate" in line 17. It is possible that Aslihan took this word at its first meaning and tried to make sense of how a celebration was appropriate there. This was probably a moment fragile enough for her that she raised this question and sought clarification. In lines 32–34, Becky further explains its meaning in context with its implications. Becky did not simply redefine the word "celebrate" or provided a dictionary definition, but provided a contextualized elaboration on the word.

Teacher candidates employed interactional strategies in both collaborative and reciprocal manners. The "let-it-pass principle" was commonly used and language errors were ignored as long as the message was understood. Clarification requests were employed only when communication broke down during fragile moments. The clarification requests were sometimes used on language differences, but also with cultural and procedural differences across the different contexts. In the example below, Aslihan is trying to make sense of how teachers are getting certified in the US context.

*Excerpt 6: clarification requests on procedural differences*

| Line | Transcript |
|---|---|
| | Denise:...I'm a Education major at Sam Houston State University, and I am trying to become an elementary school teacher! I hope to teach 2nd grade students one day! |
| | Aslihan: You wrote 'I am trying to become an elementary school teacher'. I wonder do you have a special reason for that or you are educated to be only an elementary school teacher? |
| | Denise: When we want to become teachers, and are a part of the education program here, we have to pick a specific grade and subject that we want to teach and then get certified for that grade (after we have taken all of our college level classes). I personally love little kids so I want to teach elementary! So I am getting certified to teach 1st through 6th grade! |
| | Aslihan: Wow! In Turkey we are educated for elementary, secondary and high schools. It is the government that decides which grade we go to. I liked your system. Thank you for enlightening |

In this excerpt, Aslihan's lack of understanding does not stem from a language issue, but of a difference in the teacher education procedures in these contexts. In response, Denise explains her experience in a detailed and explicit manner, which reestablishes the footing for the interaction to be maintained.

### *Entextualization: cultural and procedural differences explained*

Compared to the first three strategies, entextualization was not as commonly used by the teacher candidates. This is possibly due to the fact that teacher candidates were still learning about their peers and were not necessarily able to preemptively differentiate their language for their interlocutors. In the above examples presented in Excerpt 5 and Excerpt 6 both Denise and Becky are directed a clarification question. In their response, they choose their words carefully and explain in greater detail, monitoring their speech with sensitivity to the different competencies of their interlocutors. They effectively employ entextualization strategies so that their response to the clarification question may effectively address the question.

In another example, Becky anticipated that her name may be unfamiliar to her peers and provided its pronunciation: "My name is Rebecca, but I go by Becky (Bek-kie)." Since the teacher candidates in the United States were native English speakers, and those in Turkey and France were intermediate to advanced speakers, the let-it-pass principle was applied frequently and there were not many communication break-downs as much as language was concerned. However, there were some concepts that teacher candidates anticipated to be perceived unfamiliar or difficult to understand for their interlocutors. For these narratives, teacher candidates provided explanations preemptively before a communication break-down happens. The first example is the DACA law that was presented in Excerpt 5 in which Becky carefully explained the law to an audience who may never have heard of it. Another example is presented in Excerpt 7 below.

*Excerpt 7: preemptively explaining perceived unfamiliar concepts*

| *Line* | *Transcript* |
|---|---|
| 1 | Aysegul: Culture is like soup. It includes lots of different and important ingredients. |
| 2 | Each of them gives a remarkable flover. What are they, ingredients? Firstly, |
| 3 | language brings close a nation. Thanks to it, some significant things are hanged |
| 4 | down. From that perspective, what we share is another part of a culture. Some |
| 5 | ethical values, common history, religion, tradition etc. are transfered consciously or |
| 6 | subconciously. For example, we kiss an elder person due to respect. However, we |
| 7 | don't know the basic reason of that custom. We see, and we do subconsciously. |
| 8 | Even, when we interrogate the reason, we can be a rebellious. While the religion |
| 9 | play a significant role in some |
| 10 | situations, sometimes that is adverse. For example, there is a notion "nazar" may be |
| 11 | "evil eye" for you. This is a notion in Islam, but the a glass bead for "nazar" is |
| 12 | dependent on Shamanism. In other words, there are lots of old but continuant item |
| 13 | in our culture. Morever, the twenty-first century technology have affected us also. |
| 14 | In a short meaning, a culture changes day by day. In that alteration, we try to find a |
| 15 | identity. So as so, a culture shape lots of people. For instance, the national holidays |
| 16 | reminds us our history, and they give a national conscience. Another one is cuisine |
| 17 | culture determine our taste as from babyhood. If I figure out my country and |
| 18 | culture in some words, I say "the harmony of colours". We are both very different |
| 19 | from each other and the same. There are countless common points which make us |
| 20 | a colourful flower bouquet. |
| 21 | Becky: I love your idea of culture being like soup because it is made up of so many |
| 22 | ingredients! |
| 23 | Denise: I love your reference of soup with all the different ingredients as well and |
| 24 | the colorful flower bouquet! |

In this exchange, Aysegul explains some cultural elements and brings up concepts that are central to her culture, but might be unfamiliar to her interlocutors. She shows awareness of these differences and relates the new concept to what she thinks exists in her interlocutors' culture. In line 10, she explains that "nazar" might be "evil eye" in her interlocutors' culture. As she continues, she introduces the soup and flower metaphors that symbolize culture, and her interlocutors also comment on these metaphors. There are some ungrammatical parts in Aysegul's narrative, but overall she can communicate her main message and it receives uptake, as both Becky and Denise agree with the diversity point made with the soup and flower metaphors. In lines 8–12, Aysegul underplays the role of religion in her culture and explains the overlapping historicity of the cultural elements in an effort to portray the plurality of these cultural practices. This exchange took place later in the semester and it is possible that Aysegul made this comment on religion in case her interlocutors started to think that religion is extremely important throughout Turkey. Therefore, in order to portray a complex and multiculturally rich image of Turkey, as supported by the symbols of soup and flowers, she had to address and play down the "one religion, one people" notion in an effort to better explain the plurality and historicity of these cultural practices. We base this argument on our in-class observations that teacher candidates were concerned with the uptake they produce and how their narratives were being received by their interlocutors. They frequently brought up these points during in-class discussions and made comparisons across members of other groups.

## Discussion and conclusion

This chapter drew upon the asynchronous online discussion data from a telecollaborative project involving participants from three teacher education programs (France, Turkey, and the United States) and addressed the following questions: How do teacher candidates negotiate and construct cultural identities in online translingual contact zones? How do they use translingual negotiation strategies as they negotiate and construct these identities? As a transnational practice of TESOL teacher education, telecollaboration provides unique discursive and experiential space for participants to engage in social-justice topics with peers from different educational contexts in translingual contact zones. Our analysis suggests that participants identity negotiation and construction in such contact zones are mediated by their use of translingual negotiation strategies. The examples analyzed in this chapter illustrate the intertwined nature of language use and identity negotiation, which leads us to assert that understanding learning and identity in telecollaboration requires specific attention to language use.

Telecollaborative projects, especially in teacher education, are designed with several foci, that is, supporting intercultural competence development (Dooly, 2011), professional teacher-learning/collaboration (e.g., Tanghe & Park, 2016), cultural identity construction (Menard-Warwick, 2008), and social justice teacher education (Uzum et al., 2019). Earlier projects highlight the use and improvement of languages through virtual exchange based on various methods of communication. However, our study specifically focused on the role of language in such exchanges, especially discussing "tough" topics and explored the relationship between identity and translingual negotiation strategies. Our findings support the argument that participants' translingual skills are essential in engaging in successful intercultural conversations on social justice matters and telecollaboration should incorporate a dual focus on targeted content (e.g., intercultural competence) and translingual development. This argument points to the intersection between transnationalism and translingualism, that is, telecollaboration opens up spaces beyond physically and ideologically patrolled national borders and brings "the languages in contact, generating new forms and meanings in synergy" (Canagarajah, 2018, p. 42).

Telecollaboration gathers individuals from diverse linguistic and cultural backgrounds in a virtual space where these individuals navigate and negotiate sociocultural in-betweenness. They mobilize all semiotic resources (Blommaert, 2010) they have brought to this space and engage in collaborative meaning-making which is rife with complex and innovative uses of these resources. However, participants are not always aware of the ways in which they (need to) use translingual negotiation strategies to mobilize their semiotic resources and to enhance the transnational relationships they establish within the virtual translingual spaces. We suggest that teacher educators should integrate activities in telecollaboration to raise participants' awareness about translingual negotiation strategies and explicitly attend to the intricate relationship between language and identity. Furthermore, directing teacher candidates' attention to translingual practices can provide them sociolinguistic awareness and learning experience. Since the translingual approach adopts a conceptual lens that aims to disrupt the monolingual ideologies and the associated sociocultural hierarchization in language use, such micro-level language focus in telecollaboration can help its original transformative goal to educate participants for criticality and social justice in education. This sociolinguistic learning could transfer to teacher candidates' future language teaching practices.

In closing, telecollaboration affords a unique virtual translingual contact zone for complex, novel, and creative language use and holds a significant potential for transnational TESOL teacher education practices. Teacher educators can best use this potential if telecollaborative projects, connecting teacher candidates in an online platform and assigning them some collaborative tasks, are complemented with an explicit language focus on the ways participants' use of translingual negotiation strategies influence their intercultural and professional learning experiences in such virtual contact zones.

## Note

1 Transcripts are presented in unedited form for accuracy. Names and places are replaced with pseudonyms.

## References

Blommaert, J. (2010). *The sociolinguistics of globalization*. Cambridge: Cambridge University Press.

Canagarajah, S. (2013). *Translingual practice: Global Englishes and cosmopolitan relations*. New York, NY: Routledge.

Canagarajah, S. (2018). Transnationalism and translingualism: How they are connected. In X. You (Ed.), *Transnational writing education: Theory, history, and practice* (pp. 57–76). New York, NY: Routledge.

Chun, D. M. (2011). Developing intercultural communicative competence through online exchanges. *CALICO Journal*, 28(2), 392–419.

Çiftçi, E. Y., & Savaş, P. (2018). The role of telecollaboration in language and intercultural learning: A synthesis of studies published between 2010 and 2015. *ReCALL*, 30(3), 278–298.

Dooly, M. A. (2009). New competencies in a new era? Examining the impact of a teacher training project. *ReCALL*, 21(3), 352–369.

Dooly, M. A. (2011). Crossing the intercultural borders into 3rd space culture(s): Implications for teacher education in the twenty-first century. *Language and Intercultural Communication*, 11(4), 319–337.

Dooly, M. A., & Sadler, R. (2013). Filling in the gaps: Linking theory and practice through telecollaboration in teacher education. *ReCALL*, 25(1), 4–29.

Dooly, M., & Sadler, R. (2020). "If you don't improve, what's the point?" Investigating the impact of a "flipped" online exchange in teacher education. *ReCALL*, 32(1), 4–24.

Goffman, E. (1981). *Forms of talk*. Philadelphia, PA: University of Pennsylvania Press.

Guth, S., & Helm, F. (Eds.) (2010). *Telecollaboration 2.0.: Language, literacies and intercultural learning in the 21st century.* Bern: Peter Lang.

Gutierrez, K. D. (2008). Developing a sociocritical literacy in the third space. *Reading Research Quarterly*, 43(2), 148–164.

Hauck, M. (2007). Critical success factors in a TRIDEM exchange. *ReCALL*, 19(2), 202–223.

Helm, F. (2015). The practices and challenges of telecollaboration in higher education in Europe. *Language Learning & Technology*, 19(2), 197–217.

Kumaravadivelu, B. (2008). *Cultural globalization and language education.* New Haven, CT: Yale University Press.

Lincoln, Y. S., & Guba, E.G. (1985) *Naturalistic inquiry.* Beverly Hills, CA: Sage Publications.

Menard-Warwick, J. (2008). The cultural and intercultural identities of transnational English teachers: Two case studies from the Americas. *TESOL Quarterly*, 42, 617–640.

Menard-Warwick, J., Heredia-Herrera, A., & Palmer, D. S. (2013). Local and global identities in an EFL Internet chat exchange. *The Modern Language Journal*, 97(4), 965–980.

Muller-Hartmann, A., & Kurek, M. (2016). Virtual group formation and the process of task design in online intercultural exchanges. In R. O'Dowd & T. Lewis (Eds.), *Online intercultural exchange: Policy, pedagogy, practice* (pp. 131–149). New York, NY: Routledge.

O'Dowd, R. (Ed.) (2007). *Online intercultural exchange: An introduction for foreign language teachers.* Clevedon: Multilingual Matters.

O'Dowd, R. (2016). Emerging trends and new directions in telecollaborative learning. *CALICO Journal*, 33(3), 291–310.

O'Dowd, R., & Eberbach, K. (2004). Guides on the side? Tasks and challenges for teachers in telecollaborative projects. *ReCALL*, 16(1), 5–19.

O'Dowd, R., & Lewis, T. (Eds.) (2016). *Online intercultural exchange: Policy, pedagogy, practice.* New York, NY: Routledge.

O'Dowd, R., & Ritter, M. (2006). Understanding and working with "failed communication" in telecollaborative exchanges. *CALICO Journal*, 61(2), 623–642.

O'Dowd, R., Sauro, S., & Spector-Cohen, E. (2020). The role of pedagogical mentoring in virtual exchange. *TESOL Quarterly*, 54(1), 146–172.

Pitzl, M.-L. (2010). *English as a lingua franca in international business.* Saarbrucken: VDM-Verlag.

Risager, K. (2007). *Language and culture pedagogy: From a national to a transnational paradigm.* Clevedon: Multilingual Matters.

Schreiber, B. R. (2019). "More like you": Disrupting native speakerism through a multimodal online intercultural exchange. *TESOL Quarterly*, 53(4), 1115–1138.

Sharkey, J., & Peercy, M. M. (Eds.) (2018). *Self-study of language and literacy teacher education practices: Culturally and linguistically diverse contexts.* Bingley: Emerald Publishing.

Tanghe, S., & Park, G. (2016). "Build[ing] something which alone we could not have done": International collaborative teaching and learning in language teacher education. *System*, 57, 1–13.

Uzum, B., Akayoglu, S., & Yazan, B. (2020). Using telecollaboration to promote intercultural competence in teacher training classrooms in Turkey and the USA. *ReCALL*, 32(2), 162–177.

Uzum, B., Yazan, B., Avineri, N., & Akayoglu, S. (2019). Preservice teachers' discursive constructions of cultural practices in a multicultural telecollaboration. *International Journal of Multicultural Education*, 21(1), 82–104.

# 10 Creating authentic contexts for transnational learning and teaching in TESOL teacher education

*Sarina Chugani Molina*

## Introduction

As a director of a TESOL program situated in a department dedicated to the value of social justice, it has been a significant and critical undertaking for me to explore ways in which to realize this value in our policies, research, process, and practices from outreach and admissions to our program design and through our deliberate selections of fieldwork experiences for our teacher-candidates. Over the years, through thoughtful consideration of our values and those of other institutions, I strategically partnered with community colleges, language schools, and non-profit organizations to create opportunities for our teacher-candidates to engage in teaching and learning alongside migrant, immigrant, refugees, and international students within the US context and internationally.

Canagarajah (2018) differentiates "multinational" and "international" from "transnational" in that he considers "multinational" as a "constellation of nation states," and "international" as the "relationship or collective around geographically bounded nations." In reviewing literature around transnational language teaching, it became important for me to recognize the value of creating authentic contexts for our teacher-candidates to prepare them for the kind of work they will be doing not only in international contexts, but also within transnational contexts. The question I then began to consider was how to create such opportunities for our teacher-candidates to experience transnational language teaching "between and beyond boundaries and borders" (p. 42).

During this time, our institution named Kito International, a non-profit organization in Kenya, our international partner of the year. The mission of Kito International is to provide at-risk youth an opportunity to transition out of poverty through provision of professional development opportunities (see UN-Habitat's Safer Cities Program and Partnership for Africa's Development). As the year drew to a close, I met with the founder of Kito International to consider ways in which our TESOL program could continue to support his organization. Over several months, we collaboratively came up with the possibility of creating an online program to provide English language lessons to support the entrepreneurial goals of the Kenyan youth this organization served. As this was uncharted territory for us, I wanted to ensure that our teacher-candidates, who would serve as the language teachers in this online forum, were prepared to engage in this unique work in Kenya with a complex relationship with the English language. As such, I met with the teacher-candidates weekly to discuss and theorize about transnationalism and translingual practice in this post-colonial, post-method, and post-structural era (Kumaravadivelu, 2012). Through engaging in this experience, we began to understand the ways in which English language teaching and learning practices in Kenya is situated within its unique ecological context comprising of complex historical, political, economic, institutional, social, and cultural dimensions (Molina, 2017). In this chapter, I share the learning derived from our work with Kito International from a transnational lens.

## Guiding questions

1 What are some lessons learned from engaging in English language teaching with Kenyan youth within this transnational context?
2 What are some key competencies that are important to nurture in teacher-candidates to teach effectively in transnational contexts?

## Transnational context

Initially, this study considered this online language teaching as an international, rather than transnational, project. But, as we delved deeper into the complex linguistic and cultural identities of our Kenyan students and our teacher-candidates, it became clear that our work with Kito International was a transnational experience. This required us to go beyond the framework around teaching English as an International language to consider the process of language teaching and learning not only from "between" places, but "within" and "beyond" spaces, which will become clearer as you read this chapter.

We worked alongside the founder of Kito International and his staff members to develop an online Business English program for the youth they served with a focus on supporting them to meet their entrepreneurial goals. We piloted this project with the leadership team, who then partnered with our teacher-candidates to deliver this program to their youth in collaborative teams to support the youth in accessing and understanding the content, and navigating the technology to successfully participate in this online course.

For our teacher-candidates, one of the aims of the project was to encourage thoughtful consideration of the local, global, and transnational perspectives in English language teaching and learning, which is an epistemic shift from the traditional national and colonial approaches to language teaching and learning, particularly where positionality is concerned. We met every Friday during the semester to discuss the articles I assigned on the historical and contemporary role of English in Kenya, our curriculum, and approach to feedback. The Friday sessions provided a space for teacher-candidates to question, deliberate, and dialogue about positionality, assumptions, standards, and assessment practices unique to this transnational context.

## Participants

### *Teacher-educator background*

It is important here to provide my positionality within this context. I am an Indian national, born and raised in Japan. I attended an American International School, where I was exposed to multiple varieties of English spoken by our teachers and peers. At home, my parents spoke our native tongue, Sindhi (a region in what is now Pakistan), Hindi, and Indian English learned when they relocated to mainland India after the war. They spoke a version of Indianized or nativized British English as India was under the colonial rule of Britain from 1858 to 1947. In Japan, my father learned Japanese to engage in business transactions and my mother learned Japanese for day-to-day communication. As third, fourth, or even fifth culture child, I quickly learned to engage in what Canagarajah (2013) terms "translingual practice" within my own speech communities. I have now been in the United States for close to 25 years and find that I am continuing to de-construct, re-construct, and negotiate my identity and liminal cultural and linguistic space as an English teacher and teacher-educator.

### *Teacher-candidate background*

The teacher-candidates included six females, who ranged in age from 24 to 32. Five of them identified as white Americans and one identified as African American. All of them identified as native American English speakers. Three of them had extended international teaching experiences and one of them had friends or relationships with those who spoke other varieties of English.

### *Kenyan student backgrounds*

The Kenyan students who enrolled in this program consisted of ten males and 12 females, and ranged in age from 18 to 25. In the first two weeks of the online program, our teacher-candidates spent time assessing student proficiency levels and understanding their needs. We learned that many of them wanted to learn English to attend institutions of higher education, enhance their business skills, start their own businesses, work for multinational corporations, and empower their communities through non-profit work. We also learned that students had varying levels of proficiency in their own native tongue, Kiswahili, the Kenyan English variety and British English. As in many post-colonial countries, English remains the official language of power in Kenya in addition to one of the local languages, Kiswahili (Muriungi, 2013). Kiswahili, on the other hand, is the main language used for communication within the local sector. According to Michieka (2005), English is the language medium for national exams, the legal system, and accessing information. Dhillon and Wanjiru (2013) also note that it plays a significant role in social mobility and academic achievement. Kiswahili, on the other hand, is the main language used for communication within the local sector.

In addition, we also noted that the students demonstrated stronger writing skills than speaking skills. In our research, we found that in Kenya, because the educational system is exam-oriented, there is more focus on English literacy than creative use of language (Dhillon & Wanjiru, 2013). The students spoke a variety of native languages including Kecrew, Kikuyu, Luhya, Luo, Dholuo, and Nubian, which provided insight into their transnational space, where many of them migrated to Kenya for a variety of reasons with their native tongue being an identity marker of their family, culture, ethnicity, and home (Budohoska, 2011).

## Methodology

As both the researcher and teacher-educator in this study, I hoped to "go beyond the typical qualitative research foci and observation, interviews, and document analysis, and to become actively involved with the participants in order to bring about change" (Jiménez, 1997, p. 228), which led to my selection of formative research design as a methodology for this study. Reinking and Bradley (2004) purport that the purpose of a formative design is to accomplish pedagogical goals for the program. In this study, this approach served us on two levels. One, this iterative, cyclical paradigm informed our practice, where we planned our units based on emerging student needs and remained open and flexible to changes, which were often implemented synchronously. On an institutional level, this design served to accomplish a pedagogical goal for the program, which in this case was to understand ways in which I could create meaningful opportunities for our teacher-candidates to engage in transnational pedagogical practice. As such, this research design allowed me to simultaneously identify and respond to those challenges as they emerged (Molina, 2015b).

### *Business English curriculum*

The curriculum developed included eight unit plans in total delivered over a 16-week period including pre- and post-assessments. Our teacher-candidates spent the first two sessions with the Kenyan students getting to know their needs and goals. This pre-assessment data was collected through self-introduction writing samples and Skype interviews, and used to determine the scope and sequence of the curriculum that included both synchronous (live, in-person interactions) and asynchronous (uploaded materials and pre-recorded videos) learning opportunities. The unit plans included writing a business letter, marketing hand-made, recycled products to support Kito International, making a sales pitch, writing a résumé, researching employment opportunities, and preparing for a job interview.

### *Data collection and analysis*

The data for this study were extracted from a larger data set (see Molina, 2015a, 2016), and centered around the weekly conversations I had with my graduate students documented in my analytic notes where we discussed (1) the assigned articles on the historical and contextual role of English in Kenya, (2) our identity and positionality as English language teachers within this context, (3) our assumptions around the role of English and what constitutes standard English, (4) possible theoretical and conceptual lenses in which to consider our work with our Kenyan students, and (5) emerging challenges in our work, particularly around our feedback practice within this transnational setting.

## Findings

In this section, I highlight the learning we derived from our weekly sessions and areas that emerged as questions or challenges unique to this transnational context. The themes that emerged from our sessions documented in my analytic notes included the consideration of the unique status of English in the Kenyan context, the role of criticality in language teaching, the interplay between the framework of teaching English as an International language and teaching English as a transnational language, and assessment practices within transnational contexts.

### *Criticality in language teaching*

Through engaging in this transnational teaching and learning context, it became clear that it was important to frame this work within critical perspectives. Crookes (2013) defines critical language teaching as one that:

> does not take for granted the status quo, but subjects it to critique, creates alternative forms of practice, and does so on the basis of radical theories of language, the individual, and society that take seriously our hopes in the direction of liberty, equality, and justice for all.
>
> (p. 1)

We discussed Delpit's (1988) work on "culture of power," that is enacted in the context of any classroom, but was particularly relevant to the teacher-candidates teaching within this setting. We reflected on the power dynamics within this setting from the institutional level, curricular level, to the interactions between our teacher-candidates and the Kenyan students they served. We acknowledged the power differential between the university of higher education in the United States and the non-profit organization in Kenya and what this means within this context.

As we were teaching within this context, we were concerned about the possibility of having the dominant ideologies re-socialize us into "monolingual practices and colonizing relationships" (Canagarajah, 2013). As such, we found it important to use our Kenyan students as cultural and linguistic informants as we approached the inherent tension that characterized our work. Motha (2014) recognizes that:

> The teaching of English is frequently represented as a neutral enterprise or even a benevolent one, one that promotes equity and access, arming learning

> with skills that allow them to escape poverty, to deploy identities of privilege and power, to move ahead socially. These representations bear truth, and the proliferation of English does indeed open doors and further futures. It is undeniable that around the world, English and opportunity walk hand in hand. However, I have begun to see that as English is spread, it carries other effects. It reinforces colonial divisions of power and racial inequalities. As English is increasingly commodified, racialized, and globalized, it is implicated in the persistence of racial inequalities, in cultural and economic domination, in heritage loss, in the extinction of less-commonly-spoken-languages and their inherent epistemologies, and in inequitable distribution of global wealth and resources.
>
> (p. xxi)

We discussed how we might approach this work through collaboration based on mutual honor and trust with the Kenyan leadership team and students. To this end, we decided to pilot the project first with the Kito leadership team and then have them work alongside our teacher-candidates to work with their own students in a hand-over, take-over model, so that they can continue to adjust and use this material as they deemed appropriate for the youth in the organization.

On an ongoing basis, the teacher-candidates explored these principles of criticality as reflected on their identity and positionality as native speakers of English and the power hierarchies inherent within varieties of English, and how this played a role in their interactions, material selections, and assessment practices. Jenkins (2000) stressed the importance of adjusting methods of teaching English to be more attuned with the changing patterns of English use, which is now more often between non-native speakers of the language. Therefore, the traditional curriculum that focuses on having a native speaker model was reexamined. This discussion arose when we selected Steve Jobs's video pitch of the iPhone. Initially, we thought Steve Jobs was a global figure and that the iPhone had global presence. However, upon further reflection the teacher-candidates felt that the video and mentor texts selected with American English stylistic elements may have been in discordance with the local styles of pitching products to companies.

Kumaravadivelu (2008) defines social relevance as the need for teachers to be sensitive to the societal, political, economic, and educational environment in which L2 (second language) education takes place. L2 education is not a discrete activity; it is deeply embedded in the larger social context that has a profound effect on it. The social context shapes various learning and teaching issues such as (a) the motivation for L2 learning; (b) the goal of L2 learning; (c) the functions L2 is expected to perform at home and in the community; (d) the availability of input to the learner; (e) the variation in the input; (f) and the norms of proficiency acceptable to that particular speech community (p. 207). He defines "global cultural consciousness," as a need to treat the learner as a cultural informant, which puts a premium on their power/knowledge instead of privileging the teacher as the sole cultural informant. The Kito leadership team was able to bridge the gap between our teacher-candidates and the Kenyan students as they were able to engage in translingual practice with their youth, which was an important asset they brought to this context. In light of the readings on social and global cultural consciousness, the teacher-candidates thought it would have been better to have reached out to our Kito leadership team to select videos and texts that the students were most likely to come across in their interactions within their local contexts. Since some of the student goals also included working in multinational corporations such as Amref Health Africa, World Vision, USAID, and the United Nations, we concluded that perhaps integrating business practice norms in a range of English varieties within both international and local contexts could be beneficial so that they can be empowered to select what might work best for them in sharing their voices and meeting their goals within local, international, multinational, and transnational contexts.

### *International vs. transnational language teaching*

In the program, our teacher-candidates were introduced to the framework of teaching English as an international language as a lens in approaching our work. Sandra Lee McKay's (2002) seminal work calls on English teachers to examine the assumptions guiding their conceptual and pedagogical approaches when teaching in global contexts. They were familiar with the critical questions undergirding the framework around the ownership of English, the native-speaker model, standard English, distancing of the notion of culture as associated with particular English-speaking countries, and approaching pedagogical practice from a socio-culturally salient space (Alsagoff, McKay, Hu, & Renandya, 2012), where the needs of the local community needed to be kept in mind along with their goals and the specific model of English they wished to approximate. This foundation supported the discussions around conducting needs assessments and developing curriculum to support those needs, but fell short in terms of assessment and feedback practice. We were no longer looking at two homogeneous varieties of English, but complex, multidimensional influences on the English variety spoken by our students and the variety they wished to learn to meet their specific entrepreneurial goals both within the local context of Kenya and in multinational corporations globally. This then became an area to bear in mind when considering our assessment practice within this transnational context. It also continued to allow the teacher-candidates to reflect on their own transnational English language teacher identity, where some of them had multiple exposures to different varieties of English that influenced their understanding of student language and feedback practice. In the next section, I share specific examples of discussions around errors and challenges around assessment practices within this context.

## Assessment in transnational contexts

During each session, we reviewed student written and spoken submissions along with the feedback our teacher-candidates provided to the students. A total of 91 assignments, including 63 written submissions and 28 spoken submissions, housed on the online platform we used for this online program, were used as data for discussion. We also simultaneously read and discussed articles that described the unique features of the Kenyan English variety, which led our teacher-candidates to experience some level of cognitive dissonance, particularly as it related to their feedback practice. Initially, the teacher-candidates used American English as the standard variety in which to assess student submissions, but began to wonder which variety they should use, given that Kenya was colonized by the British and, therefore, the influence of British English was deep-rooted in their linguistic repertoire.

Examples from the feedback data generated rich discussions around the grammatical, mechanical, and pragmatic aspects of student writing as well as the phonological elements of spoken language. Feedback was much more straightforward when it included differences in spelling (e.g., tyre, learnt), stylistic elements of writing (e.g., date – 25.3.2016), phrasing (e.g., try our products and see), word choice, which were clear influences from the British English variety, and therefore not necessary to correct. The specific situation that sparked these deeper conversations was when a Kenyan student challenged one of our teacher-candidate's feedback where she noted the date should be written starting with the month, the date, and the year. The student pushed back in the chat feature, telling the teacher-candidate that this was the way in which they wrote dates in Kenya. Kang and Dykema (2017) criticize previous studies on feedback practice which they believe lack a deeper understanding of how power and identity are negotiated through the process of feedback.

Through this interaction with our Kenyan student, it became important for our teacher-candidates to frame their work with their students not as passive recipients of the feedback, but as active agents in the negotiation process of power and identity. That is to say, that the errors identified needed to be cross-checked with the students' rich linguistic backgrounds, while simultaneously continuing to engage in reflexive practice about their own identity, positionality, and variety as an English speaker framing their approach to feedback. Because the teacher-candidates were not all familiar with the conventions of the British English variety, they changed the language input source on their word document to British English, so as to raise their awareness of what they may have automatically flagged as errors.

Other errors they identified were much more challenging to navigate. These included errors such as subject-verb agreement, preposition omission, subject omission, pluralization (e.g., dropping the third person plural 's'), and sentence boundaries. They wondered if these were attributed to the students' developing English language system, English variety, Kiswahili, or influences from their native language. Budohoska (2012) believes that the Kenyan English variety has developed characteristic features of its own like many English varieties spoken around the world, where the language becomes nativized in a sense. Sharifian and Jamarani (2013) use the term "renationalized" to describe the evolution of language use through interactions between and within multilingual communities. Through an analysis of the International Corpus of English, Mwangi (2004) found that the

Kenyan English variety went through a process of syntactic simplification, where fewer overarching categories of prepositions were used in favor of subcategories of prepositions with synonymous meanings. Likewise, the omission of articles and prepositions or what the teacher-candidates considered to be a misuse of prepositions were acceptable in the descriptive use of the Kenyan language. In addition, because of the dynamic nature of language, we acknowledged that our students were also possibly engaging in code-meshing, code-switching, and using emerging vernaculars, which added to the complexity of teaching English within this setting. We also learned from the TEIL literature that many of what we considered to be "errors" were in fact pragmatic (Firth, 1996; Meierkord, 2000), grammatical (Seidlhofer, 2004), and phonological features (Jenkins, 2000) quite typical in Lingua Franca communications. Jenkins (2000) argues that, "There is really no justification for doggedly persisting in referring to an item as 'an error' if the vast majority of the world's L2 English speakers produce and understand it" (p. 160), which made us re-examine our feedback practice each time we met for our weekly sessions.

The teacher-candidates continued to struggle with the question of which variety of English to use in their assessment. Some researchers (Davies et al., 2003) believe it is important to have one standard English variety, whereas other researchers (Hu, 2012; Lowenberg, 2012) maintain that other varieties need to be acknowledged and considered in assessment practices.

Canagarajah (2007) pushes our field to re-evaluate what it means to acquire a language where he states, that it is important that "previously dominant constructs such as form, cognition, and the individual are not ignored; they get redefined as hybrid, fluid, and situated in a more socially embedded, ecologically sensitive, and interactionally open model" (p. 923). In our attempts to employ multiple lenses in our feedback practice with our Kenyan students, we became painfully aware of the challenges of providing meaningful feedback that honors the English variety of the students we served, though we made conscious efforts and erred on the side of caution in our feedback practice. In the next section, I discuss competencies that emerged as important to nurture in teacher-candidates working in transnational contexts.

### *Teacher-candidate competencies within transnational contexts*

There were three competencies that were particularly important for our teacher-candidates working within this context. These included critical reflexivity, translingual competence, and metacultural competence.

Critical reflexivity competence, when applied to this context, is the ability to engage in iterative, reflective practice on one's own subjective understandings and positionality as teachers within particular contexts so as to draw these out and become more conscious of the power dimensions that are enacted within the learning and teaching context, and the conceptual and pedagogical assumptions that undergird our practice. In this study, our weekly meetings allowed us a space to bring in questions and challenges, and to negotiate understandings of our work with our Kenyan students through our interactions with the readings and each other, and through sustained dialogue throughout this project. As a teacher educator, I engaged in spontaneous responsive mediation in order to identify areas of need and growth. Johnson and Golombek (2016) coined the term *responsive mediation* to characterize their approach to feedback that is embedded within this socio-cultural theoretical stance. They state:

> Responsive mediation requires a lot of teacher educators. First and foremost, it requires that we attend to what our teachers bring to our interactions, where they are coming from and how they understand what they are experiencing. And gaining access to such pre-understandings is no easy task.
>
> (p. 42)

They lean on Kozulin et al.'s (2003) definition of mediation which involves the process of the learning and teaching of new understandings in situations where prior understandings were inadequate (p. 380). Both the cognitive and emotional dimensions of their interactions with their teachers are recognized within their mediation practice where these "mediational supports may not always be accepted due to the emotions and motivations they bring to these interactions" (Johnson & Golombek, 2016, p. 34).

A second competence that was identified as important for our teacher-candidates within this context included translingual competence, or "the ability to use diverse codes across language varieties and settings in ways that are contextually appropriate and that facilitate successful communication" (Jain, 2014, p. 493). Canagarajah (2006) describes a related competence in his discussion of "multi-dialectal competence." Though his conceptualization of multi-dialectal competence is in reference to the call to change assessment practices in the field of English language teaching, it is essential to nurture these skills in our teacher-candidates as well. When applied to this setting, this requires that our teacher-candidates have awareness of the multiple varieties of English, socio-linguistic sensitivity to the differences between the multiple varieties of English, understanding of the contextual influences on the English variety or varieties used, awareness of linguistic and cultural identity in the usage of particular varieties of English, and negotiation skills which include having an understanding that students may be engaging in code-switching or code-meshing practices, accommodating speech and feedback to negotiate mutual understanding, and using clarification strategies such as rephrasing, repair, and circumlocution. In the same way, Kilickaya (2009) suggests that if the goal is to promote intercultural communication, or in this case, transnational communication, the focus should be on developing awareness of the many varieties of English and the various communication strategies that can be used to enhance intelligibility. Needless to say, this takes time, patience, and motivation.

Lastly, Sharifian and Jamarani's (2013) notion of meta-cultural competence emerged as an important competence to nurture within this context. He defines meta-cultural competence as "a competence that enables interlocutors to communicate and negotiate their cultural conceptualizations during the process of intercultural communication" (p. 9). This includes three interconnected elements, including: (1) conceptual variation awareness – awareness that the same language can be used to express unique cultural ideas; (2) conceptual explication strategy – strategies employed to make one's cultural conceptualizations clear to the interlocutors; and (3) conceptual negotiation strategies, which are strategies to clarify or ask for clarification when cultural conceptualizations that are being discussed are not clear (Sharifian & Jamarani, 2013, pp. 10–11). This competence was critical in our negotiations around curriculum with the Kenyan leadership team and students.

## Discussion and conclusion

The opportunity of working with Kito International to build an online Business English program and to teach the Kenyan youth expanded our conceptual and pedagogical understanding of what it means to teach within transnational contexts. Given that more and more people in this world are considered multilingual users of English with a variety of national, political, economic, and social histories, we began to question the limitations of considering our work as international. Rather, we recognized that we can no longer see our work as between nations, but beyond nations and boundaries – that our work is, in essence, *transnational* (Canagarajah, 2018, p. 42), which we find now in many ESOL classrooms within English speaking countries and beyond (see Jain, 2014).

Even in this postcolonial era, where we consider English as an international language, we were cognizant of the complex political history of the English language which includes ideological questions around the role of linguistic imperialism (Canagarajah, 1999) and linguicide (Hassanpour, 2000; Van Dijk, 2000) and racialized practices that undergird the hierarchical power (native/non-native; standard/non-standard). The imposition of the Western education system on the culture and heritage of its people (Canagarajah, 1999; Crookes, 2007) around the world has alerted us to how history can shape individuals' attitudes toward learning the English language. We had to also shift away from our traditional methods of teaching and learning, and construct our practices within our transnational context where the teacher-candidates felt empowered to theorize about teaching practice through understanding the needs of our Kenyan students that continually manifested within this unique online ELT teaching context. We honored their unique translingual practice, where we recognized that historically as their languages came in contact with others, they created their own variety of language that were "appropriated by [them] and used beyond their separate labels as suits their purposes" (pp. 42–43).

Through our Friday meetings, we confronted these challenges, which were often uncomfortable because it demanded a sense of honesty, integrity, and authenticity in our experiences as we recognized our vulnerabilities and shortcomings in our work with our students. We attempted to learn as we engaged within this complex transnational context by continually reflecting on our positionality, construction of self, and identity as language teachers (Yazan & Rudolph, 2018). It became clear that this positioning of teaching of English within this transnational context entailed a certain demand for our teachers to have a sense of critical consciousness informed by "socio-culturally sensitive pedagogical practice" (Alsagoff et al., 2012).

English language teaching in transnational contexts may be an important consideration for teacher education in TESOL as our teachers will most likely work with English speakers that transcend boundaries and positionalities. This can afford possibilities for teacher-candidates to engage in deep learning about the role of English and reflection on their own evolving identities as English teachers. Though we were able to engage in these critical discussions during our Friday meetings, in terms of pedagogical practice, the questions about which English to use, what materials and methods to use for instruction, and what assessment measures to utilize in our feedback process continue to be important areas to examine when teaching in transnational contexts.

## References

Alsagoff, L., McKay, S. L., Hu, G., & Renandya, W. A. (Eds.) (2012). *Principles and practices for teaching English as an international language*. New York, NY: Routledge.

Budohoska, N. (2011). Language as a means of expressing identity in a multilingual reality: The place of English in Kenya today. *Anglica*, 20, 37–52.

Budohoska, N. (2012). Characteristic morphological and syntactic features of English in Kenya: A corpus study (ICE). *Lingua Posnaniensis*, 54(1), 45–56.

Canagarajah, S. (1999). *Resisting linguistic imperialism in English teaching*. Oxford: Oxford University Press.

Canagarajah, S. (2006). Changing communicative needs, revised assessment objectives: Testing English as an international language. *Language Assessment Quarterly*, 3(3), 229–242.

Canagarajah, S. A. (2007). Lingua franca English, multilingual communities, and language acquisition. *The Modern Language Journal*, 91(1), 923–938.

Canagarajah, S. (2013). *Translingual practice: Global Englishes and cosmopolitan relations*. New York, NY: Routledge.

Canagarajah, S. (2018). Transnationalism and translingualism: How they are connected. In Q. You (Ed.), *Transnational writing education: Theory, history, and practice* (pp. 41–60). New York, NY: Routledge.

Crookes, G. (2007). *A practicum in TESOL: Professional development through teaching practice*. Cambridge: Cambridge University Press.

Crookes, G. (2013). *Critical ELT in action: Foundations, promises, and praxis*. New York, NY: Taylor & Francis.

Davies, A., Hamp-Lyons, L., & Kemp, C. (2003). Whose norms? International proficiency tests in English. *World Englishes*, 22(4), 571–584.

Delpit, L. (1988). The silenced dialogue: Power and pedagogy in educating other people's children. *Harvard Educational Review*, 58(3), 280–298.

Dhillon, J. K., & Wanjiru, J. (2013). Challenges and strategies for teachers and learners of English as a second language: The case of an urban primary school in Kenya. *International Journal of English Linguistics*, 3(2), 14–24.

Firth, A. (1996). The discursive accomplishment of normality: On "lingua franca" English and conversation analysis. *Journal of Pragmatics*, 26, 237–259.

Hassanpour, A. (2000). The politics of a-political linguistics: Linguists and linguicide. In R. Phillipson (Ed.), *Rights to language: Equity, power, and education* (pp. 33–39). Mahwah, NJ: Lawrence Erlbaum.

Hu, J. D. (2012). Assessing English as an international language. In L. Alsagoff, S. L. McKay, G. Hu, & W. A. Renandya (Eds.), *Principles and practices for teaching English as an international language* (pp. 123–144). New York, NY: Routledge.

Jain, R. (2014). Global Englishes, translinguistic identities, and translingual practices in a community college ESL classroom: A practitioner researcher reports. *TESOL Journal*, 5(3), 490–522.

Jenkins, J. (2000). *The phonology of English as an international language: New models, new norms, new goals*. Oxford: Oxford University Press.

Jiménez, R. T. (1997). The strategic reading abilities and the potential of five low-literacy Latina/o readers in middle school. *Reading Research Quarterly*, 32(3), 224–243.

Johnson, K. E., & Golombek, P. R. (2016). *Mindful L2 teacher education: A sociocultural perspective on cultivating teachers' professional development*. New York, NY: Routledge.

Kang, H., & Dykema, J. (2017). Critical discourse analysis of student responses to teacher feedback on student writing. *Journal of Response to Writing*, 3(2), 6–35.

Kilickaya, F. (2009). World Englishes, English as an international language and applied linguistics. *English Language Teaching*, 2(3), 35–38.

Kozulin, A., Gindis, B., Ageyev, V. S., & Miller, S. M. (Eds.) (2003). *Vygotsky's educational theory in cultural context*. Cambridge: Cambridge University Press.

Kumaravadivelu, B. (2008). *Understanding language teaching: From method to postmethod*. Mahwah, NJ: Lawrence Erlbaum Associates, Inc.

Kumaravadivelu, B. (2012). *Language teacher education for a global society*. New York, NY: Routledge.

Lowenberg, P. H. (2012). Assessing proficiency in EIL. In A. Matsuda (Ed.), *Principles and practices of teaching English as an international language* (pp. 80–103). Bristol: Multilingual Matters.

McKay, S. L. (2002). *Teaching English as an international language: Rethinking goals and approaches*. Oxford: Oxford University Press.

Meierkord, C. (2000). Interpreting successful lingua franca interaction: An analysis of non-native/non-native small talk conversations in English. *Linguistik Online*, 5(1). doi:10.13092/lo.5.1013.

Michieka, M. M. (2005). English in Kenya: A sociolinguistic profile. *World Englishes*, 24(2), 173–186.

Molina, S. C. (2015a). Transnational English language teaching: Opportunities for teacher learning and development. *English Language Teacher Education and Development*, 18, 20–28.

Molina, S. C. (2015b). Mediating teacher learning through dialogical learning spaces integrated in a TESOL practicum experience. *Journal of Teaching and Teacher Education*, 3(1), 75–88.

Molina, S. C. (2016). The complexity of providing feedback when teachers and students speak different varieties of English: A case study. *Journal of Teaching and Teacher Education*, 4(1), 61–69.

Molina, S. C. (2017). English language teaching in China: Teacher agency in response to curricular innovations. In P. C. L. Ng & E. F. Boucher-Yip (Eds.), *English language teaching: Teacher agency and policy response* (pp. 19–37). New York: Routledge.

Motha, S. (2014). *Race, empire, and English language teaching: Creating responsible and ethical anti-racist practice.* New York, NY: Teachers College.

Muriungi, P. K. (2013). The influence of mother-tongue maintenance on acquisition of English language skills among day secondary school students in Imenti south district, Kenya. *International Journal of Linguistics*, 5(1), 296–305.

Mwangi, S. (2004). Prepositions vanishing in Kenya: A case of syntactic simplification in east African English. *English Today*, 77(20), 27–32.

Reinking, D., & Bradley, B. (2004). Connecting research and practice using formative and design experiments. In N. Duke & M. Mallette (Eds.), *Literacy research methods* (pp. 149–169). New York, NY: Guilford Press.

Seidlhofer, B. (2004). Research perspectives on teaching English as a lingua franca. *Annual Review of Applied Linguistics*, 24, 209–239.

Sharifian, F. & Jamarani, M. (Eds.) (2013). *Intercultural communication in the new era.* New York, NY: Taylor & Francis.

Van Dijk, T. (2000). Discourse and access. In R. Phillipson (Ed.), *Rights to language: Equity, power, and education* (pp. 73–78). Mahwah, NJ: Lawrence Erlbaum.

Yazan, B., & Rudolph, N. (Eds.) (2018). *Criticality, teacher identity, and (in) equity in English language teaching: Issues and implications.* Switzerland: Springer.

# 11 TESOL through the reflections of transnational EMI lecturers

## A ROADMAPPING approach

*Davinia Sánchez-García and Nashwa Nashaat-Sobhy*

## Introduction

The internationalization of higher education (HE) has brought about a new teaching context where English is the lingua franca (ELF) through which disciplinary content is negotiated in class (Doiz, Lasagabaster, & Sierra, 2013; Björkman, 2013). With the spread of English medium education (EME) as a worldwide practice, non-language teachers are presented with numerous linguistic, pedagogical, and cultural challenges. Although they need not be language experts, their success as content teachers requires them to be equipped with the necessary linguistic competence to communicate meaningfully, to adapt their subject matter to the new language requirements, and to support their students' learning process. Such scenario calls for specific teacher education programs such as Two2Tango (T2T), a transnational online teacher education program which emerged to cater for the needs of university lecturers involved in EME (Valcke & Romero, 2016).

Since teachers' identities seem to largely influence their teaching practice, this chapter examines the identities of teachers from a wide range of HE institutions across Europe as they share their EME reflections and conceptualizations naturalistically with other colleagues undergoing comparable experiences and concerns in the T2T transnational community of practice.

The analytical tool used is the recently developed ROADMAPPING framework (Dafouz & Smit, 2016, 2020), which is an integrative applied linguistic model that captures the dynamic nature of English medium education in multilingual university settings (EMEMUS). The findings throw light on the linguistic and pedagogical needs of EME lecturers, who as L2 speakers of English are part of the broader TESOL community, and whose needs depict the current foreign language education landscape.

The chapter first explains the rapid expansion of EME, the main features of the ROADMAPPING model, and the role of teachers' identities on their teaching practices. Second, it describes the context, participants, and dataset used. Third, it displays and discuss the findings. Finally, possible practical implications for TESOL and directions for future research are provided.

## Theoretical framework

### *The advent of EME in Europe*

EME is entrenched in European educational and language policies as an effective way to promote individual and societal multilingualism. Higher education institutions (HEIs) have been persistent in their quest to achieve the status of global institutions. They have thus adhered to the premises in the Bologna Process (Wilkinson, 2018), whereby these institutions have promoted internationalization, that is, educational opportunities that can be regarded as mobile since they seek partnerships and connections with other HEIs across the globe (Carroll, 2015) and which bring together multi- and cross-cultural participants. When mobility is not bound by boarders, cultures or nationalities, taking the form of virtual or physical engagement, and the teachers' and/or the students' mobility varies in length, it is referred to as "transnational education," where boundaries of time and space are more open to all (Mercado & Gibson, 2013; Wilkins, 2018). Precisely resulting from this educational transnationalism and with the aim of raising the prestige of the institution, attracting international students, teachers, and researchers, and also preparing local students for global employability, HEIs have started offering educational programs that no longer use the dominant national language as the means of instruction, but use English instead. In these institutions, English becomes the language of education for the home students as well, so that the internationalization of these universities starts at home (Beelen & Jones, 2015). This phenomenon is nowadays a mainstream practice all around the world (Doiz, Lasagabaster, & Sierra, 2013; van Der Walt, 2013; Taguchi, 2014) that materializes in rather heterogeneous ways in response to diverse political, sociocultural, economic, historical, geographical, and linguistic contexts deriving from transnationalism. In the particular case of Europe, marked differences stand out between northern and southern EME implementation, with the Nordic countries offering a higher number of English-medium programs than southern countries (Hultgren, Jensen, & Dimova, 2015). Disparities in the provision of EME are often largely influenced by countless factors such as the need of northern smaller-sized populations to recruit larger numbers of international students and researchers, or English presence being greater not only in academia but in everyday life in northern countries than in southern ones (Doiz, Lasagabaster, & Sierra, 2011).

EME's uneven and complex implementation also leaves its mark on the wide terminological variation trying to define the phenomenon at tertiary education (Smit & Dafouz, 2012). Among the most used terms in the research are: (1) "Integrating Content and Language in Higher Education" (ICLHE), to address programmes that explicitly integrate content and language learning objectives; (2) "English-medium instruction" (EMI), which underscores the learning of content over language; (3) "Integrating Content and Language" (ICL), which leaves aside explicit teaching goals and focuses on teaching and learning as integral discursive practices (Smit & Dafouz, 2012, p. 7); and (4) "English-medium education in multilingual university settings" (EMEMUS), which is the one chosen for this study as it highlights the multilingual nature inherent in HE contexts where

English co-exists with other linguistic repertoires (Dafouz & Smit, 2016, 2020). EMEMUS arose from the attempt to create a theoretical basis for the EME phenomenon, as described next.

### *ROADMAPPING: conceptualizing EMEMUS*

Although a wealth of research has focused on the imperative need of analyzing the educational and linguistic outcomes derived from the implementation of EME, its wide diversity and complexity has made it difficult to reach a consensual conceptualization that serves as a common ground for further implementation and empirical investigations. Standing up for the challenge, Dafouz and Smit (2016) proposed ROADMAPPING as an integrative applied linguistic model used to capture the dynamic nature of EMEMUS present in manifold HE sites. Informed by sociolinguistics, theories on the ecology of language, language policy research, and social practices as discourses, this comprehensive and multi-dimensional conceptual framework lends itself as an analytical guide. It allows the analysis of six dimensions, namely, Roles of English, Academic Disciplines, (language) Management, Agents, Practices and Processes, and Internationalization and Glocalization with discourse as the intersecting point of access. This chapter is concerned with university teachers' conceptualizations of EMEMUS and, therefore, only three of the six ROADMAPPING dimensions will be used as the analytical access into teachers' reported conceptualizations and identities: Roles of English, Academic Disciplines, and Processes and Practices. These three dimensions allow access into teachers' identity as main agents of the teaching process, which may be influenced by how they conceive the role(s) of English as the language for classroom communication in the particular practices that enact the teaching of their academic disciplines.

### *The impact of EMEMUS on teacher identity, practices, and education*

Teaching and learning through an additional language not only brings with it a change in the language of classroom communication, but also having to accommodate the pedagogical principles that underpin the process of teaching and learning to that new language and to the academic and disciplinary needs of the students. Consequently, a major concern resulting from the burgeoning implementation of EMEMUS is the challenges that it places on non-native English-speaking university teachers. One such challenge is often represented by teachers' linguistic and communicative competence since

> whereas we may assume that experienced university academics have a tacit understanding of the academic milieu in which they work, the ability to draw upon the appropriate or necessary language for working within this milieu in a foreign language, especially in relation to oral genres in this context, cannot be assumed.
>
> (Kling, 2016, p. 225)

If teaching through one's L1 to students who also speak that L1 and its culture is not free of complications, teaching through an additional language to cohorts of students with diverse linguistic and cultural backgrounds seems even more complex (Kling, 2016). As a basic premise to face this challenge, teachers need to have sufficient competence in the language of instruction, which has led HEIs to the testing of their teachers' proficiency. Although expert authorities have conveniently agreed upon a minimum level of competence of C1 following the Common European Framework of Reference (CEFR), the type of assessment method is cause for debate. While the vast majority of universities employ standardized English tests such as the Test of English as a Foreign Language (TOEFL), Cambridge Assessment English Exams, or the International English Language Testing System (IELTS) to certify their teachers' level, a reduced number of HEIs have developed their own internal assessment methods (Dimova & Kling, 2018), acknowledging that the linguistic proficiency needed for teaching goes far beyond the generic language competence and descriptors provided by the CEFR. EMEMUS requires teachers to master general and academic English language in combination with discipline-specific language. To make matters more complex, EMEMUS typically involves communication among people who do not share their L1 and for whom English works as a lingua franca, that is, the main, if not the only, communicative medium of choice (Seidlhofer, 2011). This directly implies that in such multilingual university settings, the language and communicative competences needed are a far cry from native-likeness and closer to managing the discourse strategies (Sánchez-García, 2019) and accommodation skills that will make the teacher an effective communicator in the particular domain-specific ELF classroom (Jenkins, 2019).

As a result, to ensure the effective implementation of the internationalisation process, HEIs need to

> provide the necessary professional development and teacher training programmes that will allow HE teachers to appropriately develop their language proficiency as well as their professional and pedagogical knowledge, skills and competences and thereby empower them to ensure the quality of their teaching – and their students' learning – in the multilingual and multicultural learning space.
>
> (Lauridsen, Dafouz, Stavicka, & Wetter, 2015, p. 12)

Despite HEIs' increasing efforts to follow this recommendation, specific teacher education programs equipping teachers for teaching in internationalized settings are scarce outside the north-western part of Europe, and often ad hoc (Lauridsen, 2017). It is of much concern to tap into their conceptualization regarding EMEMUS, more specifically, their teacher identity in this new transnational educational context as influenced by their beliefs about the role of English, and whether (and if so how) it affects their disciplinary teaching practices.

Professional identity in the domain of teaching and teacher education is often described as teacher's self-concept or images of the self (Knowles, 1992). Self-representation develops over time as it is an ongoing process of reflection built through transactions with the surrounding social environment (Mead, 1934; Erikson, 1968). Teachers, therefore, construct their own identities as they experience and bring together their personal self-image and what they believe is expected from them as teachers and as dictated by their educational context. Teacher identity then is a decisive factor in shaping the way teachers carry out their professional duties, how they develop professionally, and how they react to potential educational changes (Beijaard, Meijer, & Verloop, 2004). Based on this premise, looking into in-service teachers' conceptualizations of their professional identity at the moment in which they first encounter the EMEMUS experience may contribute to a deeper understanding of the challenges they face, may throw some light on how teacher education can be designed to best cater for teachers' EMEMUS needs, and may reveal how TESOL best fits into this educational context.

Although some research has already delved into this issue (House & Lévy-Tödter, 2010), the present chapter approaches the research topic from a transnational perspective, involving teachers from 11 HEIs. Besides, the data analyzed is not research-prompted, but emerges from the natural interactions among these teachers as they share their personal teaching experiences and beliefs with other colleagues in an online teacher education program. Next, more detail about the participants, the data, and the analysis will be provided.

## Methodology

### *Research context and participants*

In response to the increasing internationalization of HE, two educational developers, one at the University of Cadiz (in Spain) and other at the Université libre de Bruxelles (in Belgium) decided to join forces to equip their teachers with the skills and competence necessary to face the challenges and opportunities of EMEMUS. This marked the beginning of TwotoTango (T2T), an innovative teacher education program that unites EME lecturers from across Europe (Valcke & Romero, 2016). They opted to design an online program that could be smoothly integrated in both institutional contexts and which targeted university teachers with diverse teaching styles, and linguistic and disciplinary backgrounds. The idea behind the program was then to create an online community of practice in which teachers could improve their English language skills for teaching purposes while reflecting and discussing on EME issues through the asynchronous interaction that only virtual learning environments can provide.

This chapter reports on the results obtained from the fourth edition of the program running December–June from the academic year 2017–18 since the latest one is still under way. In this fourth edition, the teacher participants enrolled in the program amounted to 28 coming from 11 higher education institutions from six European countries (Table 11.1). These student teachers were placed in e-tandems so that each teacher would work with a colleague from a different

*Table 11.1* Description of teacher participants

| *Name* | *Home institution* | *Country* | *Specialist field* |
|---|---|---|---|
| M.A. | Chalmers University of Technology | Sweden | Architecture – Urban Planning |
| K.A. | KEA – Copenhagen School of Design and Technology | Denmark | Production Technology |
| A.B. | University college VIVES Brugge | Belgium | Computer Science, ICT |
| J.C. | Universidad de Cádiz | Spain | Sport Sciences |
| L.C. | Karolinska Institutet | Sweden | Cardiovascular Medicine |
| A.D. | University of Applied Sciences Amsterdam | Netherlands | Nutrition |
| G.G. | Amsterdam University of Applied Sciences | Netherlands | Functional Exercise Therapy |
| N.G. | Universidad de Cádiz | Spain | Accounting |
| Y.H. | Chalmers University of Technology | Sweden | Information Literacy |
| R.L. | Tampere University of Technology | Finland | Chemistry and Bioengineering |
| E.L. | Universidad San Jorge | Spain | Chemistry |
| M.L. | Karolinska Institutet | Sweden | Bioentrepreneurship |
| L.L. | Chalmers University of Technology | Sweden | Management of Technology, Lean Product Development |
| P.L. | Université Catholique de Louvain | Belgium | Materials and Process Engineering |
| V.L. | Universidad de Cádiz | Spain | Social Psychology |
| JI.N. | Universidad de Cádiz | Spain | Psychology |
| I.N. | Universidad de Cádiz | Spain | Developmental and Educational Psychology |
| Y.N. | Chalmers University of Technology | Sweden | Industrial Biotechnology, Cell Factory Design |
| M.P. | Universidad de Cádiz | Spain | Literature |
| A.M. | Universidad Complutense de Madrid | Spain | Ancient History |
| P.R. | Universidad Complutense de Madrid | Spain | Medicine - Pediatrics |
| M.R. | Universidad de Cádiz | Spain | Software Engineering |
| S.T. | Tampere University of Technology | Finland | Industrial Engineering Management |
| V.V. | UMons | Belgium | Materials Engineering |
| K.V. | Karolinska Institutet | Sweden | Clinical Science |
| P.V. | Amsterdam University of Applied Sciences | Netherlands | Functional Exercise Therapy |
| T.W. | University college VIVES Torhout | Belgium | Economy |
| Y.G. | Chalmers University of Technology | Japan | Building Technology, Wood Engineering, Sustainable Building |

institution, a different country, and a different disciplinary expertise. A placement test was carried out, which reported that teachers' language proficiency ranged from B2 to C1+ (CEFR).

The program took seven months to complete and was conducted via the learning platform Eliademy. It consisted of six modules covering a number of EME-related topics, and English was always the language of work. Each of these six modules was broken down into three tasks as follows:

- Pre-task: participants had to read an article and watch a video on the topic individually.
- Task: participants would meet online with their corresponding e-tandem partner via Skype to orally discuss about the pre-task. The exchanges were prompted by questions based on the pre-task materials to facilitate their interactions.
- Post-task: teacher participants had to write a summary of the main personal reflections and post them in the discussion forum. Then, they had to comment on other teacher participants' contributions.

### *Data collection and analysis*

The data collected for the study belongs to the teachers' entries on the discussion forum of "*Module 2. English as a lingua franca*" of the course. This Module aims at making teachers reflect upon EME practices based on their beliefs about the English language and its role as a lingua franca, and how ELF impacts their teaching. A total number of 110 entries were gathered and analyzed following thematic analysis, as it is a research method that facilitates the process of identifying patterns or themes within qualitative data (Braun & Clarke, 2006). We read the entries thoroughly and searched for the main themes emerging in the data. Ploughing through the posts and threads in the teachers' entries to identify and classify the emerging themes was an expected challenge, which we dealt with using the aforementioned ROADMAPPING framework (Dafouz & Smit, 2016, 2020). This provided the solution since its aforementioned three selected dimensions, namely, Roles of English, Academic Disciplines, and Practices and Processes, served as the codes used to organize those data in a meaningful and systematic fashion. The identification, coding, and interpretation of the data were carried out individually by the two researchers and put in common at a later stage; thus, complying with the principle of interrater reliability. The selected three dimensions represent the main themes that will next articulate the results and discussion section.

## Results and discussion

Teachers' conceptualizations about EMEMUS and their identity as users of ELF in their professional practices have been analyzed around three dimensions of the ROADMAPPING framework. Under the premise that identity is likely to shape performance and actions, teachers' conceptualizations about EMEMUS as realized through their identity as users of ELF in the 110 collected forum entries will be analyzed in the first place, followed by how they believe that ELF arguably affects the teaching of their academic disciplines and their general classroom practices and processes.

### *Roles of English*

When discussing the roles of English in their EMEMUS practice, teachers' reflections seem to evolve around one main issue: their identity as non-native speakers of English and their subsequent belief that this status determines, to a greater or lesser extent, their capacity as teachers according to the actual distance separating their linguistic competence from nativeness.

When discussing about the roles of the English language, teachers seem to position themselves along a continuum. On the left extreme there are the teachers who acquired English at a very early age and have since used the language for regular communication in most realms of their lives. Moving along the continuum and reaching the middle of it, there are those teachers for whom English works as their professional language. They have always used English for academic purposes and it is their language of work. A shared assumption among these two groups of teachers is the potential difficulty they would find if they had to teach through their L1. As confirmed by a teacher who is struggling with such situation:

> Extract 1. "I have been using English as my professional language throughout my career and feel most comfortable teaching in English. Teaching in Swedish, despite Swedish being my mother tongue, I find quite challenging."

On the opposite right extreme of the continuum there are the teachers who have studied English as a foreign language (EFL) and for which English has never played an instrumental role until now that they have started teaching through it. What all teachers along the continuum acknowledge is that the concept of ELF is new to them. As put by two of the teacher participants:

> Extract 2. "For me the concept of a lingua franca is totally new, I didn't know it, and the truth is that it has opened a new vision of English, its learning and teaching in this language."
>
> Extract 3. "The new concept of ELF has made me consider learning English and the possibility of teaching in this language in another way. Now I understand that it is not so necessary to adhere to Oxford or Cambridge standards."

Learning about ELF has evidently meant a mindshift, especially for those teachers on the right extreme of the continuum, that is, those facing the challenge of teaching through English for the first time. While the teachers on the left side of the continuum seem to feel comfortable teaching through English and confident about their linguistic and communicative competence (Extract 4), those with little or no experience openly recognize their fears and low self-esteem in terms of language competence. They repeatedly admit to being convinced that the quality of their teaching will suffer if the language of instruction is not fully mastered. As a result of such belief, they assert that when teaching through English, most of their efforts are put into deploying a correct usage of the language, leaving intelligibility behind (Extract 5).

> Extract 4. "I try to speak as grammatically correct as possible to avoid any misunderstandings due to grammatical errors. However, I am aware that I make mistakes and I am fine with it as long as I make myself understood as I intend. We [teacher and students] are well aware we are not native speakers and it doesn't matter to have minor grammatical or pronunciation errors. What matters is the effectiveness of teaching itself."
>
> Extract 5. "I hear my speaking and I am afraid to make mistakes and it is worse in front of native speakers, while I try to mimic their tone and adapt myself to the use of advance vocabulary. That is where I found my English is in the ELF level and not EFL level. When there are native speakers among my students, I felt I paid more attention on my language than on my message."

Learning about ELF has made these teachers challenge their initial belief and contemplate the option of giving preference to the comprehensibility of what they would like to communicate over producing grammatically mistake-free utterances as long as the mistakes do not impede students' understanding of the message. This realization seems to have impacted teachers' identity and possibly their future classroom performance, as described in Extract 6.

> Extract 6. "I think ELF is more dynamic than EFL due to the different cultural impact. This knowledge increases my awareness of language variations and intercultural differences, considering that I have 20–30 students from 10+ different countries. Now I will focus more on intercultural communication understanding."

While before completing the course module on ELF, teachers usually identified themselves as speakers of EFL, their written after-thoughts reflect their new identity as ELF users. As described in Extract 7, they call into question the preconceived native speakerism that seemed to be initially deeply rooted in their identity and plan to adapt their future teaching accordingly.

> Extract 7. "Being a native speaker does not automatically mean you are a good user of the language and even less that we would be skilled in teaching in English. I have during this course reflected on my teaching in English, something I never did before. The main thing I will change is explain to students what ELF means, the emphasis on understanding, not on the correct use of the language. This may be appreciated by some students who are not yet so practiced ELF users."

At the outset of the course module, our teachers firmly believed that being users of EFL constituted a factor negatively impinging on their identity and their classroom practices despite their extensive teaching experience and disciplinary expertise. However, as they learned about ELF and shared their beliefs with their colleagues, they experienced a clear transitional change that made them believe that however important high language competence in English is to teaching, intelligibility is likely to work as an equalizer. Besides, it seems to have been revealing for teachers to find out that all speakers, even native ones, need to acquire ELF and, therefore, they should not defer to L1 English standards to judge their own English usage and their teaching capability (Seidlhofer, 2011) (Extract 8).

> Extract 8. "When the teacher does not master English fully it might be problematic. However, we [teachers and students] all have to adapt to ELF, even the native speaking students and teachers. Sometimes it is actually more difficult to understand a native speaker in this setting seeing as we all have adapted to a common ELF that is not necessarily 'correct' English."

### *Academic disciplines*

The academic disciplines taught by the teachers participating in the course are diverse (Table 11.1). However, when discussing EMEMUS, they tend to concur on similar conceptualizations and worries. First of all, all teachers firmly acknowledge the importance of mastering English for students' professional development and future practice. Therefore, they value the English learning opportunities granted by the internationalization of their HE institutions. In one teacher's own words:

> Extract 9. "You have to believe in English-medium education. If medical students want to become good medical doctors, they NEED to read, understand and speak English fluently." (Emphasis in original)

The eagerness to stand up for ELF when learning an academic discipline may be accentuated by the prolific existence of teaching and learning materials in English as opposed to other teachers' L1 languages. Teachers seem to agree that the uncontested role of English as the language of science plays in their favor when planning and preparing their lessons and saves them time and work to create or translate them.

> Extract 10. "It is actually easier to keep a course in English. In my field, Chemistry, the variety of available study material is much wider in English, which gives me more freedom of choice. It is sometimes time consuming to find all the correct translations for the technical terms in Finnish, my L1. But when the course is in English, it is not a problem."
>
> Extract 11. "In some fields like Engineering, a lot of concepts have been theorized in English and it is easier to teach them in English because we sometimes don't have the words or resources to teach them in our L1."

Teachers believe that the importance of English for becoming full-fledged members of their disciplinary community is as high as it is their self-concept as experts of their particular scientific field. A teacher participant explains it as follows:

> Extract 12. "[Being a content expert] increases the quality of my teaching. I teach technical courses and it is very important to know the technical words in English. Thus, the students learn very useful vocabulary in English that they will use in their professional career."

Our teachers hold in high esteem their skill and capability as content teachers. In fact, their assumed expertise is considered a determining factor in the quality of their teaching as well as a decisive trigger of students' successful disciplinary learning. However, this positive teachers' identity is at times counteracted by several challenges contingent upon teachers' linguistic proficiency. On the one hand, some teachers confirm that they do not encounter any difficulty when teaching the discipline-specific vocabulary and expressions that underpin their particular discipline literacy. However, they often struggle to find the most effective way to make the disciplinary declarative and procedural knowledge intelligible for their students. As explained by one of the teachers in Extract 11, teachers are experts in their discipline epistemology and the language that characterizes it, but still see themselves not equipped with more generic academic linguistic resources to be able to successfully convey and negotiate that specialized knowledge with their students.

> Extract 13. "I have to teach technical courses and the vocabulary is technical. Most of the times that is not an issue because students read those words in articles and documents. However, I think it is important in more day-to-day vocabulary to make everyone comprehend what you are saying. As a teacher I can use difficult vocabulary, but the main thing is to get your communication right."

On the other hand, some teachers' domain-specific communicative competence seems to have reached a plateau that makes it difficult for them to (1) account for and/or discuss the subtleties of their discipline in a very high-specialized level (Extract 14), and/or (2) lower down the linguistic and cognitive demand inherent in their subject matter so as to adapt it to their students' baseline level (Extract 15).

> Extract 14. "The more complicated the idea we want to convey, the more we must master the language. So I find it more difficult to participate in the debate of my scientific area in English (although I have knowledge and the jargon) than to communicate in an everyday situation because making nuanced statements requires full proficiency of the language."
>
> Extract 15. "A personal challenge for me is to be able to adapt my English to such a level that it can be understood by all non-native speakers. I find it difficult to assess what is the level of English of the students I teach."

Although participant teachers undoubtedly identify themselves as content experts, this self-image is often undermined by their reported feeling of not having sufficient linguistic resources to express their discipline-specific knowledge in a direct and intelligible manner to their students, which may be conducive to accommodations in classroom practices.

### *Practices and processes*

In the forum all teachers share the assumptions that teaching in ELF impacts their performance in fundamental ways. For example, teachers' preconceived belief that sounding native-like will benefit their teaching practices leads them to emulate native standards as close as possible. A teacher reflects upon it as follows:

> Extract 16. "I've picked up a lot of idiomatic expressions and slang from my interaction with American colleagues and, thinking about it, my students get blanked out looks when I use them. I'll try to avoid using them from now on."

Once again, learning about ELF and reflecting upon their practices provokes a change in teachers' identity that, in turn, seems to have potential implications for their future teaching performance. The teacher in Extract 16 has just discovered that attempting to be native-like may not be effective to her particular student cohort because native ways of expressing may be obscure for their international students (Jenkins, 2014). Her reflections are supported by another teacher's stance on the issue (Extract 17).

> Extract 17. "Sometimes it is actually more difficult to understand a native speaker in this setting [EMEMUS] seeing that we all have adapted to a common ELF that is not necessarily standard English."

Using ELF also seems to entail changes in teachers' classroom practices and processes in terms of loss of spontaneity and loss of improvisation. Teachers do not only confirm investing greater effort and much more time in lesson preparation, but also report having to simplify the content to facilitate students' comprehension of the lectures, and also because they have to adapt those contents to their own linguistic repertoire and language competence. As teachers' entries in Extract 18 show, the self-declared linguistic areas that teachers emphasize as being more problematic for their teaching practice and in need for improvement include: the correct use of verb tenses; their strong accents often understood by those students sharing their L1, but not by the rest; and a narrow variety of lexicon.

> Extract 18. "My vocabulary is too little. I repeat words where in my L1 I would have used many more synonyms." "My personal challenge now is to get a wider vocabulary to sound less repetitive." "My personal challenge is pronunciation. Some words are really difficult to me!" "I talk and talk but I need help with the correct use of the verbs." "It cost me more time to

prepare my lectures, both mentally and in vocabulary. I am less flexible in my answers and I am not always able to say what I think."

Additionally, teachers' own linguistic and communicative competence is not their only concern in EMEMUS. The often low linguistic level of their students is on many occasions also added to the mix. One teacher explains the extra difficulty in evaluating their students' learning as their poor written and oral production is not transparent enough:

> Extract 19. "I struggle when students have trouble expressing themselves in English, orally or in writing. Then I need to make sure that I don't assess student's English, but his knowledge of the subject."

Since ELF is nobody's L1, students also undergo the process of learning it for classroom communication. What is more, learners are not only novices regarding ELF but, if they have just started their higher education, they are apprentices in need of academic and disciplinary acculturation. It is at this point where teachers' responsibility for teaching the disciplinary-specific language resides (Sánchez-García, 2020; Dafouz, forthcoming). Although in our data teachers do not delve into this issue, they seem to be deeply concerned about the possible interference that students' L1 and, often, their already acquired disciplinary knowledge in this language may have in their learning of new disciplinary information in English. This is a teacher's description of it:

> Extract 20. "There are particular words to describe phenomena. For example, 'water', 'moisture', 'vapor', 'humidity' and 'damp' relate to some states of H20. However, the Swedish word 'fukt' can have multiple meanings of those English words, and I cannot judge if students are using the English words knowing the difference of the meanings of the English words."

Finally, the international nature of the students brought together in EMEMUS results in a further challenge in terms of teachers' practices: how to best integrate all students' cultural and linguistic backgrounds in their lessons. The following exchange among teachers illustrates this issue:

> Extract 21. "I am teaching students coming from different cultures. It is important to offer the students connections between the new things and their existing knowledge. I think my challenge is finding these connections within the variety of cultural backgrounds and language skills." "I have 10+ different countries represented in my classroom and I have to provoke communication among them. It is not very easy but at the end I become more complete when I get to integrate all students."

Participant teachers reported changes in their classroom practices give visibility to their seemingly constant process of accommodation to ELF, on the one hand, to try to ease their teaching and, on the other hand, to scaffold their students' learning through this language.

## Conclusions and implications

The results of this study on transnational teachers' identities as derived from the conceptualization of their EMEMUS experiences help depict the current foreign language education landscape and shed light on these teachers' actual linguistic and pedagogical needs. Although the 28 teachers participating in the study teach diverse discipline subjects in 11 HE institutions from six different European countries, teachers' verbalizations of their EMEMUS teaching practices are, to a large extent, common to all of them and have important implications for TESOL and TESOL teacher education programs. As shown by the study, teachers seem to face and be concerned about similar challenges regarding the impact that ELF places on their professional identity, the teaching of their academic disciplines, and their general classroom practices and processes. To ease such challenges and cater for teachers' reported needs, this study suggests the following measures. Teachers could benefit from specific language courses that equip them with a wider general and also academic language repertoire. This could include learning and practising how to articulate basic academic linguistic functions such as explaining, defining, exemplifying, or many others that are distinctive but not exclusive of their disciplines. Likewise, raising teachers' awareness of the discourse strategies that are available in their linguistic repertoire and providing them with further practice on them can also be of great value. Examples of such strategies could include approximation, circumlocution, paraphrasing, to name but a few (refer to Sánchez-García, 2019, for further examples of discourse strategies). These can be complemented by notions of social language that guide teachers on the organization and management of the lessons and on how to create good rapport with their students. Finally, teachers seem to be in need of strategies on how to deal with intercultural and mixed-ability language groups so that they can scaffold weak students' discipline-specific language needs and push forward more advanced learners while, at the same time, making good use of students' diverse backgrounds as an added value to the learning process. Against this backdrop, TESOL can inform EMEMUS in all these education needs. EMEMUS and language development are not mutually exclusive; quite the opposite, EMEMUS can build on EAP and/or ESP programs (Pecorari & Malmström, 2018). TESOL professionals are thus fundamental in supporting EME teachers' general linguistic and communicative competence while also helping them become more language-sensitive. This way, a much wished-for collaboration between language and content experts could turn into a fruitful reality in both research and practice.

In general terms, the benefits of providing teachers with chances for critical reflective practice are quite evident. T2T has afforded a transnational community of practice in which teachers not only reflect on their self-conceived teaching identities, but also share them with other colleagues who, although in different educational contexts, are undergoing similar teaching challenges and opportunities. Meaningful exchanges among colleagues are likely to promote a sense of belonging in a teaching community of experts that support and enrich each other and that, as a consequence, helps reaffirm and often improve teachers' self-concept. As reported by one teacher participant, "I feel I need to get objective feedback on my English and teaching from both students (who are not familiar with the subject yet) and from other experts in the same field (who know what I am talking about) in order to improve." For this reason, teacher education programs need to find ways that help pre-service and in-service EMEMUS teachers question their pre-established teaching assumptions and identities and exchange their concerns within a community of practice. T2T may serve as an example of bringing together and creating successful working networks among transnational teachers and/or other agents engaged in EMEMUS. T2T has been a pioneer in that sense, but more training programs of this type are much needed.

As a way of concluding, this is a teacher's personal written manifestation of the identity change experienced regarding ELF and its subsequent impact on EMEMUS teaching practices after the individual and joint reflections in the T2T forum analyzed:

> When it comes to ELF and my teaching, perhaps I need to use a different pedagogy when I teach in English. Until now, I have translated my L1 into English, and then try to do it as good as I do in L1. This leads to a feeling of inadequacy, as I never will be as good in English as in L1. I try to work interactively when I teach in L1 and in English, but perhaps the interactivity becomes even more important in the ELF-situation, as I need to understand where students are in terms of understanding. After all, they need to understand the topic AND the language. Part of the vocabulary is new regardless we use L1 or English, they do learn a new topic. In L1, it feels natural to explain new words to students, but in English, it might be harder to discern what words we need to discuss the meaning of. Being perceptive to those details makes a good ELF-teacher.

## Acknowledgments

The authors of this chapter thank the T2T team, both facilitators and participants, without whom this research would not have been possible.

## References

Beelen J., & Jones, E. (2015). Redefining internationalization at home. In A. Curaj, L. Matei, R. Pricopie, J. Salmi, & P. Scott (Eds.), *The European higher education area* (pp. 149–154). Cham: Springer International Publishing.

Beijaard, D., Meijer, P. C. M., & Verloop, N. (2004). Reconsidering research on teachers' professional identity. *Teaching and Teacher Education*, 20, 107–128.

Björkman, B. (2013). English as an academic lingua franca. Berlin: De Gruyter Mouton.

Braun, V., & Clarke, V. (2006). Using thematic analysis in psychology. *Qualitative Research in Psychology*, 3(2), 77–101.

Carroll, J. (2015). *Tools for teaching in an educationally mobile world.* London: Routledge.

Dafouz, E. (forthcoming). "So, after a week, I became a teacher of English": Physics lecturers' beliefs on the integration of content and language in English-medium higher education.

Dafouz, E., & Smit, U. (2016). Towards a dynamic conceptual framework for English-medium education in multilingual university settings. *Applied Linguistics*, 37(3), 397–415.

Dafouz, E., & Smit, U. (2020). *ROAD-MAPPING English medium education in the internationalised university.* Cham: Palgrave Pivot.

Dimova, S., & Kling, J. (2018). Assessing English-medium instruction lecturer language proficiency across disciplines. *TESOL Quarterly*, 52(3), 634–656.

Doiz, A., Lasagabaster, D., & Sierra, J. M. (2011). Internationalization, multilingualism and English-medium instruction. *World Englishes*, 30(3), 345–359.

Doiz, A., Lasagabaster, D., & Sierra, J. M. (2013). *English-Medium instruction at universities: Global challenges.* Bristol: Multilingual Matters.

Erikson, E. H. (1968). *Identity, youth and crisis.* New York: W. W. Norton & Company.

House, J., & Lévy-Tödter, M. (2010). Linguistic competence and professional identity in English medium instruction. In B. Meyer & B. Apfelbaum (Eds.), *Multilingualism at work: From policies to practices in public, medical and business settings* (Vol. 9, pp. 13–46). Hamburg: Hamburg Studies on Multlingualism (HSM).

Hultgren, A., Jensen, C., & Dimova, S. (2015). English-medium instruction in European Higher Education: From the North to the South. In S. Dimova, A. Hultgren, & C. Jensen (Eds.), *English-medium instruction in European higher education* (pp. 317–324). Berlin: de Gruyter Mouton.

Jenkins, J. (2014). *English as a lingua franca in the international university.* Oxford and New York: Routledge.

Jenkins, J. (2019). English medium instruction in Higher Education: The role of ELF. In A. Gao, C. Davison, & C. Leung (Eds.), *Second handbook of English language teaching* (pp. 2–18). Springer Nature Switzerland AG.

Kling, J. (2016). Content teachers engaged in English medium instruction in Denmark. In J. Crandall & M. A. Christison (Eds.), *Global research on teacher education and professional development in TESOL* (pp. 225–239). New York: Taylor & Francis.

Knowles, G. J. (1992). Models for understanding pre-service and beginning teachers' biographies: Illustrations from case studies. In I. F. Goodson (Ed.), *Studying teachers' lives* (pp. 99–152). London: Routledge.

Lauridsen, K. M. (2017). Professional development of international classroom lecturers. In J. Valcke & R. Wilkinson (Eds.), *Integrating content and language in higher education* (pp. 25–37). Frankfurt am Main: Peter Lang.

Lauridsen, K., Dafouz, E., Stavicka, A., & Wetter, M. (2015). IntlUni recommendations. In K. M. Lauridsen & M. K. Lillemose (Eds.), *Opportunities and challenges in the multilingual and multicultural learning space. Final document of the IntlUni Erasmus Academic Network project 2012–2015* (pp. 11–13). Aarhus: IntlUni.

Mead, G. J. (1934). *Mind, self and society.* Chicago: University of Chicago Press.

Mercado, S., & Gibson, L. (2013). The key elements of transnational education (TNE). European Association for International Education. Retrieved from www.eaie.org/blog/key-elements-transnational-education-tne.html.

Pecorari, D., & Malmström, H. (2018). At the crossroads of TESOL and English medium instruction. *TESOL Quarterly*, 52(3), 497–515.

Sánchez-García, D. (2019). "I can't find the words now…": Teacher discourse strategies and their communicative potential in Spanish- and English-medium instruction in higher education. *CLIL Journal of Innovation and Research in Plurilingual and Pluricultural Education*, 2, 43–55.

Sánchez-García, D. (2020). Internationalization through language and literacy in the Spanish EME context. In S.Dimova & J. Kling (Eds.), *Integrating content and language in multilingual higher education*. Springer.

Seidlhofer, B. (2011). *Understanding English as a lingua franca*. Oxford: Oxford University Press.

Smit, U., & Dafouz, E. (2012). Integrating content and language in higher education: An introduction to English-medium policies, conceptual issues and research practices across Europe. *AILA Review*, 25, 1–12.

Taguchi, N. (2014). English-medium education in the global society: An introduction. Special issue of *International Review of Applied Linguistics*, 52(2), 89–98.

Valcke, J., & Romero, E. (2016). It takes two to tango: Online teacher tándems for teaching in English. In S. Jager, M. Kurek, & B. O'Rourke (Eds.), *New directions in telecollaborative research and practice: Selected papers from the second conference in telecollaboration in higher education* (pp. 171–177). Research-publish.net.

van Der Walt, C. (2013). *Multilingual higher education: Beyond English medium orientations*. Bristol: Multilingual Matters.

Wilkins, S. (2018). Definitions of transnational higher education. *International Higher Education*, 95, 5–7.

Wilkinson, R. (2018). Locating the ESP space in problem-based learning: English-medium degree programmes from a post-Bologna perspective. In I. Fortanet & C. Räisänen (Eds.), *ESP in European higher education: Integrating language and content* (pp. 55–73). Amsterdam: John Benjamins.

# Part IV

# Policy, curricula, and professional learning and development

# 12 Transglocality in English language teacher education

## A transnational polyethnography of the Glendon D-TEIL experience in Cuba

*Iara Bruz, Gustavo Moura, Ruberval Maciel, Ian Martin and Brian Morgan*

Duoethnography – "a research methodology that desires to be participatory, dialogic and nonprescriptive" (Norris & Sawyer, 2016, p. 12) – was chosen to capture the experiential differences of the author-collaborators, while facilitating a potentially transformative dialogue around key themes: transglocal program design; the ethics of transnational teacher education; dealing with unpredictability; white privilege and the native English-speaking teacher; the place and purpose of English in the world; ethics and criticality; ecological thinking and epistemic location.

The chapter does not seek to resolve these thematic questions, but raising them in a transnational dialogue around a transnational teacher education project demonstrates how duo/polyethnography can allow for an extremely rich set of themes to be expressed. The D-TEIL project becomes, therefore, a site for transglocal language teacher education whose continuing validity and dynamism stem from the ongoing dialogue along the thematic lines suggested here, and elsewhere engaging a range of collaborators and participants coming together in the spirit of polyethnography.

### Introduction

This chapter brings together language teacher education (LTE) scholars from Brazil and Canada and extends a wide range of collaborative research projects that first began in 2010,[1] followed soon after by a Social Sciences and Humanities Research Council (Government of Canada) partnership development grant that involved several Canadian and Brazilian universities.[2] In 2012, the State University of Mato Grosso do Sul (UEMS) and Glendon College formalized a partnership agreement with the intention of supporting further student and faculty exchange. These various transnational activities have been highly productive, culminating in numerous co-publications and presentations, and providing many rich opportunities to study and teach across our varied sites of research and practice. Such opportunities invariably encourage critical reflection and reconsideration of our own localities and preferred beliefs and practices as language professionals.

Perhaps this is one of the most beneficial aspects of transnational work: to begin to see our own students and classrooms anew through the eyes and experiences of "distant" colleagues – what we feel is best captured in the concept *transglocality*, which we will describe in greater detail below.

The focus of such a comparative and ethnographic lens is Glendon College's Certificate in the Discipline of Teaching English as an International Language (D-TEIL) program, and more specifically, its international practicum at the E. A. Varona Pedagogical University in Havana, Cuba (Martin & Morgan, 2015, 2019; Moura, 2017; Bruz, 2018), which has facilitated this collective conversation around critically and ethically teaching our students (see Appendices 1 and 2). This chapter, therefore, combines the experiences of the five language teacher scholars, who are in different stages in their careers, in order to rethink English teaching and its purposes in the contemporary world. In thinking of English language teacher education alongside what we call transglocality in this chapter, we aim at examining and exploring how our life histories as English speakers, English learners, English teachers, and English teacher educators affect the meanings we give to our experiences. From the notion of duoethnography, our objective is to unravel our stories and work on our senses in learning experiences through the voices of the five authors of the chapter. Socio-politically and culturally speaking, we have all acquired beliefs that have influenced what we teach and learn. Therefore, we find it reasonable to approach the numerous similar and different meanings we have of a shared phenomenon through what we call a polyethnography.

## Duoethnography: a participatory research method for language teacher education

Given our number, we describe our efforts here as a polyethnography, one informed by the principles and goals of duoethnography, "a research methodology that desires to be participatory, dialogic, and nonprescriptive" (Norris & Sawyer, 2016, p. 12; Schmidt & Gagné, 2014; Breault, 2016; Sawyer & Norris, 2013). An English language teaching (ELT) duoethnography thus seeks to avoid an imposed consensus, a singular interpretive meta-narrative of the program or curricula at hand. Moreover, this collaborative work focuses not only on a shared research object, but also in promoting the transparency and experiential differences of participants to facilitate a potentially transformative dialogue.

Researchers write and use other texts and experiences to prompt their findings and construct their own meanings throughout a research process (Oberg & Wilson, 2002). For this chapter, then, the process of juxtaposing our dialogues and ideas of the same core content means to set the table for how differently each one of us relates to the various themes that emerge from the research context. Following Oberg and Wilson (2002), we have decided to negotiate and pluralize the voices in our work, which essentially represents our chosen polyethnography. Organizing ourselves through a polyethnographic methodology reflects on how each of our perspectives shows its own integrity to the theme as well as how we all offer a myriad of possibilities to approach and reframe English language teaching and teacher education. It is also particularly appropriate for the study of a complex, transglocal program such as the one we describe.

Still, a duo/polyethnography is not without its own complexities. For one, it requires sustained interaction and not mere juxtaposition, which is not easy in a profession that is often isolating. A second point relates to the effects on participants, who are challenged to recognize their individual interpretations and unacknowledged biases in respect to their favored approaches to language teacher education. Potentially, according to Fanselow (1977), even though participants generally share the same experience in a program under study (i.e., D-TEIL), it is a crucial task of duoethnography to align multiple voices and discover what is really central to the analysis amidst diverse lenses and beliefs. Indeed, by its nature, a duoethnography produces novel alignments across sites and spatio-temporal scales that might not have been discovered otherwise.

## Data analysis display

The tenets of our polyethnography allow us to escape from the universalism of describing and analysing the D-TEIL program. With that in mind, this chapter organizes all authors' individual voices drawn from three different moments of making sense of the data. The first moment portrays data from two virtual roundtables (VR). Following the dialogical notion of a duoethnographic approach, we include short transcripts as modified conversational data using ellipses and quotation marks. The excerpts we choose from the VR play an important role in the construction of this chapter as we revisit our experiences in the D-TEIL program and during our practicum in Varona University.

Then, in writing this chapter, we came across unanticipated different ways of constructing a dialogical reflection. That is, as each of us went back to listening to both of our VRs, we realized we still had commentaries we wanted to add. Therefore, we continued our dialogues and built them up adding personal reflections as we constructed the chapter. This type of data is represented in this chapter by regular font preceded by the name of the author/narrator. And lastly, as we went back and forth with the drafts of the chapter, we ended up creating a third form of textual display, which is more expository in style and function, focused on commentary, analysis, and organization. This third form of expository text is marked by *italics* and does not have individual attribution.

Within the next sections of our chapter, we will provide a brief overview of the D-TEIL program and its practicum in Havana. After this, we discuss our choice of the term transglocal over other terms, and the understanding behind the prefix "trans." Following sections will address a group of themes that first emerged in our VRs. Overall, the chapter presents some reflections around the ethics of critical transnational teacher education, exploring culture and power in north–south exchanges, as well as how to make sense of privilege. The themes are as follows: transglocal program design; the ethics of transnational teacher education; dealing with unpredictability; white privilege and the native English-speaking teacher;

rethinking the place and purpose of English in the world; and reflections on ethics and criticality.

## Discipline of Teaching English as an International Language (D-TEIL)

**Gustavo**: My understanding of the purposes of the D-TEIL program is that it includes learning about different cultures and languages and working with students from a liberal arts education who show interest in the field of English as an international language teaching. The outline of the D-TEIL certificate delves into the general principles of applied linguistics applicable to language teaching, the notions of language learning, the concepts of language and society and bi/plurilingualism, as well as the history and impact of English as a global language. Besides the required courses, pre-service teachers are responsible for partaking in a teaching practicum.

**Ian**: Following on from what Gustavo has said, we have designed the D-TEIL program as a 24-credit undergraduate certificate which can be taken by Glendon students majoring in Liberal Arts disciplines such as English, Linguistics, or International Studies. These students have varying degrees of background in bilingual (French-English) education. They are not necessarily intending to make a career of teaching English abroad, but who see D-TEIL as an international experiential learning opportunity which also opens a window on English in the World/the World in English, which the English Department curriculum holds to be an essential component of 21$^{st}$ century English Studies. The students' language repertoires are rich and varied, due both to Glendon's student body being a reflection of Toronto, a major multilingual metropolis with high levels of global immigration, as well as to Glendon's commitment to bilingual education and language learning. The result is that the formerly canonical "monolingual (English) native speaker" is not represented in the D-TEIL student body. The program has been in existence since 2006, and over 125 students have participated in its biennial international teaching practica in Cuba.

**Gustavo**: As I personally experienced in 2016, the practicum normally takes place at Varona Pedagogical University in Havana, Cuba, and it is an essential component of the certificate. The exchange agreement supports the mutual collaboration of both universities, and in the past few years, this relationship has been strengthened with the addition of Brazilian academics such as Iara, Ruberval and Clarissa (Jordão),[3] and myself in the project. In three weeks, the practicum is divided as: week 1 – observation of classes; week 2 – co-teaching with Cuban teachers; and week 3 – D-TEIL students teach a "thematic module" lesson on their own. That means student-teachers have to choose a topic of interest and develop a language teaching plan which considers the socio-cultural-political-historic implications of the topic (e.g., hip hop, ballet, vegetarianism). These topics allow the D-TEIL students to develop a more global awareness of local attitudes of students and teachers, here called the transglocality of our teaching.

## "Trans" to what? Why foreground the transglocal in LTE?

**Brian**: In the initial preparation of our chapter proposal one of the final discussion points was about how we should complete the prefix "trans" to best represent our experiences. The notion of the transnational seemed self-evident given the context and unifying theme of this book on LTE. We also agreed quite early on that the notion of the translocal was relevant as we recognized how we came to rethink our own sites of practice and related professional beliefs through our collaboration. I think it was Ian who brought forward the notion of transglocality, which we have included in our title. The choice reminded me of an acronym coined many years ago: TEGCOM (Teaching English for Glocalized Communication) by Lin, Wang, Akamatsu, and Riazi (2002). In ways that parallel our own experiences, they saw the sharing and comparing of local stories facilitating a broader understanding of the profession and a source of critique and "revisioning" of dominant LTE ideologies. What does the transglocal say about our own work and our perspectives arising from D-TEIL and the Varona practicum in Havana?

**Ian**: A word about the word: "transglocal." Clearly, it is an extension of Robertson's (1992) term "glocalization," in which "the global is brought in conjunction with the local, and the local is modified to accommodate the global" (Kumaravadivelu, 2008, p. 45). The addition of the "trans" prefix is intended to allow that glocalization works differently in different places, and the different place-based dynamics need to be taken into account, for example, in preparing "Northern" students to travel for study in the "South," or in matters of curriculum development (what generative themes "work," however differently, in Toronto, Havana, and Campo Grande), or in classroom observation assignments (e.g., what counts as "affordance" "here" and "there" and how can an observer from "here" perceive the value of affordances "there" – en route to designing place-appropriate affordances for "there"?). The third-week "thematic modules" which the D-TEIL students teach are designed by students using a transglocal approach, in which a theme (topic) is selected which includes both common (Canada–Cuba) aspects and locally distinct elements. The process includes both a provisional design brought by Glendon students to Havana, after which, in dialogue with upper-year Varona students, the module, now "grounded locally," is presented to a Varona English class, with elements brought in from Toronto and Havana, and often using texts in both English and Spanish supporting the theme.

Iara, Gustavo, how do you see elements of transglocality revealed in your observation of the practicum?

**Iara (VR)**: "One related, transglocal issue for me was in L2 pronunciation teaching in Varona. Some of the Cuban teachers treated the Canadians as a source for the right pronunciation, they would also go to the pollitos[4] and say 'oh, how do you say this in English? What is the CORRECT way to say that?' They treated them as more like a grammar and pronunciation source, than anything else. Some of the pollitos said they felt they were being used to read texts […] but they had an impact on those classrooms, we just don't know if it was an impact to show that English is global, or an impact to reinforce English as it belongs to Canada. English belongs to the Canadians."

**Gustavo**: I see transglocality through the lens of (neo)colonialism. LTE is the centre for the spread of colonial one-size-fits-all models of teaching. According to Kumaravadivelu (2012), the orientations for English teaching still focus on colonially center-based knowledge production which results in the Global North teaching the Global South what the proper ways of teaching English are. Also, given the current neoliberal agendas of governmental practices and policies, it is pivotal to be sensitive to the theories behind teaching practices. In an interview with Brian, Ferraz (Ferraz & Morgan, 2019), for instance, encourages us to reflect on how English classes can be spaces for developing critical, reflective, and ethical pedagogies. Adding to Ian's transglocal interpretation, English teachers need an awareness of the situatedness of practices that can affect global contexts. It is about my seeing how the local affects the global and vice versa.

I believe that pedagogies should reflect the localities of the host communities, and as teachers who are in the process of transnationalism, coming back and forth from one country to the other, they are able to realize and recognize their local language teaching practices through an international experience. Basically, the idea is to think locally and impact globally. In the matter of the transglocality, which we choose to work with in this chapter, we imply a group of language teachers and scholars who cross nation-state borders, revisit their theories on English teaching and teacher education, and how they impact local, national, and global teaching contexts.

**Ian**: This raises an interesting question around the value of movement (i.e., embodied transglocality) and its effect on theory in LTE. In fact, I see movement as a powerful unsettling force against center-based hegemonies in theory formation.

**Gustavo (VR)**: "Theory actually made more sense because of this moving, all this travelling. And we were not only theorizing from theories, we were actually living the theories through the mobility we got to do."

**Ruberval (VR)**: "I think in this process of being in different places, and in each place, they have to reflect about some specific things, and these things being related to ELT and teacher education, for example, as they were here with me or with Clarissa [...] I think this experience of being in different places and with different professors and different groups of students [...] I think if they were just in one place, they would have only one perception [...] It is a different process when we go there from when we are just outsiders. We are outsiders but also insiders because we have had the experience."

*Different perspectives inform a transglocal reflection on teaching. The D-TEIL program, with the international practicum, provides northern teachers and southern teachers with a chance to rethink the ethics of their teaching and helps prepare teachers to teach globally, and to recognize what the dynamics behind English teaching are in terms of white-privilege and native-speakerism. Therefore, in the following subsections of the chapter, we approach some of these ideological stances which the practicum at Varona University has afforded us to think about.*

## The ethics of transnational teacher education

**Gustavo**: As we rethink the ethics of a transnational teacher education, we agree that the D-TEIL program somehow showed us that "we need to be better as teachers. We need to be able to provide a rationale" for the theories – critical or otherwise – that we present to student-teachers (Ferraz & Morgan, 2019, p. 205). Especially in my case, my theoretical background has had a huge impact on my teaching as it should be something essentially critical. In one of the VR discussions we had as a group, my concern was of imposing a sense of criticality that sometimes does not reflect my students' contexts, nor their communities. For me, there is still a sense that some cultural communities act as if they held more knowledge than others. As we talk about English teaching and international practica, scholars such as Martin and Morgan (2015, 2019) affirm that there are ways of developing international practica that are sensitive to and supportive of local conditions and traditions of language teaching and learning.

**Gustavo (VR)**: "I don't think it would be ethical just to present my idea of something. As if just my opinion mattered [...] You can identify how different notions ... different things work out in different places [...] The classes (English as a World Language) were important to raise those ... like, to be ethically responsible for our students and their differences. At the same time, Ian's classes were focused on the Cuban culture, how students are, and how we could do something more approachable in terms of teaching English."

**Iara (VR)**: "It's interesting, because of what Gustavo said, it would be an example of what I found [...] Being a teacher is a never-ending process. Those pollitos [the Canadian student-teachers] are probably doing other things now and adding their teaching to all the things [they learned] from the D-TEIL program [...] We don't have an end [...] For teacher educators, it is about choosing what to show students. For example, in the D-TEIL program, they cannot show everything about Cuba. So, choices have to be made. And when we make those choices, there's no guarantee. What the student is going to read is going to go through their experiences, previous experiences as well."

**Iara**: The matter of choosing your ethical positionality in teaching reflects much of the ethics in a transnational context. Although we, as an outside culture, think we have made good choices, we cannot expect our students will agree and accept them. Drawing back from the notion of emancipation, as a teacher, we may think we are being neutral when in fact we are not. Thus, we have to watch and better understand the ethics of seeing our students. Duffy (2017), for instance, says teachers ethically affect students by the way they talk, the words they choose and the truths they validate.

**Brian**: In accordance with that, Iara, I'd like to comment on your important point on ethical positionality. We tend to treat our own ethical beliefs as commonsensical and universal rather than ideological and shaped by particular experiences including the preferred values and identity roles that teacher educators provide. It reminds me of a question I posed in our virtual roundtable, specifically for you and Gustavo. As graduate students of Clarissa (Jordão) and Ruberval, you could be called the 3rd generation of the University of São Paulo (USP) school of critical literacies (Novos Letramentos) in Brazil, an impressive and continuing legacy of applied linguistic thought created and guided by Lynn Mario de Souza and Walkyria Monte Mor. USP grads have moved into academic positions of scholarly influence throughout the country. My question in the roundtable was partly celebratory (i.e., the USP legacy) but also critically reflective: How would you (re) consider the ethics of your own critical training and approach as you teach your student-teachers (the 4th generation) based now on the additional, transnational experience of D-TEIL and the practicum in Havana?

**Iara**: One conclusion from my Ph.D. research (Bruz, 2018) is that there is no guarantee of achieving preestablished objectives when involved in teacher education, and I would even argue there is no guarantee in teaching in general. Taking the D-TEIL as example, the pollitos prepared themselves before going to the practicum by reading about teaching English as an International language and researching about the country they were going to go to. Moreover, even though they did a great job on preparation, they still had to face moments in which they felt unprepared or moments in which they each faced cultural shock. Adding to that, each of them went through different experiences during the practicum in Cuba, besides attending the same courses in Canada. Therefore, teachers or teacher educators cannot access what their students truly process when they are taking their courses; considering them as unique individuals, each of them expressed different perspectives during the program.

**Gustavo**: To answer your question, Brian, when observing and teaching future teachers, I believe I should reconsider my ethics of my critical training in terms of accepting that criticality should not serve as a one-size-fits-all teaching method. The USP legacy reflects practices that question and challenge hegemonic and traditional teaching methods. It indeed shows us the power of language in (re) defining ways of knowing. And that is what we should carry on with us – knowing there is no singular, universal, or context-free way to know or teach.

In this context, being ethically responsible gives you a notion of dealing with what is unpredictable. Ethics vary from person to person, and from culture to culture. Therefore, for a teacher education program, it is important to negotiate power relationships, the exploration of host communities, and making sense of privilege as English speakers.

## Dealing with unpredictability

**Ruberval (VR)**: "This is one place [D-TEIL] that is very rich to address unpredictability [...] They have to go there [Cuba], to a place with very limited resources ... and they are aware that there are many [content] aspects that they cannot address [e.g., consumerism]. Normally they [Brazilian teachers] say they [Brazilian students in public schools] don't learn because they don't have resources; the normal thing that they say here in Brazil, the lack of support or any other aspect that is negative to learn English. But this [observation of a Cuban class] is very different. I remember when they were looking at their cell phones, and the first time I thought they were, you know, looking for something on the Internet … not paying attention. But they were using their cell phones to read the text, to follow the lesson!"

**Iara (VR)**: "I'd like to comment on expecting the unexpected. Almost all the pollitos mentioned it in the interviews [for my Ph.D. thesis]. Looking back and thinking back, I think that D-TEIL does a great job of that. And it's impossible to prepare for the unexpected. What I think D-TEIL did was, 'Oh, you're going to find many different things in Cuba, everything can happen, sometimes you'll have to improvise.' But it's impossible to prepare teachers for what's really going to happen … and a classroom in another country, a country that is so unique like Cuba. So, there are no guarantees, because some pollitos dealt with that [i.e., unpredictable classroom events] much better than the others."

**Iara**: The D-TEIL program is full of examples of dealing with unpredictability. It makes sense to think of unpredictability when thinking of classrooms in general. A classroom is made of people with different backgrounds who have different perceptions about what happens around them. In this sense, when this group of teachers-to-be went to their practicum, they went through a period of preparation (Bruz, 2018; Moura, 2017; Martin & Morgan, 2015, 2019). Since the participants of the group were getting ready for this international trip to be able to complete their course, they were also creating expectations, which is rather impossible not to have and create. Most of them would be inside a classroom as teachers for the first time besides going into an international setting for their practicum. It's unimaginable that one can just stop the creation of expectations. It's more a case of how we understand this idea. As Pennycook states (2012), "expecting the unexpected is not so much a question of being ready for what we do not expect as an undoing of the lines along which our lines of expectation run" (p. 36).

**Brian**: A very interesting quote. For me, it suggests that an "unexpected" moment potentially has a productive, pedagogical effect on students and something to utilize. But it requires some prior work (or articulation) in order to be effective in terms of undoing familiar lines of expectation.

**Ian**: I agree. In D-TEIL, for example, a lot of thought has gone into helping shape the students' expectations in the pre-departure period. Exposure to videos of Varona classes, written reflections of previous years' students, academic literature on English in Cuba, as well as a course component entitled "my emergent image of Cuba" in which the Canadian students chart the deepening of their knowledge about Cuba over the three months prior to departure help. On the applied side, they are required to come up with a "personal cultural project" on Cuba, which often coincides with the requirement that they develop and design a draft "thematic module" to be taught in the third week of the practicum. Here, there is a serious applied focus on expectations of how generative the theme will be as a framework of affordances for English and content-learning by the Cuban students. Of course, we have adopted a flexible framework which lends itself to this challenge of expectations and unpredictability in local settings unfamiliar to the teacher, and this would be Kumaravadivelu's (2012) post-method approach, in particular, his parameters of possibility, practicality, and particularity.

**Iara**: As part of this framework, Kumaravadivelu (2012, p. 9) claims that "since language learning and teaching needs, wants and situations are unpredictably numerous, no idealized method can visualize all the variables in advance in order to provide situation-specific suggestions." It was not a surprise that this theme [unpredictability] showed up when the participants were interviewed (Bruz, 2018). Among what the participants mentioned about unpredictability, it had both positive and challenging sides. According to the students I interviewed, they refer to the classroom environment where anything can happen, and when a teacher has a plan, the class can either stick to the plan or deviate from it and still be a good class. Moreover, there is the sense that adaptation played a big role during the student-teachers' practicum and made them feel as if they were dealing with something that made them insecure (e.g., "I hope to float"). They all mostly had to reinvent themselves once they were in the practicum. When there is teacher education, the teacher educator has no guarantees of what their students are learning or reflecting on. Bruz (2018) reports that it is impossible to prepare teachers for unpredictability, since the word itself states uncertainty. One cannot know what exactly will happen regarding this, so there is no accurate preparation and no prior certainty of what will transpire.

## White privilege and the native English-speaking teacher

**Ian**: Iara, I'd like you to expand on a point you raised above (p. 000) on L2 pronunciation, which relates to Cuban perceptions of speaker authenticity, white privilege, and the ownership of English. My long experience in Cuba has shown me that native-speakerism is a powerful belief, which leads Cubans to feel insecure about the legitimacy of their English. What kinds of data did you collect on this phenomenon, and how did the pollitos respond?

**Brian**: Before Iara responds I'd like to remind her of a Varona class we observed in which students asked us about our favorite variety of English. When we responded together that we really liked Cuban English, the students were shocked and couldn't believe that such English could be anything but a learner's inadequate and/or "fossilized" version!

**Iara**: I do remember that episode. It's interesting that the Cubans were learning English but not realizing that they were learning and speaking a legitimate variety of English. This relates to Ian's pronunciation question and the issue of native-speakerism.

**Ian**: I remember an experience taping dialogues in which the Cuban roles (for example, the role of a Cuban waiter at a tourist restaurant), at the insistence of the Cuban teachers, had to be voiced by foreign native speakers rather than Cubans speaking fluent English!

**Iara**: And that happened all the time I was there! It was the usual practice to ask the pollitos to read passages from the textbooks out loud. In my doctoral research I was interested in how the pollitos responded to this positioning of them as model native speakers. I asked some of them about how they defined or problematized the native-speaker concept. Their answers varied, but interestingly none mentioned birth place as a defining factor. They mentioned other factors as below. In the words of a participant, this speaker can simply be someone "who speaks the language first" and this may not necessarily be related to place of birth. Another participant said this speaker is "anyone who almost speak without hesitation or without … think [too much]". In addition, this participant in special said that "they didn't know English as their first language, and yet they're still considered a native speaker. Because it is a language that they're most proficient in and have learned the most in."

**Brian**: I remember during the VR that Ruberval mentioned that Gustavo was seen or positioned as a "true" Canadian, and therefore a native speaker, based on his being racialized by Cubans as white.

**Iara**: In the VR, I remember Ruberval mentioning Gustavo's participation in the D-TEIL program, and how his appearance mattered in terms of being seen as part of the Canadian group. Not being Canadian but being considered as one of the groups in Cuba is based on the physical factor related to native speakers that is not usually reflected upon. When people think of a native speaker of English, they usually come up with one image. This image may include skin color and they may come even with a face, and this image is usually of a white person (Windle, 2017).

One of the pollitas said that her Cuban students didn't believe she was Canadian and Gustavo, just because he was positioned as white, didn't have to defend his legitimacy. They just considered him a native speaker. The pollita went on, expanding on the idea of race: in this example, the fact that the speaker was born in Canada was not relevant, nor the fact that she learned English as her first language. What mattered most was her appearance, which did not fit a Cuban expectation, because her appearance made them think she was from another country and not Canada – and perhaps a country whose people were colonized. This experience affected directly her experience in the practicum. In the interview, she said she did not initially feel legitimate as their teacher, and she had to make more effort than the other teachers-to-be.

For this matter, we can conclude that passing as a native speaker is not something we should take for granted. Also, being one and being considered one does not mean feeling legitimate as an English teacher. And thus, there were other factors related to this topic such as owning a language and feeling comfortable speaking it. Even though most of the pollitas were considered native speakers, it did not mean they did not go through struggles. And thinking about the native speaker role inside foreign language classrooms is relevant, because there is an imaginary built behind the scenes that makes students and teachers aim at a certain kind of speaker. As one of the participant pollitas mentioned:

> It's very hard to be away from that native speaker idealism because language learners will always look up at native speakers as their goal. But it's hard to make all people aware of that. And especially native speakers. There are very few native speakers that are aware … self-aware of being a native speaker.
>
> (Bruz, 2018, Appendix)

## Rethinking the place and purpose of English in the world

**Brian**: In posing my next question for our group, I'd like to reiterate that a key reason and benefit of transnational work is how we can come to see and potentially transform our own localities – the transglocality of our efforts – as a result of our ongoing dialogue and professional exchanges. Related to my own teaching, I'd like to hear from Gustavo and Iara about their experiences of auditing my D-TEIL course, English as a World Language (GL/EN 4695.3) and any recommendations they would make for it and the teaching of EWL/EIL, in general.

**Gustavo (VR)**: "[…] I thought the North Americans would be teaching me something, and we were not going to create dialogue. I was not there for them to listen to me. […] You tried to attend all the aspects of English teaching and how they are developed in different societies and cultures."

**Gustavo**: There is no doubt that English seems to have roots with its "native speakers." The positionality we take as ESL/EFL speakers grants native-speakers' English as an ideal of language. And perhaps, the need to make English teaching critical is a way I myself have found to mask the fact that I am an ESL speaker. The language of criticality has worked well in my Brazilian context since it gives me the chance to challenge the worldwide hegemony the language has taken (Canagarajah, 1999). As Ferraz (2018) presents, English is indeed the international language; therefore, the way I find to dismantle that hegemony is by presenting a critical aspect to it. Consequently, the focus I give to my English teaching does not necessarily meet the requirements of learning the system of the language.

In rethinking what the purpose of English is, there is a great imbalance between teachers' practices and teacher education programs. As Brazilian language educators, as I mentioned during our VR, I do not think we prepare new teachers to teach the language; instead, we prepare them to speak the language. When it is about the language, we learn its code and literature. When it's about teaching, we don't talk about English teaching.

In addition to Ferraz's (2018) proposition that in Brazil there is no education for educators, we understand that teachers learn how to teach as they experience it themselves. Teachers teach what they are told to teach. Going back to the unpredictability of teaching, LTE is proof of how language teachers should be open to learning what the students want to learn English for. Whether it is for having better job conditions, as in the case of Brazil and Cuba, or for learning how a culture works in a country's settings (Ferraz & Morgan, 2019), English serves people differently. And to think about English implies thinking about the ethical and critical applications of language teaching, which we will present next.

## Reflections on ethics and criticality

*In our view, ethics and criticality are two aspects of language teaching that go together. When rethinking our ethics in teaching, we open space for criticality to develop a sense of reflexivity on what we do as teachers and what our students learn from our practices. From a Brazilian perspective (Monte Mór, 2011; Menezes de Souza, 2011), criticality refers to the meaning making process and how the perceptions of the world are expanded through cultural, social, epistemological, and historical experiences. Criticality serves the citizens to visualize society and its inequities, exclusions, and issues of power. Criticality indeed leads to an ethical reflection of how diverse knowledge can be and consequently allows teachers to be self-reflexive.*

**Gustavo (VR)**: "While we reflect about critical studies and criticality in LTE [...] something I think about is why we talk so much about critical literacies in Brazil? And probably not that much at Glendon?"

**Iara (VR)**: "Well, during my defense [Ph.D. oral examination], one of the professors asked me to include critical literacies because what they do is totally critical literacies."

**Gustavo (VR)**: "And then, why are we, Brazilians, always approaching language teaching as a critical study and maybe that is not, well, mentioned in the Canadian context? [...] Why do we keep doing courses with critical implied in the courses? Also, I remember talking to Ruberval, talking to you [Brian] in the hotel in Cuba after you watched a class of mine ... with Ruberval we kind of discussed what is the real idea behind being critical in a classroom, and then you [Brian] added it's not because you need to be critical that you leave aside vocabulary aspects or grammar aspects [...] Later, back in Brazil, [teaching the same class in Campo Grande after D-TEIL] [...] I was more thoughtful of those comments. What does it mean to be critical? But then, what does it mean to teach them English because they're not there just to listen to me and ask questions and accept all answers [...] What aspects of the language itself am I teaching to those students that I wasn't before?"

**Iara (VR)**: "[Re: the difficulties of teacher preparation] On top of that, something that I question a lot is, like how can you make somebody think critically and what it is to think critically at first."

**Brian (VR)**: "How would you re-think or try to introduce [criticality] to students to reflect their particularity?"

**Gustavo (VR)**: "For me, [re: international students/classrooms] the first thing I should approach is trying to understand their notion of being critical in an English lesson. Then I wouldn't be working with my imagination and my context as a critical teacher in Brazil, because it's pretty easy to be a critical English teacher in Brazil when we have the people we have around. Once we establish what being critical in a different place means, I'd start working on more horizontal relationships with students (Kubota & Miller, 2017)."

**Iara (VR)**: "Like building knowledge with students instead of only teaching."

**Gustavo (VR)**: "[...] Maybe criticality is a process. It doesn't need an outcome right away."

**Ian**: Applying a transglocal lens to criticality, I think that the D-TEIL students were encouraged to explore what "criticality" would mean in relation to their theme (of their Week 3 module topic) in Havana and how Cuban students' criticality might differ from their own, and in quite unexpected ways.

**Gustavo**: Ethically, I agree with Ian that criticality should take into consideration the actual understanding of transformation that the host communities have in the case of transnational teaching. The D-TEIL program certainly promotes a democratic and critical world awareness among students and teachers. But rather than simply talking about or theorizing issues, as I was doing, we should look at how we are acting on them and ask ourselves why we're doing it.

## (In)Conclusions

**Iara (VR)**: "Becoming a teacher [or writing a thesis and researching] is a never-ending process."

**Gustavo (VR)**: "I think that Ruberval taught me that, too. Nothing is fixed, everything always flows, so you never have a result that is limited. It goes beyond boundaries. And research is like that, there is always something new coming up."

**Brian**: Yet, as language teacher educators, we have a responsibility to provide guidance for new teachers in terms of identifying these new things (i.e., flows and processes) coming up and to respond to them in practical and ethical ways, which should be embedded throughout our LTE course designs. There are many examples of this type of practical embeddedness in the D-TEIL program. For example, our telecollaboration project, which Ian and Ruberval have organized, and in which Gustavo and Iara have participated, is an explicit and graded component of course design that fosters transnational dialogue between peers. Also, the Issues Analysis Project, which is a final assignment option in EWL, similarly encourages a practical and critical engagement with EIL theory. Of particular importance, the three-week structure of the D-TEIL practicum in Cuba is exemplary of a process of the emergence of teacher agency as viewed through a post-colonial lens in that so-called Non-Native Speakers of English, the Cuban faculty, serve as mentors and local experts in respect to appropriate parameters of the Cuban ecology of learning and teaching English (see Appendix 2). These types of pedagogical innovations are, again, enhanced and reinvigorated through a transnational polyethnography.

**Ian**: One line of thought toward theoretical responsiveness in critical LTE – and which makes duo/poly-ethnography an especially appropriate approach for a transnational discussion of transglocality – is an ecological one; that is, one which is grounded in place-based epistemologies rather than "consensualized"/"scienticized" forms of knowledge, in which "placelessness" is held up as an ideal worth striving for. My view is that both duoethnography and transglocality partake of what Lorraine Code (2006), a York University philosopher, called "ecological thinking," which is grounded in epistemic location. Following Code, and from a pedagogical standpoint, Lang (2007) describes ecological thinking as "an imaginary of negotiated, rather than 'given' hegemonic empiricism; of embodied, socially-morally-politically situated knowledges and knowers" (p. 87). The specificities of their ecological location – including their specific geographical-cultural climates – are enacted as they craft their self-understandings, and so duoethnography, with its emphasis on multi-vocal, multi-positional dialogue and negotiation, its engaged enquiry in the service of ever-emergent ethics, commitments, agendas, and values (cf. Brazil's Novos Letramentos) and its abhorrence of ending up with a master narrative, is a perfect format for representing this kind of ecological thinking.

*In many ways, ecological thinking has been realized in the ongoing conversational process of (re)writing that has informed our polyethnography across our transglocal sites of practice. The chapter itself, however, does not adequately reveal the collaborative and interactive processes of change (i.e., reconceptualizations, revisionings, synergies, etc.) that have preceded the permanence of the printed page. As well, the chapter itself cannot predict and measure the ways in which we might become better teachers and teacher educators in Canada, Cuba, and Brazil as a result of this experience. Also, in terms of ecological flows and processes, it's important to note that D-TEIL graduates have been teaching internationally (and hence transglocally) in places such as Japan, Korea, China, France, and Costa Rica. Others are doing graduate work inspired by their D-TEIL experiences. These flows and processes suggest possibilities of further widening the conversational and collaborative potential for transglocal language teacher education.*

## Notes

1 That is, Brian's participation in the Second Seminar of the New Literacies/Novos Letramentos national project at the University of São Paulo.
2 Brazil-Canada Knowledge Exchange, 2011–14; principal investigator: Diana Brydon of the University of Manitoba, including the State University of Mato Grosso do Sul (UEMS; Ruberval and Gustavo), the Federal University of Paraná (UFP; Iara), and Glendon College/York University (Ian and Brian).
3 Dr. Clarissa Jordão, from Universidade Federal do Paraná, another Brazilian researcher who was in Cuba during the D-TEIL program in 2015. She is also Iara's thesis advisor.
4 **Ian**: "Pollitos" (from Sp., pollo "chicken," plus -ito diminutive) is the endearing nickname given to the Glendon students by the first Varona colleague – Dr. Alejandro Torres – to receive and mentor the early groups of Glendon D-TEIL students in their Varona practicum. He would see me and my Glendon colleague Prof. Rosalind Gill marching from our on-campus guest houses to the Foreign Languages Faculty, two teachers in front and 20-odd students following along, like chicks following their mother. The name has stuck, and thanks to Iara's thesis, seems to have entered the lexicon of Applied Linguistics.

## References


Breault, R. A. (2016). Emerging issues in duoethnography. *International Journal of Qualitative Studies in Education*, 29(6), 777–794.

Bruz, I. M. (2018). Formação inicial de professores de língua inglesa como língua internacional: uma experiência transnacional. Doctoral dissertation. Retrieved from www.acervodigital.ufpr.br/handle/1884/57360.

Canagarajah, S. (1999). *Resisting linguistic imperialism in English teaching*. Oxford: Oxford University Press.

Code, L. (2006). *Ecological thinking: The politics of epistemic location*. Oxford and New York: Oxford University Press.

Duffy, J. (2017). The good writer: Virtue ethics and the teaching of writing. *College English*, 79(3), 229–250.

Fanselow, J. F. (1977). Beyond Rashomon—Conceptualizing and describing the teaching act. *TESOL Quarterly*, 11(1), 17–39.

Ferraz, D. M. (2018). English (mis)education as an alternative to challenge English hegemony. In M. Guilherme & L. M. T. Menezes de Souza (Eds.), *Glocal languages and critical intercultural awareness: The south answers back*. New York: Routledge. https://doi.org/10.4324/9781351184656.

Ferraz, D. M., & Morgan, B. (2019). Transnational dialogue on language education in Canada and Brazil: How do we move forward in the face of neoconservative/neoliberal times? *Trabalhos em Linguística Aplicada*, 58(1), 195–218. https://dx.doi.org/10.1590/010318138654861490091.

Kubota, R., & Miller, E. R. (2017). Re-examining and re-envisioning criticality in language studies: Theories and praxis. *Critical Inquiry in Language Studies*, 14(2–3), 129–157. Retrieved from https://doi.org/10.1080/15427587.2017.1290500.

Kumaravadivelu, B. (2008). *Cultural globalization and language education*. London: Yale University Press.

Kumaravadivelu, B. (2012). *Language teacher education for a global society: A modular model for knowing, analyzing, recognizing, doing, and seeing*. New York: Routledge.

Lang, J. (2007). Review of ecological thinking: The politics of epistemic location. *Paideusis*, 16(3), 87–92.

Lin, A., Wang, W., Akamatsu, N., & Mehdi Riazi, A. (2002). Appropriating English, expanding identities, and re-visioning the field: From TESOL to Teaching English for Glocalized Communication (TEGCOM). *Journal of Language, Identity & Education*, 1, 295–316.

Martin, I., & Morgan, B. (2015). Preparing teachers for "unequal Englishes": The D-TEIL experience in Cuba. In R. Tupas (Ed.), *Unequal Englishes*. London: Palgrave Macmillan.

Martin, I., & Morgan, B. (2019). A transnational approach to language teacher education: The Glendon D-TEIL experience in Cuba and Brazil. In W. M. Silva, W. R. Rodrigues, & D. M. Campos (Eds.), *Desafios da Formação de Professores na Linguística Aplicada*. Campinas: Pontes.

Menezes de Souza, L. M. (2011). Para uma redefinição de Letramento Crítico: conflito e produção de Significação. In R. F. Maciel & V. A. Araújo (Eds.), *Formação de professores de línguas: ampliando perspectivas*. Jundiaí: Paco Editorial.

Monte Mór, W. (2011). Critical literacies in the Brazilian university and in the elementary/secondary schools: The dialectics between the global and the local. In R. F. Maciel & V. A. Araújo (Eds.), *Formação de professores de línguas: ampliando perspectivas*. Jundiaí: Paco Editorial.

Moura, G. (2017). Um olhar para a formação de um professor de língua inglesa em contexto transnacional/transcultural: Brasil-Canadá-Cuba [A look to an English language teacher education in transnational/transcultural context: Brazil-Canada-Cuba]. Master's dissertation. Letras, State University of Mato Grosso do Sul. Campo Grande, MS, Brazil.

Norris, J., & Sawyer, R. D. (2016). Toward a dialogic methodology. In J. Norris, R. D. Sawyer, & D. Lund (Eds.), *Duoethnography: Dialogic methods for social, health, and educational research*. New York: Routledge. Retrieved from https://ebookcentral.proquest.com.

Oberg, A., & Wilson, T. (2002). Side by side: Being in research autobiographically. *Educational Insights*, 7(2). Retrieved from http://ccfi.educ.ubc.ca.uml.idm.oclc.org/publication/insights/v07n02/contextualexplorations/wilson_oberg/.

Pennycook, A. (2012). *Language and mobility: Unexpected places*. Bristol: Multilingual Matters.

Robertson, R. (1992). *Globalization: Social theory and global culture.* London and Los Angeles: Sage Publications.
Sawyer, R. D., & Norris, J. (2013). *Duoethnography: Understanding qualitative research.* Oxford: Oxford University Press.
Schmidt, C., & Gagné, A. (2014). Diversity and equity in an educational research partnership: A duoethnographic inquiry. *IJE4D Journal*, 3, 1–19.
Windle, J. (2017). Social identity and language ideology: Challenging hegemonic visions of English in Brazil. *Gragoatá*, 22(42), 370–392.

## *Appendix 1*

Description of the D-TEIL Certificate courses offered at the English Department, Glendon College, York University, Toronto, Canada.

Recently the Certificate was revised, and the new curriculum requires students to take 24 credits as follows:

EN 1903 3.0 English in the World; the World in English

EN 3606 3.0 Learning English as a Second Language

EN 3570 6.0 Nuts and Bolts: Grammar for Teaching and Learning

EN 4695 3.0 English as a World Language

EN 4696 9.0 Teaching English as an International Language, and 3-week International Practicum in Cuba (E.A. Varona Pedagogical University, Havana) or Brazil (State University of Mato Grosso do Sul, Campo Grande)

Students are strongly encouraged to have taken at least an introductory course in Latin American Spanish or Brazilian Portuguese, depending on the site of their practicum.

## *Appendix 2*

Description of the three-week practicum at E. A. Varona Pedagogical University in Havana, Cuba

### *First week: observation week*

Canadian students meet their Cuban class and their English teacher, a member of the Varona faculty. They observe the English class all week, taking notes and writing reflections. Group discussions. "Getting to know Havana" excursions, and starting work on their "personal cultural project" with help from Cuban students. This project is intended to focus on a generative theme, which is relevant both to Canada and Cuba, and which may inform their third week "thematic module" presentation. Peer friendships begin to form between Canadian and Cuban students. Familiarization with living in and getting around Havana.

### *Second week: co-teaching week*

The Varona English teachers assign lesson components of their regular lessons to the Glendon students (one-hour long on average, twice or three times in the week) and offer comments on their performance; Varona students – future teachers of English – also offer comments; this is written up in two reflective essays and submitted to the accompanying Glendon teacher for comment and grading; Glendon teacher also observes portions of students' performances. Continued work by students on "personal cultural project," continued excursions in Havana. Celebration of May 1 National Holiday.

### *Third week: thematic module presentation*

The Canadian students present a two-lesson content-based module (three hours on average, spread over two days) which they have designed and may relate to their "personal cultural project." This is observed by both the Varona teacher and a Glendon teacher; and the students are asked to offer comments on the module. The Glendon students submit a reflection on each day to a Glendon faculty member for comments and grading.

# 13 Transnationalism to further transform TESOL education

*Kyle Perkins and Xuan Jiang*

## Introduction

One result of globalization is the bi-directional movement of people and their ideas across geographical and national boundaries into new communities while these people maintain economic, social, political, and cultural connections with their old community (Sun, Zhang, & Cheung, Chapter 3, this volume). According to Sun et al. (Chapter 3, this volume), contemporary globalization contributes to the emergence of transnationalism, a topic that has become increasingly prominent in anthropology, education, and linguistics research (Hornberger & McCarty, 2012).

Warriner (2017) provides a very cogent description of transnationalism:

> The construct of transnationalism has been used to describe and examine how people maintain connections with their homeland while learning about and participating in the practice of the receiving context. This notion has influenced a great deal of research that seeks to capture how transnational connections are created and sustained and how participation in an adopted society's practices might co-exist with continued engagement with the people and practices in another space.
>
> (p. 50)

Many results of transnational connections have implications for TESOL teacher education because mobility and movement, among other related phenomena, influence teaching and learning and should therefore be reflected in TESOL teacher education policy, practices, and theory. Sun et al. (Chapter 3, this volume), however, point out that the impact of transnationalism on graduate TESOL teacher education has not been well represented in the existing literature and there is a paucity of international/transnational teaching practica in graduate TESOL teacher education programs. Following Sun et al.'s (Chapter 3, this volume) lead, we list some phenomena that we believe should merit the inclusion of transnationalism in TESOL teacher education preparation, as the "why" component.

## Global mobility, plurality of English, demographics shift, and overseas study in TESOL

Global mobility can produce changes in cultural and personal identity (Casinder, 2014). There is an increase in the number of culturally and linguistically heterogeneous students (some in monolingual English classrooms) who bring assets to the classroom that benefit ESL instruction. Some of these learners are likely to use different varieties of English (Rose, 2017). Wright (2015) maintains that "home language and literacy skills can be transferred to support English literacy development" (p. 186), which is a "language-as-resource" orientation (Ruiz, 1984).

There are more varieties of English (i.e., "Englishes") being taught in ESL classrooms as well as more non-native English-speaking teachers (NNESTs) teaching ESL and enrolled in TESOL teacher education programs. According to Flores and Aneja (2017), the number of international candidates enrolled in TESOL teacher education programs worldwide is on the rise. With more diversity in ESL classrooms, there have been more opportunities to attenuate linguistic imperialism (Phillipson, 1992a) and English hegemony (Sun et al., Chapter 3, this volume), both of which will be elaborated on in the subsequent section.

A related phenomenon is the practice of focusing on native-speaker norms as the center of ESL teaching practices, which has been challenged (Rose, 2017). Non-native English-speaking teachers and immigrants have accumulated "transnational funds of knowledge" that can be effectively utilized in ESL classrooms (Dabach & Fones, 2016, p. 8). This phenomenon creates the need for more culturally responsive teaching practices which reflect the impact of transnational mobility (Song, 2011).

Studying in a different country as part of students' graduate programs would allow them to develop intercultural competence with real-life acquaintances, which seems to be not reflected in the current TESOL teacher education programs. It may be the case that the programs have not yet completed the inclusion of transnationalism in their courses or have not updated their course descriptions if they have included transnationalism in their courses. It has been our experience that catalog course descriptions sometimes lag behind updates in the courses and in the curricula. We enthusiastically endorse Sun et al.'s (Chapter 3, this volume) recommendation that the impact of transnationalism should be reflected in TESOL teacher education coursework, and, as a result, we advance the notion that transnationalism should be included as a curriculum unit or module in graduate TESOL teacher education degree programs. We believe that we have answered the "why" question about including transnationalism in teacher education in the paragraphs above.

In the following sections of the chapter, we will present four potential themes or topics to be included in the module, as the "what": (1) the hegemony of English and its effect on teaching and testing throughout the world; (2) the need for teachers to understand that there are different varieties and norms of English that their current and future students use, due to overseas study; (3) NNESTs in preservice and in-service teachers should be welcomed and valued, because they have valuable transnational assets to offer in the classroom; (4) and, translanguaging, codeswitching, and codemeshing.

## Linguistic imperialism and the hegemony of English and its effect on teaching and testing

The hegemony of English or of any language is associated with the transfer of a dominant language to other people as the result of colonization or globalization in terms of economic power or military conquest (Phillipson, 1992a). This phenomenon is known as linguistic imperialism. Because language and culture cannot be separated, aspects of the dominant culture can also be transferred with the language as well. Language identities may also be affected by the transfer of a dominant language.

With the increase of transnational teachers and learners who bring diverse identities and literacy practices into TESOL teacher education, researchers and practitioners are calling into question the dominant ideology of linguistic imperialism (Phillipson, 1992a; Sun et al., Chapter 3, this volume). We acknowledge that English hegemony needs to be re-examined in light of the introduction of diverse identities and diverse literacy practices due to transnationalism, and we believe that TESOL teacher education candidates need to have some perspective on language hegemony, which we provide as follows. Hornberger and McCarty (2012) report that in Northern Thailand, middle-class children are marginalized for speaking Kam Muang, the Northern Thai regional vernacular. This practice serves to centralize power in standardized (central) Thai. The idea of standardizing one language over others is tightly bound with the question of nation-state development (Carter & Callesano, 2018, p. 70). Language remains "a fundamental symbolic resource in nation-building efforts and national languages, particularly the constructed 'standard' varieties, are therefore tightly bound up with national identity the world over" (Tetel Andresen & Carter, as cited in Carter & Callesano, 2018, p. 70).

In Europe, where English is involved, it is a dominant foreign language in continental European education systems, which is generally accepted (Phillipson, 2001). The demand for English arose as an inheritance historically from the British Empire and contemporarily from the hegemonic status of the United States (Edge, 2003; Phillipson, 2003). Pennycook (2008) points out that global English is seen as a monolingual enterprise leading to local pedagogical practices being "denigrated and despised" (p. 35). One result of this approach, according to Pennycook (2008), is that English is perceived as a threat to European languages and cultures (p. 37). In a discussion of younger immigrants in UK compulsory schooling, Sharples (2017) states "[i]ncreasingly complex patterns of transmigration in Europe mean that education systems and young immigrants are increasingly at odds: for the former, the dominant expectation is that new arrivals will settle, adapt to the norms of schooling and become invisible" (p. 170). Such a decision of assimilation and sacrifice was made to become "a truly integrated member of the school community ... as soon as possible," which Derrick depicted over 40 years ago (1977, p. 16).

In this neo-colonial era, English-speaking nation-states play a significant role in global capitalism, the world's economy, militarization, politics, commerce, entertainment, military links, and culture (Phillipson, 2001). Phillipson (1992a, 2001) and Pennycook (1994) comment on how English-speaking nation-states have maintained language policies of colonial times in post-colonial societies. Such maintained domination of the English language from monolingual nation-states threatens the continuing existence of some, if not many, languages (Skutnabb-Kangas, 2000).

English use marginalizes other languages, and English-speaking nation-states' dominance in curriculum and assessment are augmented. One example of the influence of English-based textbook publishing is that some language pedagogy textbooks have been found to be Eurocentric and not compatible in some regions of the world (Toh, 1999). Educational Testing Services and the University of Cambridge Local Examinations Syndicate probably hold a monopoly on English-language testing worldwide. And there are implications of testing for immigrants and refugees. Warriner (2007) points out that:

> test scores (and the credentials or job opportunities they allow) serve as an extremely effective gate-keeping mechanism for immigrants and refugees trying to establish new lives by securing a place in local/global economies communities … The act of testing, along with the uses to which test scores are put, serve to support and privilege certain pedagogical practices over others.
>
> (p. 306)

Standard language varieties are associated with language hegemony beyond teaching and testing, as mentioned above; they, as we summarize from existing literature, help either create or reinforce "stratification of sociolinguistic resources" (Hornberger & McCarty, 2012, p. 4). According to Bourdieu (1984, 1991), Lippi-Green (1997), and Carter and Callesano (2018), standard language varieties usually have social elite dialect varieties as their base. Bourdieu (1984, 1991) claims that language is a form of social capital which the dominant groups use to reinforce their dominance. Lippi-Green (1997) defines standard language ideology as "bias toward an abstracted, idealized, homogenous spoken language, which is imposed and maintained by dominant bloc institutions and which names as its model written language, but which is drawn primarily from the spoken language of the upper middle class" (p. 64). Carter and Callesano (2018) present a further entailment of standard language ideology in education that "children whose home dialect corresponds to the school standard are automatically exceptional, gifted, and prepared for school, while children who speak nonstandard dialects in the home are automatically rendered remedial, deficient, or underprepared for school" (p. 69).

## Awareness of "Englishes" students speak

An emerging population of transnational learners (Song, 2011) and an increasing number of international candidates enrolled in TESOL teacher education programs worldwide (Flores & Aneja, 2017) virtually guarantee that different "Englishes" will be used in these two types of educational settings—ESL classrooms and the TESOL programs. For these reasons, we include a section on "Englishes," because World Englishes is a central construct in a discussion of transnationalism, NNESTs, and other associated phenomena. According to Lok (2012), "Kachru conceived his model of the Three Concentric Circles to counter the hegemony of the so-called 'native' user" (p. 424). Kachru (1996, p. 135) defined "Englishes" as follows:

> The term "Englishes" is indicative of distinct identities of the language and literature. "Englishes" symbolizes variation in form and function, use in linguistically and cultural distinct contexts, and a range of variety in literary creativity. And above all, the term stresses the *WE*-ness among the users of English, as opposed to *us* vs. *them* (native and non-native).

The number of World Englishes continues to grow. Galloway and Rose (2018) provided the following list: Japanese English, New Zealand English, Scottish English, Singaporean English, Australian English, Egyptian English, Kenyan English, Malaysian English, Nigerian English, Patois (Jamaican English Creole), Philippine English, Quebec English, Saudi Arabian English, and South African English.

There are numerous implications of World Englishes that TESOL teacher education candidates need to be aware of. Some of the implications are comprehension of deviations from the "standard" should be included in teaching methodology, and there is a movement away from the native English benchmark (Galloway & Rose, 2018). Successful communication can be achieved without adhering to native English-speaking norms (Canagarajah, 2011). The "norm in the study of English" is equated with diversity (Canagarajah, 2013, p. 75), including that from students; however, sometimes teachers "fail to acknowledge the Englishes that their students bring into the classrooms as valid and valuable" (Jain, 2014, p. 490) and "have not kept pace with these 21$^{st}$ century realities, and persistently display a monolingual orientation more consistent with 20$^{th}$ century ideologies" (Jain, 2014, p. 491).

TESOL teacher education candidates also need to be aware that due to transnational educational migration, their target students having had previous overseas study experiences are learning different varieties of English other than "standard English" and norms. Song (2011) describes a practice of assisting school-aged children and young people to acquire English as a global language as soon as possible. Song notes that, for example, middle-class Chinese and Korean mothers will accompany their children for long-term stays in the Philippines and Singapore. Song continues, "Parents in this group believe that their children can gain access to global membership" (p. 750). Song (2011) proposes "Englishes" as a continuum over a dichotomy, which implies a critical perspective to be developed in TESOL, explained as below:

> teacher education needs to help language teachers develop a critical approach toward different varieties of English and norms, moving away from the

> dichotomous "native" and nonnatives perspective to a "plural" perspective that enables them to be open to different varieties of English in which the learners have competence.
>
> (p. 754)

Given the concept of plural "Englishes," marginalized forms in students' "Englishes" also deserve more attention. Such a focus and consideration "can be a force for dismantling local and global linguistic hierarchies" (Hornberger & McCarty, 2012, p. 6). In terms of instruction and corrective feedback, classroom teachers would need to have a preference for higher-order concerns (i.e., content, logic, and organization of a text) versus lower-order concerns (i.e., surface features), rethinking the term "standard" (Conference on College Composition and Communication, 1974). Plurality of "Englishes" should be "used in negotiated context" (Pennycook, 1994, p. 39) and such negotiations focus on meaning rather than form. For instance, errors in article usage would not interfere with meaning too much, thus they might be considered with less priority than substantial components in academic writing.

"English is always a language in translation" in terms of its plurality and interactivity with other languages (Pennycook, 2008, p. 37). Accordingly, TESOL should move forward from "a monolingual enterprise" (Pennycook, 2008, p. 33) to an arena where "postcolonial speakers of English creatively negotiate the place of English in their lives" (Canagarajah, 2006, p. 200). Moreover, English itself is in dynamic evolution. For example, the words *data* and *media* are plural nouns; however, many persons use these two words as if they were singular nouns, for instance, *The media is biased.*

## Non-native-English-speaking teachers' input as a transformative impetus

TESOL candidates need to know the importance, presence, and influence of NNESTs who have rapidly increased in English language teaching over the past three decades. For far too long, the common belief in the English language teaching community was that native speakers of English teachers (NESTs) were the ideal English models and teachers for English language learners (ELLs)—a belief that Phillipson (1992a) referred to as the *native speaker fallacy.* This fallacy has been interrogated by many scholars (e.g., Canagarajah, 1999; Watson Todd & Pojanapunya, 2009).

Watson Todd and Pojanapunya (2009) provided three arguments against the native speaker model:

> First, with the growth of English as an international language, the use of native speakers as the target for language learning becomes irrelevant with proficient non-native speakers a more attainable and relevant target. Second, a realization of the strengths of non-NESTs and the weaknesses of NESTs has led to NESTs and non-NESTs being seen as simply different rather than one being superior to the other. Third, whatever the arguments for and against

> NESTs and non-NESTs, other issues related to professionalism, such as dedication and willingness to develop, are more important than native-speakerhood in determining effective teachers.
>
> (p. 24)

Beginning in the 1990s, scholars such as Medgyes (1994) began to acknowledge NNESTs' strengths which were summarized by Moussu and Llurda (2008, p. 322), as follows:

1 They provide a good learner model to their students.
2 They can teach language learning strategies very effectively.
3 They are able to provide more information about the language.
4 They understand the difficulties and needs of the students.
5 They are able to anticipate and predict language difficulties.
6 In EFL settings, they can use the students' native language to their advantage.

In addition, Cook (2005) points out that NNESTs have more knowledge of the local education system than expatriate NESTs from another country. And Phillipson (1992b) notes that since NNESTs have been ESL learners themselves, they are more aware of their students' cultural and linguistic needs than expatriate NESTs from another country.

NNESTs, unfortunately, can potentially face hardships in the English Language Teaching (ELT) community for the following reasons. Menard-Warwick (2008) reports that a consensus is building that NNESTs have been unfairly discriminated against, because it is assumed that they lack knowledge about the target language and its associated cultural norms (p. 617). Other scholars (e.g., Nemtchinova, 2005) who opposed the assumption argue that NNESTs' biculturality and interculturality are classroom assets, not liabilities, because they can "make explicit cross-cultural comparison and contrasts … and weave these observations into their teaching" (Nemtchinova, 2005, p. 254).

An approach of NEST–NNEST teamwork has been proposed and empirically studied. Jang, Nguyen, and Yang (2010), for instance, delineate the following advantages that accrue from NEST–NNEST cross-cultural teaching teamwork:

> closer ties between Asian and Western countries in terms of cultural and language exchange … improvement of communicative competence, enhancement of cross-cultural awareness, active involvement of both teachers and students (Liu, 2006; Wang, 2008) … attract students into ESL/EFL classrooms, especially in China and Korea (Moussu, 2006) … and contributes effectively to the professional growth of both teachers by sharing knowledge, experience and observing each other's teaching strategies, techniques and styles.
>
> (pp. 250–251)

In addition to the advantages mentioned above, there is the possibility that NEST–NNEST team teaching in the classroom could preclude or ameliorate mismatches in the classroom. For example, Matalene (1985) discussed rhetorical differences between Chinese and English that result in miscommunication between NESTs and their Chinese students. NESTs' and Chinese students' differences in cultural backgrounds could lead to mismatches in communication styles. See Liu (2006) for more details and for further discussion about these important issues.

Definitely, contextual considerations might be embedded in such teamwork building. Scholars such as Amin (2004), Kamhi-Stein (2016), and Thomas (1999) point out that the native-speaker construct was associated with colonialism and nativism, a consequence of which is that non-whiteness may be perceived to suggest potential incompetence, producing a negative effect on NNESTs' self-esteem and professionalism. Aneja (2016) discusses deficit framing of non-nativeness on preservice NNESTs. Wang and Lin (2014) suggest "the presence of NESTs might affect NNESTs' self-image and self-perception, making NNESTs feel that they are less competent than NESTs, 'second class citizens' in the workplace, and in a disadvantaged position in the ELT workplace" (p. 8).

Such considerations should not be used to ignore the demographics and the need for NNESTs in reality. As a matter of fact, Young and Walsh (2010) report that L1 English users are becoming a smaller minority. To be specific, Graddol (2006) estimates that there are currently approximately "350 million L1 speakers of English (NES), as opposed to over a billion NNES" (p. 125). The NNESTs from Kachru's (1992) Outer and Expanding circles greatly outnumber NESTs in the Inner Circle. Canagarajah (1999, 2005), Kachru (1996), and Ma (2012) provide an estimate that approximately 75 percent of the ESL and EFL teachers worldwide are NNESTs. TESOL candidates also need to be aware of the increase in NNESTs; some of the candidates in TESOL-related degree programs are NNESTs themselves.

As the previous discussion has shown, the labels of NESTs and NNESTs constitute a dichotomy. That being said, NNESTs' input should be valued and considered in the TESOL field for the sake of more breadth in a pedagogical and an ideological continuum and for a smoother "Englishes" transition across borders and cultures. Such transnational traffic or transcultural interaction can be seen in the following ways: (1) NNESTs come to the United States to learn TESOL and then go abroad to teach; (2) NNESTs come to the United States to learn TESOL and then stay in the United States to teach; (3) NESTs learn TESOL and teach in the United States; (4) and, NESTs learn TESOL in the United States and then teach abroad. Due to the historical lack of NNESTs' input, TESOL educators need to pay more attention, recognize, and incorporate those traditionally non-mainstream cultures and knowledge brought by NNESTs as vital and as a transformative impetus.

Many readers and publishers may not agree with the ideologies that World Englishes are acceptable targets for ESL and EFL learners and that NNESTs have advantages over NESTs (R. F. Young, personal communication, September 2, 2019). Throughout the chapter, we have made references to (1) the transnationalism movement poses a threat to center-based hegemonies in theory formation

(Bruz, Moura, Maciel, Martin, & Morgan, Chapter 12, this volume); (2) there is a call for a focus on "globalism from below" (Hornberger & McCarty, 2012, p. 2), that is, World Englishes; (3) and, there are more NNESTs teaching ESL and they have valuable and unique "transactional funds of knowledge" to apply in the classroom (Dabach & Fones, 2016, p. 8). We concede that funding agencies sponsoring ESL students in English teaching programs may not look favorably upon NNESTs teaching their students. We also acknowledge that, for some, World Englishes may not be acceptable targets for ESL and EFL learning; however, the preponderance, use, and distribution of World Englishes is likely to increase as well as the number of NNESTs. These realia cannot be ignored or denied.

## Translanguaging, codeswitching, and codemeshing

Transnational learners, due to the impact of transnational mobility, bring funds of knowledge from their homes, communities, and native languages and cultures to the ELLs' classes where they can be utilized in teaching and learning (Dabach & Fones, 2016; Gonzalez, Moll, & Amanti, 2005). These learners and their accompanying diversity invite culturally responsive teaching practices that respond to the impact of transnational mobility (Song, 2011). We advocate translanguaging as an example of culturally responsive teaching.

Garcia (2009) describes translanguaging as follows:

> When describing the language practices of bilinguals from the perspective of the users themselves, and not simply describing bilingual language use or bilingual contact from the perspective of the language itself, the language practices are examples of what we are here calling translanguaging … translanguagings are multiple discursive practices in which bilinguals engage in order to make sense of their bilingual worlds.
>
> (p. 45)

One classroom practice to consider is having ELLs discuss prewriting activities such as determining the purpose of the writing assignment, and determining the audience, the main idea, and the supporting details in their home language with the help of a paraprofessional or a bilingual teacher. If the ELLs can write in their home language, they could create outlines using graphic organizers and their first draft in their home language (Wright, 2015). The teacher could then assist her students in choosing the correct rhetorical organization for the writing assignment and help them with sentence starters, sentence frames, sentence structures, and function vocabulary in the target language.

We also advocate for codeswitching and codemeshing in the ELLs' classrooms. Codeswitching has been defined as the "oral use of two or more languages either within or across sentences … in ways that are syntactically coherent" (Escamilla et al., 2014; Lee & Handsfield, 2018, p. 160). As Canagarajah (2011, p. 403) notes, codeswitching "treats language alternation as involving bilingual competence and switches between two different systems." Codeswitching can occur at sentence or clause boundaries (Li, 2000), within a sentence or clause (Myers-Scotton, 1989), within a word itself (Myers-Scotton, 1989), and with the switching of a tag phrase or a word from one language to another (Li, 2000). Conversationally, multilingual speakers may codeswitch between two or more languages or varieties of language in order to fit in, to integrate, to flatter someone in order to curry favor, or to maintain a sense of identity and a sense of more than one linguistic variety, maintaining the consistency of the phonology and syntax of each variety.

Before the 1980s, many people viewed codeswitching as a substandard use of language, that is, lazy, or "sloppy" use of language (Weinreich, 1953). Codeswitching, however, is now considered a natural result of bi- and multilingual language use (Brice & Brice, 2009). In our opinion, codeswitching is an example of linguistic creativity and so is codemeshing.

Codemeshing is understood as oral or written blending of other languages with English (Young & Martinez, 2011) or as a writing practice, in particular within sentences, with languages that are intentionally integrated (Canagarajah, 2011; Lee & Handsfield, 2018, p. 160). Codemeshing involves "mixing vernacular with standard written English ... [and] treats the language as part of a single integrated system" (Canagarajah, 2011, p. 403). Codemeshing occurs when multilingual users combine local, vernacular, colloquial, and world dialects of English in daily conversation and in formal assignments. Codemeshing allows multilingual users to communicate with a broader audience by combining their native language with "standard English," to pluralize their academic writing, and to further enhance attained proficiency of their multiple languages for transnational relationships.

## Course descriptions

Sun et al. (Chapter 3, this volume) reported that the impact of transnationalism on graduate TESOL teacher education has not been well represented in existing literature. Accordingly, we have elected to examine the course descriptions of the required courses offered by the graduate TESOL degree programs in seven US universities to ascertain the extent to which transnationalism and related topics were mentioned. We selected those doctoral universities, in various geographic locations, with high research activity and well-known and long-established graduate programs in applied linguistics and TESOL teacher education.

Sixty-five core courses from seven programs were examined. Not a single course description mentioned transnationalism. Nine courses (13.85 percent of the 65 courses) included tangential descriptors that could be used in a discussion of transnationalism. And those descriptors explored language and social identity; social, political, and educational perspectives; immigration patterns in the United States; theories of ethnicity; theories related to language and culture; equitable and culturally responsive classrooms; relationships of school and society in different cultural areas of the world; pedagogical implications of World Englishes; discourse and identity; discourse and ideology; cross-linguistic influences; and language, culture, and multilingualism.

It is our fervent hope that as this volume becomes promulgated throughout the TESOL teacher education community, more direct references to transnationalism will appear in future curricular and course descriptions in future audits such as this one.

## The why?

In previous sections of this chapter, we have answered the question "Why should transnationalism be included as a curriculum unit or a module in graduate TESOL teacher education degree programs?"

## The what?

We suggested four potential themes or topics for inclusion: hegemony/linguistic imperialism, different varieties and norms of English, non-native English-speaking teachers, and translanguaging, codeswitching, and codemeshing. There is nothing nomothetic about our choice of themes; other scholars could provide lists of topics that might also be as appealing, or more appealing than ours. That said, our topics have been investigated and analyzed by a broad spectrum of respected scholars from around the world. We acknowledge that there might not be unanimous agreement about World Englishes or about the acceptance of NNESTs, but vigorous debate and an examination of opposing viewpoints constitute one means of validating position statements, theory, and research.

## The when?

Many graduate TESOL teacher education programs have courses (or parts of courses) devoted to research, theory, policy, and practice. Our suggested topics would probably be best situated in policy and practice. Policy is where discussions occur about how to link education and language policy to decision making. Practice can be connected to theory, research, and policy. Where these modules fit into a TESOL teacher education degree program is a decision that is best left to the instructor of the course.

## The how?

As the editors of this volume point out, there is a broad spectrum of opportunities available for collaborative learning in the delivery of language teaching education, a few of which include practica, study abroad, online teacher education, and social media platforms (Chapter 1, this volume). To that list we suggest the addition of mini courses as well.

We foresee the use of Learning Management Systems (LMSs) such as Blackboard, Canvas, Moodle, or LinkedIn Learning for the delivery of the modules. LMSs can deliver online content synchronously or asynchronously. Professors might argue that their syllabi are already at capacity because of advancements in the field, and because of learning objectives that must be included in order to meet disciplinary, state, and/or national accreditation standards. LMS delivery of the modules would not impinge on classroom time-on-task. LMSs can deliver documents such as assigned readings (papers) and videos. There must be several hours of YouTube presentations featuring Noam Chomsky discussing hegemony, for example, that a professor might want to include with the hegemony module. LMSs can be used to create content, which the LMS then hosts as text, video, or audio. Student collaborative learning, which we advocate and highly recommend, is possible by students setting up a school website.

Skype, Zoom, or similar Teleconferencing Platforms (TP) might be considered. Audio, images, and text may be transmitted by TP, in addition to video conference calls. TP in the classroom can provide live collaboration projects and classroom-to-classroom connections. We recommend that TESOL teacher education students collaborate with each other in their own class, with their ilk in other universities in their home country, and/or with other graduate students in universities across the world, for example, students at the Chinese University of Hong Kong collaborating with students at the State University of Mato Grosso do Sul.

We envision a professor presenting a lecture about one of the topics, which can be viewed live or be posted on an LMS platform for future viewing; posting the required readings and/or videos about the topic; posting the assignment based on the modules, and posting the scoring/grading rubric that will be used to evaluate the student's completed work. The scoring rubric could be a primary trait rubric, the focus of which is on one trait, a holistic rubric with which the instructor makes a judgment about the product as a whole, or an analytical scoring rubric which consists of separate scales for each aspect of the evaluation. An LMS offers the possibility that students can submit their work in progress to their classmates for peer evaluation and discussion, or they can submit their in-progress work to the professor for feedback and suggestions for revision.

We offer a few examples of potential assignments for consideration:

1. Describe how movement and mobility influence the teaching and learning of English in your country.
   Suggested readings: Appadurai (1996/2003); Warriner (2017); Wimmer and Glick Schiller (2002).
2. How do capital and power influence second language teaching and learning?
   Suggested readings: Rose (2017); Warriner (2007).
3. Describe the in focus from the top-down to the bottom-up in transnationalism studies and research.
   Suggested readings: Appadurai (2001); Block (2008); Blommaert (2010); Canagarajah (2005); Hornberger and McCarty (2012);
4. Describe how test scores serve as a gate-keeping mechanism in your choice of country.
   Suggested reading: Warriner (2007).
5. Critically analyze cultural representations found in any genre of instructional materials and/or tests taking into consideration globalization and the resulting transnational flow of information, goods, and people.
   Suggested reading: Curdt-Christiansen and Weninger (2015).

## Limitations

Some professors may complain that there is no room in their syllabi to add the transnationalism modules proposed in this chapter. A solution to this dilemma would be to offer the modules in a mini-course. Others may offer other topics for modules that appeal to broader audiences in the transnationalism research community. We chose topics that we consider to be at the forefront of transnationalism practice, policy, and research. Some universities may lack the technological infrastructure platforms that we suggested in this chapter. Perhaps, what we have suggested in terms of using LMSs could be accomplished by email. The number of universities whose course descriptions we audited is small and may not be representative of the graduate TESOL teacher education programs that have included the impact of transnationalism in their programs and have in place international/transnational teaching practice. And, finally, many readers and publishers may not agree with the thoughts that World Englishes are acceptable targets for ESL and EFL learners and that NNESTs have advantages over NESTs.

## References

Amin, N. (2004). Nativism, the native speaker construct, and minority immigrant women teachers of English as a second language. In L. D. Kamhi-Stein (Ed.), *Learning and teaching from experience: Perspectives on nonnative English-speaking professionals* (pp. 61–84). Ann Arbor, MI: University of Michigan Press.

Aneja, G. A. (2016). (Non) native speakered: Rethinking (non) nativeness and teacher identity in TESOL teacher education. *TESOL Quarterly*, 50, 572–596.

Appadurai, A. (1996/2003). Sovereignty without territoriality: Notes for a postnational geography. In S. M. Low & D. Lawrence-Zuniga (Eds.), *The anthropology of space and place: Locating culture* (pp. 337–349). Malden, MA: Blackwell.

Appadurai, A. (2001). Grassroots globalization and the research imagination. In A. Appadurai (Ed.), *Globalization* (pp. 1–21). Durham, NC: Duke University Press.

Block, D. (2008). Multilingual identities and language practices in a global city: Four London case studies. *Journal of Language, Identity, and Education*, 7, 1–5.

Blommaert, J. (2010). *The sociolinguistics of globalization*. New York: Cambridge University Press.

Bourdieu, P. (1984). *Distinction: A social critique of the judgement of taste*. Cambridge, MA: Harvard University Press.

Bourdieu, P. (1991). *Language and symbolic power*. Cambridge, MA: Harvard University Press.

Brice, A., & Brice, R. (2009). *Language development: Monolingual and bilingual acquisition*. Old Tappan, NJ: Merrill/Prentice Hall.

Canagarajah, S. (1999). Interrogating the "native speaker fallacy": Non-linguistic roots, non-pedagogical results. In G. Braine (Ed.), *Non-native educators in English language teaching* (pp. 77–92). Mahwah, NJ: Lawrence Erlbaum.

Canagarajah, S. (Ed.). (2005). *Reclaiming the local in language policy and practice*. Mahwah, NJ: Lawrence Erlbaum.

Canagarajah, S. (2006). Interview. In R. Ruby & M. Saraceni (Eds.), *English in the world: Global rules, global roles* (pp. 200–212). London: Continuum.

Canagarajah, S. (2011). Codemeshing in academic writing: Identifying teachable strategies of translanguaging. *The Modern Language Journal*, 95(3), 401–417.

Canagarajah, S. (2013). *Translingual practice: Global Englishes and cosmopolitan relations.* New York: Routledge.

Carter, P. M., & Callesano, S. (2018). The social meaning of Spanish in Miami: Dialect perceptions and implications for socioeconomic class, income, and employment. *Latino Studies*, 16, 65–90.

Casinder, N. (2014). *Culture, transnational education and thinking: Case studies in global schooling.* Abingdon, UK: Routledge.

Conference on College Composition and Communication. (1974). Students' right to their own language. *College Composition and Communication*, 25(3), 1–32.

Cook, V. (2005). Basing teaching on the L2 learner. In E. Llurda (Ed.), *Non-native language teachers: Perceptions, challenges and contributions* (pp. 47–61). New York: Springer.

Curdt-Christiansen, X. L., & Weninger, C. (2015). Introduction: Ideology and the politics of language textbooks. In X. L. Curdt-Christiansen & C. Weninger (Eds.), *Language, ideologies and education: The politics of textbooks in language education* (pp. 1–8). New York: Routledge.

Dabach, D. B., & Fones, A. (2016). Beyond the "English learner" frame: Transnational funds of knowledge in social studies. *International Journal of Multicultural Education*, 18(1), 7–27.

Derrick, J. (1977). *Language needs of minority group children.* Slough, UK: National Foundation for Educational Research.

Edge, J. (2003). Imperial troopers and servants of the Lord: A vision of TESOL for the 21st century. *TESOL Quarterly*, 37(4), 701–709.

Escamilla, K., Hopewell, S., Butvilofsky, S., Sparrow, W., Soltero-González, L., Ruiz-Figueroa, O., & Escamilla, M. (2014). *Biliteracy from the start: Literacy squared in action.* Philadelphia, PA: Caslon.

Flores, N., & Aneja, G. (2017). "Why needs hiding?" Translingual (re) orientations in TESOL teacher education. *Research in the Teaching of English*, 51, 441–463.

Galloway, N., & Rose, H. (2018). Incorporating Global Englishes into the ELT classroom. *ELT Journal*, 72(1), 3–14.

Garcia, O. (2009). *Bilingual education in the 21st century: A global perspective.* Malden, MA: Wiley-Blackwell.

Gonzalez, N., Moll, L., & Amanti, C. (2005). *Funds of knowledge.* Mahwah, NJ: Lawrence Erlbaum.

Graddol, D. (2006). *English next.* London: British Council.

Hornberger, N. H., & McCarty, T. L. (2012). Globalization from the bottom up: Indigenous language planning and policy across time, space, and place. *International Multilingual Research Journal*, 6, 1–7.

Jain, R. (2014). Global Englishes, translinguistic identities, and translingual practices in a community college ESL classroom: A practitioner researcher reports. *TESOL Journal*, 5(3), 490–522.

Jang, S. H., Nguyen, B. H., & Yang, Y. (2010). Enhancing pedagogical roles of ESL/EFL native and non-native teachers through team teaching: How to make this "international partnership" successful. *International Journal of Learning*, 17(9), 249–257.

Kachru, B. B. (Ed.). (1992). *The other tongue: English across cultures* (2nd ed.). Urbana, IL: University of Illinois Press.

Kachru, B. B. (1996). World Englishes: Agony and ecstasy. *Journal of Aesthetic Education*, 30, 135–155.

Kamhi-Stein, L. D. (2016). The non-native English speaker teachers in TESOL movement. *ELT Journal*, 70(2), 180–189.

Lee, A. Y., & Handsfield, L. J. (2018). Code-meshing and writing instruction in multilingual classrooms. *The Reading Teacher*, 72(2), 159–168.

Li, W. (Ed.). (2000). *The bilingualism reader*. London: Routledge.

Lippi-Green, R. (1997). *English with an accent: Language ideology and discrimination in the United States*. London: Routledge.

Liu, L. (2006). Co-teaching between native and non-native teachers: An exploration of co-teaching models and strategies in the Chinese primary school context. *ESL/EFL Actions on English Language Teaching*, 7(2), 103–118.

Lok, I. M. C. (2012). World Englishes and postcolonialism: Reading Kachru and Said. *World Englishes*, 31(4), 419–433.

Ma, L. P. F. (2012). Strengths and weaknesses of NESTs and NNESTs: Perceptions of NNESTs in Hong Kong. *Linguistics and Education*, 23(1), 1–15.

Matalene, C. (1985). Contrastive rhetoric: An American writing teacher in China. *College English*, 47(8), 789–808.

Medgyes, P. (1994). *The non-native teacher*. London: Macmillan.

Menard-Warwick, J. (2008). The cultural and intercultural identities of transnational English teachers: Two case studies from the Americas. *TESOL Quarterly*, 42(4), 617–640.

Moussu, L. M. (2006). Native and nonnative English-speaking English as a Second Language teachers: Student attitudes, teacher self-perceptions and intensive English administrator beliefs and practices. Unpublished doctoral dissertation, Purdue University, West Lafayette, IN.

Moussu, L., & Llurda, E. (2008). Non-native English-speaking English language teachers: History and research. *Language Teaching*, 43, 315–348.

Myers-Scotton, C. (1989). Codeswitching with English: Types of switching, types of communities. *World Englishes*, 8(3), 333–346.

Nemtchinova, E. (2005). Host teachers' evaluations of nonnative-English-speaking teacher trainees: A perspective from the classroom. *TESOL Quarterly*, 39, 235–261.

Pennycook, A. (1994). *The cultural politics of English as an international language*. Harlow: Longman.

Pennycook, A. (2008). English as a language always in translation. *European Journal of English Studies*, 12(1), 33–47.

Phillipson, R. (1992a). *Linguistic imperialism*. Oxford: Oxford University Press.

Phillipson, R. (1992b). ELT: The native speaker's burden? *ELT Journal*, 46(1), 12–18.

Phillipson, R. (2001). English for globalization or for the world's people? *International Review of Education*, 47(3–4), 185–200.

Phillipson, R. (2003). *English only Europe? Challenging language policy*. London: Routledge.

Rose, H. (2017). A global approach to English language teaching: Integrating an international perspective into a teaching methods course. In A. Matsuda (Ed.), *Preparing teachers to teach English as an international language* (pp. 169–180). Bristol: Multilingual Matters.

Ruiz, R. (1984). Orientations in language planning. *NABE Journal: Journal of the National Association for Bilingual Education*, 8(2), 15–34.

Sharples, R. (2017). Local practice, translocal people: Conflicting identities in the multilingual classroom. *Language and Education*, 31(2), 169–183.

Skutnabb-Kangas, T. (2000). *Linguistic genocide in education-or worldwide diversity and human rights?*Mahwah, NJ: Lawrence Erlbaum Associates.

Song, J. (2011). Globalization, children's study abroad, and transnationalism as an emerging context for language learning: A new task for language teacher education. *TESOL Quarterly*, 45(4), 749–758.

Thomas, J. (1999). Voices from the periphery: Non-native teachers and issues of credibility. In G. Braine (Ed.), *Non-native educators in English language teaching* (pp. 5–15). Mahwah, NJ: Lawrence Erlbaum.

Toh, G. K. P. (1999). Primary school English textbooks in Singapore: An examination of cultural and ideological content. Ph.D. thesis. School of Education, Curtin University of Technology, Perth, Australia.

Wang, L.-Y., & Lin, T.-B. (2014). Exploring the identity of pre-service NNESTs in Taiwan: A social relational approach. *English Teaching: Practice and Critique*, 13(3), 5–29.

Wang, Y. (2008). The teaching behavior differences between native and non-native English speaking teachers. A case study at a public primary school in Taiwan. Unpublished master thesis. National Taiwan University of Science and Technology, Taiwan.

Warriner, D. S. (2007). "It's just the nature of the beast": Re-imagining the literature of schooling in adult ESL education. *Linguistics and Education*, 18, 305–324.

Warriner, D. (2017). Theorizing the spatial dimensions and pedagogical implications of transnationalism. *Curriculum Inquiry*, 47(1), 50–61.

Watson Todd, R., & Pojanapunya, P. (2009). Implicit attitudes towards native and non-native speaker teachers. *System*, 37, 23–33.

Weinreich, U. (1953). *Languages in contact.* The Hague: Mouton.

Wimmer, A., & Glick Schiller, N. (2002). Methodological nationalism and beyond: Nation-state building, migration and the social sciences. *Global Networks*, 2(4), 301–334.

Wright, W. E. (2015). *Foundations for teaching English language learners: Research, theory, policy and practice* (2nd ed.). Philadelphia, PA: Caslon Publishing.

Young, T. J., & Walsh, S. (2010). Which English? Whose English? An investigation of "non-native" teachers' beliefs about target varieties. *Language, Culture, and Curriculum*, 23(1), 123–137.

Young, V. A., & Martinez, A. Y. (Eds.). (2011). *Code-meshing as world English: Pedagogy, policy, performance.* Urbana, IL: National Council of Teachers of English.

# 14 Human rights as a performative context for transnationalism

## Working with difference in Brazilian teacher education

*Joel Windle*

### Introduction

The present chapter presents a reflection on teaching using principles of social justice and critical pedagogy under increasingly tense geopolitical conditions. Whereas Paulo Freire's appeal to read "the world" in order to read "the word" initially focused on local contexts and relations of colonial inferiorization felt in the global periphery (Freire, 1986), more recent critical approaches have been rescaled to incorporate global and transnational flows (Ndimande, 2015; Pennycook, 2010). Current neoconservative, neonationalist, and neoliberal trends undermine and potentially stifle such critical engagements with transnationalism, even as they provide vehicles for new transnational tendencies. This contradictory dynamic of restrictive transnationalism is evident in Brazil, where conservative political movements can be felt from below and above in English language teacher education, the empirical and theoretical setting under discussion. These tensions emerge in a context that opens up little or no space for socio-political debate in the university classroom, with undergraduate training for English teachers focused almost exclusively on linguistic structures and the teaching of surface linguistic features.

The tensions felt in Brazilian teacher education, as conservative movements gain force, result, in large measure, from the massive expansion of higher education and the inclusion of large numbers of poor and black students, who disrupt and challenge elitist curriculum and pedagogical practices. By 2018, the majority of undergraduate students attending federal universities came from poor households, were black, and had parents who had not attended university (de Souza, 2019). This shift is the result of new courses and universities opening, race and socio-economic-based affirmative action programs, strong economic growth in the period up to 2012, and income redistribution policies, such as *bolsa família* (a welfare payment for poor families with children attending school). The partial democratization of access to higher education has placed the injustices and oppressions suffered by the "new" student populations at the center of debates, particularly as these groups and their social gains have come under increasingly strident attack. The workers', feminist, black, and LGBTIQ movements that built support for the expansion of higher education provide discourses that many students have taken up.

At the most immediate level, two types of adversity shaped the pedagogical practices addressed in this chapter. The first is longstanding discourses of intolerance, circulating in society and the media, as well as amongst students. In this, as in other critical pedagogy settings, discussion of social power and language connected to race, class, gender, and sexuality has the potential to come into conflict with conservative political, cultural, and religious movements, as well as institutionalized form of oppression, such as racism (Janks, 2009; Kumashiro, 2008). More recent challenges are presented by the Brazilian federal government's moves to shut down discussions of society and politics in schools and universities, including through political screening of examinations and calling upon students to record and denounce teachers to the Ministry of Education. Some local governments have also passed by-laws restricting teachers' work, for example, by prohibiting the teaching of so-called "gender ideology," or even mention of the word "gender" in municipal schools, following globally circulating moral panics (Laje & Márquez, 2016).

Top-down restrictions as well as diffuse forms of intolerance thus provide a set of conditions in which many teachers feel at a loss as to how to construct a social justice orientation in their classrooms. Such experiences are not unique to the present moment in Brazil, but are part of the wider political landscape of "culture wars" (Apple, 2006; Hunter, 1992), in which education is a key terrain for contestation. My goal here, therefore, is to point to some ways in which a transnational dialogue can fortify critical pedagogy at a time when the latter is under attack. This is an important task for educators who, like myself, seek to further the democratization of access and participation in education while actively combating multiple forms of oppression.

Theoretically, the notions of sociolinguistic scales (Blommaert, 2015) and scaling as a semiotic practice (Carr & Lempert, 2016) are useful for thinking about how transnational contact and dialogue is related to different levels of political and discursive activity, including in light of new digital technologies and spaces. Classroom discussions and dialogues with those in other spaces, through social media, for example, index and mobilize a range of wider discourses that are in local or global circulation, resignifying them through the process of entextualization (Moita-Lopes, Fabrício, & Guimarães, 2018; Silverstein, 2009). Scales such as global and local are understood here as neither rigidly separate from each other, nor predetermined. Rather, they are constructed through discursive practices and interactional performances. The idea of transnationalism, for example, implies a given territorial scale that is complicated by transit through, and identification with, mobile, often virtual, social and linguistic spaces (Windle & Ferreira, 2019). As Canagarajah and de Costa observe, the relationship between scales may also vary: "the fact that scales function in one way in relation to schooling does not mean that the same scales with similar values, resources and influences apply to other social domains, such as international relations, corporate organisations, and virtual chatrooms" (Canagarajah & De Costa, 2016, p. 3).

Transnational contacts and dialogue, within a pedagogical setting, therefore gain meaning through the construction and counter-posing of multiple contexts through discursive activity and indexing. Some of these contexts can provide alternative sources of authority, and strategies for resignifying diversity and difference in empowering ways – such as the discourse of human rights – while others – such as Islamophobia – reinforce intolerance (to take two "universalizing" examples). Over the past 60 years, human rights has provided a central mediating discourse for shifting local concerns to a global scale and expanding notions of community (Guilherme, 2002). Other multi-scalar discourses, particularly connected to translocal experiences of marginalization, are more "bottom-up," such as the global hip-hop movement. Mobilizing multi-scalar discursive resources involves rethinking problems defined variously in laws, policy, and social and artistic movements. The practices of rescaling and reframing present possibilities for a resistant pedagogy – both in the sense of withstanding hostile political conditions and responding more actively to injustice. Some previous classroom research has suggested that rescaling does not always occur, and in fact may be a difficult process (Russell & Suárez, 2017). For example, Russell and Suarez found that human rights discourse was used primarily to discuss global problems or those from other national settings, whereas local issues were avoided, or treated within nationalistic conceptions of citizenship. With Brazil's President Jair Bolsonaro winning office in 2018 on the back of the campaign "Brazil above all-else, God above all of us," the conditioning of citizen-rights to nationalist loyalties is made explicit, and put in tension with the idea of rights that transcend national citizenship. A further slogan, popular with the Bolsonaro government, provides another example of an exclusionist vision of rights that do not apply to those cast as undesirable, deviants or unworthy: "human rights for righteous humans."

The contribution of this chapter, therefore, is to identify possibilities for learning about and participating in intercultural citizenship at local and translocal scales, and the potential of translocal contacts to disrupt tendencies toward homogenizing discourses of national values. The research presented sought to investigate undergraduate students' attitudes toward discussion of diversity in the language classroom, and their response to pedagogical activities that invited them to reflect on perspectives on diversity from other cultures. These perspectives were presented to students through audio-visual narratives drawn from the French-produced documentary *Human* and through live video-links with four individuals from various countries (Iraq, Australia, South Africa, and the United States). Student attitudes and responses were investigated through classroom-based research undertaken by the teacher and via a questionnaire.

## Research setting and methods

The research was undertaken in a Brazilian public university located in a major urban center, in an undergraduate course for teachers of English as a foreign language. Most students had not traveled outside of Brazil and had little or no contact with foreigners, except through online communities, in some cases, and through commercial media representations. Although Brazilian education policies define the role of schools as promoting active citizenship, language classes and teacher preparation focus on grammar and communicative competencies, steering away from "controversial" or "uncomfortable" issues, that are seen as outside of the purview of foreign language education. Further, English is associated with a culturally narrow range of social identities, reinforced by the predominance in textbook representations of white individuals engaged in elite professional and leisure activities (de Jesus Ferreira, 2019). Nevertheless, some recent legislation requires school curricula, and, hence, teacher education, to include Afro-Brazilian and indigenous cultures and to address domestic violence.

The research was conducted following principles of classroom research (Ellis, 1997), in a 60-hour course on applied linguistics undertaken by students in the final semester of a five-year course. A mixed-methods approach was adopted, involving a quantitative survey of student attitudes regarding diversity and its treatment as a topic in the language classroom, and qualitative examination of the student responses to a pedagogical intervention entitled "critical dialogues" (outlined further below). Data were gathered through a questionnaire administered prior to, and at the conclusion of, the course; student diaries; field-notes made by the teacher (the author of this chapter); and student work.[1] The analysis sought to identify how the participants situate issues of diversity in local and global contexts, including through discursive shifts between family, social, and educational contexts. Thus, the analysis of interactions in the classroom sought to understand the movements of practices, values, and discourses between interconnected spaces, whether local or global. Analysis of student work sought to identify discourses and positions that could guide an interpretative, ethical, and critical pedagogical framework to address issues raised by intercultural education, that is, how students took up positions as they encountered different cultures, values, or forms of expression.

A total of 26 undergraduate students participated in the "critical dialogues" pedagogical intervention and completed the questionnaire. The average age was 25 (ranging from 21 to 42), and all but three of the students were female. Eighteen identified as white and eight as black (an over-representation of white students compared to the wider population and some other courses). The class was conducted in English, however the questionnaire was administered in Portuguese (the items reported here have been translated in Table 14.1).

The pedagogical intervention investigated was framed by the notion of intercultural citizenship education (Byram, 2008), which focuses on discussion and negotiation of collective values and actions. In Byram's framework, intercultural experiences occur when people from different social groups and with different beliefs and practices meet. When reflections on these experiences result in social and political action involving people from different social and cultural groups, citizenship comes into play. A further level of reflection and change involves analyzing and rethinking one's relationship with others based on instances of intercultural citizenship. Pedagogically, intercultural citizenship education involves comparisons, the establishment of a communicative and action-oriented community, and critical (self)awareness of unequal power relations within any given social

*Table 14.1* Response to the question "what is the importance of the following types of discussion when the objective is to develop respect for diversity in the English classroom"

| | *Very important* | *Important* | *Somewhat important* | *Not important* |
|---|---|---|---|---|
| Human rights | 20 (77%) | 6 (23%) | 0 | 0 |
| News and current affairs | 14 (54%) | 12 (46%) | 0 | 0 |
| Personal experiences | 14 (54%) | 11 (42%) | 1 (4%) | 0 |
| Comparative topics in cooking, behavior, or accents | 11 (42%) | 13 (50%) | 2 (8%) | 0 |
| Differences of opinion within the family unit | 6 (23%) | 14 (54%) | 6 (23%) | 0 |

context (Byram, 2008; Gorski, 2008). The intervention focused on the topic of gender relations and inequalities, and consisted of the following stages:

1 Presentation to the class of first-person narratives on the topic of "women" taken from the documentary *Human*. These narratives are the product of interviews with individuals from Africa, Asia, Europe, and North America, and are spoken in a wide range of languages. We used transcripts of the English subtitles for more detailed discussion and reflection on forms of diversity connecting the narratives to students' own experiences.
2 Transformation by the participants of the narrative transcripts into learning activities aimed at secondary school students.
3 Collective development of interview questions and identification of interviewee profiles for video-link interviews focused on gender and diversity.
4 Video-link interviews conducted by participants and recorded.
5 Production of teaching sequences for secondary-level English classes based on the video-link interviews and other texts related to gender and diversity.

## Scaling the intercultural encounter

Students were presented with a range of situations for discussing diversity in the classroom (Table 14.1), based on common strategies for intercultural education. While they considered all of the approaches suggested to be important, they expressed the strongest preference for tasks based on human rights (77% considered "very important"), placing cultural differences onto a universal scale. This is connected to the use of news and current affairs (considered "very important" by 54%). However, students also valued approaches scaled on an individual level and through comparative topics. Perhaps surprisingly, students placed least value on discussion of differences of opinion within the family unit. Nevertheless, in actual classroom discussions and in student-generated pedagogical proposals for high-school English classes, personalized experiences and family conflicts were a common focus.

The first stage of the pedagogical intervention involved screening scenes from the documentary *Human*, a title which already invokes a universalizing scale and which aligned with the class preferences for this broad framing of diversity. Produced by French director Yann Arthus-Bertrand (2015), the film presents a selection from interviews with more than 2,000 people around the world, conducted over five years. The interviewees report their experiences, beliefs, and values about themes such as love, work, poverty, education, God, and women. The interviews take place in various languages, and all are available with English subtitles on YouTube. The documentary is notable for the presentation of narratives that do not identify the countries of origin, or other contextual elements. The interviewees, facing the camera, and with a black background, report their life experiences. These testimonies are interrupted only by panoramic sections of landscape footage – the localities featured in these sequences also do not receive any identification – again emphasizing a single, global scale.

Thus, the film represents, to a certain extent, the hypothesis of a global society, in which the individual appears divorced from national instances (Ramirez, Suárez, & Meyer, 2007), as well as other collective scales. The lack of historical and contextual elements means that viewers must "fill in the gaps" to speculate on, and contribute to, collective construction of meanings, conflicts, and changes in power relations. The documentary reveals individual stories, leaving only clues of how they might be connected to the scale of "national" cultures or ideologies. The following narrative illustrates this point:

> At home, on weekends, I do the cooking. One day, a friend came to my house.
> He said: "You do the cooking?"
> I said: "Yes."
> "Is your wife sick?"
> I said: "No, she's resting."
> "What? You do the cooking while your wife has a rest?"
> "Yes, she needs rest."
> He said: "My wife will never come visit you. You'd put ideas in her head. When she comes home, she'll ask me to cook too."
> I said to him: "You must understand that they need to rest."
> Anyway, I enjoy cooking for my family.
>
> (*Human* narrative on topic of women 6)

The narrative identifies two temporal scales (the regular habits and the singular encounter with a neighbour), and the institutionalized social scale of the family, composed of husband and wife connected by the domestic activity of cooking in the home. The interaction pragmatically signals a point of tension in norms of gender relations within the family, shown by indications of surprise ("what?"), and explanatory attempts ("you must understand …"). Ultimately, conflict appears to be deferred or avoided by the acceptance of difference as long as it is maintained in the sphere of the home. The narrator justifies adopting a role his interlocutor sees as improper by resorting to his "enjoyment" in cooking for the family, rather than taking the discussion to a wider scale of gender relations or norms, avoiding appealing to any higher social or religious authority.

Student responses, for their part, frequently undertook this rescaling work of making connections to social norms and sources of authority (family, church, government, village), which they also relativized and evaluated against their own experiences. One interesting strategy for shifting the scalar perspective was provided by a student who proposed the following classroom activity in the second phase of the pedagogical intervention:

> As a warm up I would make questions to them related to gender roles, asking them if they do some work at home (for example: who does the chores?). After that I would make them work in pairs and do a role play game when the boys will be the women for a moment and the girls will be the men. Then, they will act as they were their parents and reflect about the roles each of them have in the house. This activity aims to make the boys aware of the hard work women have at home to keep up with the house even after they've spent most part of their days working outside.
>
> (Samantha, 23, female)[2]

In this proposed activity, students are asked to reposition themselves in multiple situations – in an interaction in which they must speak from a differently gendered position (a more general interactional scale), and then take on the very specific positionality of their own parent in the domestic setting. The objective of the activity is implicitly couched in the feminist concept of the double-shift undertaken by women who both work outside of the home and take on the vast majority of domestic labor.

## Transnational dialogue as a rescaling pedagogy

Based on the discussions emerging from the *Human* narratives, in the third stage of the pedagogical intervention the class identified types of people they would like to interview in order for us to create a transnational dialogue that would be relevant to the concerns students themselves were facing. I then approached people I knew who fitted these interests, resulting in interviews with an Iraqi refugee living in Australia, who is a single mother and identifies as a Muslim and a feminist; an Australian professor of gender studies who was a member of the activist group "The Lesbian Avengers"; an American former military officer and Spanish teacher married to a Brazilian; and a South African professor of multicultural studies who lived in Texas (the only male in the group). Interviews were conducted by either the whole class or groups of students, based on questions written by students and sent in advance to the interviewees. When technology failed, some parts of the interview were conducted by texting.

Based on student journals, perhaps the strongest impact was made by the interview with Taghreed Jamal Al-deen (see Figure 14.1). Students were astounded to see a feminist discourse being joined together with a religious discourse that contradicted media portrayals of Islam as an oppressive and violent religion.

Not only did Taghreed dissociate misogyny and violence against women from a simple religious foundation, she identified a range of gender norms in different cultural and national contexts. She further complicated the semiotic scale on which the *hijab* may be read (see partial student transcript in Figure 14.1), pointing to agencies involved in the work of scaling (the media, global politics, western nations), and a conceptual vocabulary for relativizing social practices (beliefs, norms, values, meanings). Recognition of the instability and mobility of the meanings of symbols such as the *hijab* is an important prerequisite for rescaling as a reflective and pedagogical process. Questioning of this stability is, to large extent, outside of the realm of human rights, which is based on foundational categories, including of what counts as woman, man, and child.

Other types of rescaling are evident in the interview response texted by the South African participant, Bekisizwe Ndimande, in reply to the question "In Brazil, black women are the ones who suffer more with domestic violence and misogyny. Do you think it is the same in South Africa?" (see Figure 14.2).

The reply initially scales domestic violence as a universal question, before identifying economic and racial dimensions to the issue (institutional scales). He also makes a comment on the situation in Brazil ("Afro-Brazilian"), introducing a national scale; and then moving to a more local geographical and situational scale of access to specific forms of transport that offer protection and escape from violence (cars; public transportation). He further complicates the concept of domestic violence by identifying specific forms – street violence, physical violence, emotional violence. He provides an account based on reasoning, examples, and an appeal to

"The hijab is a religious obligation. Therefore, it has multiple meanings. It can be a symbol of women's submission to men, or a symbol of religious succeed, symbol of political protest. It is really hard to capture the meaning of hijab. And why Muslim women are victims of racial abuse? They have experienced discrimination, racism... Unfortunately, in global politics uniting Islam to terrorism have complicated the legitimacy of a symbolic representation of Islam identity in public, segregating women wearing hijab. So, I think media thoughts about terrorism, international militancy against terrorism have made Muslim in general, in the West, more visible (...) I think the media that is worsening the situation of Muslim women and the representation of Islam and Muslim as culturally incompatible with values, norms, and interests of Western nations. Media constructs socially shared knowledge, beliefs, norms, and values that form our minds. (...) The representation of Islam as a terrorist religion, as a backward religion (...) that's why Muslim women experiences racial abuse."

**Taghreed Jamal Al-deen**, Iraqi refugee.
Lives in Melbourne, Australia.
Researches motherhood in context of
migration and Islam

*Figure 14.1* Excerpt of Skype interview with Taghreed Jamal Al-deen, reproduced in a student-produced poster

Ok

1. All women around the world face domestic violence

2. However, White and wealthy women are not as violently abused as are Afro-Brasilain women, especially those that are poor

3. Some white and all wealthy women can leave their partners and go a different because they can afford to do that

4. Poor women cannot have that ability

5. But White and Wealthy women can have cars that can shield them away from what I call street violence

7. Statistics show that many poor working class and Black depend on public transportation; hence are more susceptible to street violence

8. All women are subjected not just to physical violence, but emotional violence as well

Maybe this is ok for now, unless you have questions

Muito Obrigado☺

*Figure 14.2* Excerpt of interview with Bekisizwe Ndimande

statistics. He generates a much-appreciated connection with the interviewing class by signing-off in Portuguese.

Student reflections show that human rights remains an important way of framing these dialogues pedagogically, as the following extract from a student journal illustrates:

> It is very important that we lead our students to think about diverse cultures and themes, to discuss relevant human rights problems, such as religious intolerance, misogyny, and racism. Moreover, we should break stereotypes and promote an intercultural teaching that is more faithful to reality … By proposing an education that considers the strengthening of respect for human rights, fundamental freedom, minorities, and tolerance, it is also necessary to consider that there will be difficulties in its implementation.

This statement mobilizes and extends the discourse of human rights, while avoiding the dichotomy between the isolated "human" and the lofty institutions legislating their rights. Importantly, it also acknowledges the political dimension of struggles for recognition and equality by pointing to potential opposition ("there will be difficulties in its implementation").

Ideas of community-building entered into this gap between the individual and the universal in student discussions and proposals. For example, one classroom activity planned by a student involved the use of hashtags to run a solidarity campaign:

> The first activity is based on a campaign that started spontaneously in Australia. As Taghreed mentioned, after a terrorist attack people see Muslim

| |
|---|
| *Gender equality: the lack of women in prestigious positions* |
| *Muslim women: prejudice & information, an equation to be resolved* |
| *Discussing domestic violence inside the school context: how women face domestic violence?* |
| *Deconstructing sexism: the role of women in Society* |
| *Abusive relationships: different types of violence against women* |
| *Should I stay or should I go? Domestic violence within language* |
| *Discussing gender roles* |
| *Women are not objects: how women are treated in Society* |
| *Gender roles and stereotypes* |
| *Approaching the theme of violence against women* |
| *Then princess. Now, generals: how women are portrayed in society* |
| *Violence against women: the importance of bringing real issues to the classroom* |

*Figure 14.3* Examples of poster titles

> people with bad eyes, especially Muslim women, because of the hijab. So, after a post in Twitter, many Australians started tweeting messages to support Muslims fearing backlash and the campaign reached great proportions. We planned this activity to provoke a more critical thinking on students.

The titles of student-produced posters containing proposals for secondary-school classes in the final phase of the pedagogical intervention further give an indication of the discourses they drew upon and drew together. These included discourses on destabilizing boundaries ("deconstructing sexism"), denouncing oppression ("women are not objects"), and naming specific forms of oppression ("different types of violence against women") (see Figure 14.3).

At the end of the course, students were asked about they felt affected by the transnational contacts and dialogues of the pedagogical intervention. The students unanimously agreed that the contacts had helped them to rethink their own values, and this appears to be largely a produced of the discursive and intellectual work involved in rescaling. A final scaling and rescaling agency has perhaps been neglected from the analysis – myself as teacher. Indeed, students asked to conduct an interview with me before the end of semester, but time was too short. This would have been an interesting shift in the teacher–student relationship, particularly following the students' development of extremely probing interview questions for the other participants. If it is possible to think about student learning in terms of scaling, then it is certainly also appropriate to identify scaling as part of the work of the teacher.

## Conclusion

This chapter analyzed how students in a Brazilian teacher education program position themselves in relation to situations of transnational contact, in an applied linguistics course that drew on concepts of critical intercultural citizenship education (Byram, 2008). Theoretically, the chapter sought to trouble the separation of geographically bound contexts that frame educational engagement with transnationalism by considering ways in which contexts are invoked in moments of contact, conflict, and reflection. In this case, mobilization of a human rights discourse, and to a lesser extent, discourses of social struggle, served to produce contexts for transnational communicative interactions that involved multiple spatio-temporal scales. Transnational staging for a nexus of political, social, and cultural concerns was provided by narratives from the documentary *Human* and Skype interviews, which provided the basis for teaching activities. With the rise in Brazil of a right-wing authoritarian government that seeks to eliminate "ideology" and thinkers such as Paulo Freire from schools, the discourse of human rights, despite its individualist and legalist limitations, provides legitimacy for resistance that indexes multiple transnational contexts, even as it contributes to the creation of these contexts. It is the productive capacity of rescaling to generate acts of transnational solidarity that is most relevant to promoting and defending critical teacher education.

I began the chapter outlining concerns about hostile conditions facing social justice education and critical pedagogy – enacted here through principles articulated in intercultural citizenship education. Walking carefully between different sociolinguistic and discursive scales can help to reinforce and make resistant such work:

1 Transnational contact and dialogue take the focus away from immediate, local political pressures, allowing space for comparing and reframing values and practices.
2 The scale of the transnational lends itself to discussions framed by the highly legitimized, universalizing scale of human rights discourse. Unlike previous studies, the examples presented here did not suggest that human rights was used mainly to talk about "other" societies rather than local issues (Suárez, 2006).
3 Local laws (state and national) can further offer concrete support, often being integrated into human rights discourses, as is the case of the law obliging schools to teach about domestic violence ("Make teenagers, youth and adults, students and teachers, who make up the school community, aware of the importance of respecting human rights, particularly those which promote gender equality, preventing and avoiding, thus, violence against women" (Rio de Janeiro State Law 7.477, 2016)).
4 Discussion of collective struggles and strategies invokes the idea of community, which implies construction and possibilities for new forms of cooperation and mutual recognition. As Mbembe notes, the idea of the universal (with which human rights is associated) implies a set of pre-existing structures, which exclude from definitions of humanity large sections of the global population seen as "disposable," outside of the concerns of justice and legality, and subject to government by types of arbitrary and constant violence

(Mbembe & Meintjes, 2003). Community-building thereby offers a counter-point to universalizing discourses, particularly when placed within social struggles and conflicts.

Ultimately, the weight of the social transformations that are already underway in Brazilian education and society make a major contribution to the ways in which classroom discourses are entextualized. The large and active black rights, student and feminist movements are vibrant and well-organized, and this influences how rights and diversity are perceived and defended. Therefore, it is impossible to divorce the practice of (re)scaling from who is doing this work, and under what political circumstances it is undertaken. The semiotic resources drawn upon in such a task gain their meaning as part of a project for social justice within an epistemology of border-crossing, dissidence, and struggle.

### *The wider implications of the study*

Framed by principles of critical pedagogy, transnational contact can offer much more to intercultural education than comparisons at the level of the nation-state. Thus, transnationalism can be integrated into a multiscalar approach that makes links between broad discourses (such as human rights), local struggles (translocal perspectives), and specific social questions (such as the position of women in society). As such, a scalar orientation contributes to a redefinition of intercultural communication as the interaction between discourse systems, rather than ethnically or nationally distinct groups (Hua & Kramsch, 2016). This perspective is valuable for the language classroom, as it 'scales' culture not as a fixed entity, but as being produced through the ways that discourses are mobilized and put into dialogue with each other. The classroom interactions here are examples of the potential of "interdiscourse" communication (Scollon & Scollon, 2001), drawing out the "co-constructive aspects of communication and social change" (Hua & Kramsch, 2016, p. 375).

## Notes

1 The full questionnaire (in Portuguese) can be accessed here: https://tiny.cc/hl9sdz.
2 The original as written by the student in English have been maintained, without corrections.

## References


Apple, M. W. (2006). *Educating the "right" way: markets, standards, God, and inequality* (2nd ed.). New York: Routledge.

Blommaert, J. (2015). Chronotopes, scales, and complexity in the study of language in society. *Annual Review of Anthropology*, 44, 105–116.

Byram, M. (2008). *From foreign language education to education for intercultural citizenship: Essays and reflections* (Vol. 17). Bristol: Multilingual Matters.

Canagarajah, S., & De Costa, P. I. (2016). Introduction: Scales analysis, and its uses and prospects in educational linguistics. *Linguistics and Education*, 34, 1–10.

Carr, E. S., & Lempert, M. (2016). *Scale: Discourse and dimensions of social life*. Oakland, CA: University of California Press.
de Jesus Ferreira, A. (2019). Social identities of black females in English language textbooks used in Brazil and Cameroon: Intersectionalities of race, gender, social class and critical racial literacy. *Revista X*, 14(4), 20–40.
de Souza, A. (2019). Alunos negros e de renda baixa são maioria nas universidades federais. *O Globo*. Retrieved from https://oglobo.globo.com/sociedade/alunos-negros-de-renda-baixa-sao-maioria-nas-universidades-federais-23672937.
Ellis, R. (1997). *SLA research and language teaching*. New York: Oxford University Press.
Freire, P. (1986). *Pedagogy of the oppressed*. New York: Continuum.
Gorski, P. C. (2008). Good intentions are not enough: A decolonizing intercultural education. *Intercultural Education*, 19(6), 515–525.
Guilherme, M. (2002). *Critical citizens for an intercultural world: Foreign language education as cultural politics*. Clevedon: Multilingual Matters.
Hua, Z., & Kramsch, C. (2016). Symbolic power and conversational inequality in intercultural communication: An introduction. *Applied Linguistics Review*, 7(4), 375–383.
Hunter, J. D. (1992). *Culture wars: The struggle to control the family, art, education, law, and politics in America*. New York: Basic Books.
Janks, H. (2009). *Literacy and power*. New York: Routledge.
Kumashiro, K. K. (2008). *The seduction of common sense: How the right has framed the debate on America's schools*. New York: Teachers College Press.
Laje, A., & Márquez, N. (2016). *El libro negro de la nueva izquierda: ideología de género o subversión cultural*. Buenos Aires: Unión Editorial.
Mbembe, J.-A., & Meintjes, L. (2003). Necropolitics. *Public Culture*, 15(1), 11–40.
Moita-Lopes, L. P., Fabrício, B. F., & Guimarães, T. F. (2018). Scaling queer performativities of genders and sexualities in the periphery of Rio de Janeiro in digital and face-to-face semiotic encounters. In *Language and culture on the margins* (pp. 127–144). New York: Routledge.
Ndimande, B. S. (2015). Pedagogy of the periphery: A letter to Paulo Freire. In S. Nieto (Ed.), *Dear Paulo: Letters from those who dare teach* (pp. 166–171). New York: Routledge.
Pennycook, A. (2010). Critical and alternative directions in applied linguistics. *Australian Review of Applied Linguistics*, 33(2), 1–16.
Ramirez, F. O., Suárez, D., & Meyer, J. W. (2007). The worldwide rise of human rights education. In *School knowledge in comparative and historical perspective* (pp. 35–52). New York: Springer.
Russell, S. G., & Suárez, D. F. (2017). Symbol and substance: Human rights education as an emergent global institution. In *Human rights education: Theory, research, praxis* (pp. 19–46). Philadelphia: University of Pennsylvania Press.
Scollon, R., & Scollon, S. W. (2001). Discourse and intercultural communication. In D. Schiffrin, D. Tannen, & H. Hamilton (Eds.), *The handbook of discourse analysis* (pp. 538–547). Oxford: Blackwell.
Silverstein, M. (2009). Pragmatic indexing. In K. Brown (Ed.), *Concise encyclopedia of pragmatics* (pp. 756–759). London: Elsevier.
Suárez, D. (2006). Education professionals and the construction of human rights education. *Comparative Education Review*, 51(1), 48–70.
Windle, J., & Ferreira, B. B. P. (2019). Plurilingual social networks and the creation of hybrid cultural spaces. *Trabalhos em Linguística Aplicada*, 58(1), 139–157.

# 15 Doing TESOL postgraduate studies overseas

## Teacher training, studying abroad, and/or a master's degree?

*Dandan Zhu and Jim McKinley*

### Introduction

The concept of transnationalism can be used to refer to the multiple types of relationships and exchange that happen across borders (Anderson, 2019). Students who pursue their TESOL postgraduate studies overseas, crossing national borders, are engaged in such transnational exchange. This chapter examines how TESOL teacher education and transnationalism may intersect by exploring overseas postgraduate TESOL students' expectations of their MA program.

Postgraduate studies in TESOL, particularly in Anglophone countries (e.g., UK, Australia, and New Zealand, in particular, as the one-year TESOL master's is often more desirable than the two-year master's in the United States and Canada), are often comprised of international students who may have different interpretations of the degree. The MA (or MEd, or MSc) program in TESOL may be viewed by students and academic staff alike as a teacher training program. Some students may understand the degree to be an advanced theory-based program designed to facilitate "mastery" of the field of TESOL and a prerequisite for further (doctoral) studies in the field. Additionally, with some students seeking to improve their English language proficiency through further studies, it may be perceived as a study abroad year. While it is certainly arguable that these three interpretations could be understood together to provide a single way of describing postgraduate studies in TESOL, we argue that they indicate different types of students, with different sets of intentions, that are deserving of attention by TESOL teacher education curriculum developers.

As Phakiti and Li (2011) noted, increasing opportunities have become available for international ESL students around the world to pursue their master's or PhD studies in TESOL in Anglophone countries. With this trend, it is important to understand more about the expectations of these students. This chapter offers a contribution to the current discussion around international postgraduate TESOL students by focusing on understanding the interpretations of these students and related expectations in their MA program in a UK university. An impetus for the specific focus in this chapter on *expectations* is hearing, year after year, the same questions from students when they begin their postgraduate studies in TESOL, such as "When do we get our classroom placements?", "How can I make local friends so I can learn local culture and improve my English?" and "Now that I am a master's student, can I apply for a PhD?" There are three distinctly different initiatives in these questions, suggesting three very different ideas about why these students have enrolled in a TESOL master's program overseas, which will be further explored in the findings section.

The data reported in this chapter is the first phase of a longitudinal project that examines the expectations and experiences of 20 international students as they go through a one-year MA TESOL course in the UK. In this chapter, we take an in-depth look at their interpretations of the program to reveal insights—concerning TESOL teacher education in an increasingly transnational world—into why international students may have different objectives, and how those objectives may relate to their expectations of their TESOL studies.

## Previous research on transnationalism and international TESOL postgraduate students

In TESOL postgraduate studies, the influence of neoliberalist ideas and globalization have led to increased focus on transnationalism, most commonly connected to internationalization. This idea of transnationalism has been described, citing Altbach (2004) and Altbach and Knight (2007), as "a process involving student body, faculty, and curricula change; enrolment trends; knowledge conglomeration; push-pull factors impacting globally mobile students and the sending and receiving countries; and the economic, social, and educational consequences" (Anderson, 2019, p. 228). As theoretical constructs, transnationalism and internationalization allow researchers to focus on the individual experiences of students in investigating their socialization into the academic discourses and communities of postgraduate TESOL studies.

These constructs proved very useful for theorizing our study, and in our review of relevant literature, we found much of the research on internationalized postgraduate TESOL studies focused on curriculum concerns and/or language issues. For example, in their investigation of the association between globalization and postgraduate TESOL in the UK, Hasrati and Tavakoli (2015) found that MA TESOL programs were responding, however slowly, to the need for change to address the increasingly international profile of student cohorts. These changes were noted in the literature as being required for issues related to these students' approaches to learning, as well as concerns about their language proficiency. Given that the majority of both TESOL practitioners and TESOL postgraduate students are L2 users of English (Liu, 1999), much of the research of these students' experiences targets the difficulties that they may have with the use of academic language in their postgraduate studies (e.g., Nguyen and Pramoolsook, 2016; Phakiti and Li, 2011). Drawing on analysis of diary entries from ESL/EFL students in an MA TESOL program in the United States, Lee and Lew (2001) explored students' perceptions of the demands of their postgraduate studies. Their results demonstrate that students may experience a sense of inferiority and anxiety due to their perceived deficiency in their English language proficiency, compared to their more proficient peers.

The research also points toward these students' interest in international postgraduate TESOL studies specifically in Anglophone (so-called "native speaking") countries. More than 20 years ago, Liu (1998) argued that ethnocentrism was a problem in TESOL studies in these countries, as the students' own contexts in which they will teach were typically not considered in the curriculum. Overseas TESOL postgraduate students were expected to take on the English teaching practices and ideas, including "native speaker norms," of the country where they studied, not where they would teach. Current research suggests that this is still the case in some cases (see Fagan, 2019; Nuske, 2018).

These students may be "killing two birds with one stone" (Berry, 1990)—gaining a further degree and at the same time developing their English language skills. Cullen (1994) reported on the incorporation of language development in TESOL teacher training programs, in response to an obvious need of the students enrolling on these programs. Some larger TESOL master's programs have added language development components, such as the University of Sydney's unit "English in Academic Settings" offered only to English L2 students on the MEd TESOL program, first offered in 2004.

In another Australian university, Inoue and Stracke (2013) investigated how postgraduate TESOL students may perceive the meaning and value of the degree, focusing on ideas related to English linguistic imperialism and students' beliefs that native English-speaking teachers are advantaged. Findings from the study show that these students valued the degree because a postgraduate degree in TESOL from an English-speaking country was considered to be more likely to put them in a better position than other non-native English-speaking teachers in their country.

While brief, this review of relevant literature points toward the need for investigation into current developments concerning the thoughts of international, and specifically English L2, TESOL postgraduate students, when it comes to *why* they choose to do the degree overseas, and in what ways this influences their expectations of the program.

To further our understanding of the experience of TESOL international students, the following research questions were asked:

1 How are postgraduate TESOL studies interpreted by international students at the start of such a program in the UK?
2 What do these students identify at the start of the program as aspects of postgraduate TESOL studies relevant to their objectives?

## Methods

### *Research procedure*

To explore the expectations of international postgraduate TESOL students, we arranged to interview 20 students near the start of their MA TESOL studies, to be conducted only by Dandan, who was a postgraduate TESOL student. This was to encourage more open responses from participants (see Rose et al., 2020). The research procedure involves face-to-face semi-structured interviews conducted at three points: at the beginning of the course, in the fifth month of the course, and after they finish the course. In the interviews, participants were invited to reflect on their expectations as they go through the course, aiming to uncover their motivations, their expectations of the course, and the challenges they may face in undertaking their postgraduate studies.

Focusing specifically on initial thoughts identified at the start of the MA TESOL program, this chapter draws on the data from the interviews that were conducted in the first month of their postgraduate study, which focused on their backgrounds and perceptions of the MA program.

Each participant was interviewed for approximately 30–40 minutes. Transcripts were shared with participants in accordance with ethics approval to confirm accuracy, for the option to clarify statements, and in case they wish to make any amendments.

### *Participants*

Regarding the sample, the 20 students identified as participants were all volunteers. We recognize this as a limitation of the study, as these potentially more motivated students are unlikely to be representative of the larger cohort (see Rose et al., 2020). This particular program regularly has approximately 100 students in the MA course, majority Chinese nationals. After an invitation to participate was sent out to the whole cohort, these 20 students volunteered to participate in the project by contacting the researchers.

All participants are in their early twenties; 18 participants are females, and two males. Among the 20 informants, 17 obtained their bachelor's degree from Chinese universities. Two students hold degrees from Sino-British universities based in China. Additionally, another student studied in a "2+2 program," a cooperation scheme between two universities, where she had studied in a Chinese university for two years before continuing her undergraduate study in a university in the United States for another two years. While all 20 participants held beliefs about the TESOL program that fit into the key themes, due to limited space, the data reported in this chapter are presented as extracts from interviews with just seven of the students that exemplify the themes. Table 15.1 shows the background information of these seven participants. All names are pseudonyms to protect the identity of the participants, in accordance with ethical approval.

### *Language of the interviews*

The interviews were conducted in the language the participant preferred—all of the participants decided to use English to start the interview. In setting up the data collection procedure, we anticipated that code-switching might occur, as we

*Table 15.1* Participants' background information

| *Name* | *Gender* | *Undergraduate programs studied* |
|---|---|---|
| Zitong | Female | International Business |
| Mingli | Female | Finance |
| Wencan | Female | English Education |
| Ning | Female | Business English |
| Yihan | Female | Portuguese |
| Lanting | Female | Business English |
| Haoran | Male | Applied Linguistics |

understand that it can allow for increased efficiency in expressing ideas (McKinley & Sakamoto, 2008). Based on our transcripts, nine used Chinese at some point in the interview, code-switching for several words or switching to Chinese for an extensive amount of time. This occurred in particular instances: to confirm understanding, to ask for a translation, to allow for more convenient communication, to enact thinking processes in Chinese, or to express certain ideas more effectively said in Chinese.

### *Data analysis*

Once all 20 interviews were completed, transcribed, and checked by the participants for accuracy, we employed thematic analysis, understood from a "qualitative content analysis" approach as identifying "thematic segmentation," focusing on the content of what participants said (Selvi, 2020). Through this analysis, we did independent preliminary coding of the transcripts, which were then compared and adjusted to develop a coding frame based on the key themes. Three key themes were identified as particularly prominent across the dataset regarding students' interpretation of the program and their related expectations in the course. The seven participants were identified according to their responses as fitting into one of three themes, outlined in the next section.

## Findings

In spite of the differences in the participants' language learning expectations, their undergraduate studies and career goals, three prominent themes emerged in the interview data regarding their interpretations of the MA TESOL program. The first theme identified is the interpretation of the MA TESOL study as a teacher training program. The second theme is the perception of viewing the program as an advanced degree. Finally, the most prevalent theme was found in students' considerations of their MA studies in TESOL as a study abroad year. Our responses to the two research questions are presented with examples of the three themes, which is followed by individual participants' expectations related to those objectives in their MA studies.

### *A teacher training program*

The following two extracts exemplify the points regarding how students view their MA TESOL studies as a teacher training program, which they link closely with their future career as teachers of English. Such students perceive the MA TESOL program as a way to enhance their career prospects by gaining practical teaching skills that can be applied to their future teaching practice. As a result of such objectives, both participants here felt that the course, which appeared to focus mainly on theoretical content, did not fit with what they expected. We can see from the data that Zitong, in Extract 1.1, was attempting to find ways to link the theoretical perspectives in the course to her initial objective. Mingli, in Extract 1.2, who viewed "theories" and "practice" to be disconnected, also found that the MA program was not meeting her expectations.

*Extract 1.1: "I think it's all about the teaching skills"*

> I think it's all about the teaching skills because it's really like applying to practice major ... So I applied this course because I want to improve my, not improve, maybe gain some knowledge about teaching skills ... like how we conduct a course, how, what we usually do in the classroom, before the class, what we need to do. Like a procedure of the whole teaching.
>
> (Zitong)

> I found that it's not really about teaching skills, but there are some theories and how do you apply them into the practice. It actually is a bit different from what I thought before. But right now, I think it's fine because when I read a lot of pre-readings, I found that it actually will help our teaching, maybe skills, and also, like a mindset, like what we need to do in the future.
>
> (Zitong)

Pre-service teachers such as Zitong considered the TESOL program to be a teacher training program that can equip them with practical teaching skills that can facilitate their professional development. As a result, at the start of her post-graduate studies, where she encountered much more concentration on theories than she had anticipated, she tried to actively link what she has learned in the program with her future teaching practice.

*Extract 1.2: "it's practice, compared with theory"*

> I'm not so, an academic person, so I choose this course ... I choose the MA TESOL. And it's practice, compared with theory ... Just, let you to know how to, and not some vague concepts, yeah, the course to tell me what to do in class, and how to prepare for your work, and how to communicate with students, or what kind of approaches or techniques you can use in your

> teaching process ... Cuz think, the future is career oriented. So you should know more about practice, rather than theory. The theory, you read more, but you don't know how to do with it.
>
> (Mingli)

> I have said, I am not a so ... academic person. Maybe too many theories, especially in [the name of a module], this module, and [the name of another module], there are so many frameworks or ideas made by some authors ... I think the program can add more courses. [The modules that we currently have] [j]ust tell you some approaches or some theories, uh, prior authors have developed or have written. But in the reality, we still don't know how to be a teacher ... [I would like the program to] [j]ust tell us how to prepare, uh, and how to find all materials, or some approaches to get connect with your students more closely.
>
> (Mingli)

Although Mingli and Zitong shared a common concern with acquiring practical skills for their future career, students such as Mingli may view "practice" and "theory" as two disconnected components (and even *mutually exclusive* for her and some other student participants) in their MA studies. Participants alike have expressed their lack of interest in the modules that engage with key theories in the field of TESOL, as they find it to be irrelevant to their objectives of career development. This may also partly explain why some TESOL students have been particularly interested in getting a teaching placement in their MA course, seeing teaching practice as the primary objective of a TESOL program, more along the lines of a CELTA (The Cambridge Certificate in Teaching English to Speakers of Other Languages).

### *Advanced degree*

Another key theme that emerged from the data is viewing the program mainly as an advanced degree. Three types of expectations, or sub-themes, related to this theme are: viewing their MA TESOL course as (1) a theory-based program that enables a "mastery" of the field of TESOL ("acquiring enough knowledge" and "acquiring advanced theories" were two of the frequently mentioned concepts in this sub-theme), (2) a prerequisite for further doctoral study in TESOL, and (3) a degree that enhance employability. The following three extracts will exemplify these three strands of objectives.

*Extract 2.1: "I want to learn more about those theories"*

> So the reason why I choose TESOL ... is because previously I have some teaching experience, but they may have some contradiction to those theories that I have learned in class. So I want to learn more about those theories and

> try to find a way to cope with those contradictions … But now I found that those theories [in the MA course] are actually things I have learned in my bachelor … uh, during my bachelor's degree … So, I don't know if I can find the suggestions to those contradictions … So previously, we may say that every student is an independent individual, so we respect them, and love them, and try to find a way to make the study more suitable for them. And you also need to, like, encourage them, and don't scold at them. But, when I was teaching a student that have some learning problems, like uh, he cannot settle down to listen. And you may find that you don't have other ways, because except for scold and to ask him to settle down … So one way I try to solve this is to have more stable understanding of those theories.
>
> (Wencan)

In her account, Wencan demonstrated an expectation of gaining a stable "mastery" of the field of TESOL from her MA study. She had expected the MA TESOL course to offer theoretical content that would be different from what was learned in her undergraduate course. Aiming to clear up the confusion from her previous teaching experience, she assumed that the MA course would differ from her undergraduate program in enabling her to achieve a stable understanding of theories.

*Extract 2.2: "I hope I can get exposed to some very advanced theories or research"*

> I hope I can get exposed to some very advanced theories or research. And maybe I will get interested one of them, and I want to dig deeper … I have always wanted to be, like, a PhD, or something like that. But think I have to find my true interest, my academic interest, in this way, I will be willing to spend four years to do it. But right now, I think I haven't found my interest.
>
> (Ning)

Ning demonstrated her interpretation of the program as a prerequisite for doctoral study in TESOL. Some other participants also expressed their aspirations for pursuing PhD studies after finishing their MA. Some students like Ning viewed further studies as a process to explore their research interests, whereas some other participants appeared to be more interested in gaining a doctorate to apply for TESOL-related positions in higher education.

*Extract 2.3: "I just want to get a master's degree"*

> Expectations. Um, to be honest … I just want to get a master's degree … I didn't major in English … I wasn't that much good in my IELTS … If I want to work in, like, in the area which is related to English teaching and things like that, it would be pretty difficult for me to get a job. I would not be that much competent … [W]orking for English learning App, usually they show a page … And you have to have a really solid background to support the

> idea that you can teach them well. Even that it's not essential to the fact that if you can teach them well, but just for marketing purposes … to support that idea that we can really help you … Like, having a degree is a point. And also, I think, yeah, you have to be really passionate in this area so that you can teach well, not just because you have a degree … But you need that to make the Chinese believe in you.
>
> (Yihan)

> I just want to get a degree. Yeah, I did have concerns. I'm still having concerns, actually, about my … [a]ssignments and the final report, because … I never wrote anything in academic English … So I'm concerned about my ability to write something academically in a foreign language. So yeah, because I'm not even familiar with the requirements to write academically … It's not just the English proficiency level … I have problems with all the points. I have to find, how to find an idea that you want to say, and how to support your idea.
>
> (Yihan)

With the goal being only to obtain the *degree* in TESOL that is considered as a necessary enhancement of her employability, Yihan expressed concerns regarding the level of academic work required to get the degree. Not having prior experience in understanding conventions of academic writing in English, she was particularly concerned with the assignment requirements at the beginning of her study. As intuitive as this expectation seems, this is an important objective for several participants that can have an impact on their views on what to prioritize in their studies. Yihan viewed "getting a degree" as her only objective at the time of the interview, which may lead to the prioritization of understanding assessment requirements. Some other participants talked extensively about their expectations of the value of the master's degree in TESOL in the UK in enhancing their prospects for TESOL-related positions. This may explain why some students seemed to be more proactive and concerned about considering their final assessment at the beginning of course. This objective seemed to be especially prominent in interviews with students coming from an academic background that was not directly related English language teaching. Such participants expressed their expectations to use the TESOL degree to gain access to positions in the field of English language teaching.

These three strands of objectives suggest that students may see the program primarily as an advanced degree that can provide them with crucial or even necessary opportunities related to their aspirations in the field of TESOL. While the first two examples exemplified aims to pursue and/or identify their intellectual curiosity, these aims can be seen as incentives to pursue intellectual enhancement by exploring a (potential) area interest they have chosen. However, in the third example, the participant came with a clear idea about her career goal, viewing the MA study as a degree that enhances her career prospects. With a priority of gaining the degree, she showed a very different focus in study priorities.

### *A study abroad year*

"Studying abroad" was the most frequently discussed concept in the first phase of interviews. Aspects of being an English L2 student having gone overseas to study in the UK were emphasized repeatedly. Concepts mentioned repeatedly in the interviews related to this theme include, for example, "improving English," communicating with "foreigners"/"foreign students"/"international students," and "understanding local culture." Reasons for raising these aspects were often related to the anticipated struggle to achieve such aspects on a program where the student cohort is entirely Chinese. There was little recognition by participants of the inappropriateness of sometimes using the word "foreigner" to refer to anyone not Chinese, suggesting the possibility of a sustained sense of *foreignness* during the year-long study that will end with a return to China. The following two cases demonstrate how students may view their MA TESOL studies as a study abroad year, with expectations related to linguistic and cultural aspects related to their TESOL studies in the program. It was found that students may perceive their MA year to be an opportunity to experience a sense of *difference* overseas.

#### *Extract 3.1: "You are here to practice English"*

> Actually, I was a little disappointed because I saw all of my classmates were Chinese. Yeah, I thought it was [about] English teaching, so maybe this course may involve some, not local people, but foreigners, like Indians or Americans, like that. But I saw all Chinese, so I was a little disappointed ... Because [if] there are some foreigners, you have to talk in English, right? ... [W]hen we discuss question in our study group, we just use Chinese. I think it's, um, flaws, right? Because you are here to learn English. You are here to practice English, so you need to use English as often as possible. But it's very difficult for all people to say English in your study group, because you are all Chinese, so you can talk more smoothly and you can actually understand what they are talking about in Mandarin.
>
> (Lanting)

> Um, foreigners, for example, I think it's like "alarm" that you need to, or you have to speak English so they can understand you. And I think they have different thinking pattern. Yeah, so when you communicate together, or when there is a foreigner in your study group, you can actually, you can actually share your different thinking patterns and your opinions about this question, about this program, about this essay, so I think it's a great learning process.
>
> (Lanting)

Viewing the MA course as an English language-related program, Lanting considered her postgraduate study in TESOL to include opportunities to communicate with students from different countries. She positioned herself as *a learner of English abroad*, so she needed to grasp opportunities to improve her language proficiency. For this objective, she perceived opportunities to engage with students from other countries as an effective way to practice her spoken English. An interesting point relating to this account is the construction of a "foreigner" image, which has certain traits that the participant presumed to be part of the valuable assets that the program could have offered.

*Extract 3.2: "You go abroad, you have the opportunity to communicate. That's a part of the investment"*

> [I]n this program, we have, all of them, Chinese students … we don't have international students … I'm somehow disappointed … [B]efore people go abroad … they expect, uh, first of all, different education system, different education environment, different living environment, different people they can communicate … But they will find out that's not the case. They have different education system. They have different education environment. But they will have the same people to communicate with … I think that's the point where people think "not worth the money," because they come here, they expect to know all those people outside … I, to some extent, also think that … [Y]ou have the opportunity to communicate. That's a part of the investment … Your investment to a journey abroad [which includes] [m]oney … all the efforts you put in [that were] spread out several years … So we have, uh, rehearsed in our mind many times that we will be working in a leading university in the UK, experience different things, and develop academically and professionally, having different experience, like, broaden our horizon.
>
> (Haoran)

> "International students" is a general term that we use back in China to refer to the students that isn't Chinese. But here, because there are too many Chinese students, we cannot identify ourselves as international students, although we are international students … We are here in the UK, we need to identify ourselves, first of all, as Chinese. And secondly, as a student, as an international student. But because there are too many Chinese students, we are in the same community, whether it's speech community … the same cultural background … same social community, yeah. Same academic community.
>
> (Haoran)

Similar to the disappointment shown by Lanting in the previous extract regarding not having "foreigners" peers in the program, Haoran was also disappointed about not having "international students" in his MA course, which he considered to be an essential component of his expectations of studying abroad. The difficulty in positioning himself as an "international student" may stem from viewing his cohort as a linguistically, culturally, and socially homogeneous community. By viewing his peer students as a homogeneous group, it was difficult for students like

Haoran to conceptualize how opportunities would be available for them to achieve intercultural communication for their postgraduate studies. Developing intercultural competence can be an inherent goal for going abroad for international postgraduate students, who may have to adapt themselves to unfamiliar contexts to facilitate their learning (McKinley et al., 2019).

Previous studies have shown that international TESOL students in a program with both native and non-native speakers of English may view their previous experience in learning English to be a valuable contribution to the postgraduate program (Lee & Lew, 2001). However, in this program, students who consider their MA TESOL studies as a study abroad year, by seeing the entire group as a homogenous one, may find it more difficult to identify themselves as a member of a group that has diverse insights into the field of TESOL.

Additionally, Haoran's account reveals that students may consider their TESOL studies as a study abroad year with significant devotion of money, time, and effort—they expect multiple gains from their MA studies. This view resonates with Edwards and Ran's (2009, p. 191) point, that studying abroad can entail "enormous financial sacrifices by the family."

## Discussion

### *(Failure to meet) transnational expectations*

As Anderson (2019) points out, universities generally place great significance on internationalization in terms of recruiting international students, aiming for a more culturally and academically diverse environment and greater economic benefits. This suggests that value has been placed on the international student cohort and the transnational experience. Many of these globally mobile postgraduate TESOL students in our study had assumed they would "cross borders" to study. The participants in this study described expectations of their MA TESOL program that arch beyond the academic aspects. Specifically, the "studying abroad" theme reveals that these international students had the expectations related to transnational experiences, such as learning local culture and interacting with students from diverse backgrounds, which they expected to be embedded in their learning experience in the program.

This consensus on the importance of transnational experiences suggests the possibility of a certain level of reciprocity in transnationalism. However, our study shows a potential discrepancy between what the universities aim(/claim) to offer and what students may expect regarding transnational experiences. A strong sense of disappointment was identified across the dataset, as many students felt they would not be able to have the transnational experiences they had expected with the student cohort that they identified as homogeneous. This was especially evident in one participant's difficulties in identifying himself as an "international student" in the TESOL program.

Though the number or rate of international students in a university may generally be used as a proxy for how "international" the university is, as our study shows, having international students may not itself constitute a diverse learning environment. We need to acknowledge that programs like TESOL, with its distinctive interests of the teaching of English to EFL/ESL learners, are likely to attract students coming from certain countries. Based on the interview data, students in such a cohort may find that the transnational experience they were promised was hard to achieve in the program.

We argue that a certain level of reciprocity in the transnational experience between the MA TESOL program and the international students need to be promoted with overt intervention. The data in this study challenges the presuppositions that entail the current understanding of what a TESOL program can be. By exploring the various expectations of these students from a transnational perspective and demonstrating the possible discrepancy between what the university offers and what students may expect, we argue that the quality of reciprocity should be emphasized more in the TESOL programs.

For MA TESOL programs to better achieve transnational objectives, we highlight the needs to address the reality in TESOL programs in relation to the reciprocity of transnational experience. Built-in activities in TESOL teacher education that acknowledge, address, and facilitate such reality would be crucial. The implications of this study suggest that to better align the program with students' expectations, factors such as "studying abroad experience" need to be taken into account by postgraduate TESOL education curriculum developers.

Our findings indicate that international students may share the same transnational agenda with universities. To promote reciprocity, universities may start by acknowledging the diverse needs of the student cohort and that a transnational experience may not be readily available in postgraduate programs such as TESOL. This is an argument to be constructed and negotiated within individual universities that can acknowledge that having a large proportion of international students does not *make* the program international. The lack of overt approaches in the program may miss the opportunities to support students to have the transnational experience overseas they expected (that they *paid for*), which would align with the internationalization agenda of universities.

### *Rectifying three different interpretations*

While our participants' interpretations of the TESOL program varied, they fit generally into three key themes with three different objectives: studying abroad, teacher training, and an advanced degree. These interpretations do not necessarily conflict, but they do not currently function as three approaches forming a holistic program.

Concerning research showing interpretations of international MA TESOL programs as teacher training programs, findings are compelling. With the data from program websites in 2014, Stapleton and Shao (2018) surveyed over 200 MA TESOL programs in 16 countries. By analyzing the frequencies of the fields of knowledge that these programs offered, their findings demonstrate that language teaching methods were the most frequent focus of these courses. Along with the findings from our own small study, this suggests a strong interpretation for postgraduate TESOL studies as teacher-training programs. However, some institutions, such as the University of Greenwich, resist this interpretation, as they explicitly point out that their MA TESOL course is not about teacher training: "This MA is an academic course of study and not a teacher training course" (University of Greenwich, 2020).

As much as we can argue that the MA TESOL course is not a teacher training program and/or a study abroad year, we must acknowledge that students come into the program with their individual experiences and expectations, which are likely to influence their experience of the course. The relevance of such interpretations may even go beyond their postgraduate studies. A recent study conducted by Hennebry-Leung et al. (2019) shows that TESOL graduates from MA TESOL programs may face multiple challenges in their transition between being students in a master's program and practitioners in the classroom. Their investigation focused on understanding how participants may draw on what they have learned in their MA programs to inform their classroom practice, emphasizing participants' views on the relationship between "theory" and "practice." This is an indication that students' interpretations of the course and their experiences in the course are likely to form an arch that extends beyond their studies in the program. Therefore, it is important for course designers to strike a balance in meeting these diverse needs. Our participants' MA TESOL program appeared to have offered scant activities that might address the students' expectations of the program as a study abroad experience, such as interacting with local residents.

As TESOL programs generally target students who are interested in teaching English in ESL/EFL contexts, it is likely that the courses will continue attracting a large number of international students from certain countries. As shown in our data, many participants take the studying abroad experience as part of their expectations of doing TESOL studies overseas. In contrast to studies that explore the experience of international students in TESOL programs that have both students from ESL/EFL backgrounds and local, so-called "native" English speakers, where international students tend to demonstrate a sense of linguistic inferiority in terms of their use of English in the program (see Lee & Lew, 2001), students in our project viewed students from different cultural and linguistic backgrounds as facilitators of improving language proficiency. However, they did not appear to see interacting with other Chinese students as a beneficial aspect of meeting their expectation of study abroad experience. Notably, the interpretation of viewing the studies as a study abroad year may not just be restricted to this MA program. Research that examines the experience of Chinese students in UK universities has also highlighted such interpretations. For example, Edwards and Ran's (2009, p. 191) research shows that some Chinese students in UK universities wanted to seek friendship from students with different nationalities to improve English proficiency and to gain "a different life style."

Not being able to conceptualize the cohort as culturally diverse, some students became quickly disillusioned as the cohort was less diverse than what they had expected, in terms of nationalities and/or ethnicity. However, as researchers have pointed out, viewing international students who are Chinese speakers as a homogeneous group is problematic as there are significant differences across regions in China (Edwards & Ran, 2009). Also, China has a diverse range of "social, ethnic and linguistic groups" (Dervin, 2015, p. 3). It is therefore important for teacher educators to help students who may see themselves in a homogenous group to acknowledge what they can individually bring with them into their TESOL studies, and to build this facilitation into the postgraduate TESOL curriculum as a way of supporting their transnational experience.

These objectives can be taken individually and holistically, as it was observed that the interplay of such interpretations can influence individual experiences in the program. As discussed, international students come with different priorities and deal with the studies differently. As teacher educators and curriculum developers, embracing all three aspects in considering what to include in the course can be helpful. Insights about these objectives can also be helpful to create information that can better inform and support students' preparations for entering their postgraduate TESOL studies.

Postgraduate TESOL curriculum can be adjusted to facilitate active ongoing discussion about the expectations of students and can help facilitate their reflections on their interpretations of the course. With different students exchanging their different interpretations, those who previously saw little use of theory in their future practice may start to see the value of theoretical content and may become more actively engaged in their classroom behaviors. This can also help students to recognize the valuable diverse attributes they can bring to the classroom. Additionally, TESOL teacher educators can encourage students who may see themselves being in a homogeneous group to acknowledge the individual value of their prior experiences and ideas. Curriculum developers may also take students' cultural expectations of the course into consideration by having built-in activities that link with the course content to facilitate students' intercultural communication.

### *Limitations of the study*

While we are drawing on some bigger generalizations here, we recognize that a major limitation of this study is the lack of generalizability from the limited data. That is, due to the approach taken and the sampling strategy, the findings of this research cannot be generalized outside of the study context. In problematizing the stereotypes associated with Asian students in the field of TESOL, Kumaravadivelu (2003, p. 710) observed that there has been "a remarkable readiness to forge a causal connection between the classroom behavior of Asian students and their cultural beliefs even though research findings are ambiguous and even contradictory." This reminds us of the danger of our findings being interpreted as stereotypes and homogenization associated with TESOL international students from China. It is important to recognize that these international students' experience of the program are results that related to a complex interplay of different variables, among which their expectations may simply be one of the factors. What this research contributes are students' voices in what they expect and how they interpret their TESOL studies, which are constructs that we need to recognize as possible interpretations of TESOL studies from international students.

## Conclusion and direction for future research

This small, qualitative study has been enlightening regarding postgraduate TESOL students' expectations about their program, and their concerns about it depending on the way they initially interpret the program. The research in this area has been rich, but it has not specifically focused on the current development in TESOL international students' expectations. As Hasrati and Tavakoli's (2015) research shows, MA TESOL programs have witnessed changes in student profile and curriculum in a globalized higher education context. By connecting globalization with MA TESOL programs in the UK, their study is an indication of the value of international students' perspectives in further modifications of MA TESOL programs. What we see in this study focusing on students doing overseas TESOL studies is that, with ideas echoing previous studies, it points to new insights into changes that might take place in the MA TESOL programs.

Having gained insights into student participants' interpretations of TESOL postgraduate studies, we can now conceptualize the ways to work toward integrating them in the program; importantly, we do not suggest that future research should argue one objective over the other. Based on the analysis, all the three strands of expectations are valid interpretations, demonstrating relevance in how the students may perceive the course at the commencement of their study, which can be significant in their transition stage. Thus, in recognizing such a diverse range of interpretations of TESOL, the next step in the research agenda can investigate the feasibilities to address these objectives holistically in developing program curriculum and activities. Drawing on the findings presented in this chapter, three possible research directions for future studies can be considered.

In terms of extending and utilizing the knowledge on understanding students' interpretations of the program, future research can start to examine how to integrate these different interpretations. Also, further research may investigate other possible interpretations of the TESOL postgraduate studies in different contexts.

Regarding the positionings of students, existing research has looked at how supervisors may perceive students from ESL/EFL backgrounds in MA TESOL programs (see Llurda, 2005). Future research efforts can be directed to understanding students' own perspectives on how they position themselves. Also, in such explorations, labels such as "non-native students" and "international students" may require more interrogation. As shown in our study, students may find it hard to identify with the identity marker "international student." Further research may aim to scrutinize the labels ascribed to TESOL students and discuss the implications it may have on the identities of TESOL students. This is a consideration of a further limitation of the study, as it may simply be that we are assuming students would or might identify in these ways.

Additionally, by integrating the three objectives, future research may examine how international MA TESOL programs are addressing the future career needs of the cohort of students. Research on employability of graduate international TESOL students can provide further insights into the contexts and types of TESOL-related positions students will be likely to engage with after graduation.

## References

Altbach, P. (2004). Globalisation and the university: Myths and realities in an unequal world. *Tertiary Management*, 1, 1–20.

Altbach, P., & Knight, J. (2007). The internationalization of higher education: Motivations and realities. *Journal of Studies in International Education*, 11, 290–305.

Anderson, T. (2019). Reproductions of Chinese transnationalism: Ambivalent identities in study abroad. *Applied Linguistics*, 40(2), 228–247.

Berry, R. (1990). The role of language improvement in in-service teacher training: Killing two birds with one stone. *System*, 18(1), 97–105.

Cullen, R. (1994). Incorporating a language improvement component in teacher training programmes. *ELT Journal*, 48(2), 162–172.

Dervin, F. (2015). Introduction. In F. Dervin (Ed.), *Chinese educational migration and student-teacher mobility: Experiencing otherness*. New York: Palgrave Macmillan.

Edwards, V., & Ran, A. (2009). Building on experience: Meeting the needs of Chinese students in British higher education. In T. Coverdale-Jones & P. Rastall (Eds.), *Internationalising the university: The Chinese context*. New York: Palgrave Macmillan.

Fagan, K. P. (2019). The problems of communicative language teaching for Chinese student teachers in an American TESOL practicum and our post-lesson dialogue for solutions. Ph.D. thesis, Vanderbilt University.

Hasrati, M., & Tavakoli, P. (2015). Globalisation and MA TESOL programmes in the UK. *Higher Education*, 69(4), 547–565.

Hennebry-Leung, M., Gayton, A., Hu, X. A., & Chen, X. (2019). Transitioning from master's studies to the classroom: From theory to practice. *TESOL Quarterly*, 53(3), 685–711.

Inoue, N., & Stracke, E. (2013). Non-native English speaking postgraduate TESOL students in Australia: Why did they come here? *University of Sydney Papers in TESOL*, 8, 29–56.

Kumaravadivelu, B. (2003). Problematizing cultural stereotypes in TESOL. *TESOL Quarterly*, 37(4), 709–719.

Lee, E., & Lew, L. (2001). Diary studies: The voices of nonnative English speakers in a Master of Arts program in Teaching English to Speakers of Other Languages. *The CATESOL Journal*, 13(1), 135–149.

Liu, D. (1998). Ethnocentrism in TESOL: Teacher education and the neglected needs of international TESOL students. *ELT Journal*, 52(1), 3–10.

Liu, D. (1999). Training non-native TESOL students: Challenges for TESOL teacher education in the West. In G. Braine (Ed.), *Non-native educators in English language teaching*. New York: Routledge.

Llurda, E. (2005). Non-native TESOL students as seen by practicum supervisors. In E. Llurda (Ed.), *Non-native language teachers: Perceptions, challenges and contributions to the profession*. New York: Springer.

McKinley, J., Dunworth, K., Grimshaw, T., & Iwaniec, J. (2019). Developing intercultural competence in a "comfortable" third space: Postgraduate studies in the UK. *Language and Intercultural Communication*, 19(1), 9–22.

McKinley, J., & Sakamoto, M. (2008). Exploring language+ identity: Nature of code-switching among Japanese Students. *Bulletin of Sophia University Faculty of Foreign Languages*, 42, 1–28.

Nguyen, L. T. T., & Pramoolsook, I. (2016). Citations in literature review chapters of TESOL master's theses by Vietnamese postgraduates. *Journal of Language Studies*, 16(2), 17–32.

Nuske, K. (2018). "I mean I'm kind of discriminating my own people": A Chinese TESOL graduate student's shifting perceptions of China English. *TESOL Quarterly*, 52(2), 360–390.

Phakiti, A., & Li, L. (2011). General academic difficulties and reading and writing difficulties among Asian ESL postgraduate students in TESOL at an Australian University. *RELC Journal*, 42(3), 227–264.

Rose, H., McKinley, J., & Briggs Baffoe-Djan, J. (2020). *Data collection research methods in applied linguistics*. London: Bloomsbury.

Selvi, A. F. (2020). Qualitative content analysis. In J. McKinley & H. Rose (Eds.), *The Routledge handbook of research methods in applied linguistics*. Abingdon: Routledge.

Stapleton, P., & Shao, Q. (2018). A worldwide survey of MA TESOL programs in 2014: Patterns and perspectives. *Language Teaching Research*, 22(1), 10–28.

University of Greenwich (2020). TESOL, MA, postgraduate prospectus. Accessed February 14, 2020 from www.gre.ac.uk/postgraduate-courses/ach/tesol-ma.

# 16 Afterword

## COVID-19, transnationalism, and TESOL teacher education

*Li Wei*

As I am reading the manuscript of this book, we are in a lockdown in London because of COVID-19, as most people are in big urban centers across the globe. Teaching is continuing online. We can see and hear our colleagues and students through Teams, Zoom, Skype, and other technological means. My university has a taskforce to support online working – we have always had online platforms to support our teaching in any case and there are distance learning versions of our teaching programs. University libraries and publishers have made many more publications accessible free of charge. It seems certain that online teaching will continue well into the next academic year. Universities in the UK are worried about the loss of income from international students' fees. So they are trying very hard to promote the idea that online teaching is just as good and effective as face-to-face teaching. Whilst there is no doubt that our colleagues are working extremely hard under very difficult circumstances to deliver high quality teaching and we are fully committed to supporting our students, we all know very well that teaching and learning online is not the same as teaching and learning face-to-face in the same physical space. So what are the challenges of online teaching? And how can we turn them into opportunities for innovation? These are some of the key questions the present volume is addressing, albeit not specifically COVID-19-related or narrowly focused on online teaching.

COVID-19 has highlighted significant differences in policy and practice between nations as well as the complex political, economic, and cultural connections between them. No one nation can survive the pandemic on their own and the final solution, both in terms of a vaccine and in terms of geopolitics and economics, requires collective efforts across the globe. National and ideological boundaries are being challenged. Politicians' and businesses' self-interests are being exposed. These, I believe, are what transnationalism, the theme of this book, is about: challenging the economic and social significance of boundaries between nation-state and promoting interconnectivities between people. As an ideology, transnationalism promotes an economic process whereby the production of any goods involves and occurs in different countries, usually with the aim of minimizing costs and maximizing profits. Multinational corporations are a form of economic transnationalism through organizing their operations in the most cost-efficient means possible irrespective of political boundaries. Economic or capitalist transnationalism has, one may argue, facilitated the flow of people, currency, and goods across nations, and led to technological innovations such as the development of the internet and other wireless and digital information and communication technologies. Consequently the flow of ideas has increased, giving rise to critical realization of the impact of economic transnationalism on the world systems and on people and their communities. The latter – people and communities – has been neglected in transnational capitalism with increasing concentration of capital by dominant groups in the global economy and various power blocs.

Language and language education have always played a key role in economic development in different nations. In my view, the teaching of English to speakers of other languages has been part and parcel of the economic transnational movement. Teachers, as well as students, are moving across national borders for employment and learning opportunities. They make and pay a good deal of money. Many are doing so on their own initiative, but some are directly or indirectly managed by multinational corporations including recruitment agencies. Nowadays, TESOL is a truly transnational enterprise, with products such as the various international language testing regimes, textbooks, and online resources.

In this context, TESOL teacher education is also an integral part of the transnational movement. We see many teacher training programmes and professional associations offering support to teachers in diverse contexts, leading to various degrees of harmonization and integration. For example, in order to teach internationally, a teacher needs to possess an internationally recognized teaching qualification, and there are international professional standards that apply to teaching practices in different countries. New spaces are being created all the time for multinational and multilevel professional development activities, such as regional TESOL networks. These activities have certainly helped to enhance contacts between teachers from different backgrounds and afford opportunities for professional collaboration, as some of the studies in this book show.

Yet, the tendency to focus primarily on specific pedagogical practices and curriculum issues in many of the professional development programmes is a matter of concern. It is therefore very timely for the editors and contributors of the present volume to raise the critical issues concerning TESOL teacher development in relation to transnationalism. Drawing on evidence from a vast range of geographical, cultural, political, and educational contexts, the chapters in this fascinating and thought-provoking volume critique transnationalism in TESOL teacher education. We are reminded of the global ecological and inequality crises that are happening around us, the ideological tensions that have led to some teachers to reject the transnationalism discourses, and the importance of human rights in professional training and practices.

Returning to the COVID-19 crisis at hand. The lockdown and social distancing rules in many countries have made us realize the importance of the human touch (literally). Yes, technology is allowing us to remain connected and we can see our colleagues and students on screen. But it is what we do not see on the computer screen that often makes the difference. When I called for a staff meeting recently for our applied linguistics and TESOL group at UCL, two colleagues immediately said that the time of the meeting I originally proposed would not work for them because they have young children to home school. We have colleagues whose partners are "key workers," people who are considered to provide an essential service, e.g., National Health Service staff, teachers, police, firefighters, transport workers, etc. Many of us have caring responsibilities. From our conversations we also learned that most of us know people who are really struggling with the inequality that COVID-19 has exposed. For instance, a family with three school-aged children in London has only one desktop computer, one laptop, and one printer. Working and schooling online at the same time for the five of them is impossible. And this is actually a reasonably well-off family. We know families who are desperate to send their children to school because the children are entitled to free school lunches; keeping the children at home means that they have to provide extra lunches which they simply could not afford. We also know elderly people who do not have internet access at home. Our international students are now located in different parts of the world, in different time zones. Not everyone can attend live online lectures at the same time; some have to watch the recording at a different time. Joining in discussions with fellow students therefore becomes problematic. Some countries have restricted internet access and not all online platforms are equally available to students in the same course. These may be First World problems, but they are real and can impact on the quality of teaching and learning in a very significant way.

Online teaching and learning also raises interesting questions about what constitutes a "classroom," what "classroom interaction" means under the circumstances, and what role can the teacher have in this context. The internet and digital technologies have facilitated transnational flows and helped to break down boundaries between nations. But have they also created barriers between different social groups and enhanced the control of authorities? These and many more questions need to be considered in the context of transnationalism and TESOL teacher education. The present book has opened up a new and important venue for reflection and debate. It will stimulate further research with critical impact on policy and practice.

# Index

Made in the USA
Las Vegas, NV
29 October 2024

3c276d3a-3bee-4ae5-b6ac-aa50a865c288R01